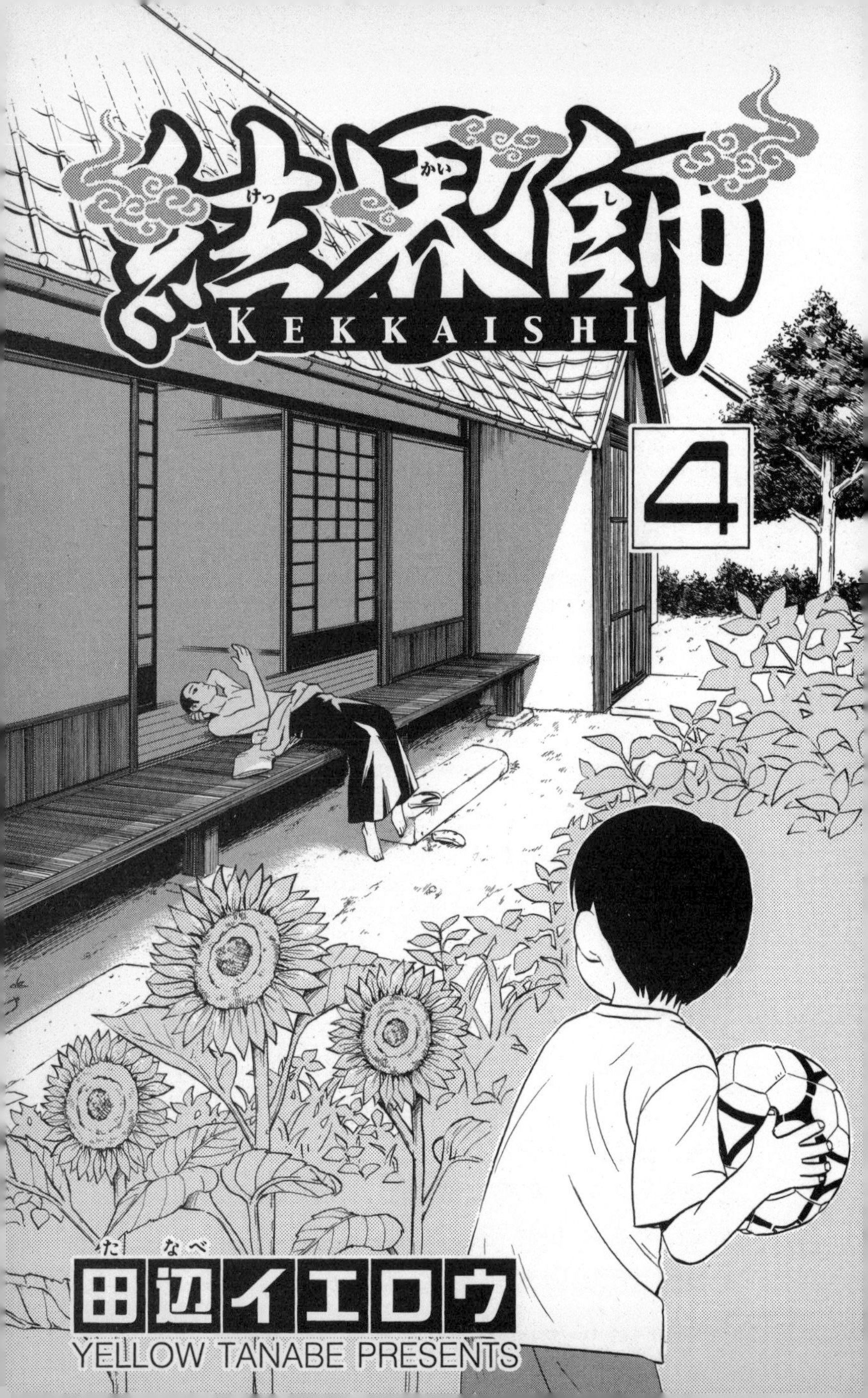
結界師
けっかいし
KEKKAISHI
4
たなべ
田辺イエロウ
YELLOW TANABE PRESENTS

The Story Thus Far

Yoshimori Sumimura and Tokine Yukimura have a special mission, passed down through their families for generations. Their mission is to protect Karasumori from supernatural beings called *ayakashi*. People with this gift for terminating ayakashi are called *kekkaishi*, or barrier masters.

A ferocious ayakashi demon dog named Koya shows up at the Karasumori site and everyone is shocked to find out that Koya is an old friend of Madarao, the Sumimura family's demon dog. Madarao wants to be the one to bring Koya down, but in order to do so, the collar that limits his full power must be removed. Yoshimori reluctantly releases Madarao from his collar and an epic canine battle ensues.

Madarao manages to defeat Koya, but Yoshimori's lack of training causes Madarao to endure horrible pain while Yoshimori struggles to reseal the collar. Yoshimori regrets that he is not more skilled as a kekkaishi, but he does manage to tie the collar around Madarao's neck. Having come through this ordeal together, the relationship between Madarao and Yoshimori is strengthened, and for the first time Madarao fully acknowledges Yoshimori as his true master.

KEKKAISHI VOL. 4
TABLE OF CONTENTS

Chapter 27: Resonance, Part 1 5
Chapter 28: Resonance, Part 2 24
Chapter 29: Resonance, Part 3 43
Chapter 30: Big Brother and Little Brother 61
Chapter 31: Masamori Sumimura 79
Chapter 32: Hoin 105
Chapter 33: Running Forest 123
Chapter 34: Over the Sky 141
Chapter 35: Resolution 159

Chapter 27: Resonance, Part 1

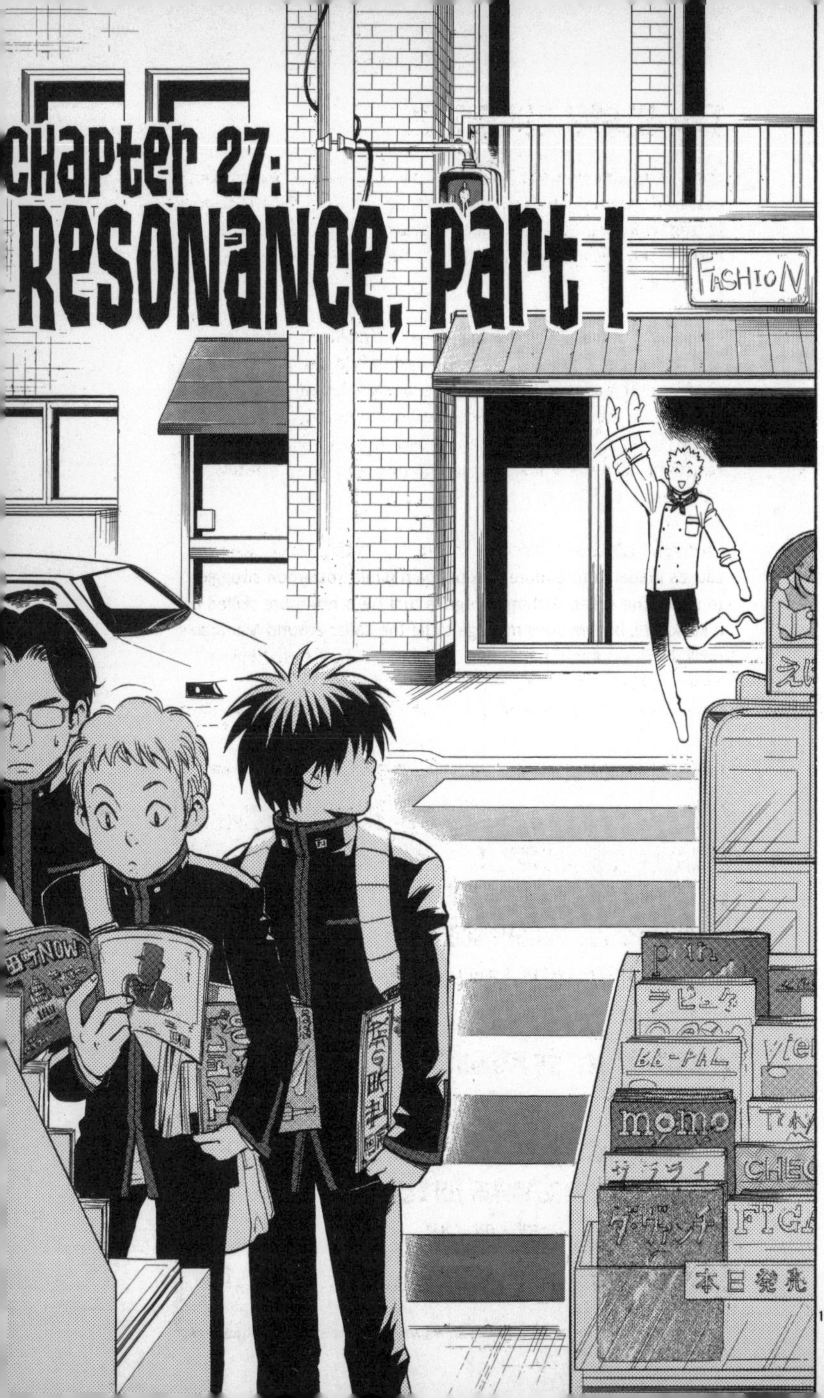
FASHION
momo
本日発売

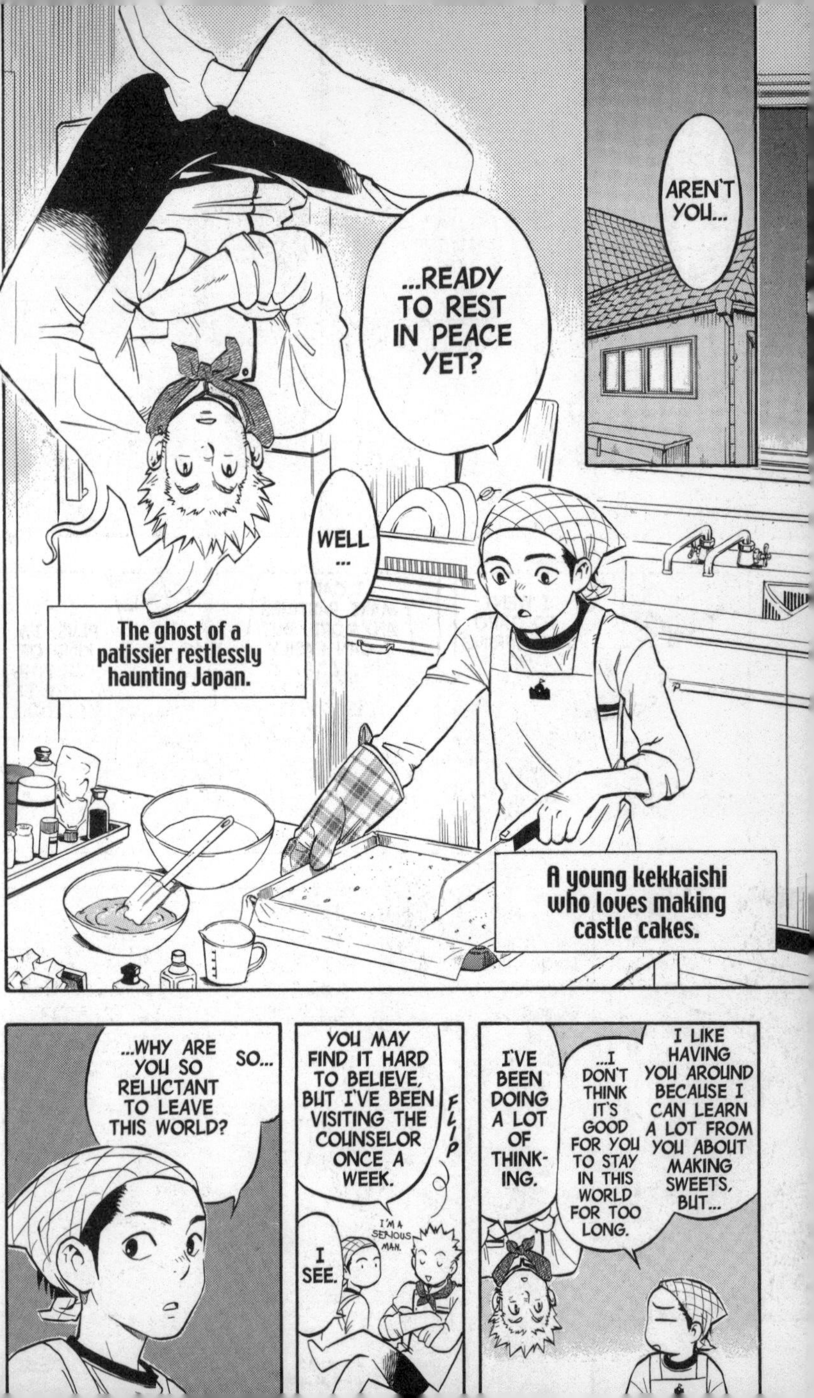
AREN'T YOU...
...READY TO REST IN PEACE YET?
WELL ...
The ghost of a patissier restlessly haunting Japan.
A young kekkaishi who loves making castle cakes.
I LIKE HAVING YOU AROUND BECAUSE I CAN LEARN A LOT FROM YOU ABOUT MAKING SWEETS, BUT...
...I DON'T THINK IT'S GOOD FOR YOU TO STAY IN THIS WORLD FOR TOO LONG.
I'VE BEEN DOING A LOT OF THINK-ING.
YOU MAY FIND IT HARD TO BELIEVE, BUT I'VE BEEN VISITING THE COUNSELOR ONCE A WEEK.
FLIP
I'M A SERIOUS MAN.
I SEE.
SO...
...WHY ARE YOU SO RELUCTANT TO LEAVE THIS WORLD?

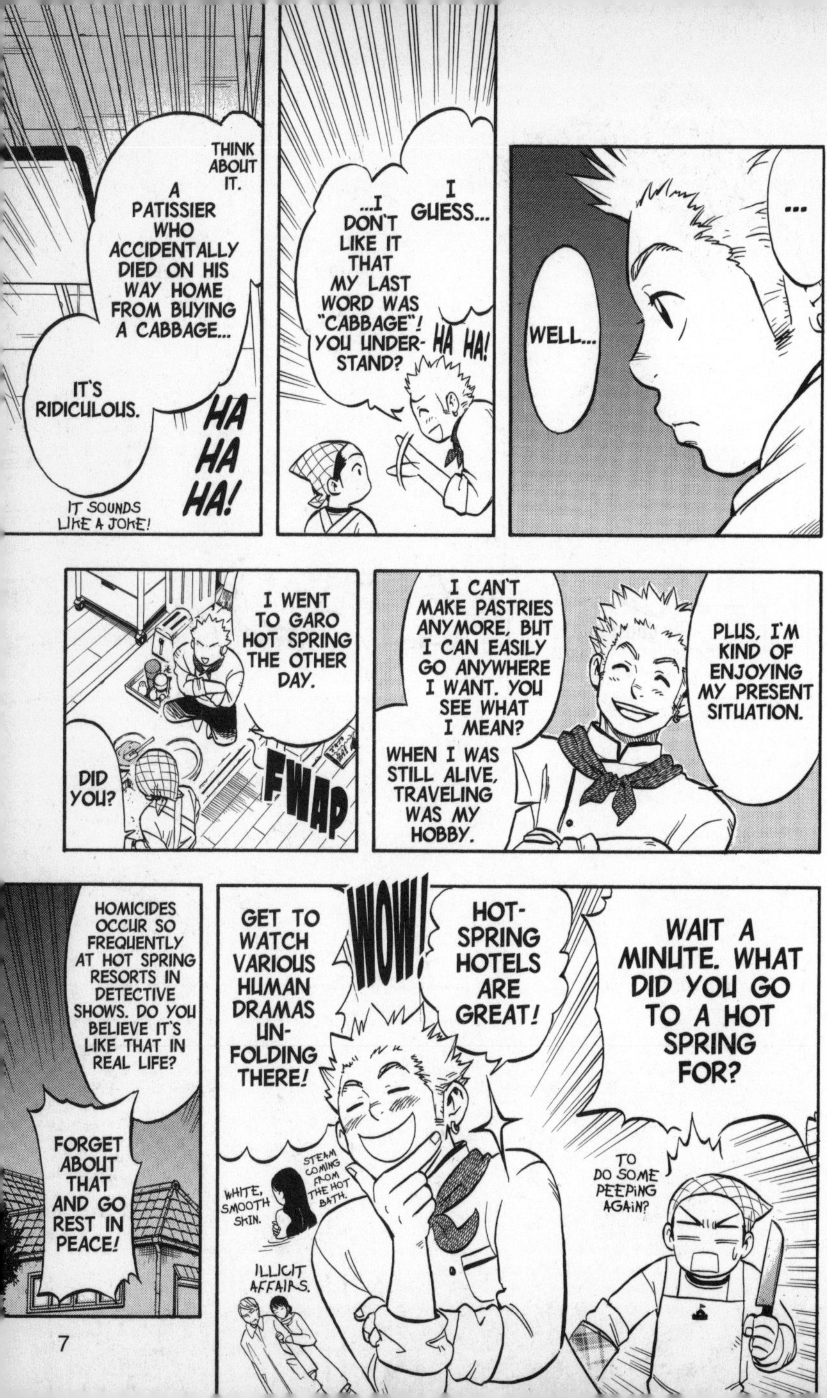
...
WELL...
I GUESS...
...I DON'T LIKE IT THAT MY LAST WORD WAS "CABBAGE"! YOU UNDERSTAND?
HA HA!
THINK ABOUT IT.
A PATISSIER WHO ACCIDENTALLY DIED ON HIS WAY HOME FROM BUYING A CABBAGE...
IT'S RIDICULOUS.
HA HA HA!
IT SOUNDS LIKE A JOKE!
PLUS, I'M KIND OF ENJOYING MY PRESENT SITUATION.
I CAN'T MAKE PASTRIES ANYMORE, BUT I CAN EASILY GO ANYWHERE I WANT. YOU SEE WHAT I MEAN?
WHEN I WAS STILL ALIVE, TRAVELING WAS MY HOBBY.
I WENT TO GARO HOT SPRING THE OTHER DAY.
FWAP
DID YOU?
WAIT A MINUTE. WHAT DID YOU GO TO A HOT SPRING FOR?
TO DO SOME PEEPING AGAIN?
HOT-SPRING HOTELS ARE GREAT!
WOW!
GET TO WATCH VARIOUS HUMAN DRAMAS UNFOLDING THERE!
STEAM COMING FROM THE HOT BATH.
WHITE, SMOOTH SKIN.
ILLICIT AFFAIRS.
HOMICIDES OCCUR SO FREQUENTLY AT HOT SPRING RESORTS IN DETECTIVE SHOWS. DO YOU BELIEVE IT'S LIKE THAT IN REAL LIFE?
FORGET ABOUT THAT AND GO REST IN PEACE!

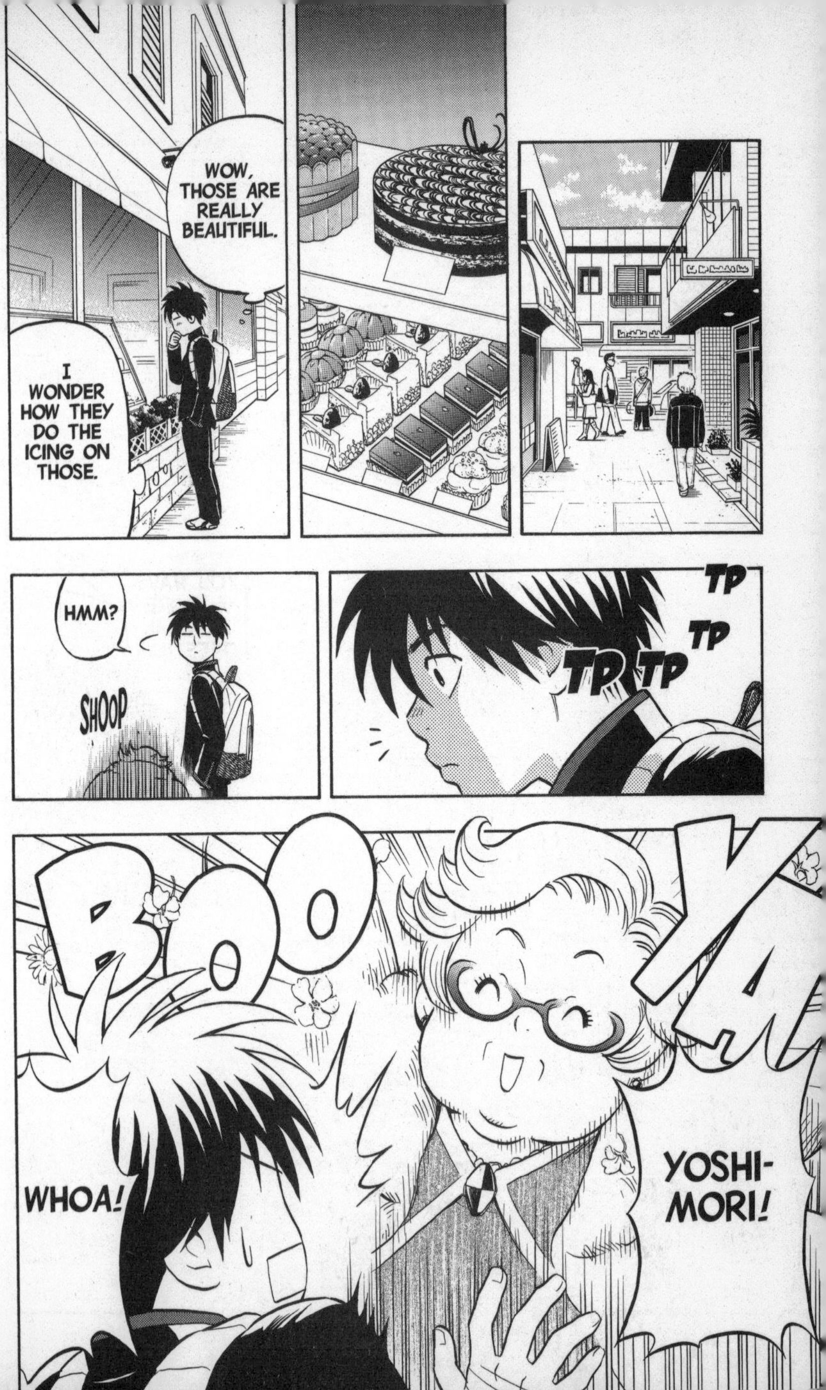
WOW, THOSE ARE REALLY BEAUTIFUL.
I WONDER HOW THEY DO THE ICING ON THOSE.
TP TP TP TP
HMM?
SHOOP
BOOYA
YOSHI-MORI!
WHOA!

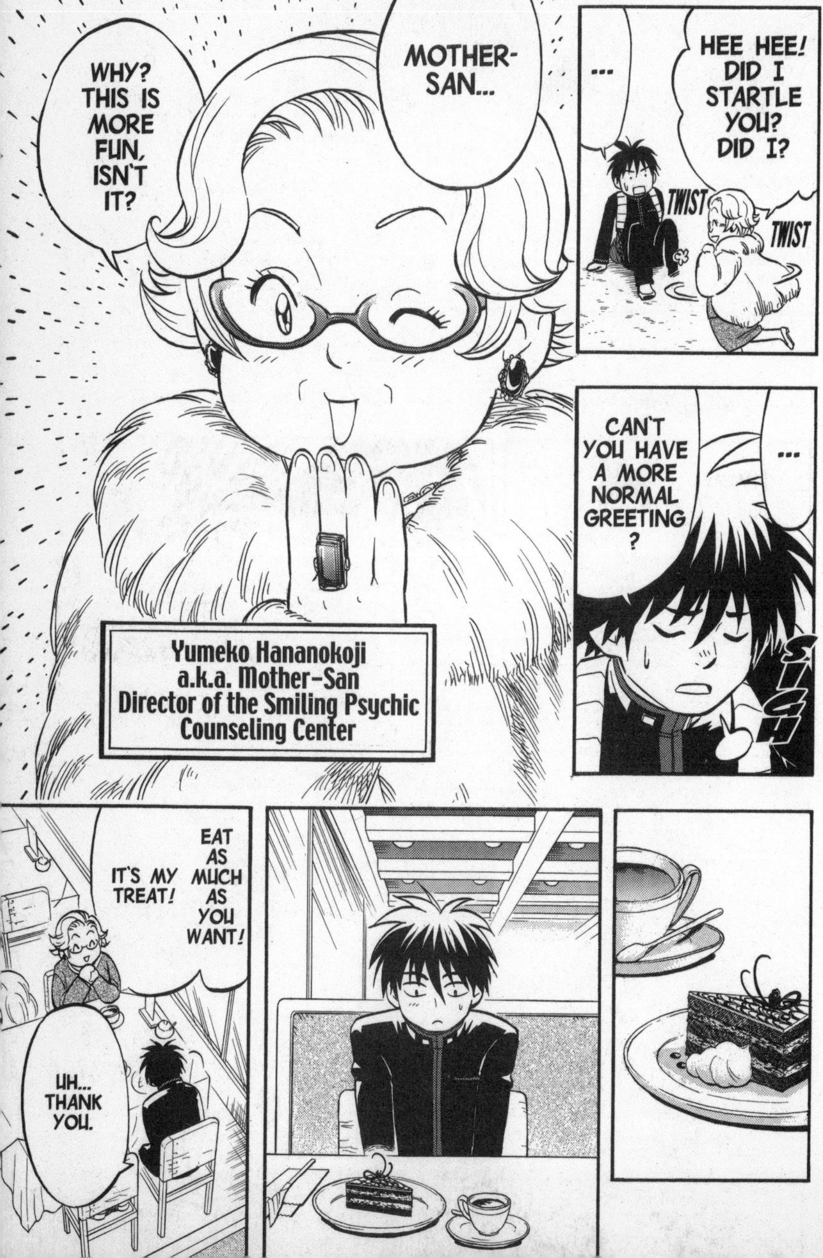
HEE HEE! DID I STARTLE YOU? DID I?
...
TWIST
TWIST
...
CAN'T YOU HAVE A MORE NORMAL GREETING?
SIGH
MOTHER-SAN...
WHY? THIS IS MORE FUN, ISN'T IT?
Yumeko Hananokoji
a.k.a. Mother-San
Director of the Smiling Psychic Counseling Center
EAT AS MUCH AS YOU WANT!
IT'S MY TREAT!
UH... THANK YOU.

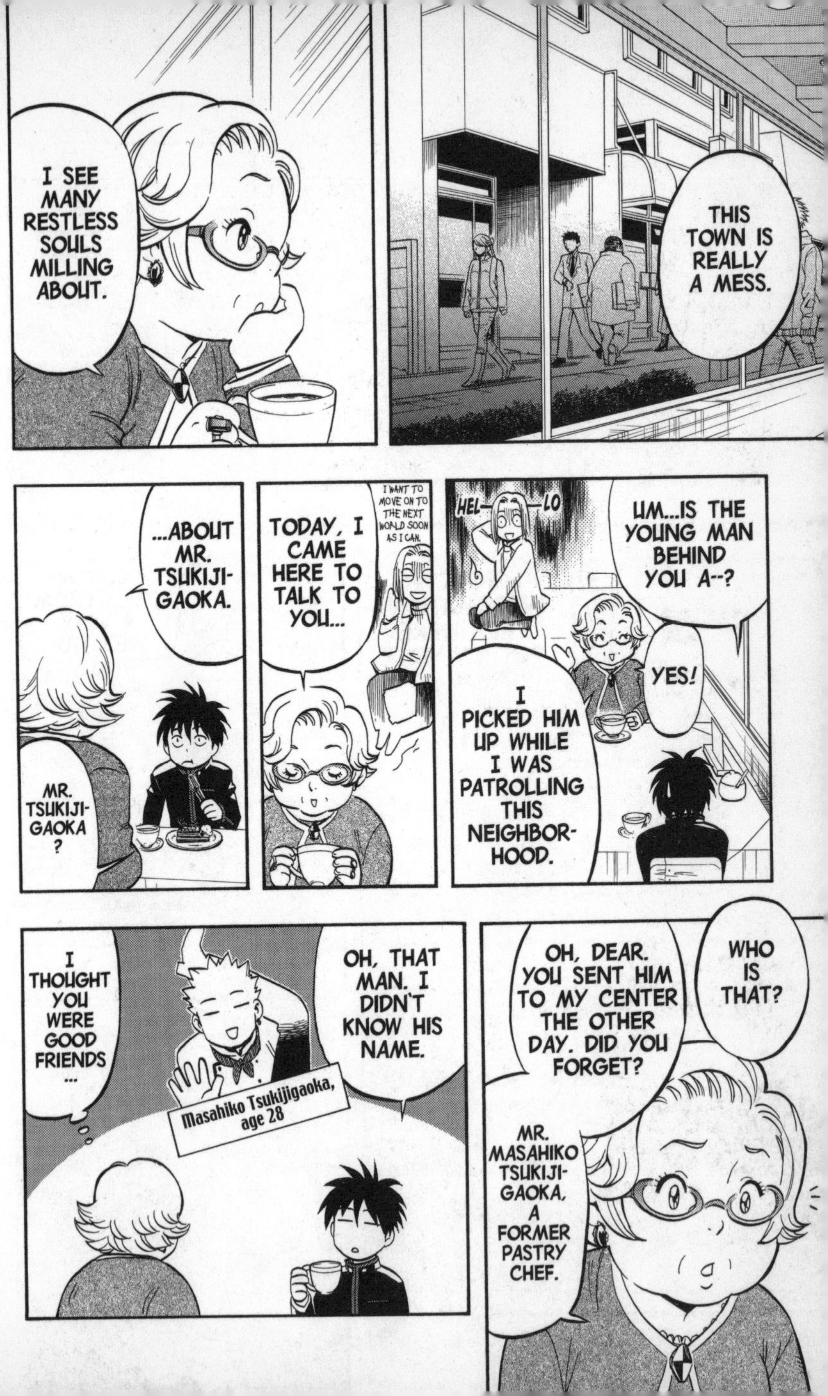
THIS TOWN IS REALLY A MESS.
I SEE MANY RESTLESS SOULS MILLING ABOUT.
UM...IS THE YOUNG MAN BEHIND YOU A--?
HEL-LO
YES!
I PICKED HIM UP WHILE I WAS PATROLLING THIS NEIGHBOR-HOOD.
I WANT TO MOVE ON TO THE NEXT WORLD SOON AS I CAN.
TODAY, I CAME HERE TO TALK TO YOU...
...ABOUT MR. TSUKIJI-GAOKA.
MR. TSUKIJI-GAOKA?
WHO IS THAT?
OH, DEAR. YOU SENT HIM TO MY CENTER THE OTHER DAY. DID YOU FORGET?
MR. MASAHIKO TSUKIJI-GAOKA, A FORMER PASTRY CHEF.
OH, THAT MAN. I DIDN'T KNOW HIS NAME.
Masahiko Tsukijigaoka, age 28
I THOUGHT YOU WERE GOOD FRIENDS...

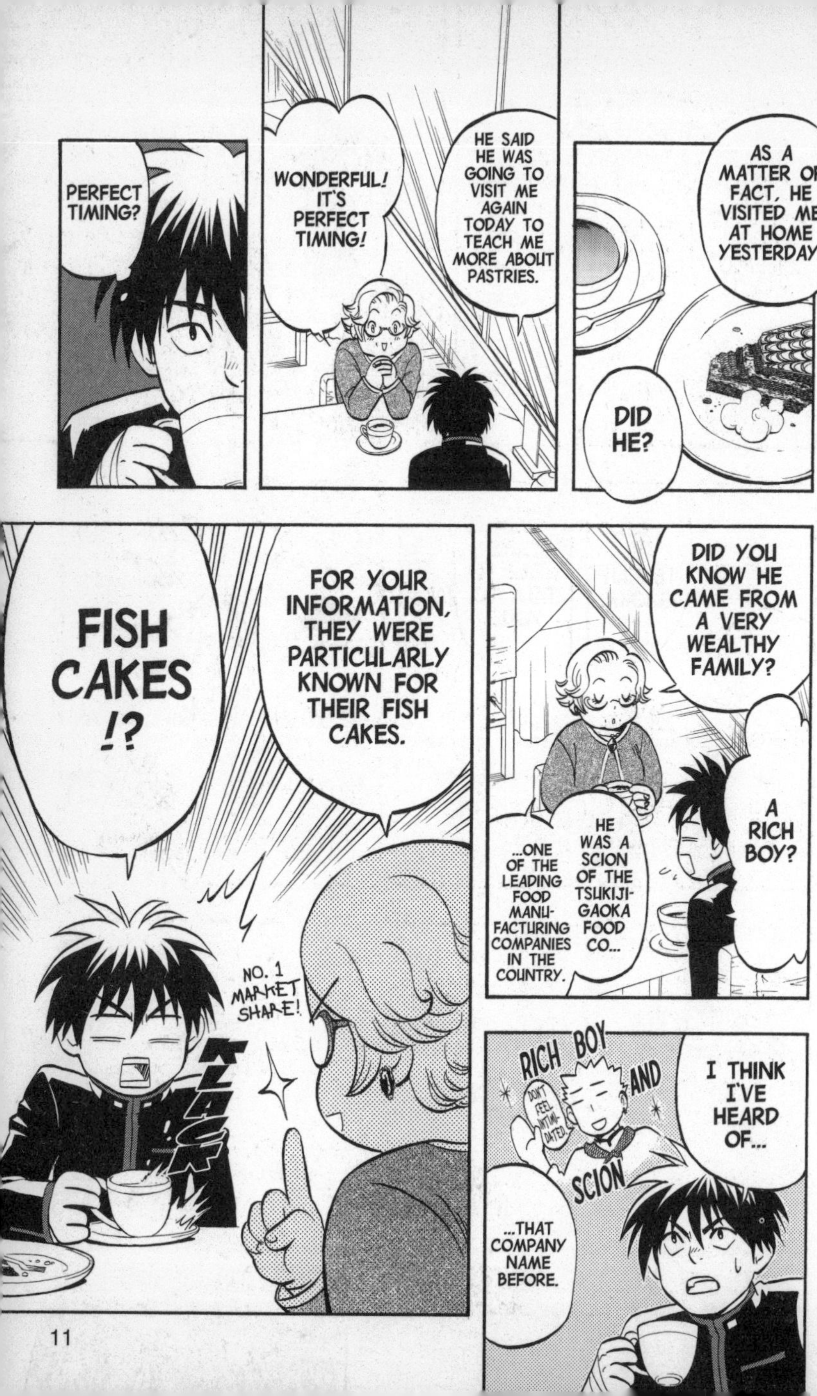
AS A MATTER OF FACT, HE VISITED ME AT HOME YESTERDAY.
DID HE?
HE SAID HE WAS GOING TO VISIT ME AGAIN TODAY TO TEACH ME MORE ABOUT PASTRIES.
WONDERFUL! IT'S PERFECT TIMING!
PERFECT TIMING?
DID YOU KNOW HE CAME FROM A VERY WEALTHY FAMILY?
A RICH BOY?
HE WAS A SCION OF THE TSUKIJI-GAOKA FOOD CO...
...ONE OF THE LEADING FOOD MANUFACTURING COMPANIES IN THE COUNTRY.
I THINK I'VE HEARD OF...
RICH BOY AND SCION
DON'T FEEL INTIMIDATED.
...THAT COMPANY NAME BEFORE.
FOR YOUR INFORMATION, THEY WERE PARTICULARLY KNOWN FOR THEIR FISH CAKES.
FISH CAKES !?
NO. 1 MARKET SHARE!
KLACK

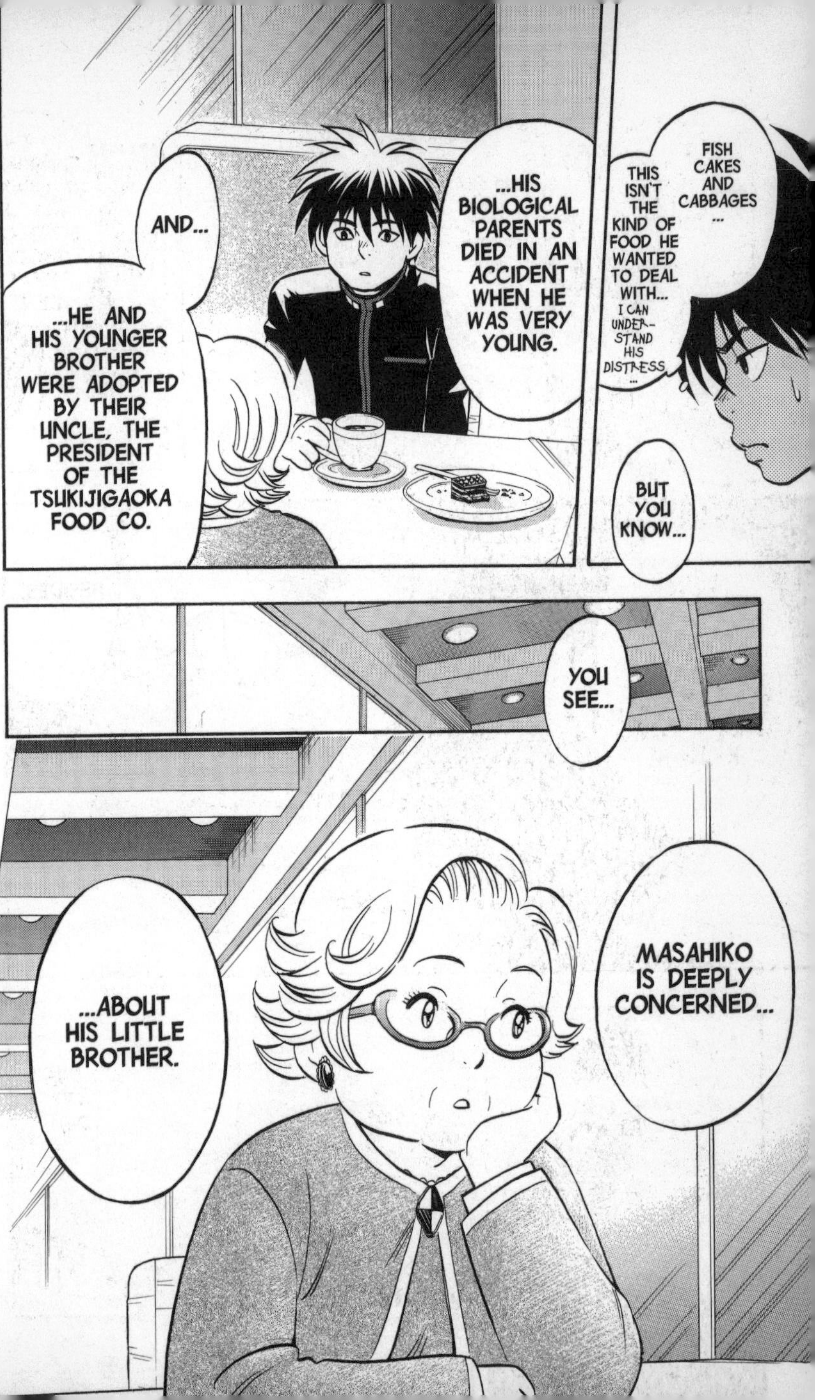
FISH CAKES AND CABBAGES ...
THIS ISN'T THE KIND OF FOOD HE WANTED TO DEAL WITH... I CAN UNDER-STAND HIS DISTRESS ...
BUT YOU KNOW...
...HIS BIOLOGICAL PARENTS DIED IN AN ACCIDENT WHEN HE WAS VERY YOUNG.
AND...
...HE AND HIS YOUNGER BROTHER WERE ADOPTED BY THEIR UNCLE, THE PRESIDENT OF THE TSUKIJIGAOKA FOOD CO.
YOU SEE...
MASAHIKO IS DEEPLY CONCERNED...
...ABOUT HIS LITTLE BROTHER.

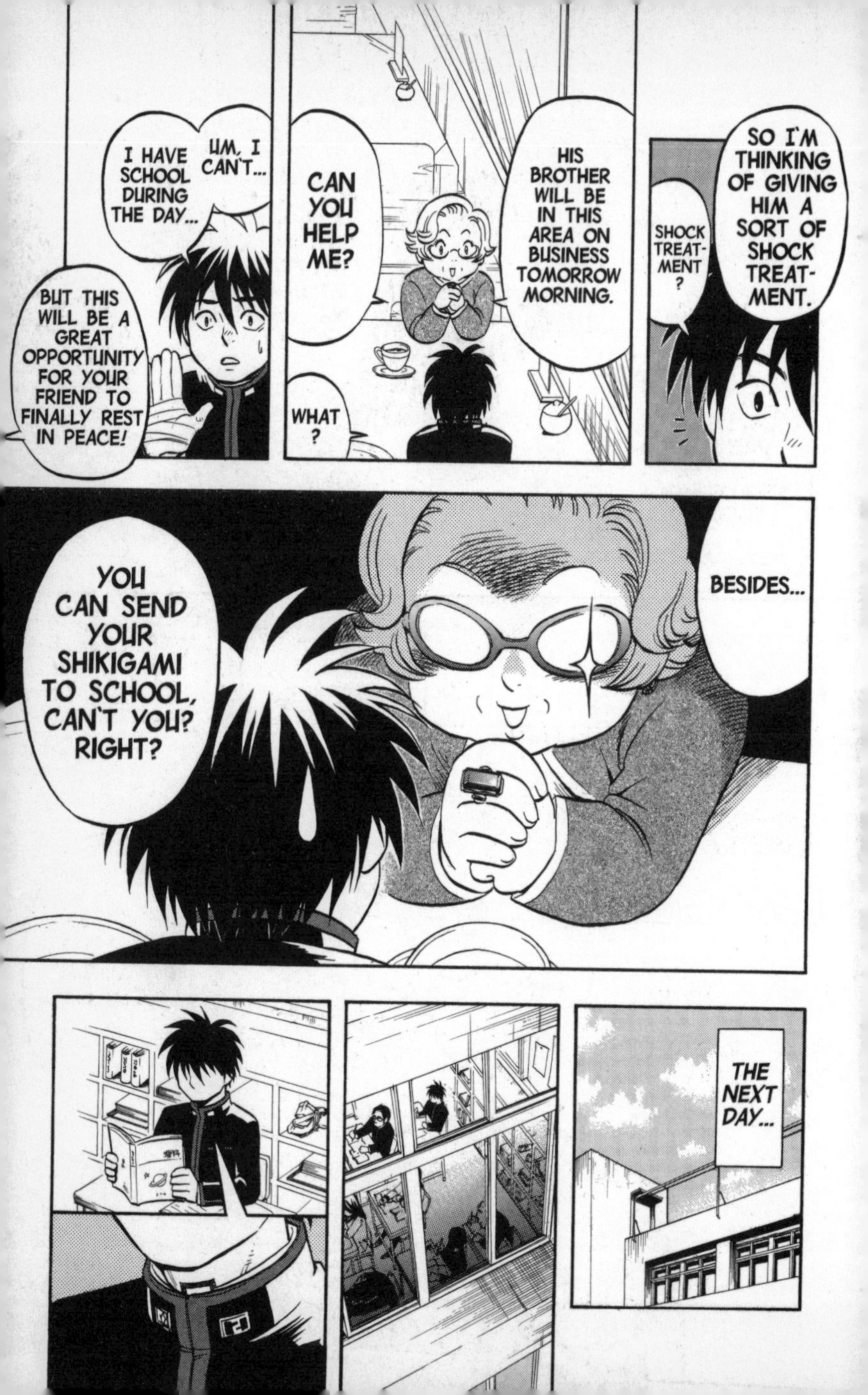
SO I'M THINKING OF GIVING HIM A SORT OF SHOCK TREATMENT.
SHOCK TREATMENT?
HIS BROTHER WILL BE IN THIS AREA ON BUSINESS TOMORROW MORNING.
CAN YOU HELP ME?
WHAT?
UM, I CAN'T...
I HAVE SCHOOL DURING THE DAY...
BUT THIS WILL BE A GREAT OPPORTUNITY FOR YOUR FRIEND TO FINALLY REST IN PEACE!
BESIDES...
YOU CAN SEND YOUR SHIKIGAMI TO SCHOOL, CAN'T YOU? RIGHT?
THE NEXT DAY...

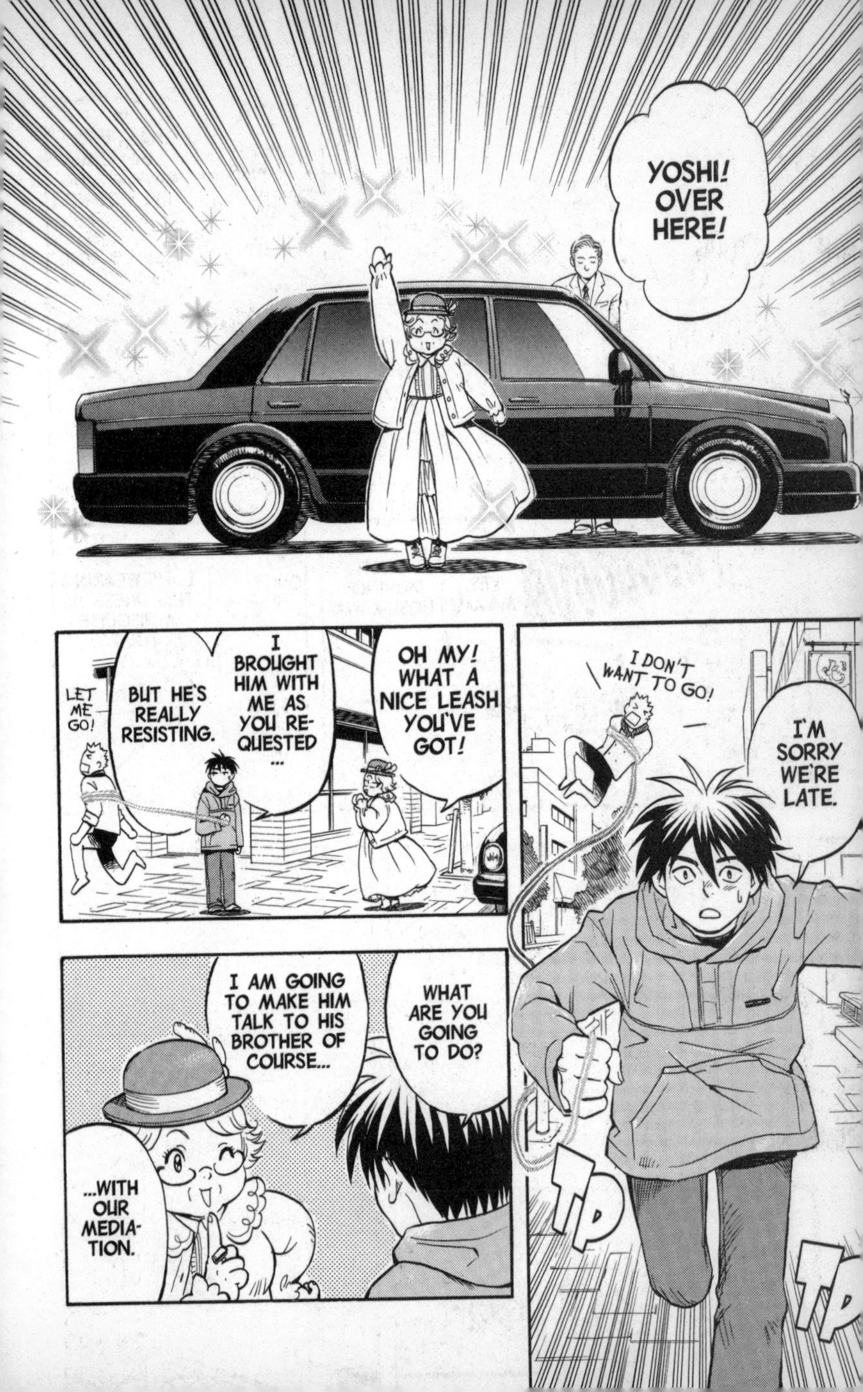
YOSHI! OVER HERE!
I'M SORRY WE'RE LATE.
I DON'T WANT TO GO!
TP
TP
OH MY! WHAT A NICE LEASH YOU'VE GOT!
I BROUGHT HIM WITH ME AS YOU REQUESTED ...
BUT HE'S REALLY RESISTING.
LET ME GO!
WHAT ARE YOU GOING TO DO?
I AM GOING TO MAKE HIM TALK TO HIS BROTHER OF COURSE...
...WITH OUR MEDIATION.

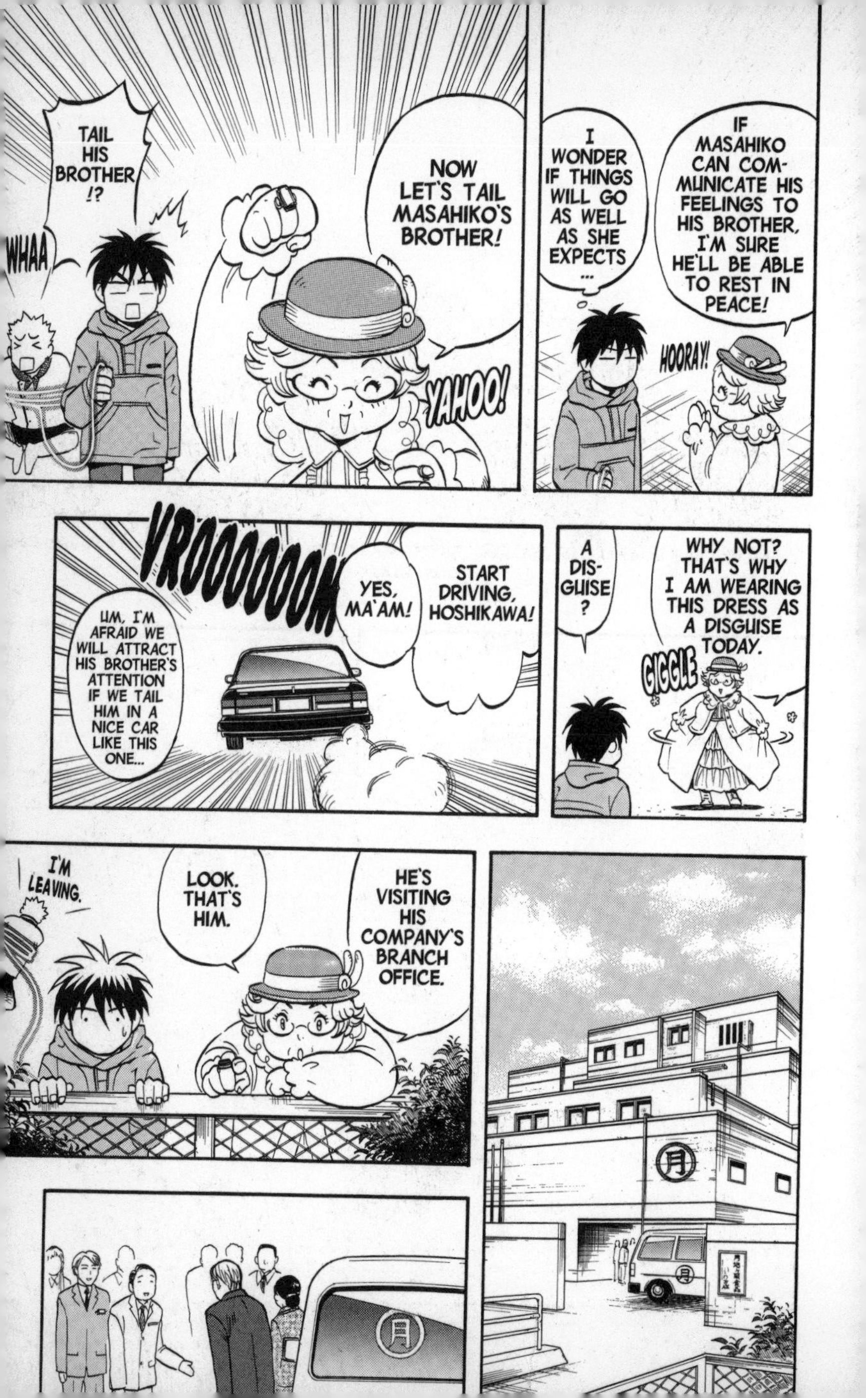
IF MASAHIKO CAN COMMUNICATE HIS FEELINGS TO HIS BROTHER, I'M SURE HE'LL BE ABLE TO REST IN PEACE!
I WONDER IF THINGS WILL GO AS WELL AS SHE EXPECTS ...
HOORAY!
NOW LET'S TAIL MASAHIKO'S BROTHER!
YAHOO!
TAIL HIS BROTHER !?
WHAA
WHY NOT? THAT'S WHY I AM WEARING THIS DRESS AS A DISGUISE TODAY.
A DISGUISE?
GIGGLE
START DRIVING, HOSHIKAWA!
YES, MA'AM!
VROOOOOOOM
UM, I'M AFRAID WE WILL ATTRACT HIS BROTHER'S ATTENTION IF WE TAIL HIM IN A NICE CAR LIKE THIS ONE...
HE'S VISITING HIS COMPANY'S BRANCH OFFICE.
LOOK. THAT'S HIM.
I'M LEAVING.

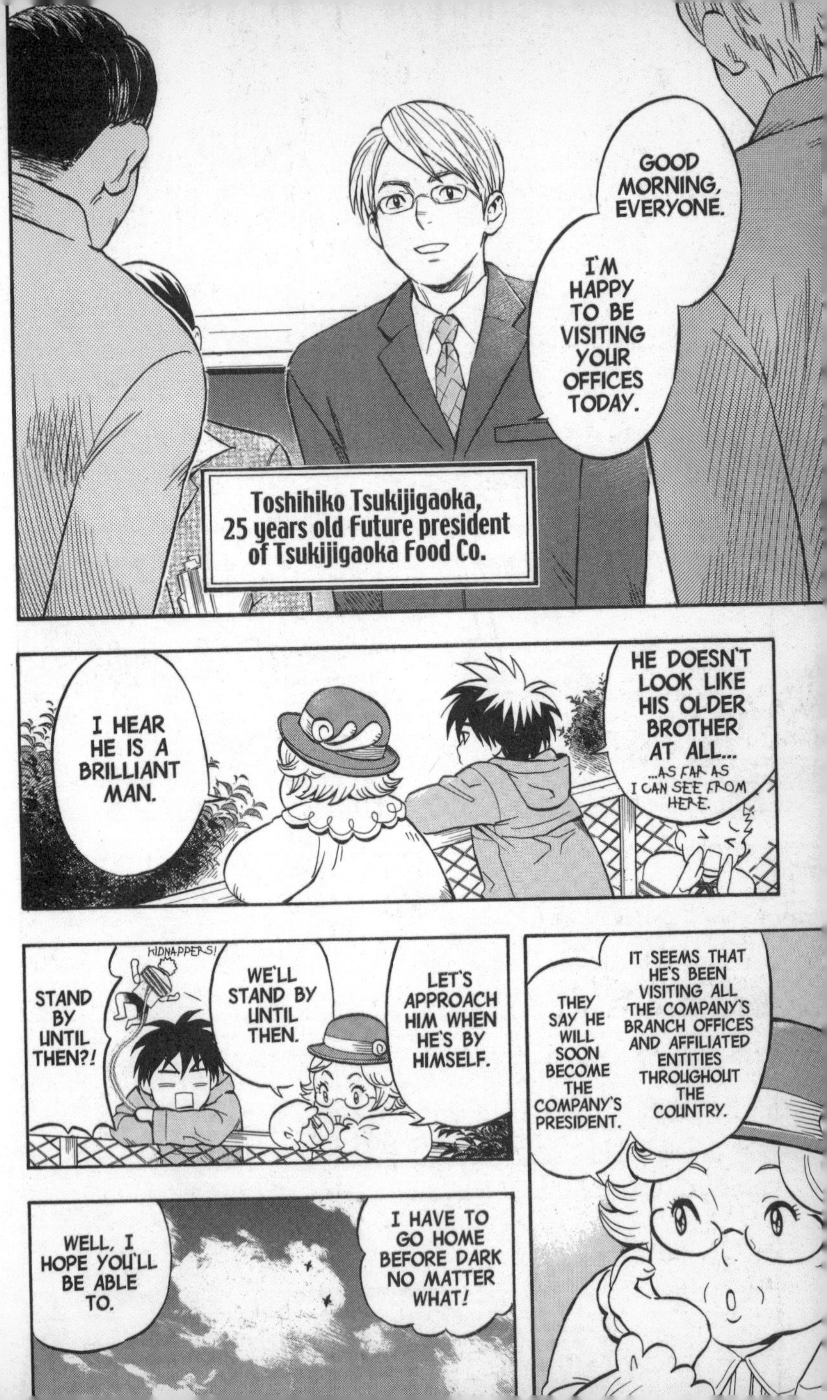
GOOD MORNING, EVERYONE.
I'M HAPPY TO BE VISITING YOUR OFFICES TODAY.
Toshihiko Tsukijigaoka, 25 years old Future president of Tsukijigaoka Food Co.
HE DOESN'T LOOK LIKE HIS OLDER BROTHER AT ALL...
...AS FAR AS I CAN SEE FROM HERE.
I HEAR HE IS A BRILLIANT MAN.
IT SEEMS THAT HE'S BEEN VISITING ALL THE COMPANY'S BRANCH OFFICES AND AFFILIATED ENTITIES THROUGHOUT THE COUNTRY.
THEY SAY HE WILL SOON BECOME THE COMPANY'S PRESIDENT.
LET'S APPROACH HIM WHEN HE'S BY HIMSELF.
WE'LL STAND BY UNTIL THEN.
STAND BY UNTIL THEN?!
KIDNAPPERS!
I HAVE TO GO HOME BEFORE DARK NO MATTER WHAT!
WELL, I HOPE YOU'LL BE ABLE TO.

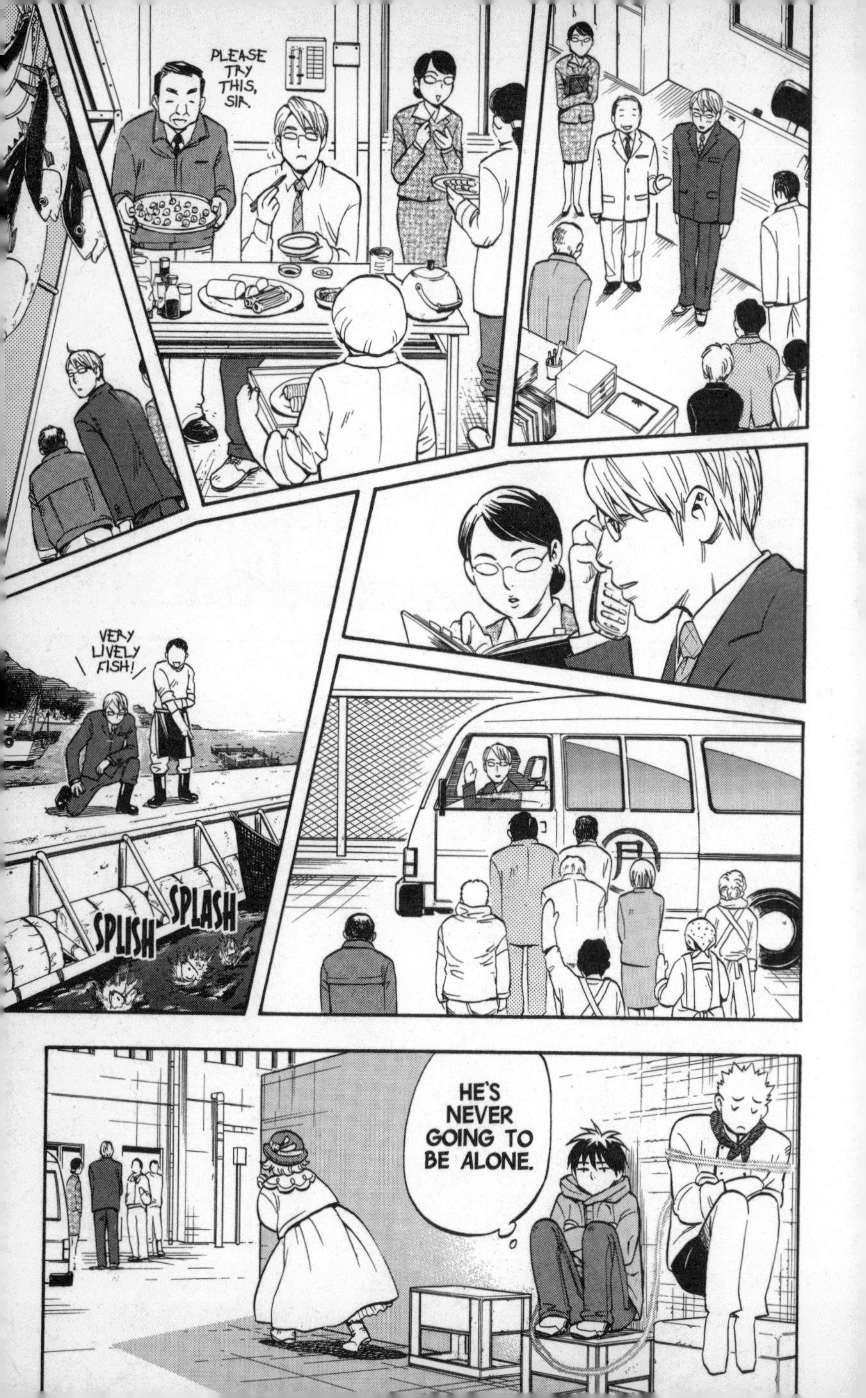
PLEASE TRY THIS, SIR.
VERY LIVELY FISH!
SPLASH
SPLISH
HE'S NEVER GOING TO BE ALONE.

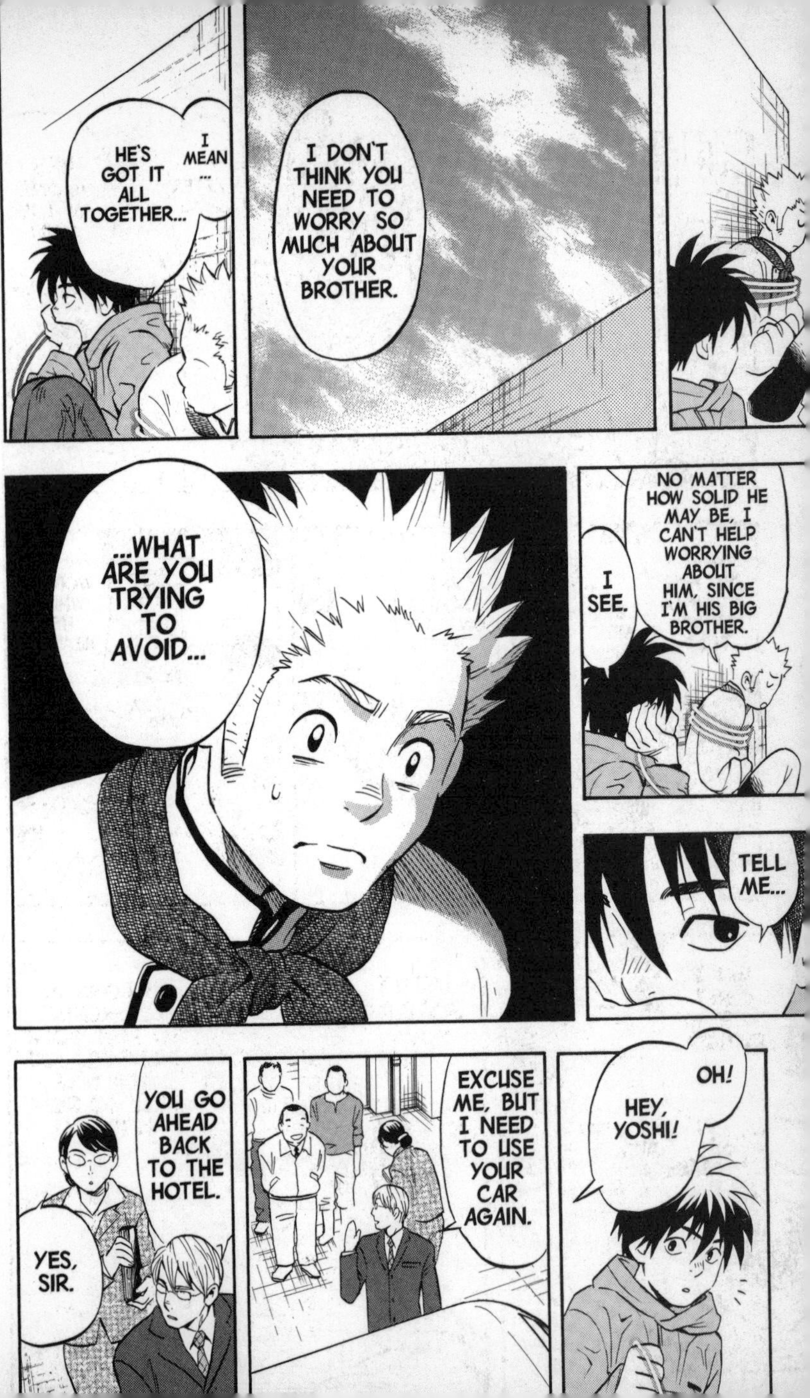
I DON'T THINK YOU NEED TO WORRY SO MUCH ABOUT YOUR BROTHER.
I MEAN ...
HE'S GOT IT ALL TOGETHER...
NO MATTER HOW SOLID HE MAY BE, I CAN'T HELP WORRYING ABOUT HIM, SINCE I'M HIS BIG BROTHER.
I SEE.
TELL ME...
...WHAT ARE YOU TRYING TO AVOID...
OH!
HEY, YOSHI!
EXCUSE ME, BUT I NEED TO USE YOUR CAR AGAIN.
YOU GO AHEAD BACK TO THE HOTEL.
YES, SIR.

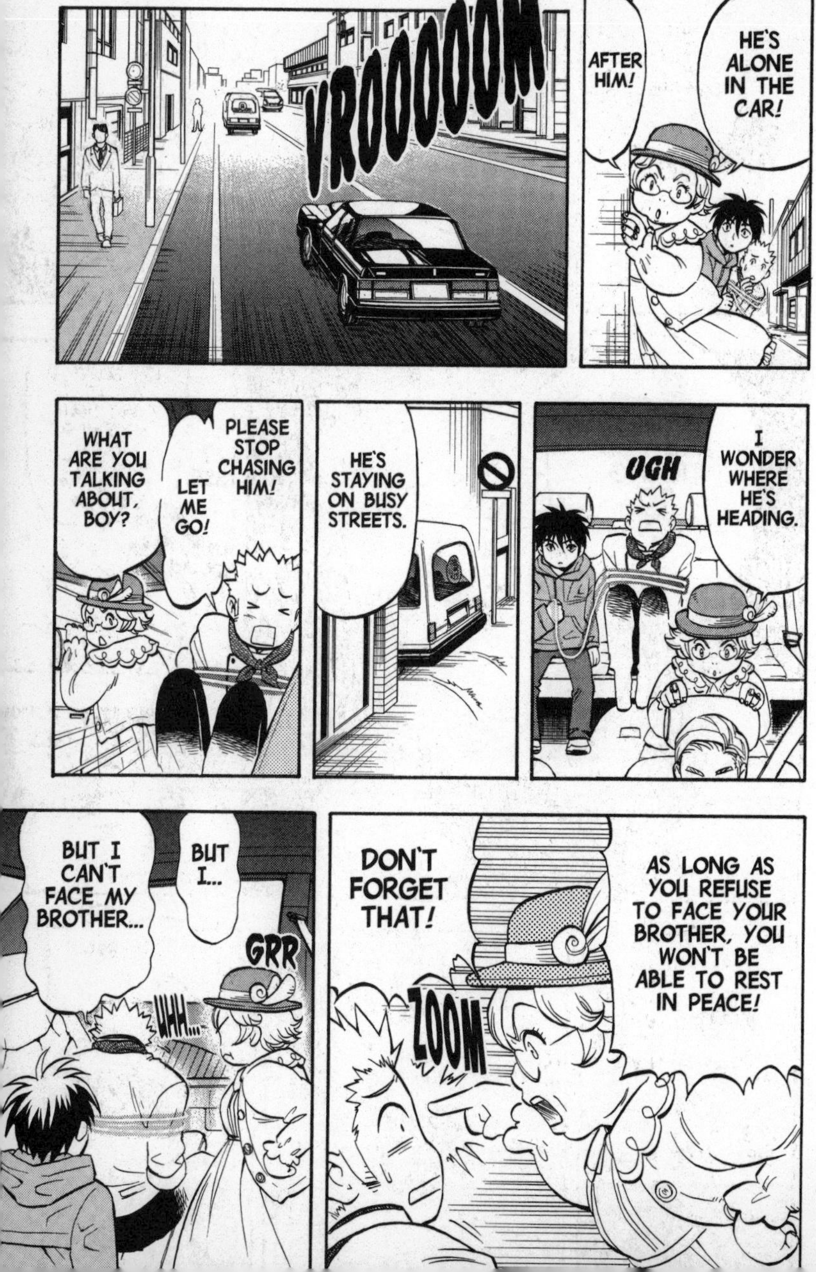
HE'S ALONE IN THE CAR!
AFTER HIM!
VROOOOOM
I WONDER WHERE HE'S HEADING.
UGH
HE'S STAYING ON BUSY STREETS.
PLEASE STOP CHASING HIM!
LET ME GO!
WHAT ARE YOU TALKING ABOUT, BOY?
AS LONG AS YOU REFUSE TO FACE YOUR BROTHER, YOU WON'T BE ABLE TO REST IN PEACE!
DON'T FORGET THAT!
ZOOM
BUT I...
BUT I CAN'T FACE MY BROTHER...
GRR
UHH...

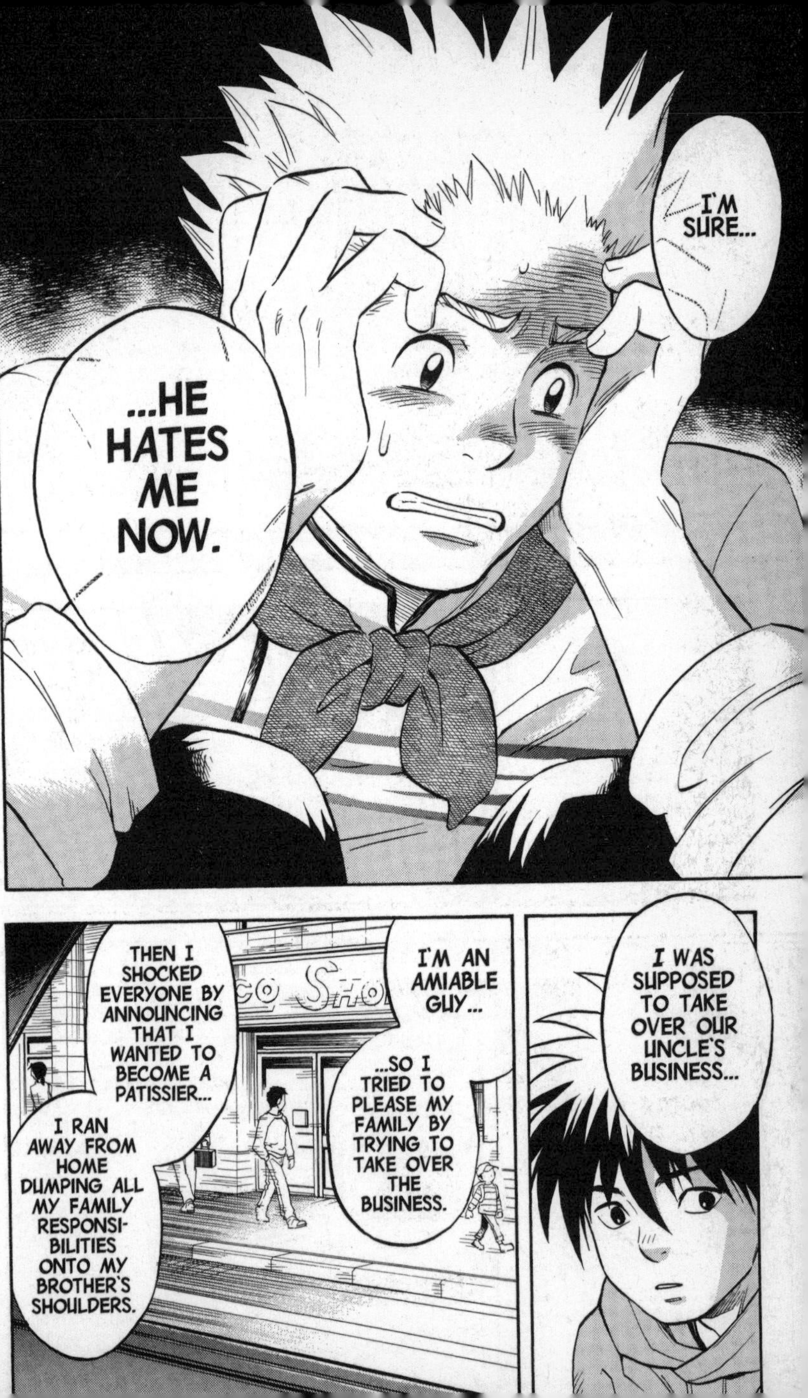
I'M SURE...
...HE HATES ME NOW.
I WAS SUPPOSED TO TAKE OVER OUR UNCLE'S BUSINESS...
I'M AN AMIABLE GUY...
...SO I TRIED TO PLEASE MY FAMILY BY TRYING TO TAKE OVER THE BUSINESS.
THEN I SHOCKED EVERYONE BY ANNOUNCING THAT I WANTED TO BECOME A PATISSIER...
I RAN AWAY FROM HOME DUMPING ALL MY FAMILY RESPONSI-BILITIES ONTO MY BROTHER'S SHOULDERS.

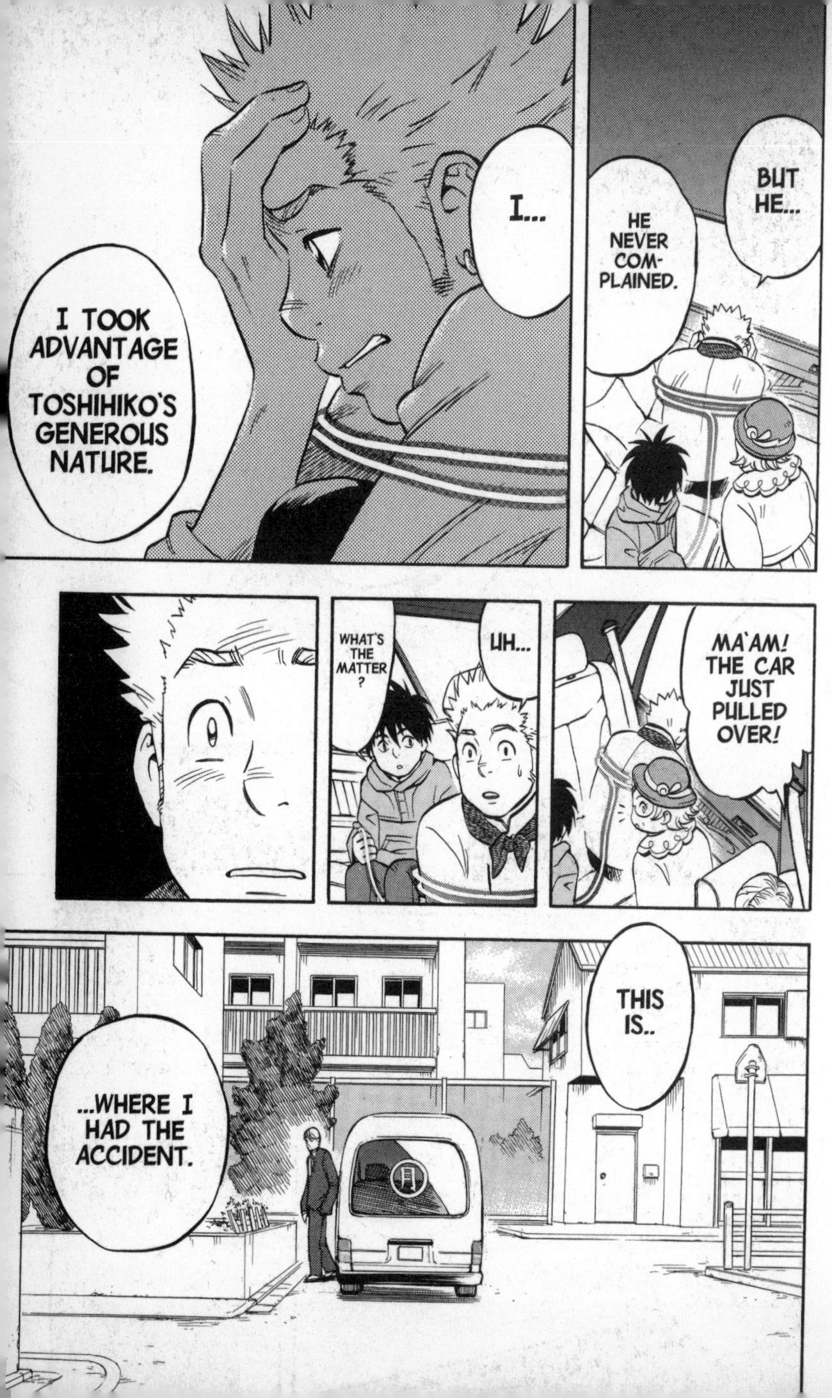
BUT HE...
HE NEVER COM-PLAINED.
I...
I TOOK ADVANTAGE OF TOSHIHIKO'S GENEROUS NATURE.
MA'AM! THE CAR JUST PULLED OVER!
UH...
WHAT'S THE MATTER?
THIS IS..
...WHERE I HAD THE ACCIDENT.

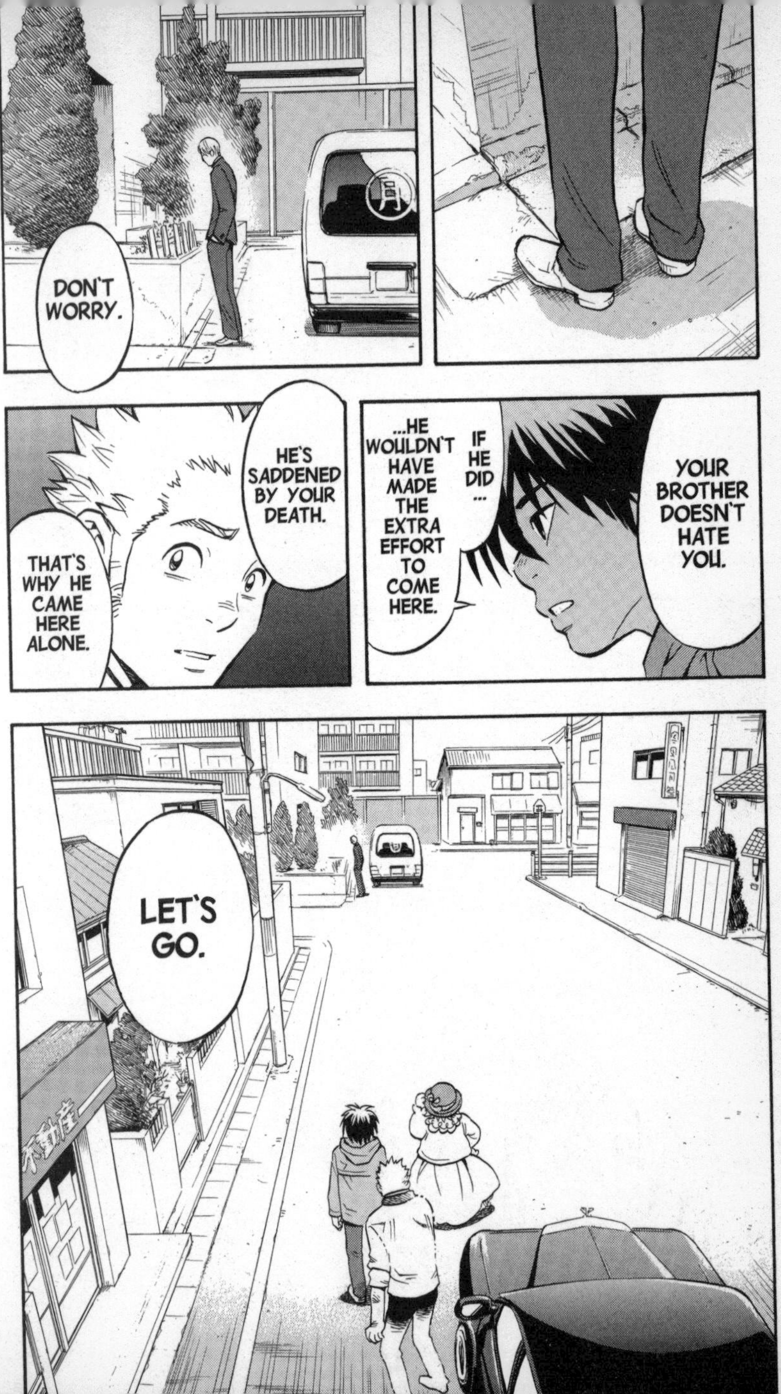
DON'T WORRY.
YOUR BROTHER DOESN'T HATE YOU.
IF HE DID ...
...HE WOULDN'T HAVE MADE THE EXTRA EFFORT TO COME HERE.
HE'S SADDENED BY YOUR DEATH.
THAT'S WHY HE CAME HERE ALONE.
LET'S GO.
不動産

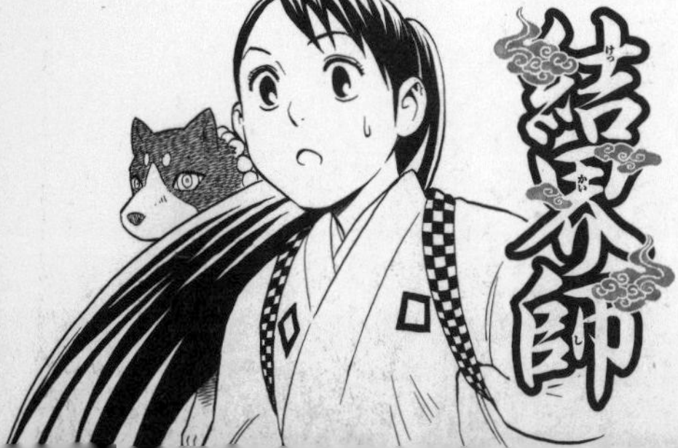
結界師

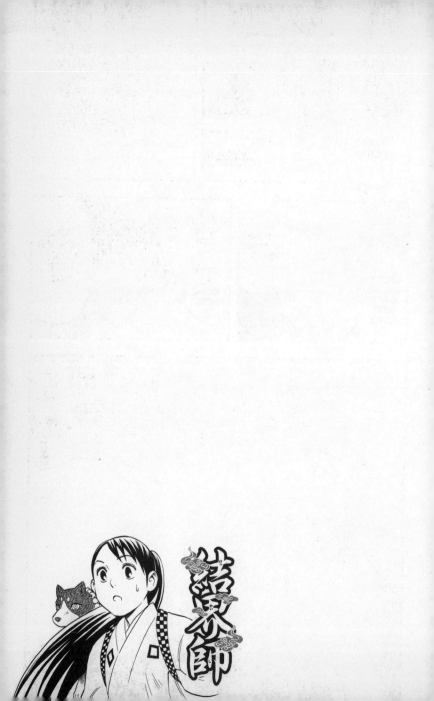

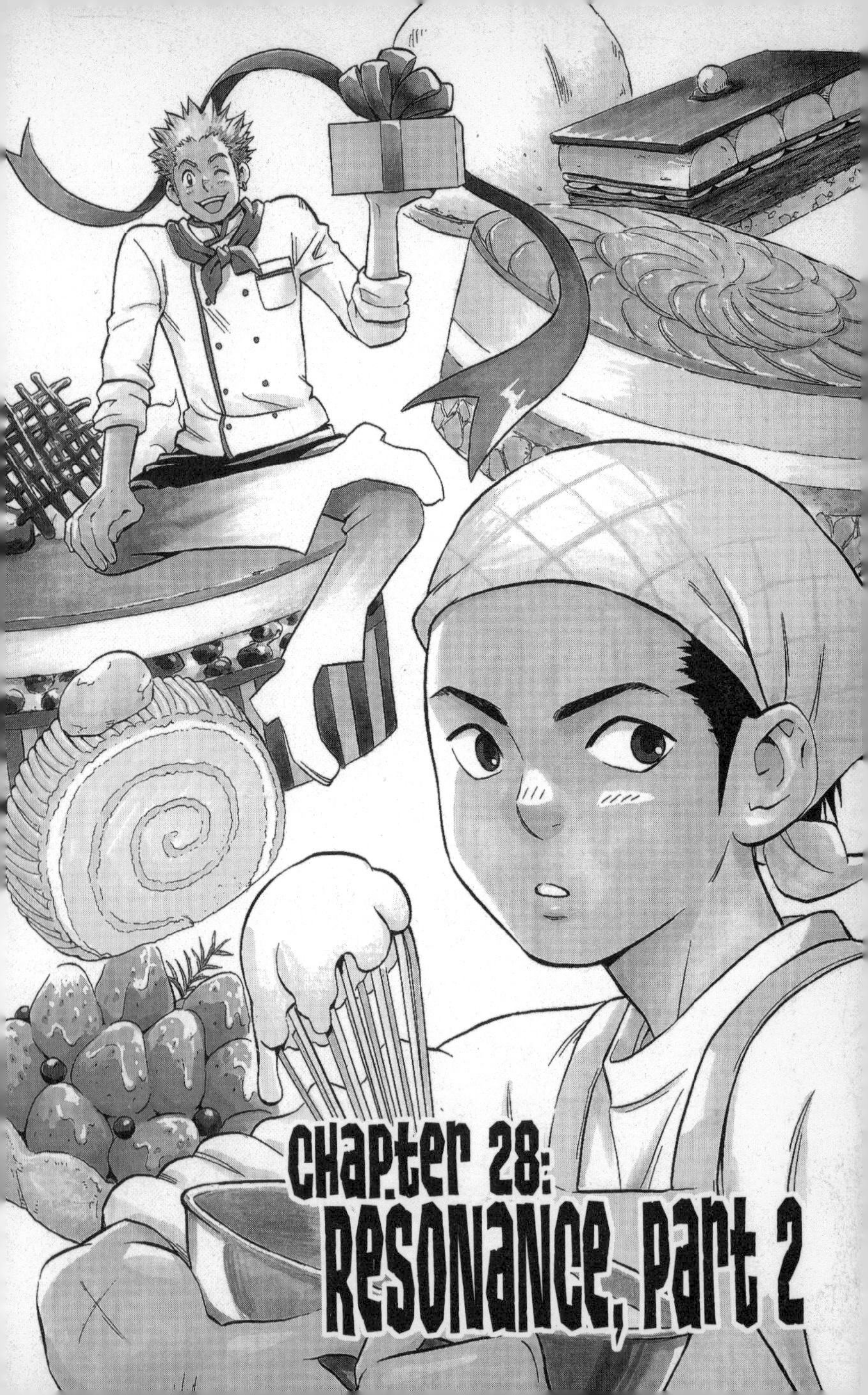
Chapter 28:
Resonance, Part 2

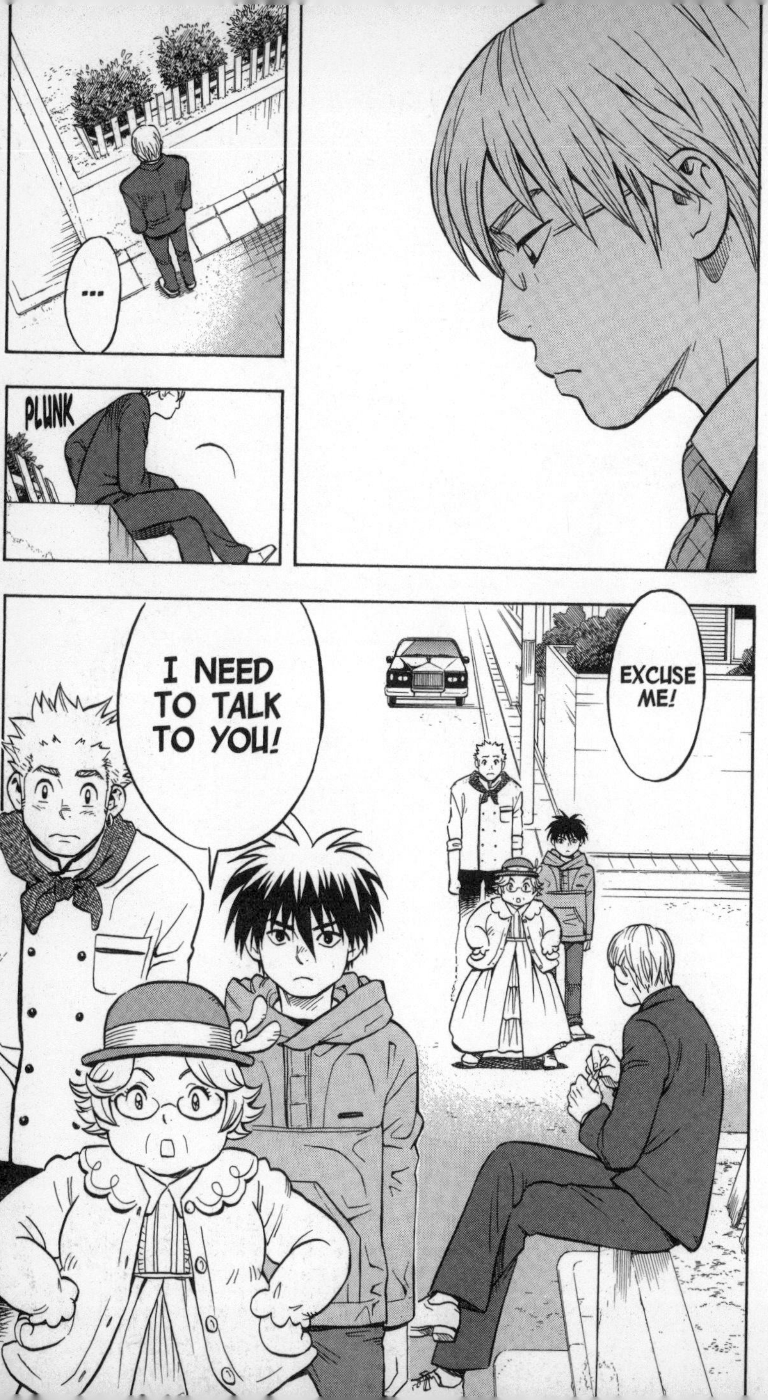
...
PLUNK
EXCUSE ME!
I NEED TO TALK TO YOU!

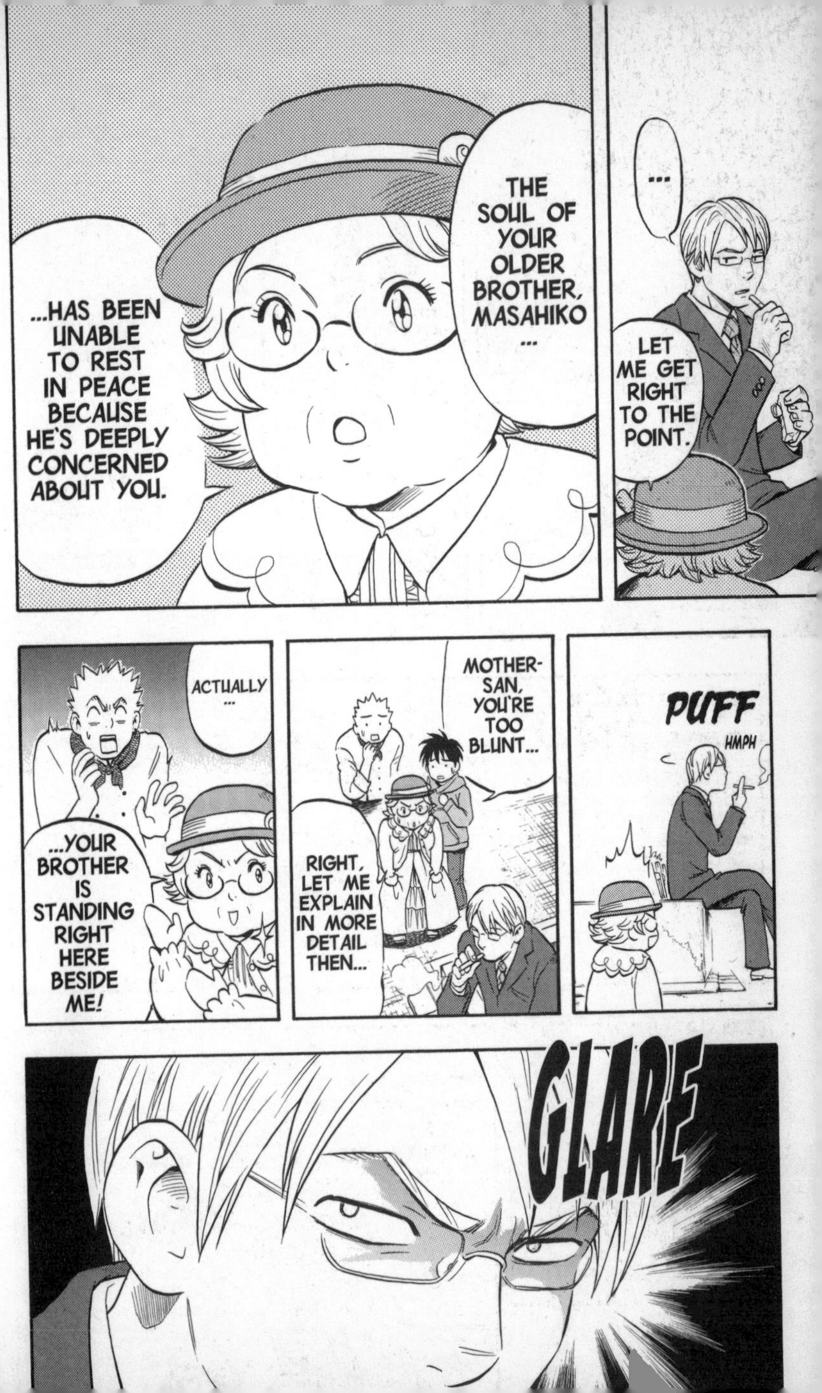
...
LET ME GET RIGHT TO THE POINT.
THE SOUL OF YOUR OLDER BROTHER, MASAHIKO ...
...HAS BEEN UNABLE TO REST IN PEACE BECAUSE HE'S DEEPLY CONCERNED ABOUT YOU.
PUFF
HMPH
MOTHER-SAN, YOU'RE TOO BLUNT...
RIGHT, LET ME EXPLAIN IN MORE DETAIL THEN...
ACTUALLY ...
...YOUR BROTHER IS STANDING RIGHT HERE BESIDE ME!
GLARE

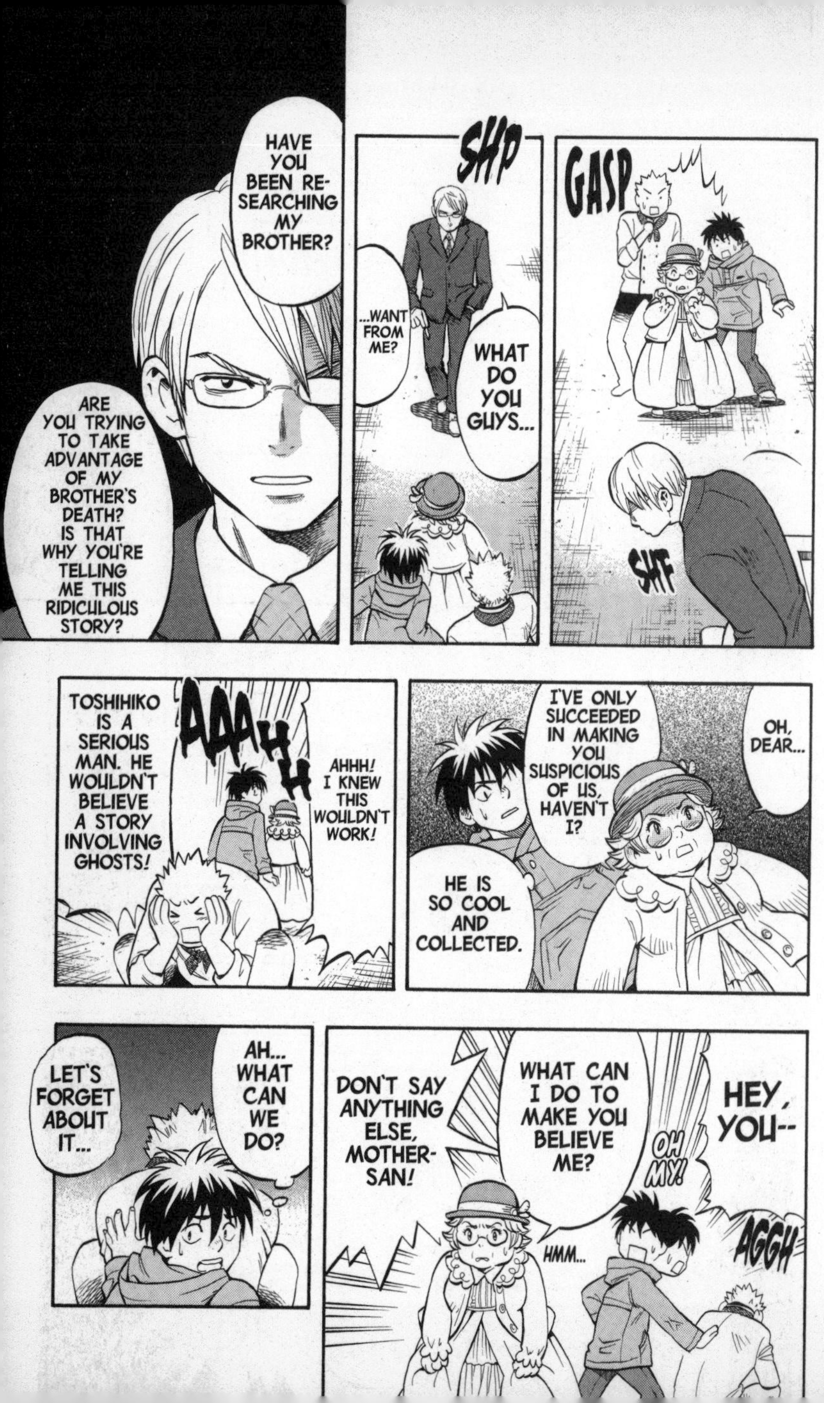
GASP
SHF
SHP
WHAT DO YOU GUYS...
...WANT FROM ME?
HAVE YOU BEEN RE-SEARCHING MY BROTHER?
ARE YOU TRYING TO TAKE ADVANTAGE OF MY BROTHER'S DEATH? IS THAT WHY YOU'RE TELLING ME THIS RIDICULOUS STORY?
OH, DEAR...
I'VE ONLY SUCCEEDED IN MAKING YOU SUSPICIOUS OF US, HAVEN'T I?
HE IS SO COOL AND COLLECTED.
AHHH! I KNEW THIS WOULDN'T WORK!
AAAHH
TOSHIHIKO IS A SERIOUS MAN. HE WOULDN'T BELIEVE A STORY INVOLVING GHOSTS!
HEY, YOU--
WHAT CAN I DO TO MAKE YOU BELIEVE ME?
OH MY!
DON'T SAY ANYTHING ELSE, MOTHER-SAN!
AGGH
HMM...
AH... WHAT CAN WE DO?
LET'S FORGET ABOUT IT...

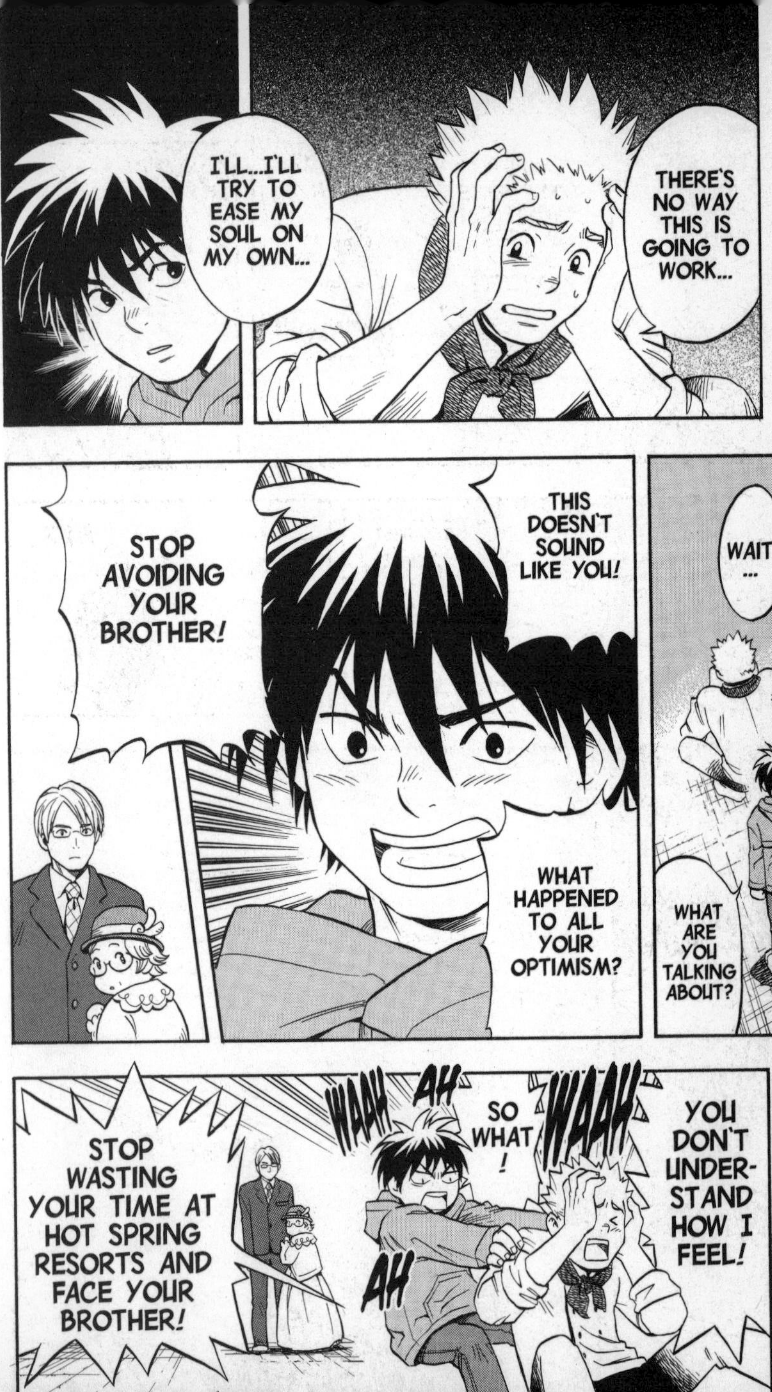
THERE'S NO WAY THIS IS GOING TO WORK...
I'LL...I'LL TRY TO EASE MY SOUL ON MY OWN...
WAIT ...
WHAT ARE YOU TALKING ABOUT?
THIS DOESN'T SOUND LIKE YOU!
STOP AVOIDING YOUR BROTHER!
WHAT HAPPENED TO ALL YOUR OPTIMISM?
YOU DON'T UNDER-STAND HOW I FEEL!
WAAH
SO WHAT!
AH
WAAH
STOP WASTING YOUR TIME AT HOT SPRING RESORTS AND FACE YOUR BROTHER!
AH

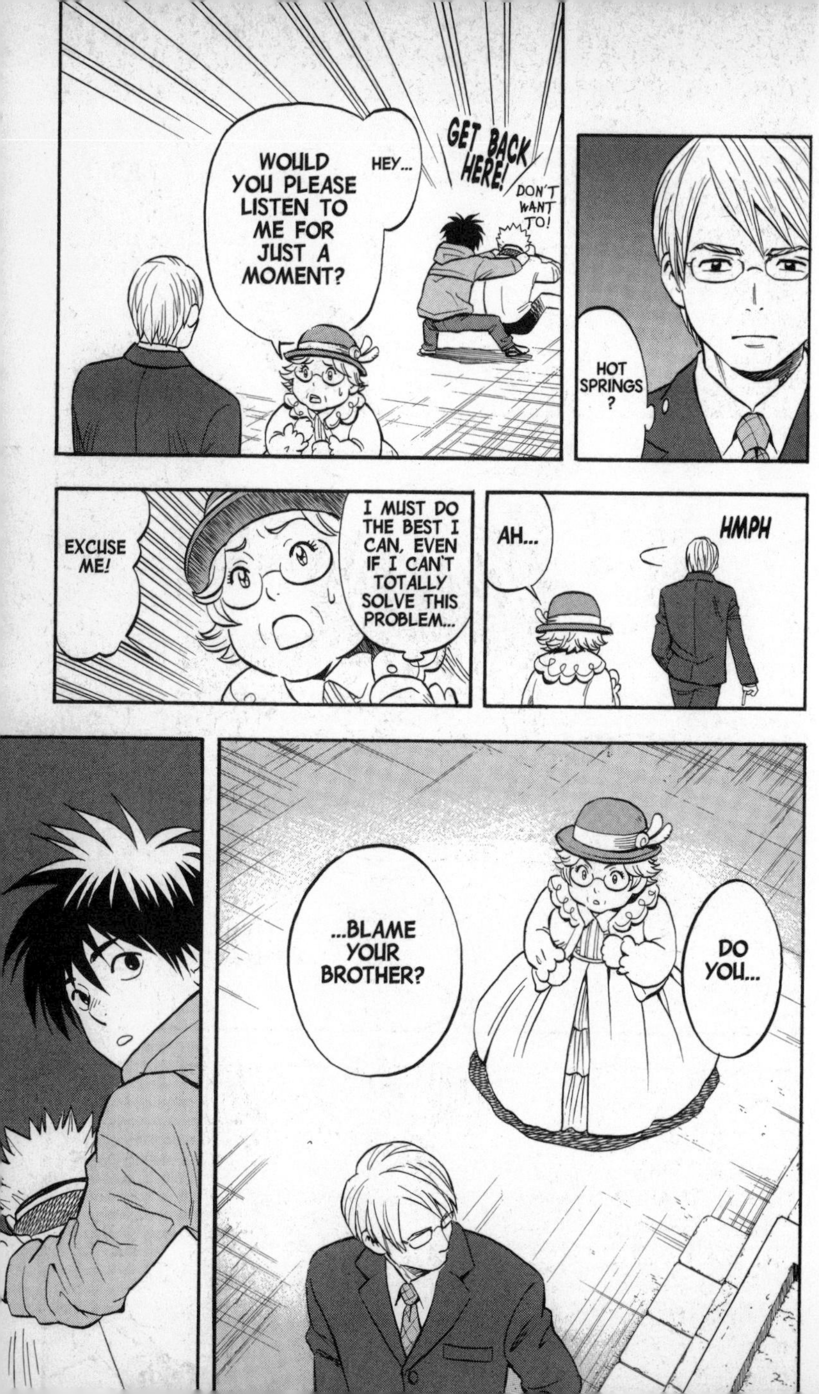
HOT SPRINGS?
GET BACK HERE!
DON'T WANT TO!
HEY...
WOULD YOU PLEASE LISTEN TO ME FOR JUST A MOMENT?
HMPH
AH...
I MUST DO THE BEST I CAN, EVEN IF I CAN'T TOTALLY SOLVE THIS PROBLEM...
EXCUSE ME!
DO YOU...
...BLAME YOUR BROTHER?

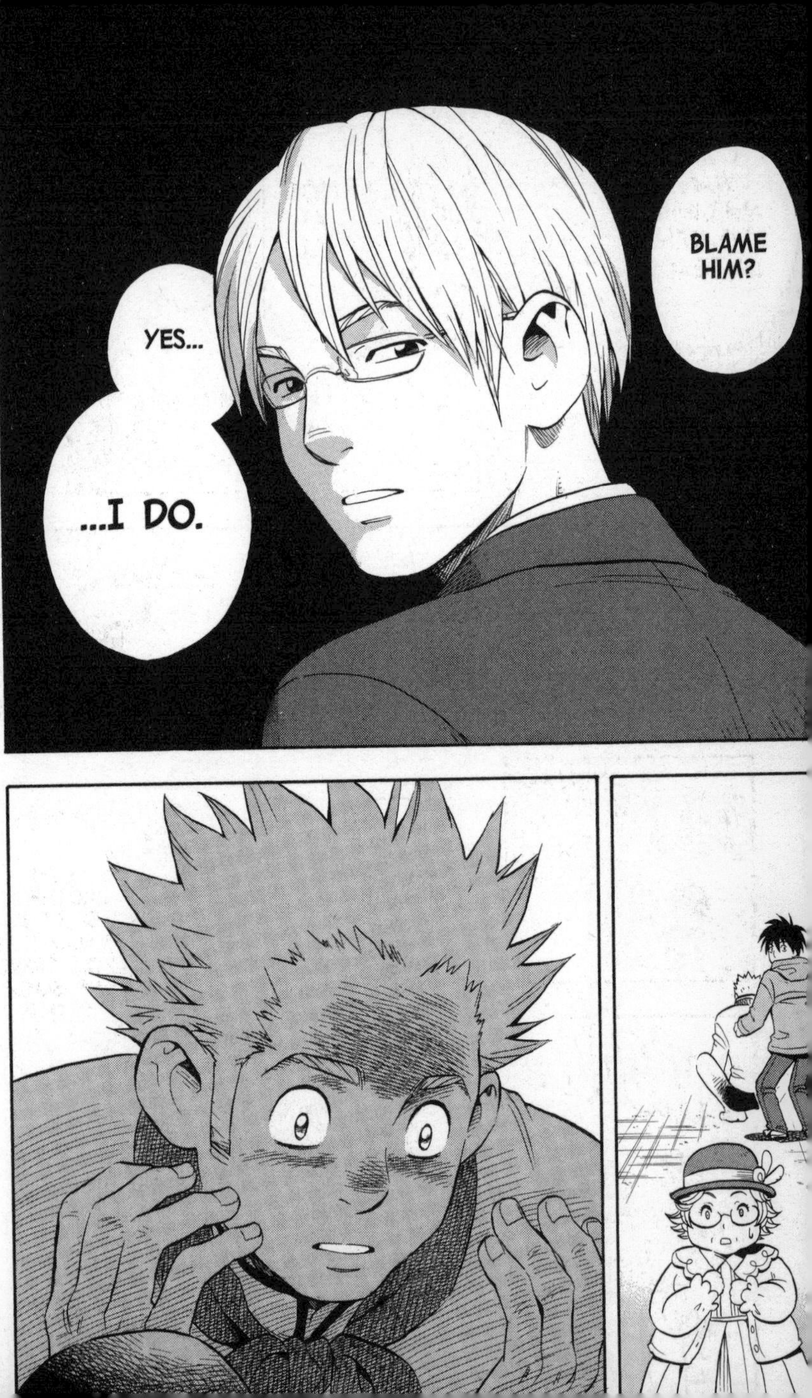
BLAME HIM?
YES...
...I DO.

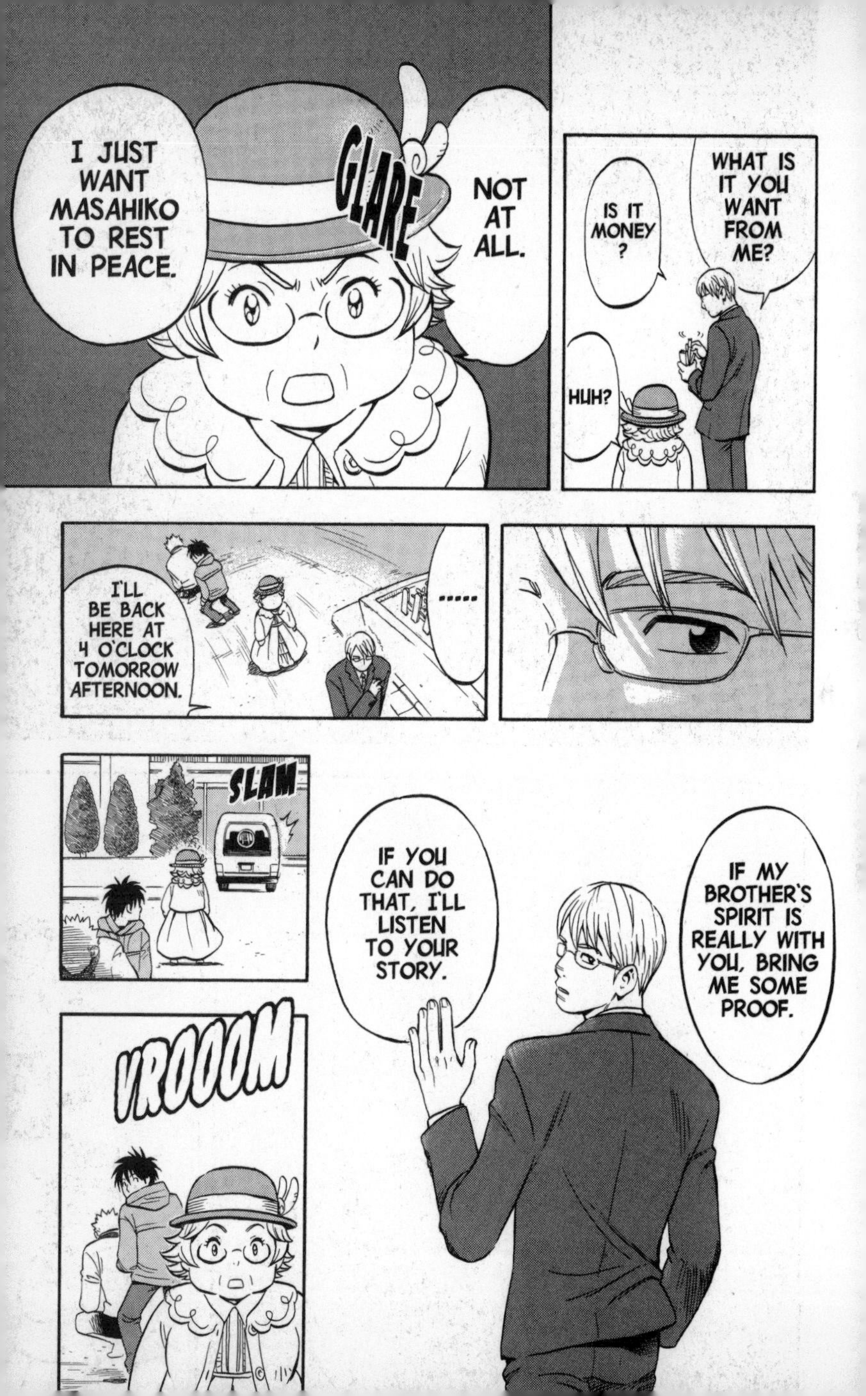
WHAT IS IT YOU WANT FROM ME?
IS IT MONEY?
HUH?
NOT AT ALL.
GLARE
I JUST WANT MASAHIKO TO REST IN PEACE.
.....
I'LL BE BACK HERE AT 4 O'CLOCK TOMORROW AFTERNOON.
IF MY BROTHER'S SPIRIT IS REALLY WITH YOU, BRING ME SOME PROOF.
IF YOU CAN DO THAT, I'LL LISTEN TO YOUR STORY.
SLAM
VROOOM

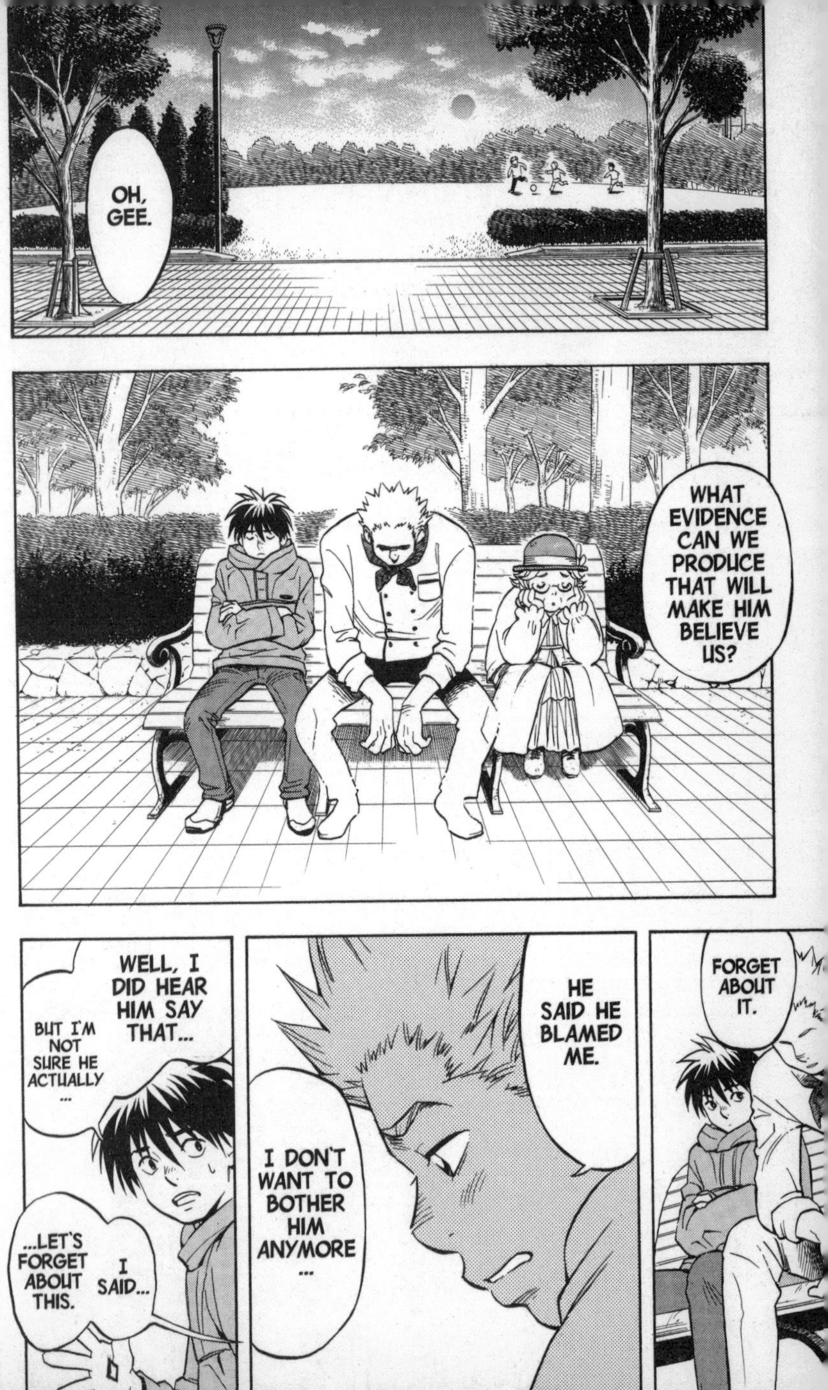
OH, GEE.
WHAT EVIDENCE CAN WE PRODUCE THAT WILL MAKE HIM BELIEVE US?
FORGET ABOUT IT.
HE SAID HE BLAMED ME.
I DON'T WANT TO BOTHER HIM ANYMORE...
WELL, I DID HEAR HIM SAY THAT...
BUT I'M NOT SURE HE ACTUALLY...
I SAID...
...LET'S FORGET ABOUT THIS.

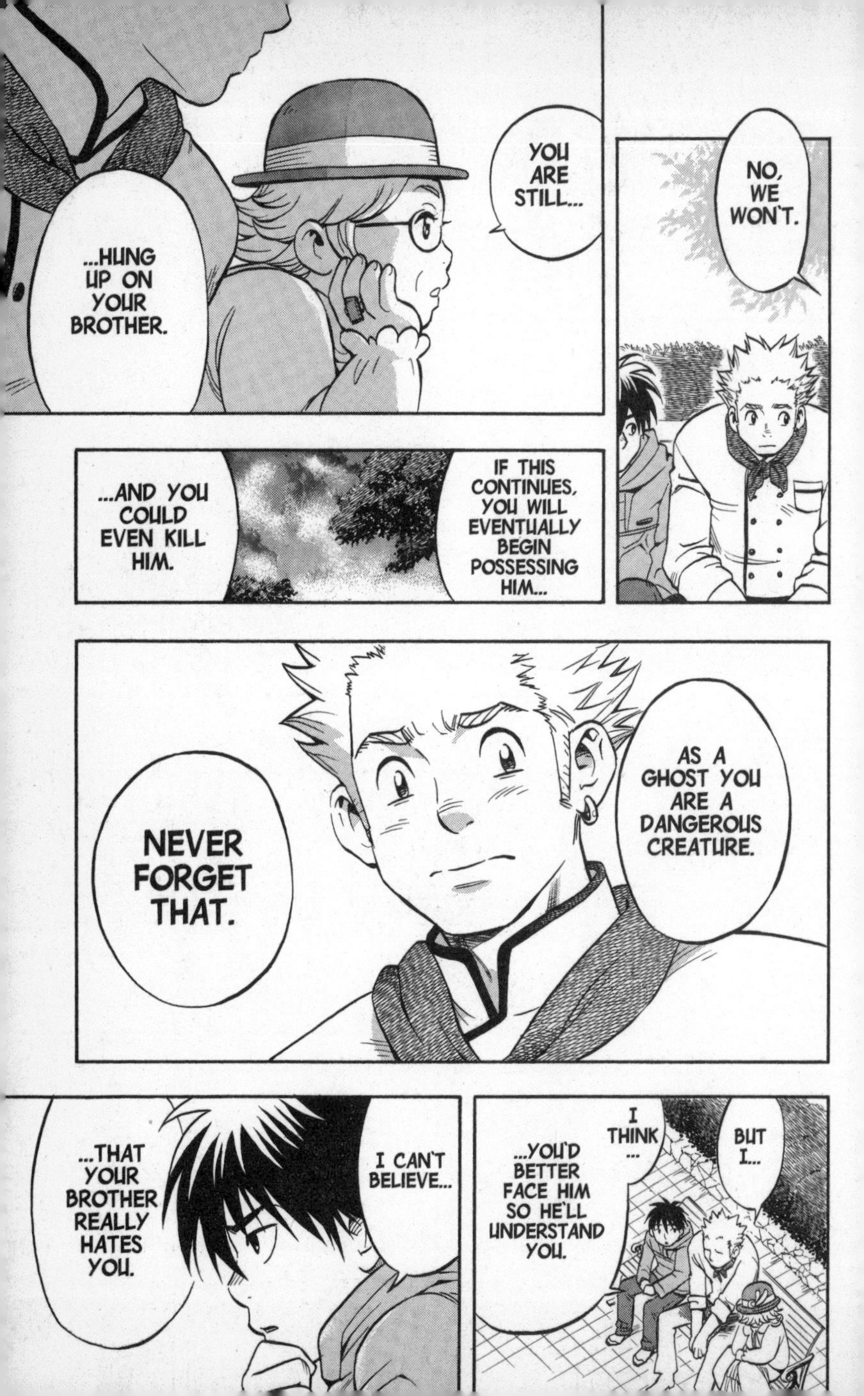
YOU ARE STILL...
...HUNG UP ON YOUR BROTHER.
IF THIS CONTINUES, YOU WILL EVENTUALLY BEGIN POSSESSING HIM...
...AND YOU COULD EVEN KILL HIM.
NO, WE WON'T.
AS A GHOST YOU ARE A DANGEROUS CREATURE.
NEVER FORGET THAT.
BUT I...
I THINK...
...YOU'D BETTER FACE HIM SO HE'LL UNDERSTAND YOU.
I CAN'T BELIEVE...
...THAT YOUR BROTHER REALLY HATES YOU.

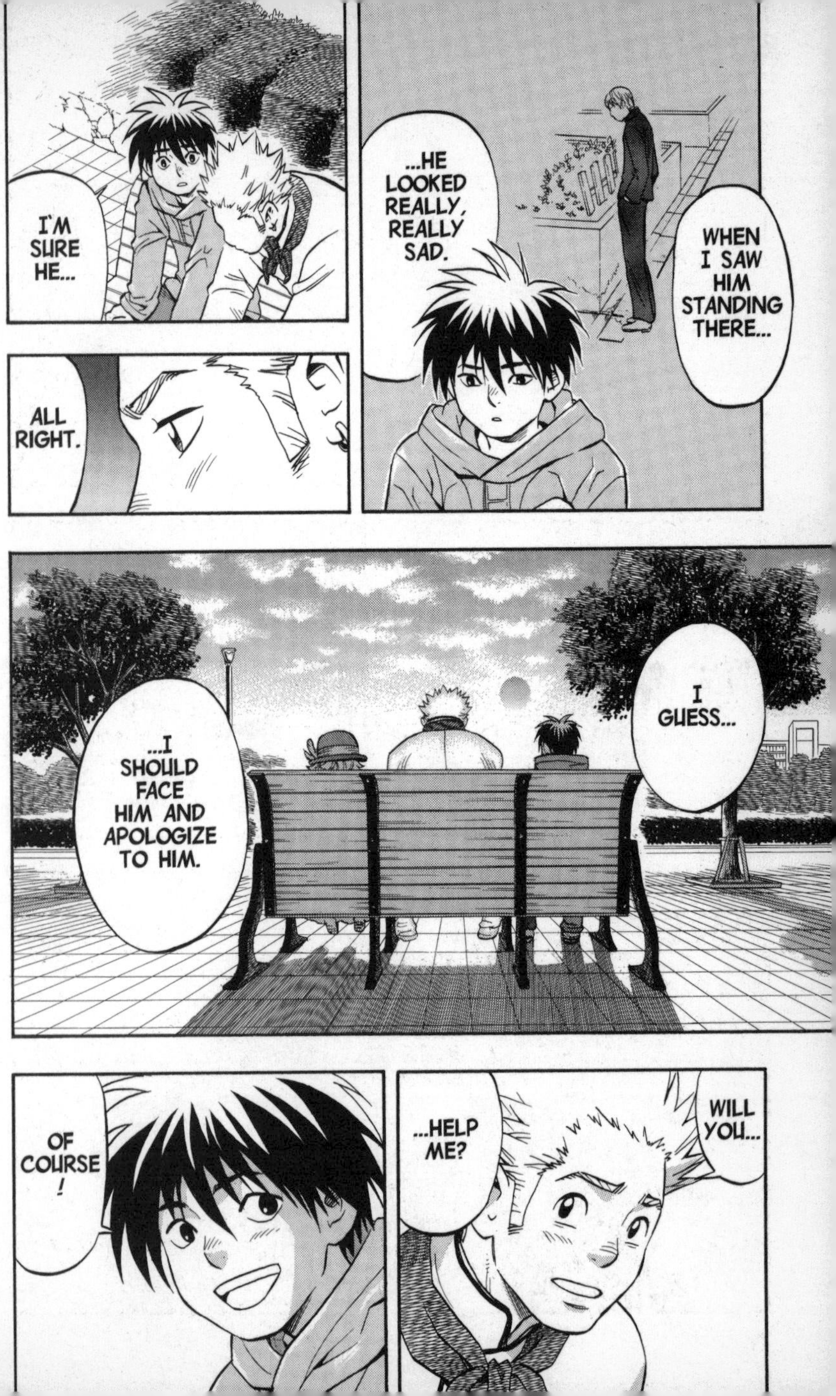
WHEN I SAW HIM STANDING THERE...
...HE LOOKED REALLY, REALLY SAD.
I'M SURE HE...
ALL RIGHT.
I GUESS...
...I SHOULD FACE HIM AND APOLOGIZE TO HIM.
WILL YOU...
...HELP ME?
OF COURSE!

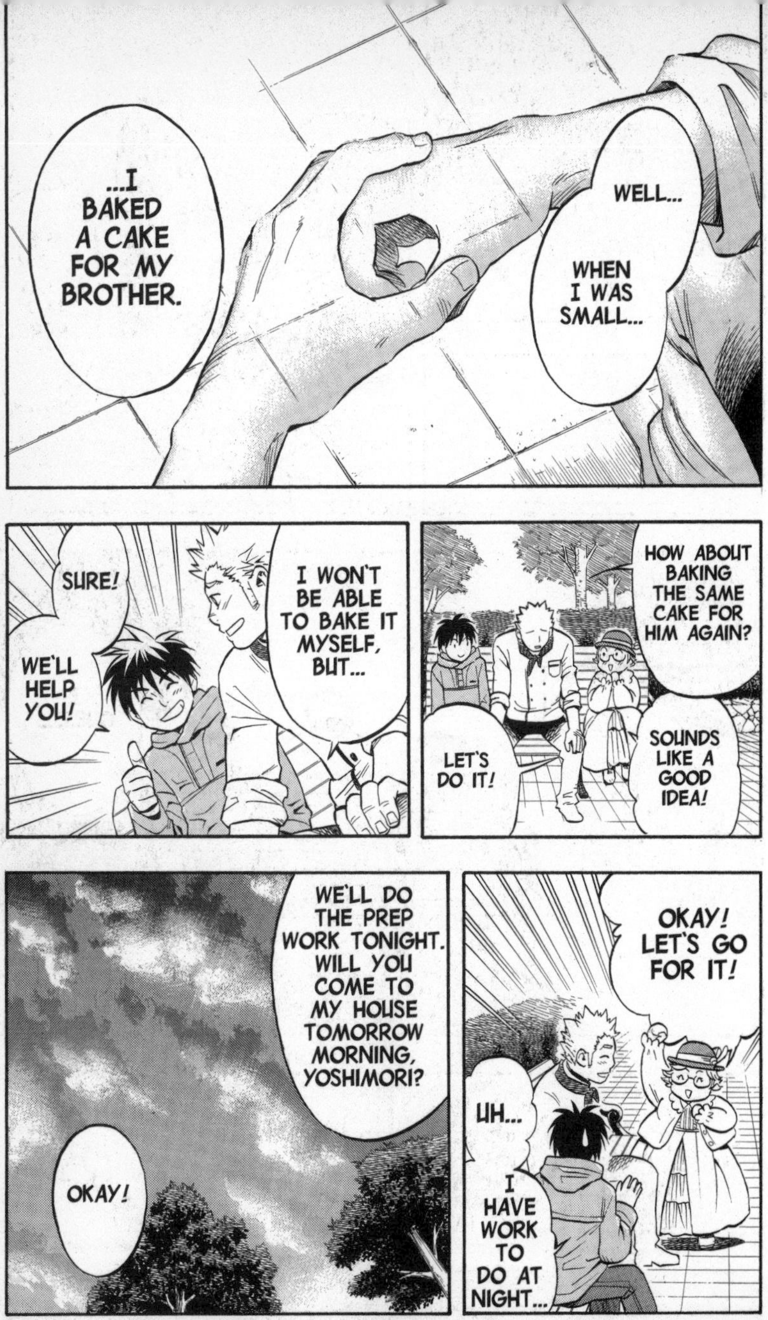
WELL...
WHEN I WAS SMALL...
...I BAKED A CAKE FOR MY BROTHER.
HOW ABOUT BAKING THE SAME CAKE FOR HIM AGAIN?
SOUNDS LIKE A GOOD IDEA!
LET'S DO IT!
I WON'T BE ABLE TO BAKE IT MYSELF, BUT...
SURE!
WE'LL HELP YOU!
OKAY! LET'S GO FOR IT!
UH...
I HAVE WORK TO DO AT NIGHT...
WE'LL DO THE PREP WORK TONIGHT. WILL YOU COME TO MY HOUSE TOMORROW MORNING, YOSHIMORI?
OKAY!

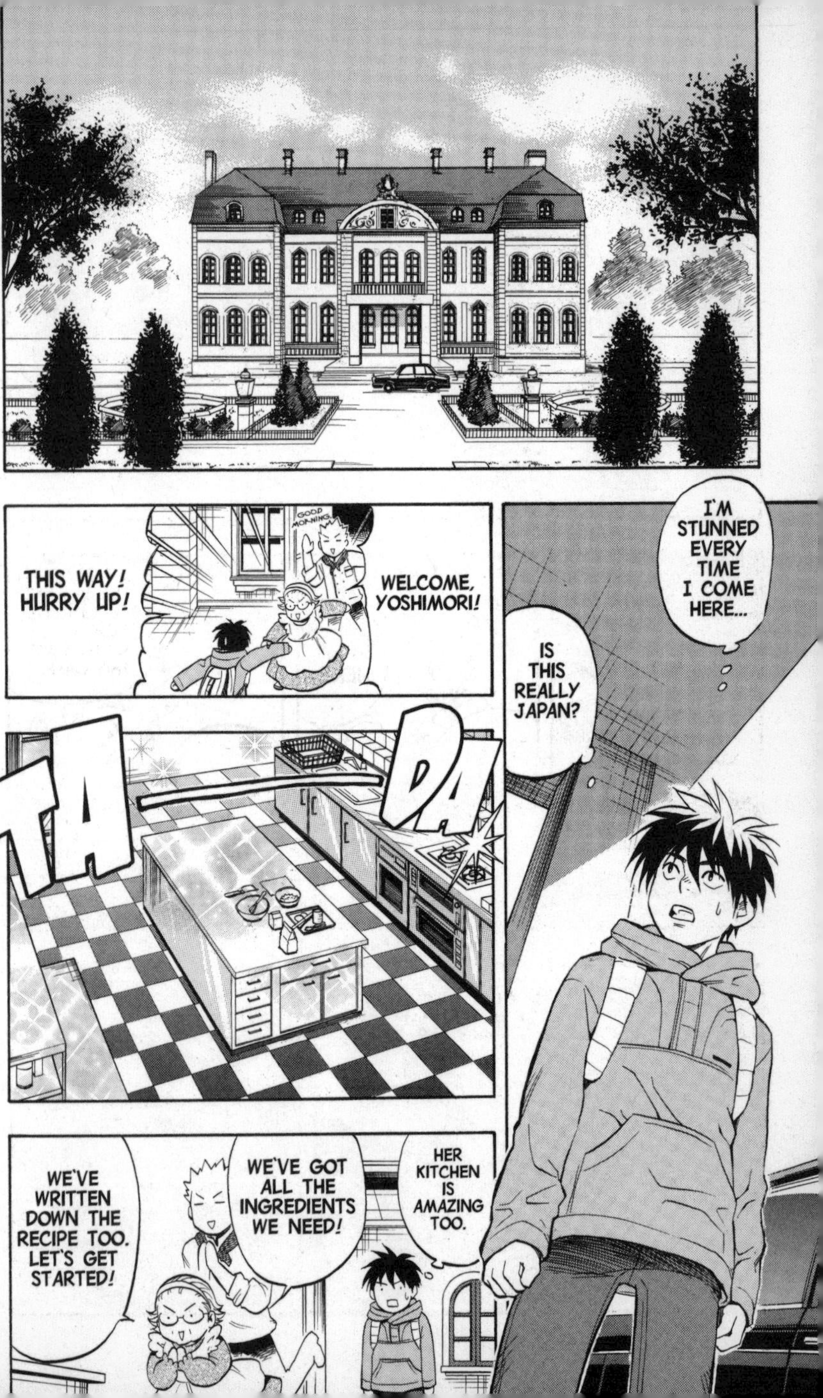
I'M STUNNED EVERY TIME I COME HERE...
IS THIS REALLY JAPAN?
GOOD MORNING
WELCOME, YOSHIMORI!
THIS WAY! HURRY UP!
TA—DA
HER KITCHEN IS AMAZING TOO.
WE'VE GOT ALL THE INGREDIENTS WE NEED!
WE'VE WRITTEN DOWN THE RECIPE TOO. LET'S GET STARTED!

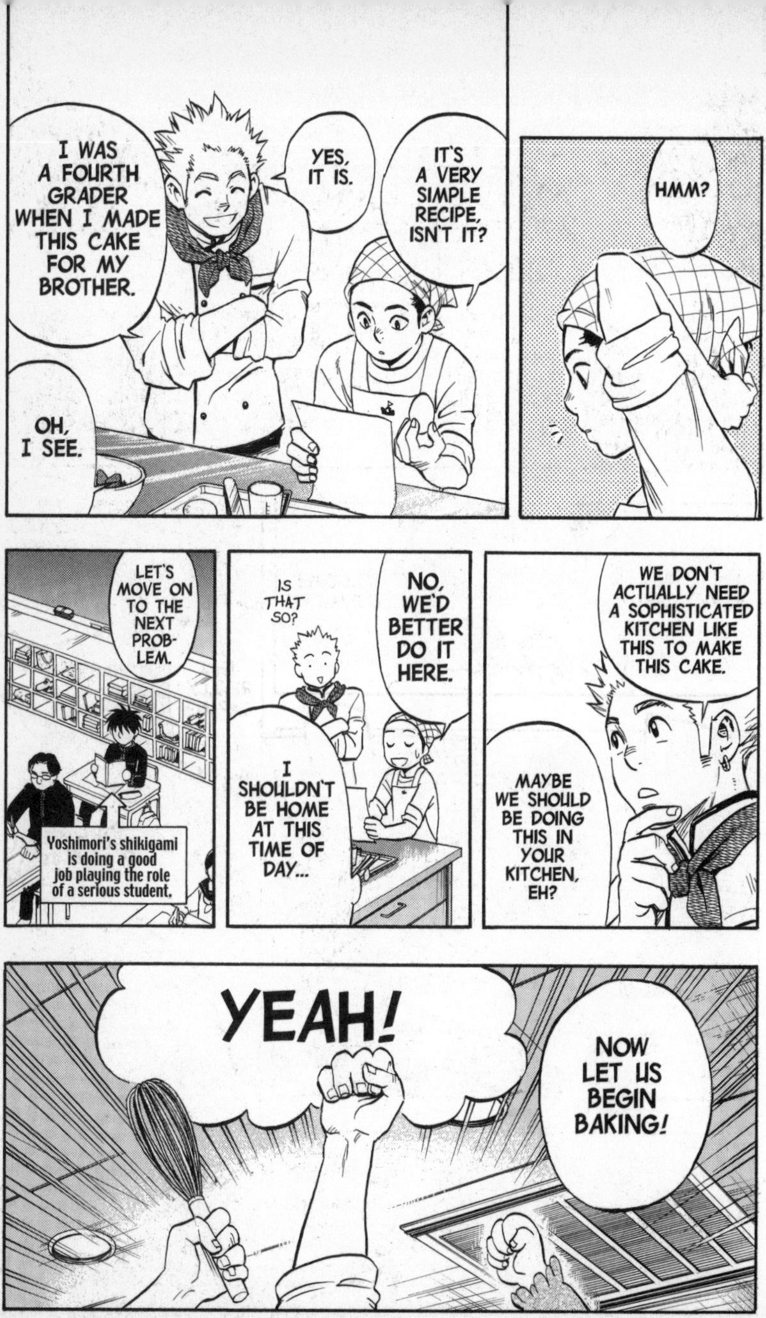
HMM?
IT'S A VERY SIMPLE RECIPE, ISN'T IT?
YES, IT IS.
I WAS A FOURTH GRADER WHEN I MADE THIS CAKE FOR MY BROTHER.
OH, I SEE.
WE DON'T ACTUALLY NEED A SOPHISTICATED KITCHEN LIKE THIS TO MAKE THIS CAKE.
MAYBE WE SHOULD BE DOING THIS IN YOUR KITCHEN, EH?
NO, WE'D BETTER DO IT HERE.
IS THAT SO?
I SHOULDN'T BE HOME AT THIS TIME OF DAY...
LET'S MOVE ON TO THE NEXT PROB-LEM.
Yoshimori's shikigami is doing a good job playing the role of a serious student.
NOW LET US BEGIN BAKING!
YEAH!

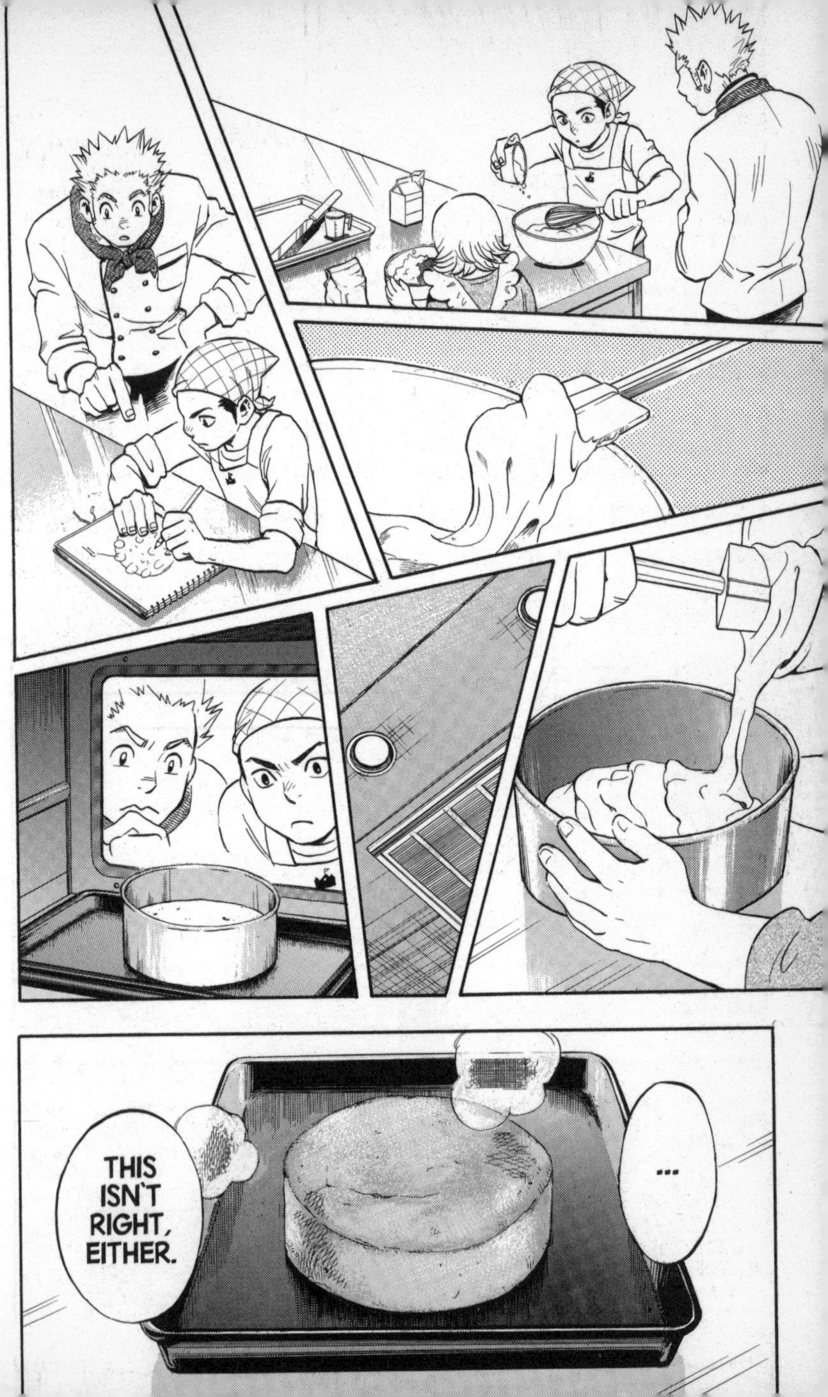
...
THIS ISN'T RIGHT, EITHER.

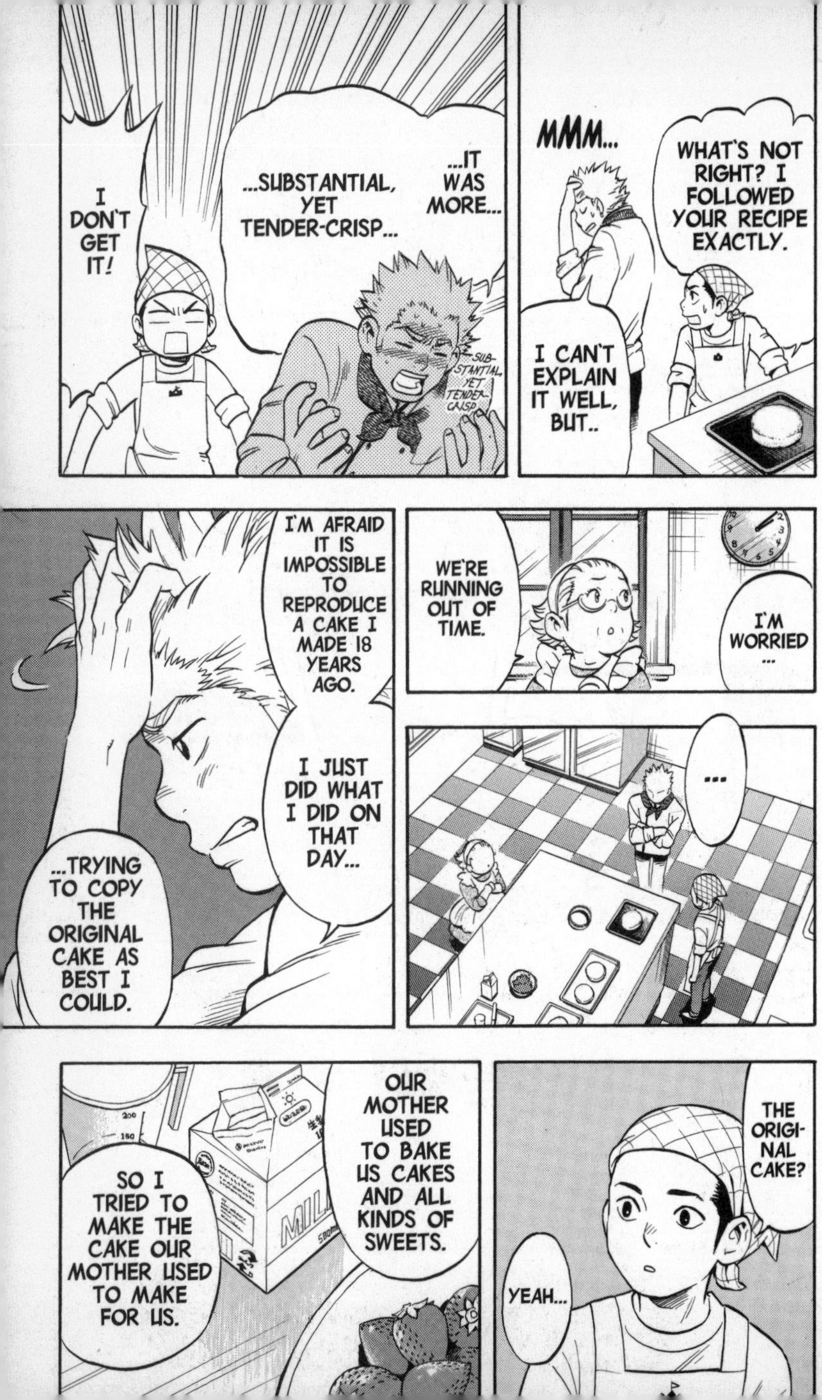
WHAT'S NOT RIGHT? I FOLLOWED YOUR RECIPE EXACTLY.
MMM...
I CAN'T EXPLAIN IT WELL, BUT..
...IT WAS MORE...
...SUBSTANTIAL, YET TENDER-CRISP...
SUBSTANTIAL, YET TENDER-CRISP
I DON'T GET IT!
I'M WORRIED...
WE'RE RUNNING OUT OF TIME.
...
I'M AFRAID IT IS IMPOSSIBLE TO REPRODUCE A CAKE I MADE 18 YEARS AGO.
I JUST DID WHAT I DID ON THAT DAY...
...TRYING TO COPY THE ORIGINAL CAKE AS BEST I COULD.
THE ORIGINAL CAKE?
YEAH...
OUR MOTHER USED TO BAKE US CAKES AND ALL KINDS OF SWEETS.
SO I TRIED TO MAKE THE CAKE OUR MOTHER USED TO MAKE FOR US.

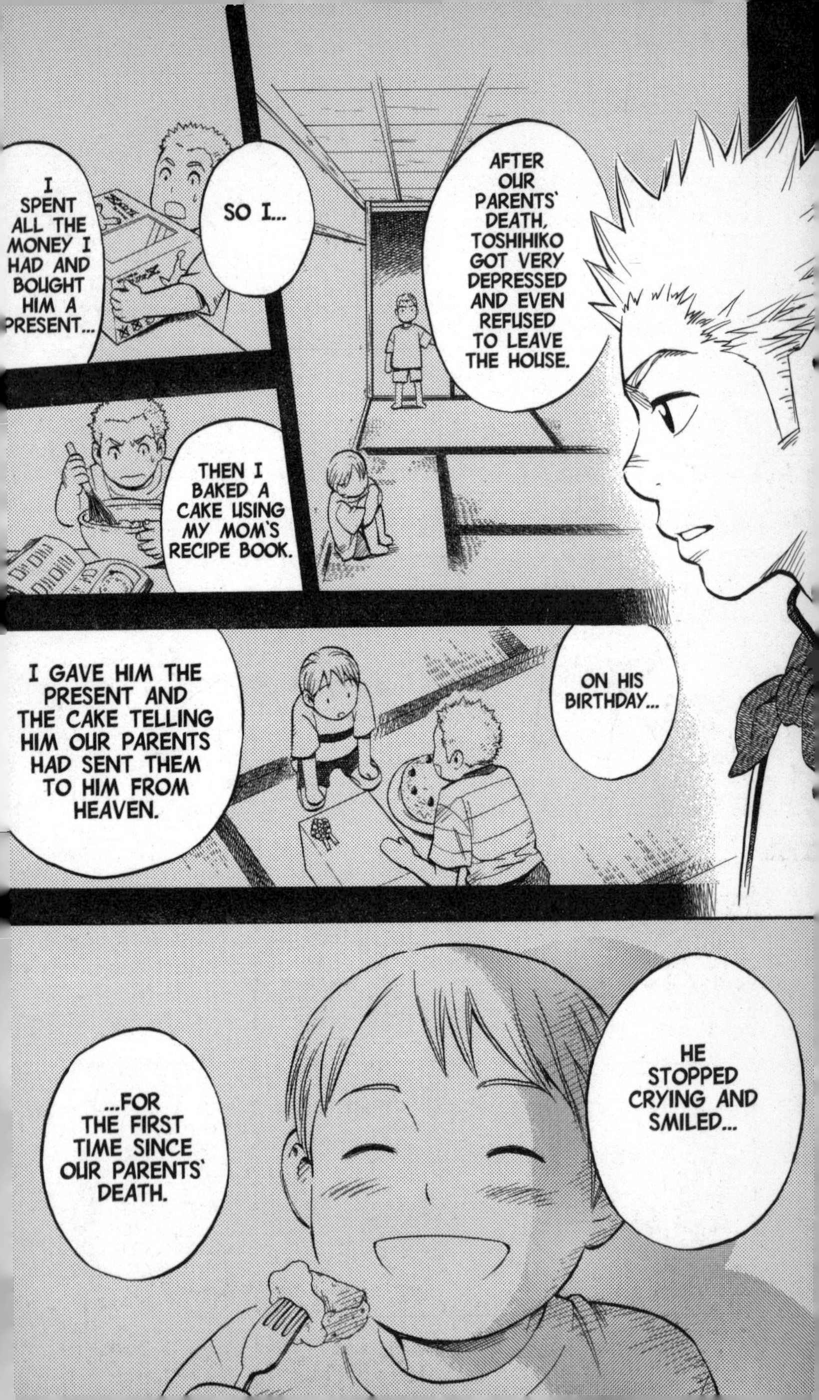
AFTER OUR PARENTS' DEATH, TOSHIHIKO GOT VERY DEPRESSED AND EVEN REFUSED TO LEAVE THE HOUSE.
SO I...
I SPENT ALL THE MONEY I HAD AND BOUGHT HIM A PRESENT...
THEN I BAKED A CAKE USING MY MOM'S RECIPE BOOK.
ON HIS BIRTHDAY...
I GAVE HIM THE PRESENT AND THE CAKE TELLING HIM OUR PARENTS HAD SENT THEM TO HIM FROM HEAVEN.
HE STOPPED CRYING AND SMILED...
...FOR THE FIRST TIME SINCE OUR PARENTS' DEATH.

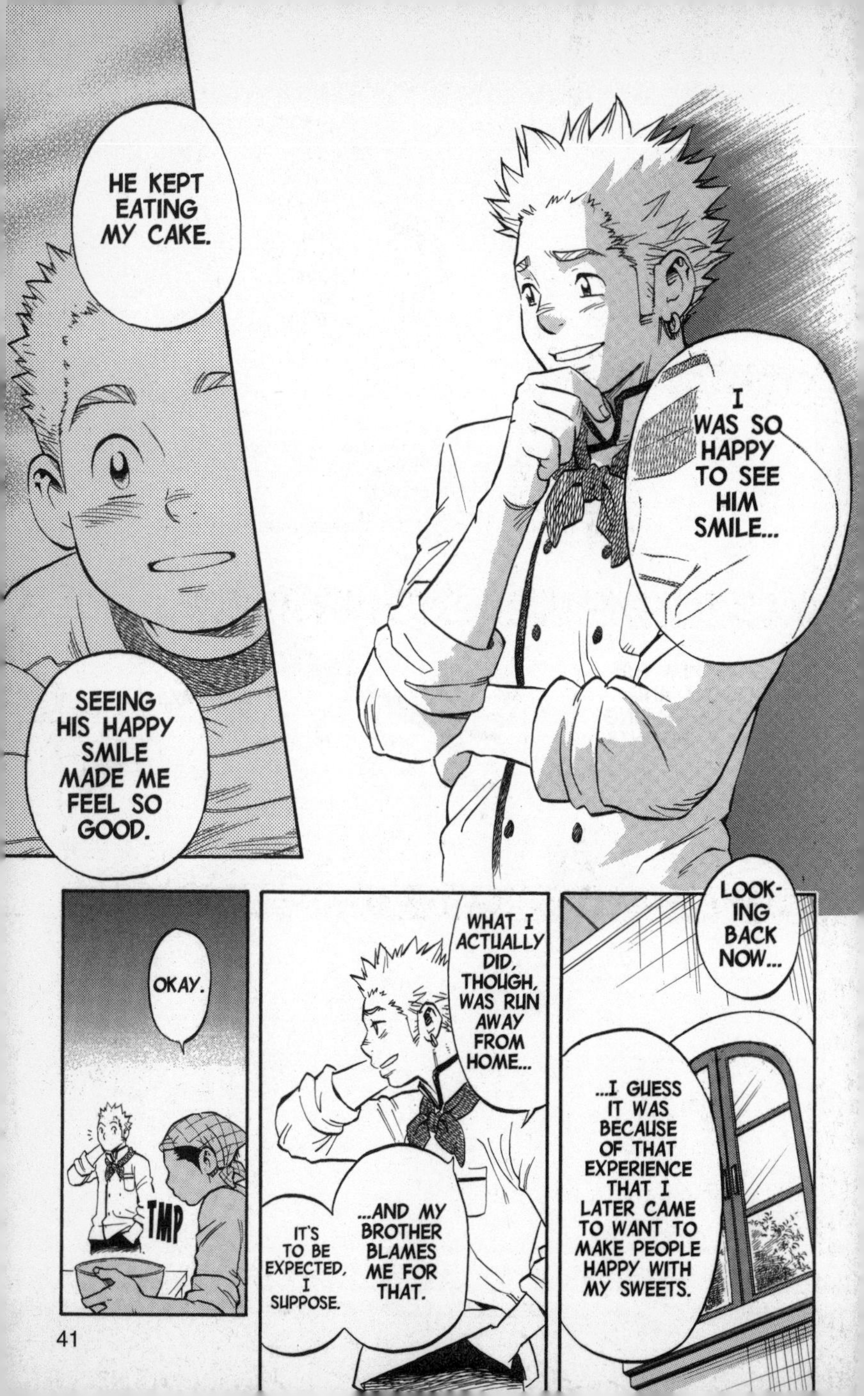
I WAS SO HAPPY TO SEE HIM SMILE...
HE KEPT EATING MY CAKE.
SEEING HIS HAPPY SMILE MADE ME FEEL SO GOOD.
LOOKING BACK NOW...
...I GUESS IT WAS BECAUSE OF THAT EXPERIENCE THAT I LATER CAME TO WANT TO MAKE PEOPLE HAPPY WITH MY SWEETS.
WHAT I ACTUALLY DID, THOUGH, WAS RUN AWAY FROM HOME...
...AND MY BROTHER BLAMES ME FOR THAT.
IT'S TO BE EXPECTED, I SUPPOSE.
OKAY.
TMP

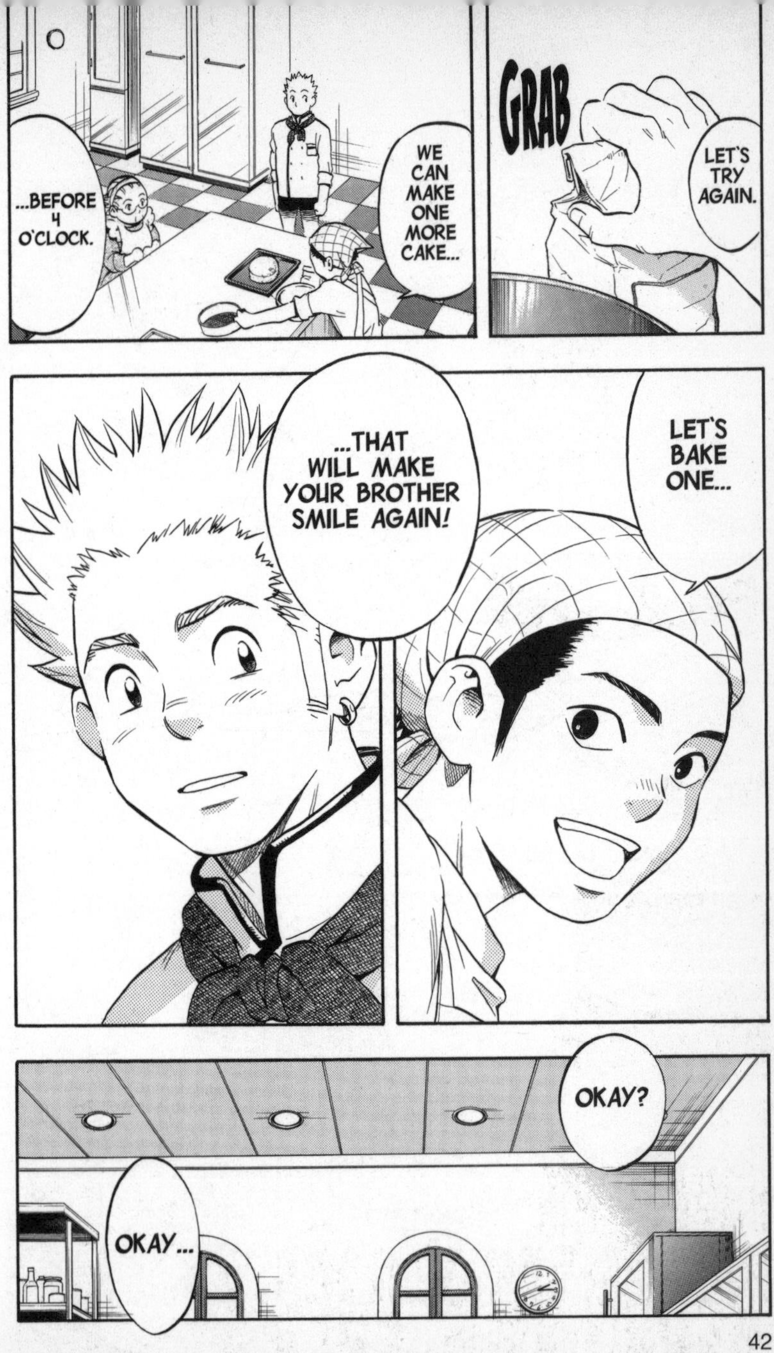
GRAB
LET'S TRY AGAIN.
WE CAN MAKE ONE MORE CAKE...
...BEFORE 4 O'CLOCK.
LET'S BAKE ONE...
...THAT WILL MAKE YOUR BROTHER SMILE AGAIN!
OKAY?
OKAY...

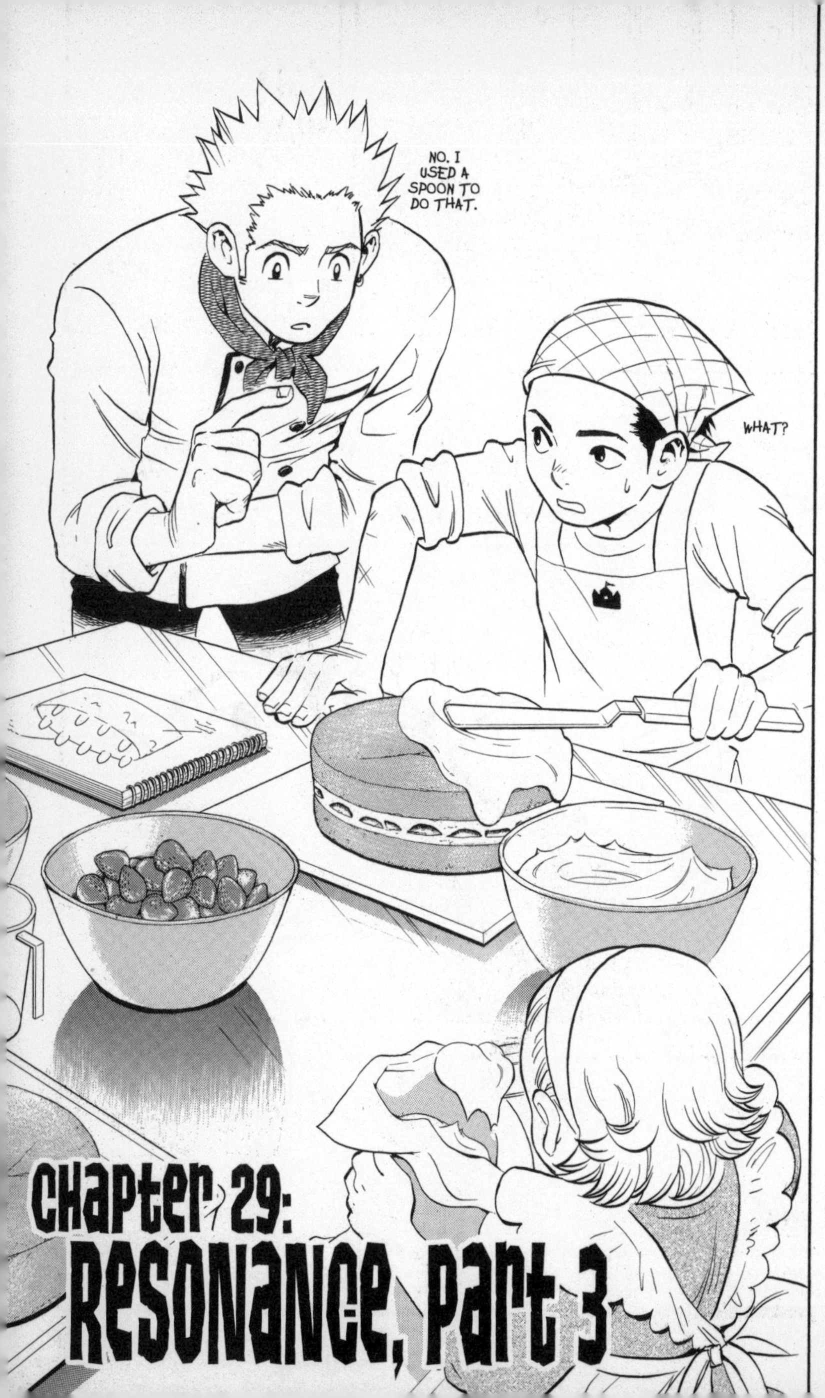
WHAT?
NO. I USED A SPOON TO DO THAT.
CHAPTER 29:
RESONANCE, PART 3

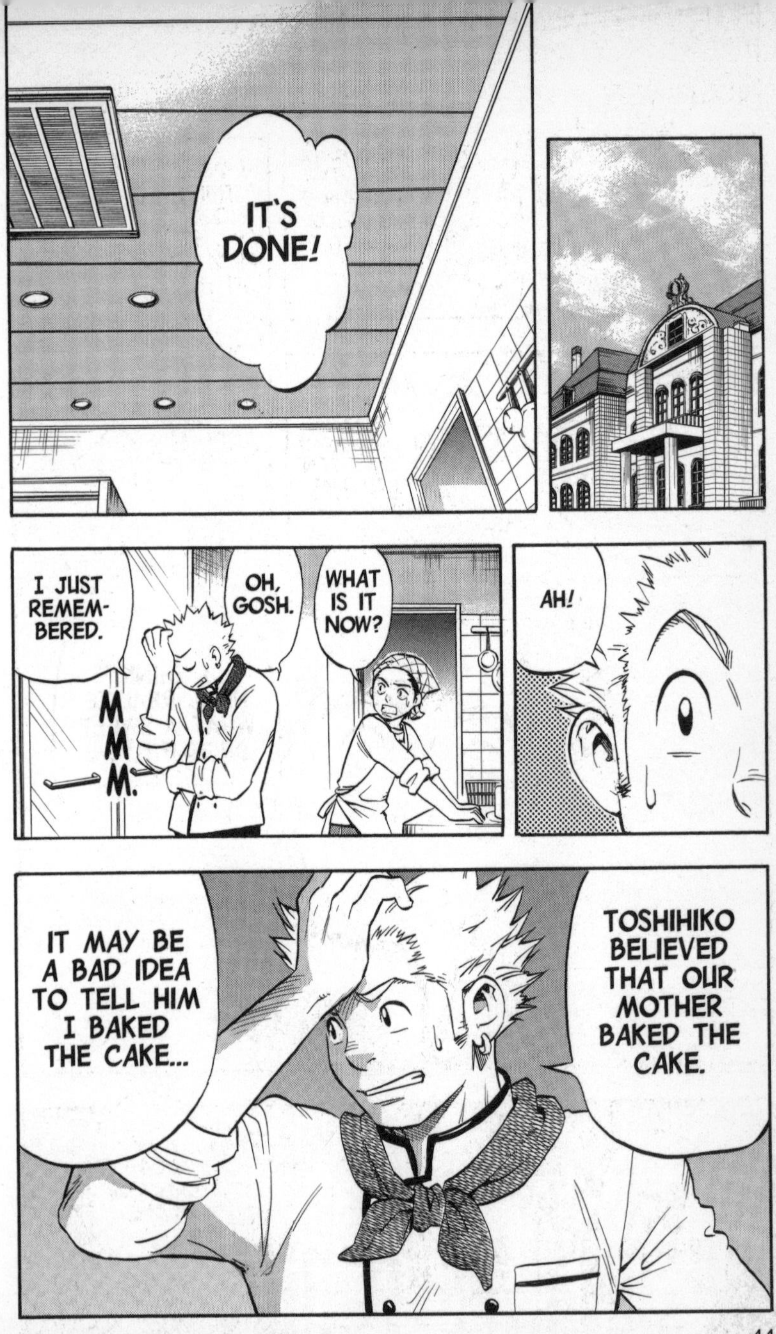
IT'S DONE!
AH!
WHAT IS IT NOW?
OH, GOSH.
I JUST REMEMBERED.
MMMM.
TOSHIHIKO BELIEVED THAT OUR MOTHER BAKED THE CAKE.
IT MAY BE A BAD IDEA TO TELL HIM I BAKED THE CAKE...

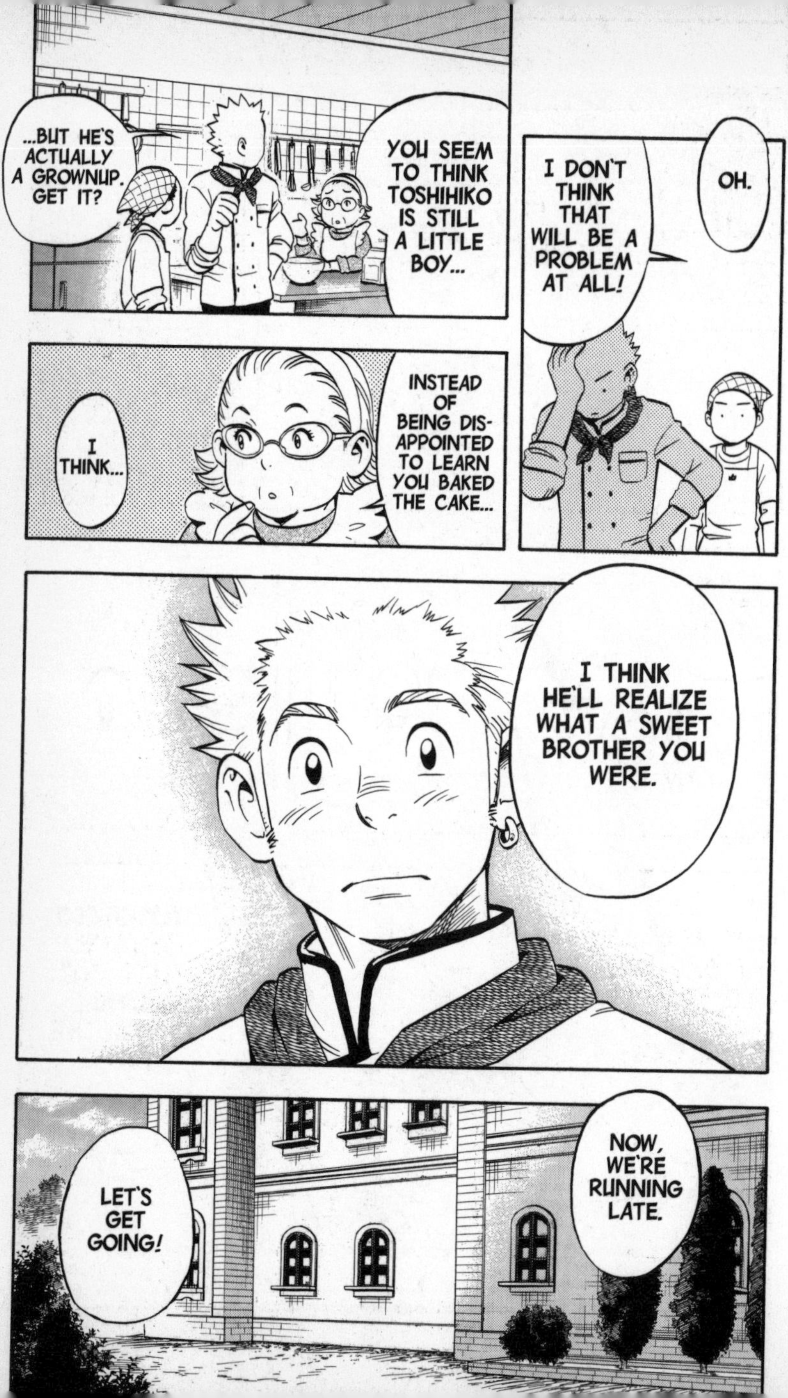
YOU SEEM TO THINK TOSHIHIKO IS STILL A LITTLE BOY...
...BUT HE'S ACTUALLY A GROWNUP. GET IT?
OH.
I DON'T THINK THAT WILL BE A PROBLEM AT ALL!
INSTEAD OF BEING DIS-APPOINTED TO LEARN YOU BAKED THE CAKE...
I THINK...
I THINK HE'LL REALIZE WHAT A SWEET BROTHER YOU WERE.
NOW, WE'RE RUNNING LATE.
LET'S GET GOING!

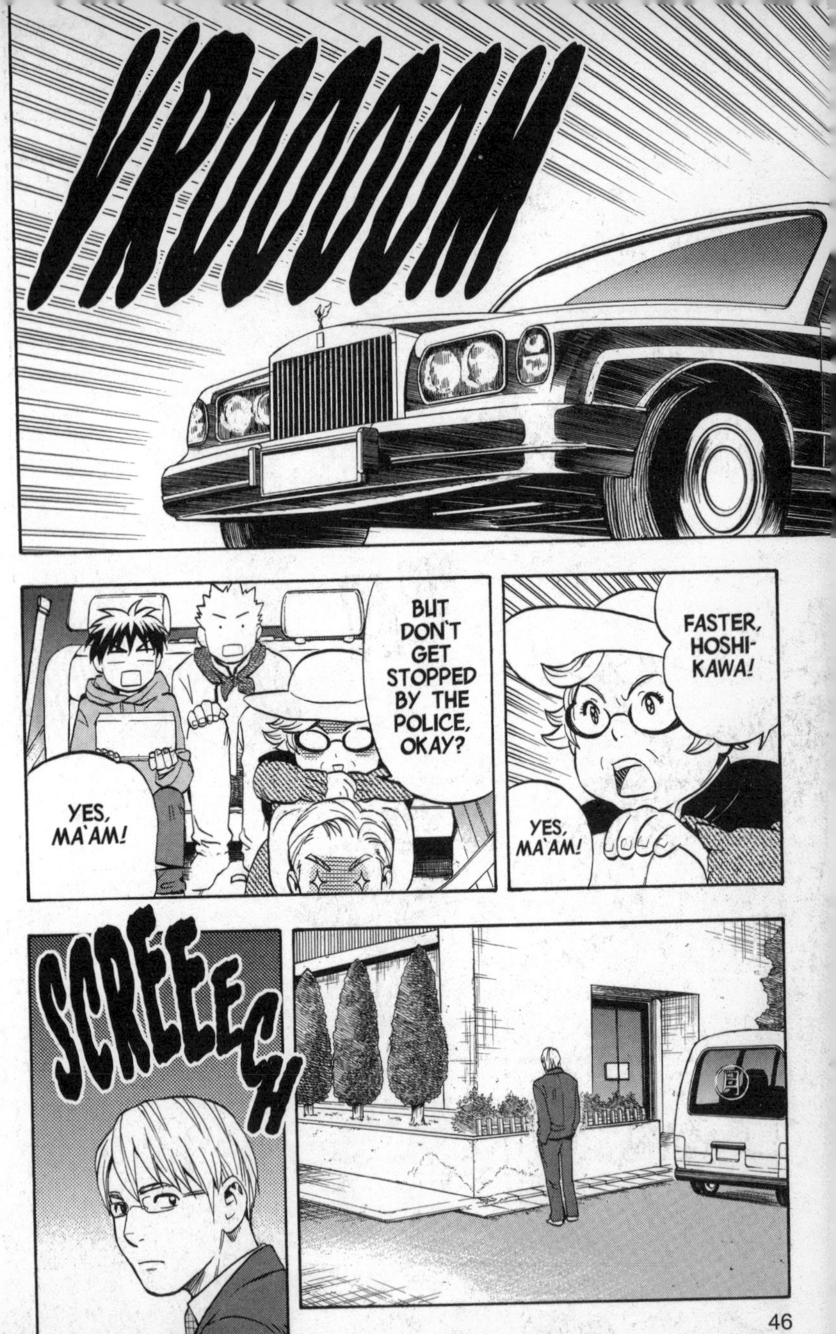
VROOOOM
FASTER, HOSHI-KAWA!
YES, MA'AM!
BUT DON'T GET STOPPED BY THE POLICE, OKAY?
YES, MA'AM!
SCREEECH

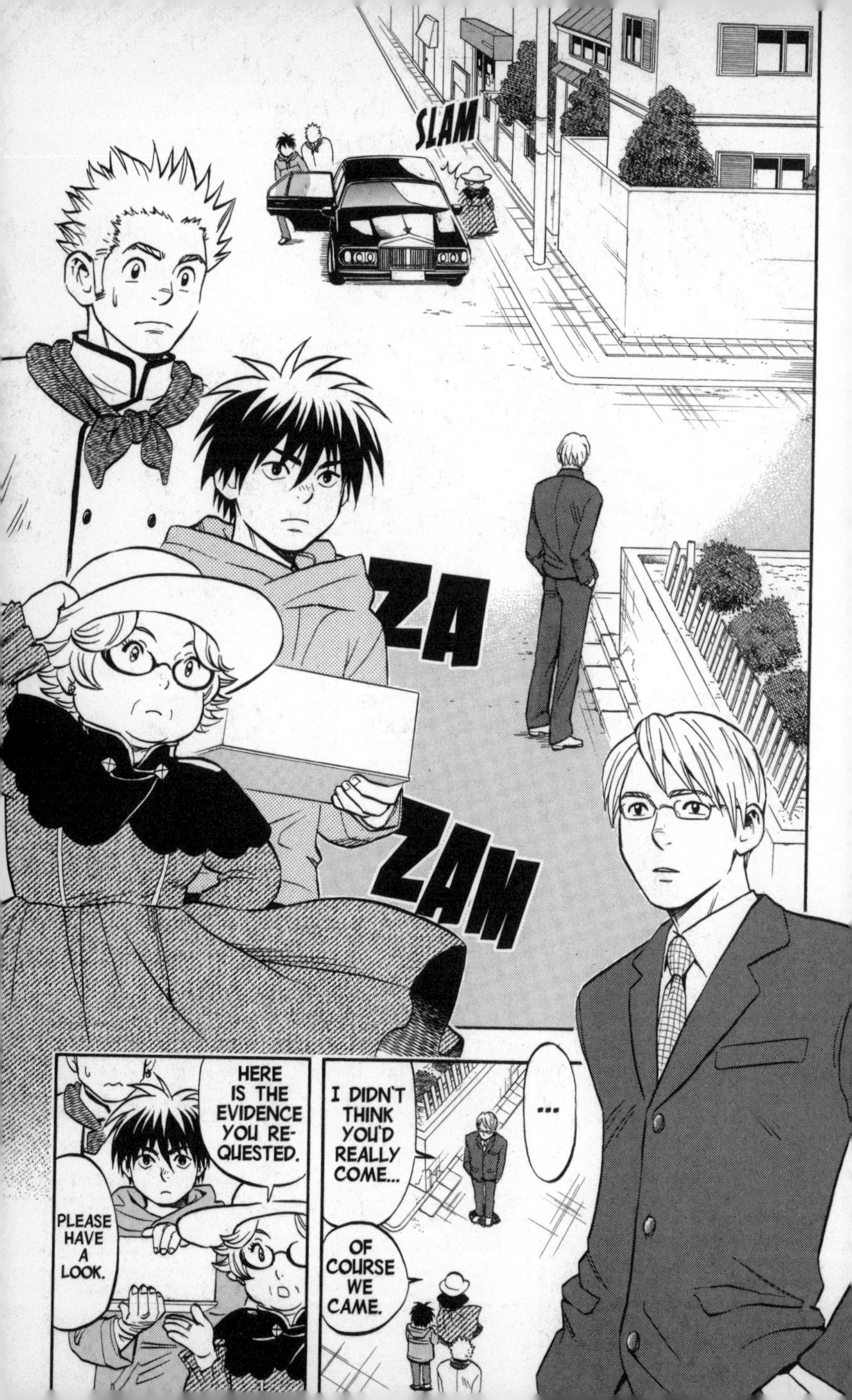
SLAM
ZA
ZAM
...
I DIDN'T THINK YOU'D REALLY COME...
OF COURSE WE CAME.
HERE IS THE EVIDENCE YOU RE-QUESTED.
PLEASE HAVE A LOOK.

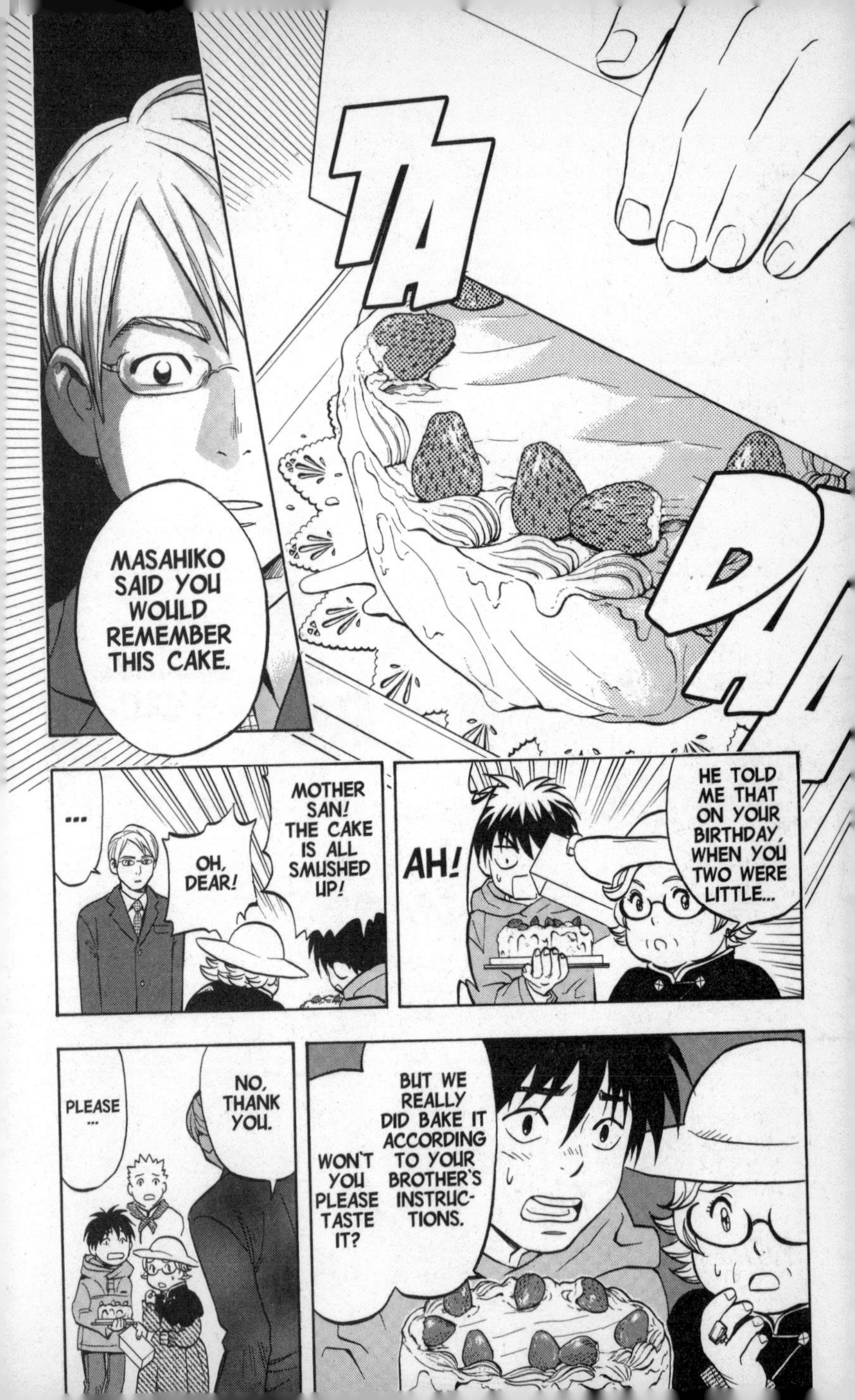
TA
DA
MASAHIKO SAID YOU WOULD REMEMBER THIS CAKE.
HE TOLD ME THAT ON YOUR BIRTHDAY, WHEN YOU TWO WERE LITTLE...
AH!
MOTHER SAN! THE CAKE IS ALL SMUSHED UP!
OH, DEAR!
...
BUT WE REALLY DID BAKE IT ACCORDING TO YOUR BROTHER'S INSTRUCTIONS.
WON'T YOU PLEASE TASTE IT?
NO, THANK YOU.
PLEASE ...

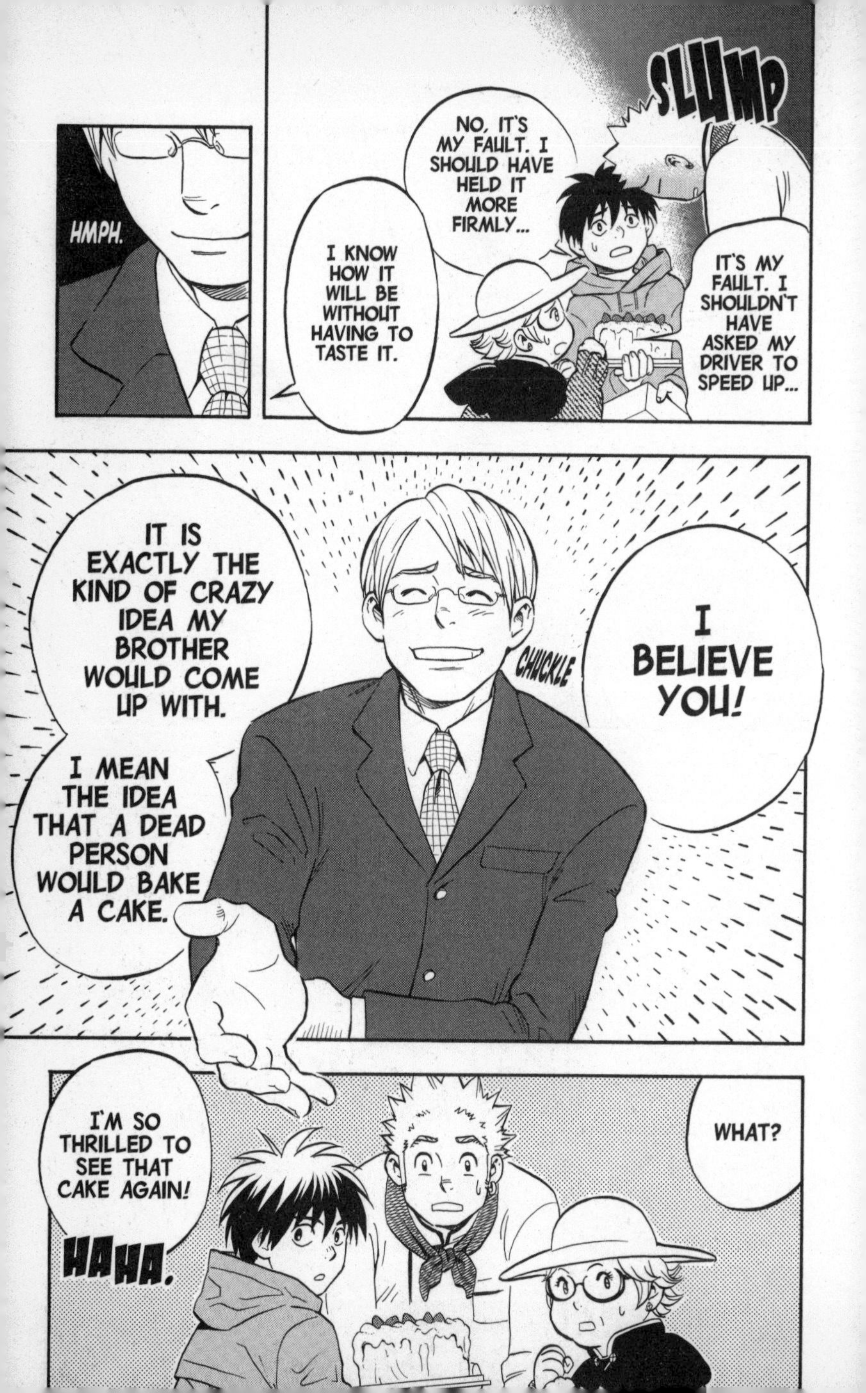
SLUMP
IT'S MY FAULT. I SHOULDN'T HAVE ASKED MY DRIVER TO SPEED UP...
NO, IT'S MY FAULT. I SHOULD HAVE HELD IT MORE FIRMLY...
I KNOW HOW IT WILL BE WITHOUT HAVING TO TASTE IT.
HMPH.
I BELIEVE YOU!
CHUCKLE
IT IS EXACTLY THE KIND OF CRAZY IDEA MY BROTHER WOULD COME UP WITH.
I MEAN THE IDEA THAT A DEAD PERSON WOULD BAKE A CAKE.
WHAT?
I'M SO THRILLED TO SEE THAT CAKE AGAIN!
HAHA.

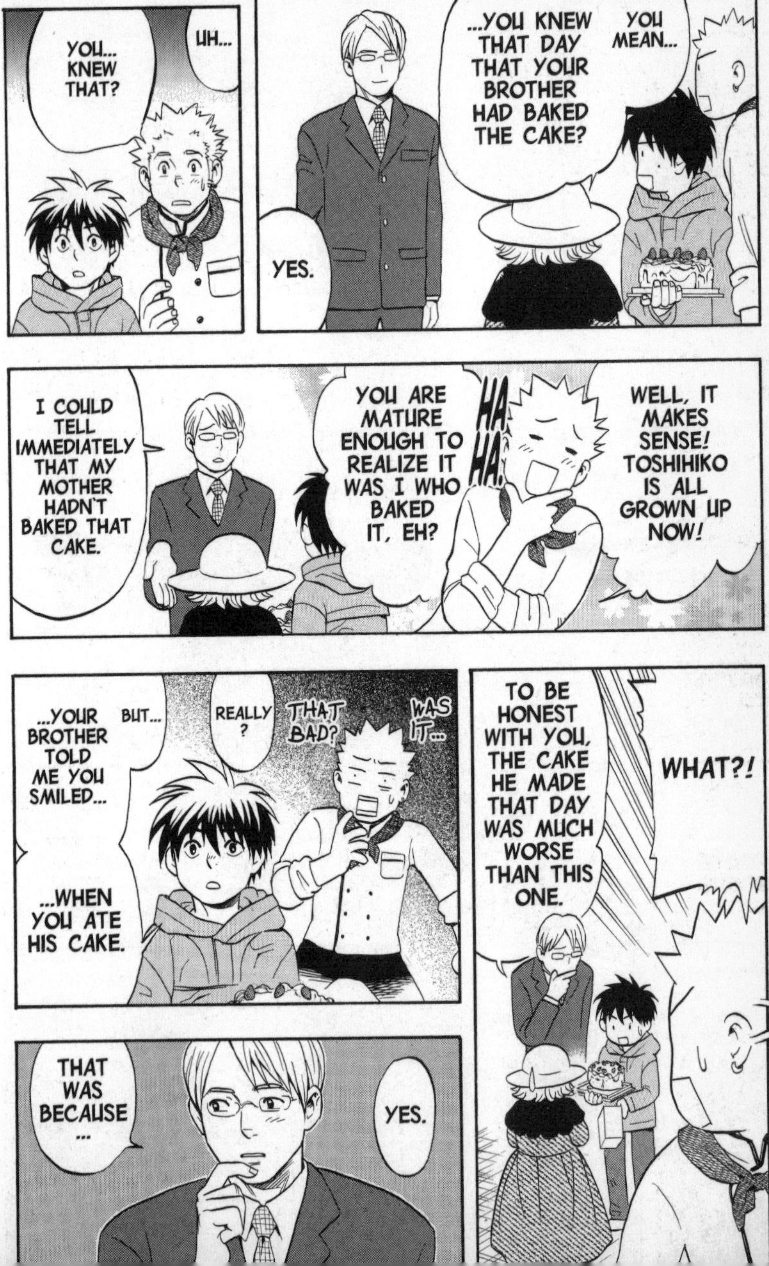
YOU MEAN...
...YOU KNEW THAT DAY THAT YOUR BROTHER HAD BAKED THE CAKE?
YES.
UH...
YOU... KNEW THAT?
WELL, IT MAKES SENSE! TOSHIHIKO IS ALL GROWN UP NOW!
HA HA.
YOU ARE MATURE ENOUGH TO REALIZE IT WAS I WHO BAKED IT, EH?
I COULD TELL IMMEDIATELY THAT MY MOTHER HADN'T BAKED THAT CAKE.
TO BE HONEST WITH YOU, THE CAKE HE MADE THAT DAY WAS MUCH WORSE THAN THIS ONE.
WHAT?!
WAS IT...
THAT BAD?
REALLY?
BUT...
...YOUR BROTHER TOLD ME YOU SMILED...
...WHEN YOU ATE HIS CAKE.
YES.
THAT WAS BECAUSE ...

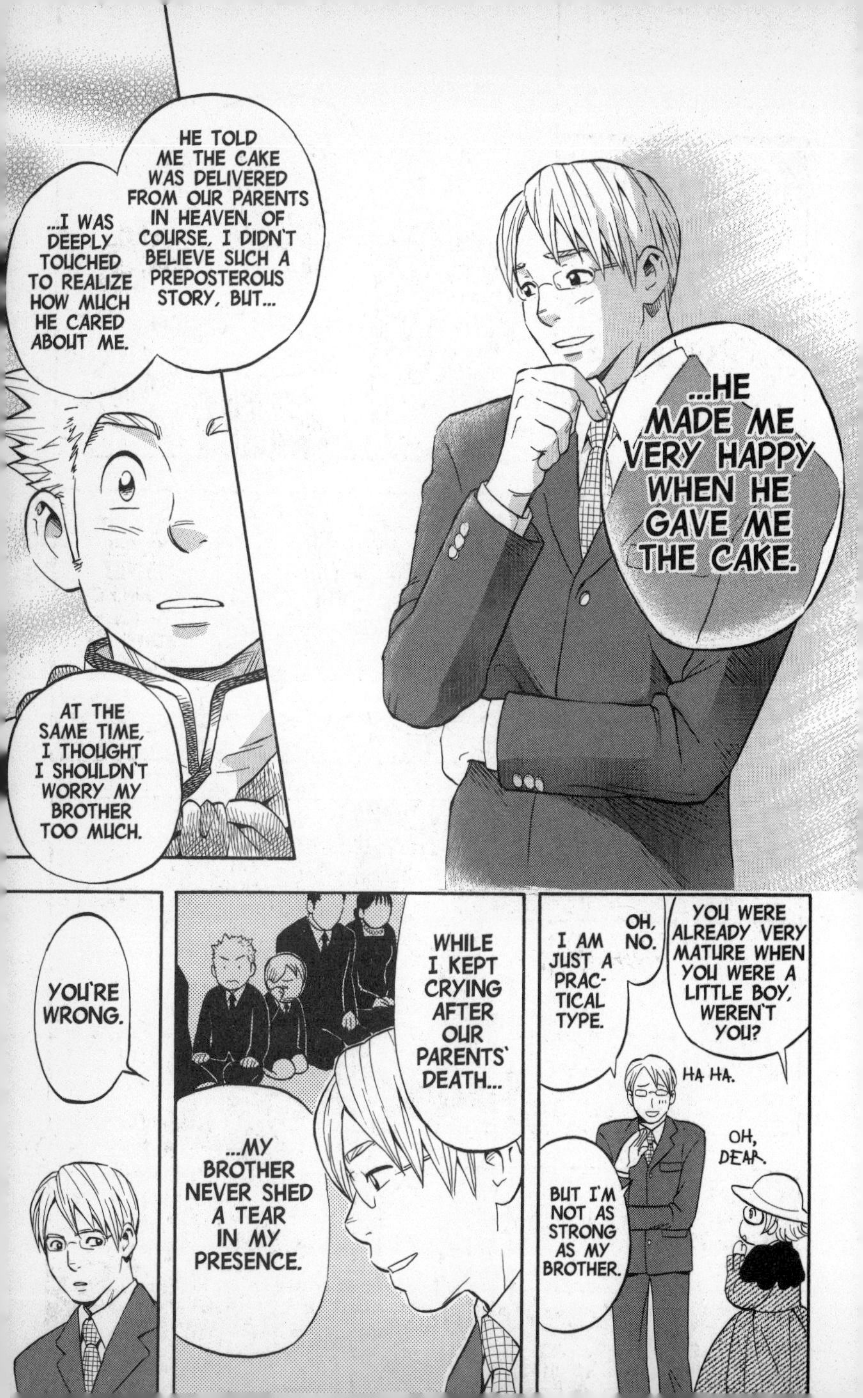
...HE MADE ME VERY HAPPY WHEN HE GAVE ME THE CAKE.
HE TOLD ME THE CAKE WAS DELIVERED FROM OUR PARENTS IN HEAVEN. OF COURSE, I DIDN'T BELIEVE SUCH A PREPOSTEROUS STORY, BUT...
...I WAS DEEPLY TOUCHED TO REALIZE HOW MUCH HE CARED ABOUT ME.
AT THE SAME TIME, I THOUGHT I SHOULDN'T WORRY MY BROTHER TOO MUCH.
YOU WERE ALREADY VERY MATURE WHEN YOU WERE A LITTLE BOY, WEREN'T YOU?
OH, NO.
I AM JUST A PRAC-TICAL TYPE.
HA HA.
OH, DEAR.
BUT I'M NOT AS STRONG AS MY BROTHER.
WHILE I KEPT CRYING AFTER OUR PARENTS' DEATH...
...MY BROTHER NEVER SHED A TEAR IN MY PRESENCE.
YOU'RE WRONG.

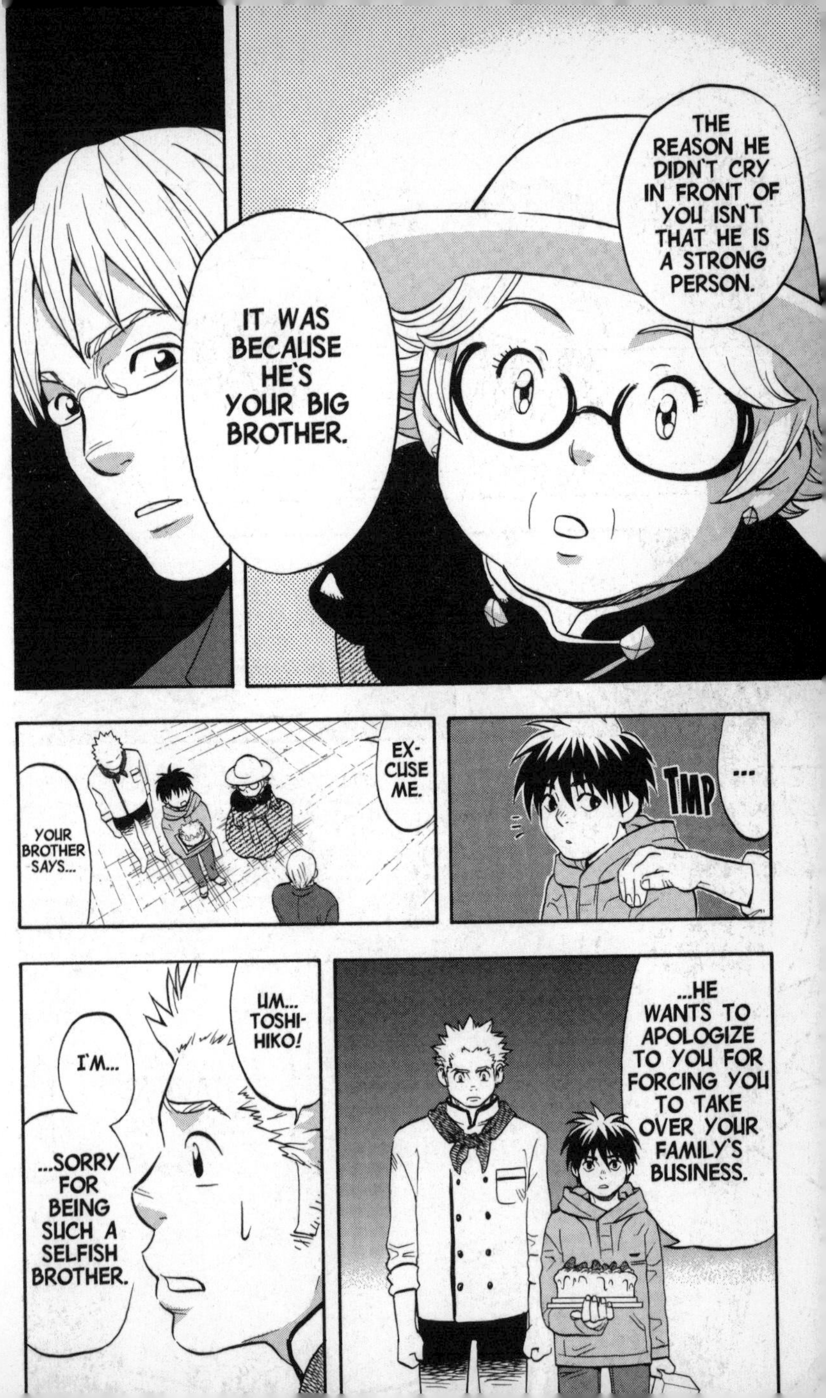
THE REASON HE DIDN'T CRY IN FRONT OF YOU ISN'T THAT HE IS A STRONG PERSON.
IT WAS BECAUSE HE'S YOUR BIG BROTHER.
...
TMP
EX-CUSE ME.
YOUR BROTHER SAYS...
...HE WANTS TO APOLOGIZE TO YOU FOR FORCING YOU TO TAKE OVER YOUR FAMILY'S BUSINESS.
UM... TOSHI-HIKO!
I'M...
...SORRY FOR BEING SUCH A SELFISH BROTHER.

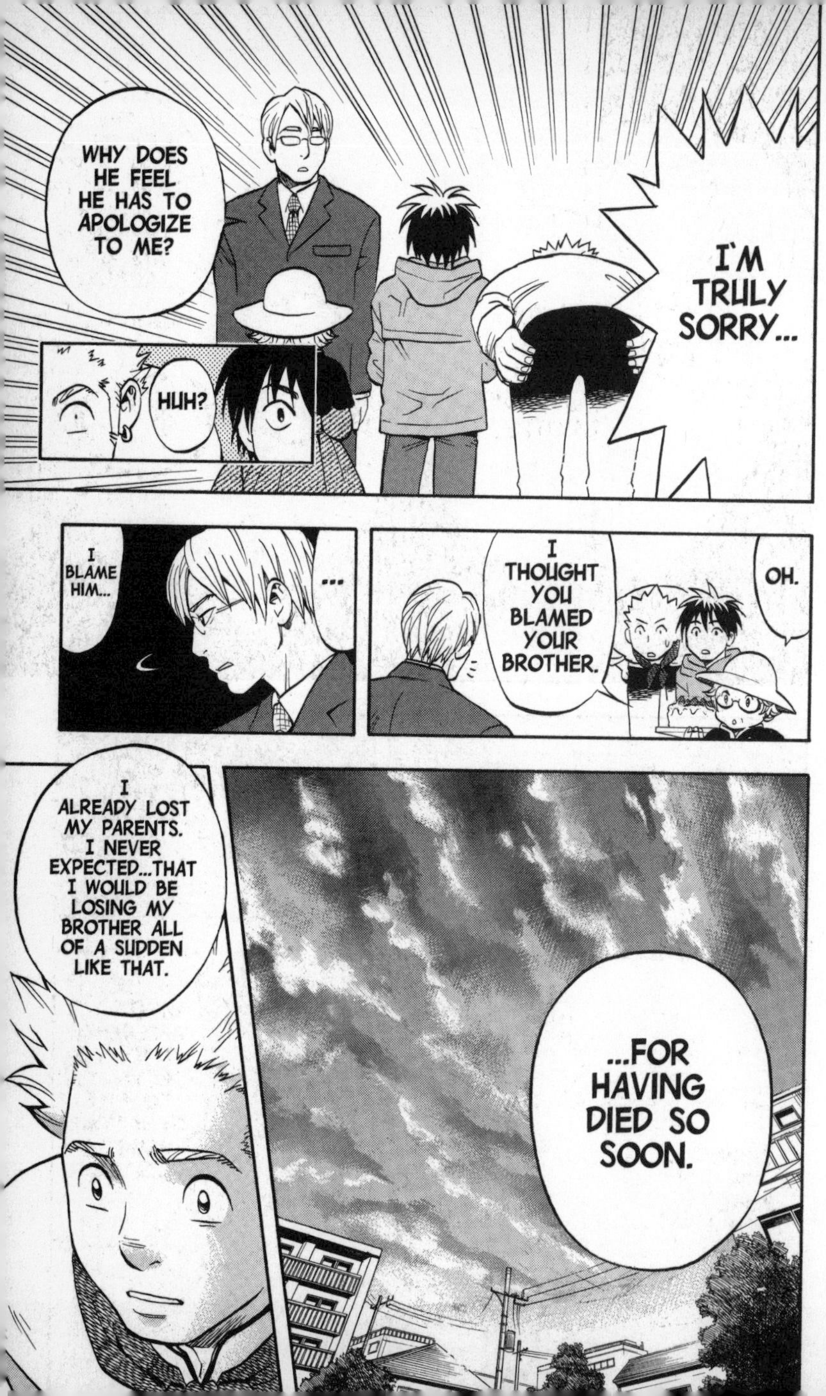
I'M TRULY SORRY...
WHY DOES HE FEEL HE HAS TO APOLOGIZE TO ME?
HUH?
OH.
I THOUGHT YOU BLAMED YOUR BROTHER.
...
I BLAME HIM...
...FOR HAVING DIED SO SOON.
I ALREADY LOST MY PARENTS. I NEVER EXPECTED...THAT I WOULD BE LOSING MY BROTHER ALL OF A SUDDEN LIKE THAT.

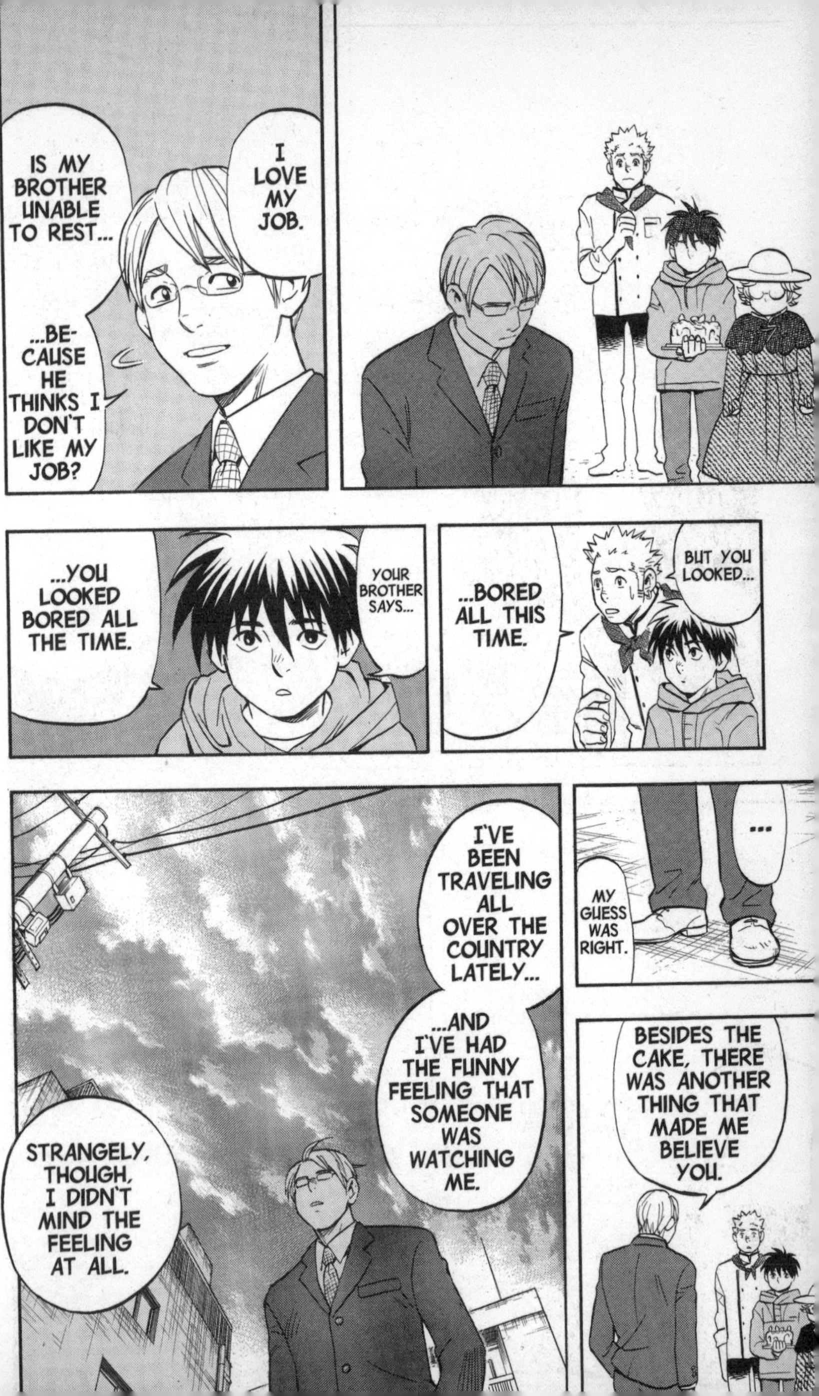
I LOVE MY JOB.
IS MY BROTHER UNABLE TO REST...
...BE-CAUSE HE THINKS I DON'T LIKE MY JOB?
BUT YOU LOOKED...
...BORED ALL THIS TIME.
YOUR BROTHER SAYS...
...YOU LOOKED BORED ALL THE TIME.
...
MY GUESS WAS RIGHT.
BESIDES THE CAKE, THERE WAS ANOTHER THING THAT MADE ME BELIEVE YOU.
I'VE BEEN TRAVELING ALL OVER THE COUNTRY LATELY...
...AND I'VE HAD THE FUNNY FEELING THAT SOMEONE WAS WATCHING ME.
STRANGELY, THOUGH, I DIDN'T MIND THE FEELING AT ALL.

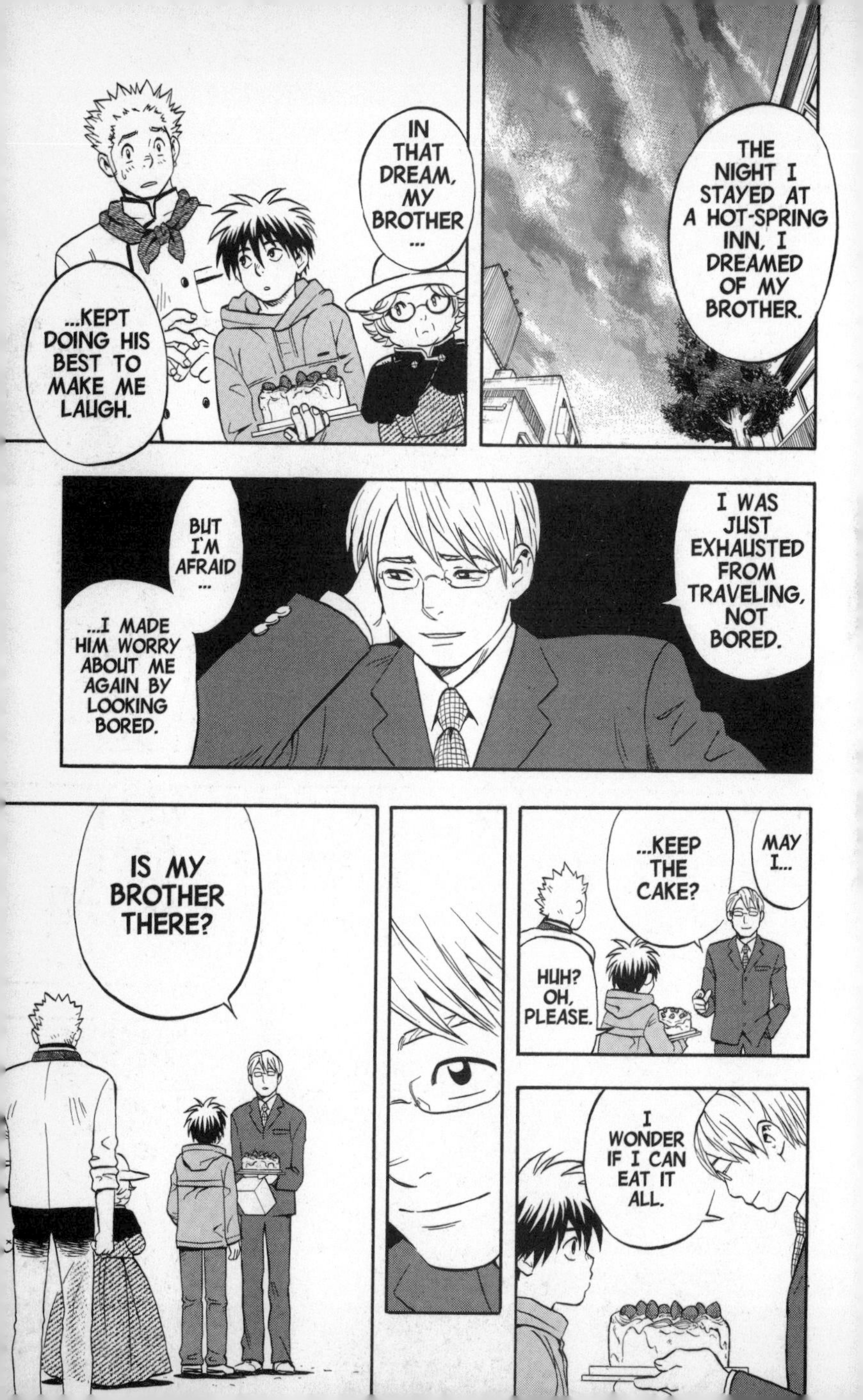
THE NIGHT I STAYED AT A HOT-SPRING INN, I DREAMED OF MY BROTHER.
IN THAT DREAM, MY BROTHER ...
...KEPT DOING HIS BEST TO MAKE ME LAUGH.
I WAS JUST EXHAUSTED FROM TRAVELING, NOT BORED.
BUT I'M AFRAID ...
...I MADE HIM WORRY ABOUT ME AGAIN BY LOOKING BORED.
MAY I...
...KEEP THE CAKE?
HUH? OH, PLEASE.
I WONDER IF I CAN EAT IT ALL.
IS MY BROTHER THERE?

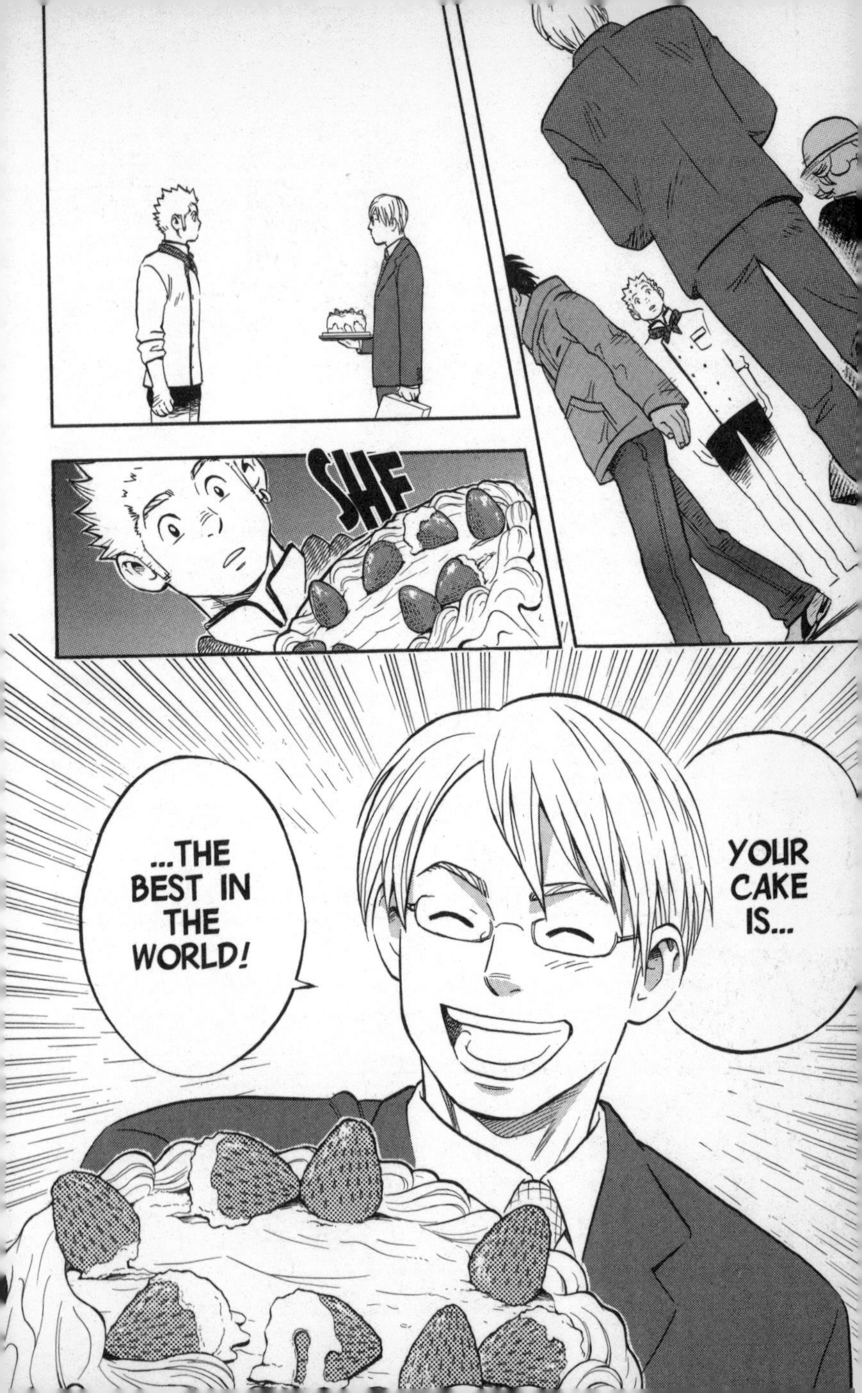
SHF
YOUR CAKE IS...
...THE BEST IN THE WORLD!

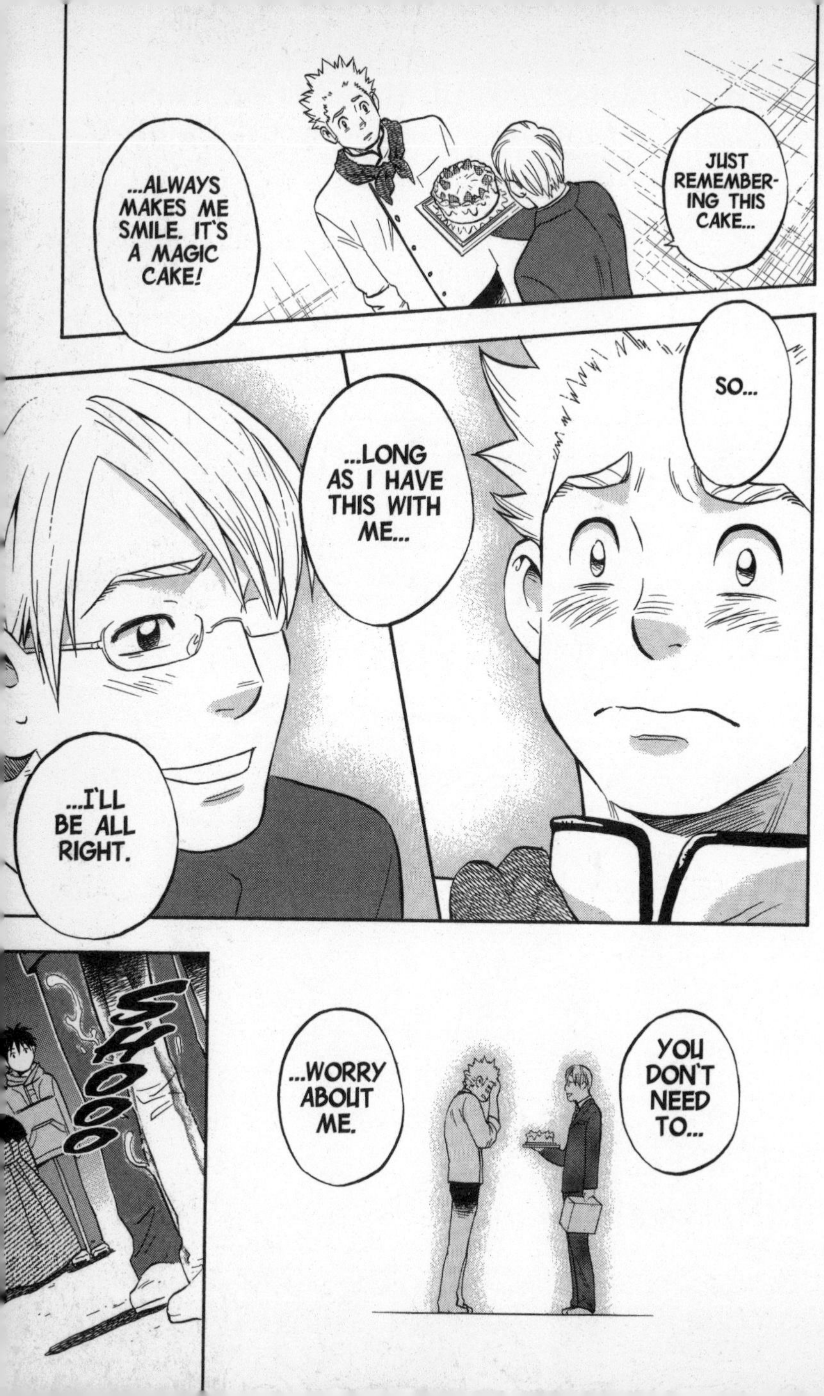
JUST REMEMBERING THIS CAKE...
...ALWAYS MAKES ME SMILE. IT'S A MAGIC CAKE!
SO...
...LONG AS I HAVE THIS WITH ME...
...I'LL BE ALL RIGHT.
YOU DON'T NEED TO...
...WORRY ABOUT ME.
SHOOOO

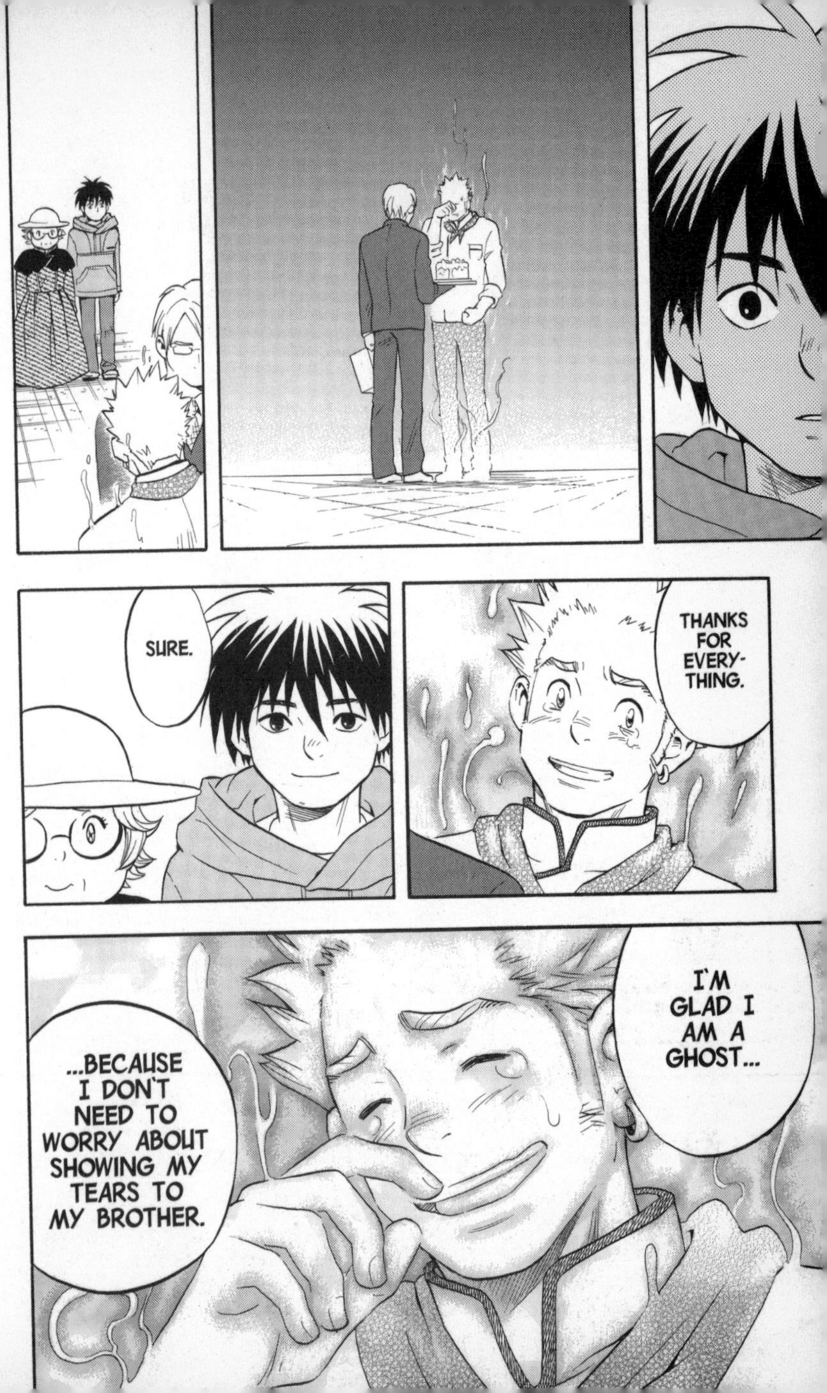
THANKS FOR EVERY-THING.
SURE.
I'M GLAD I AM A GHOST...
...BECAUSE I DON'T NEED TO WORRY ABOUT SHOWING MY TEARS TO MY BROTHER.

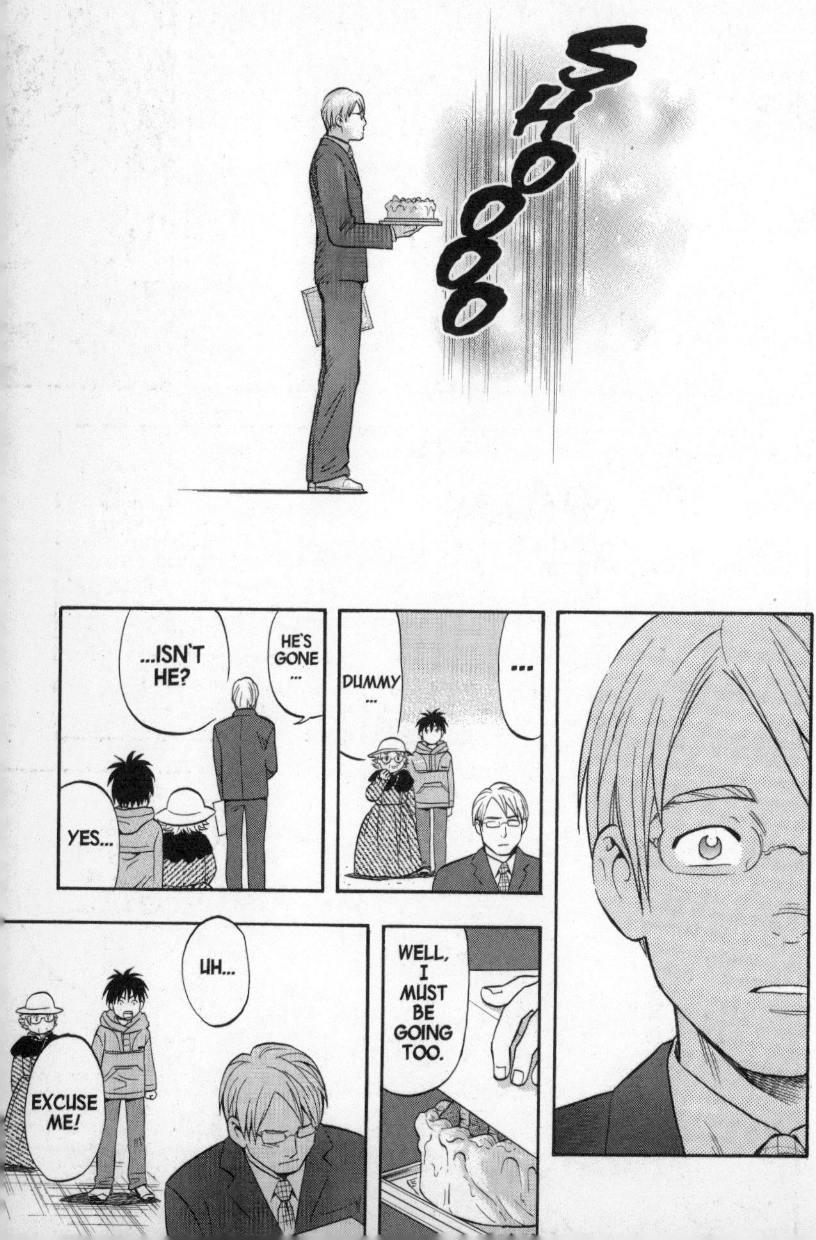
SHOOOO
...
DUMMY ...
HE'S GONE ...
...ISN'T HE?
YES...
WELL, I MUST BE GOING TOO.
UH...
EXCUSE ME!

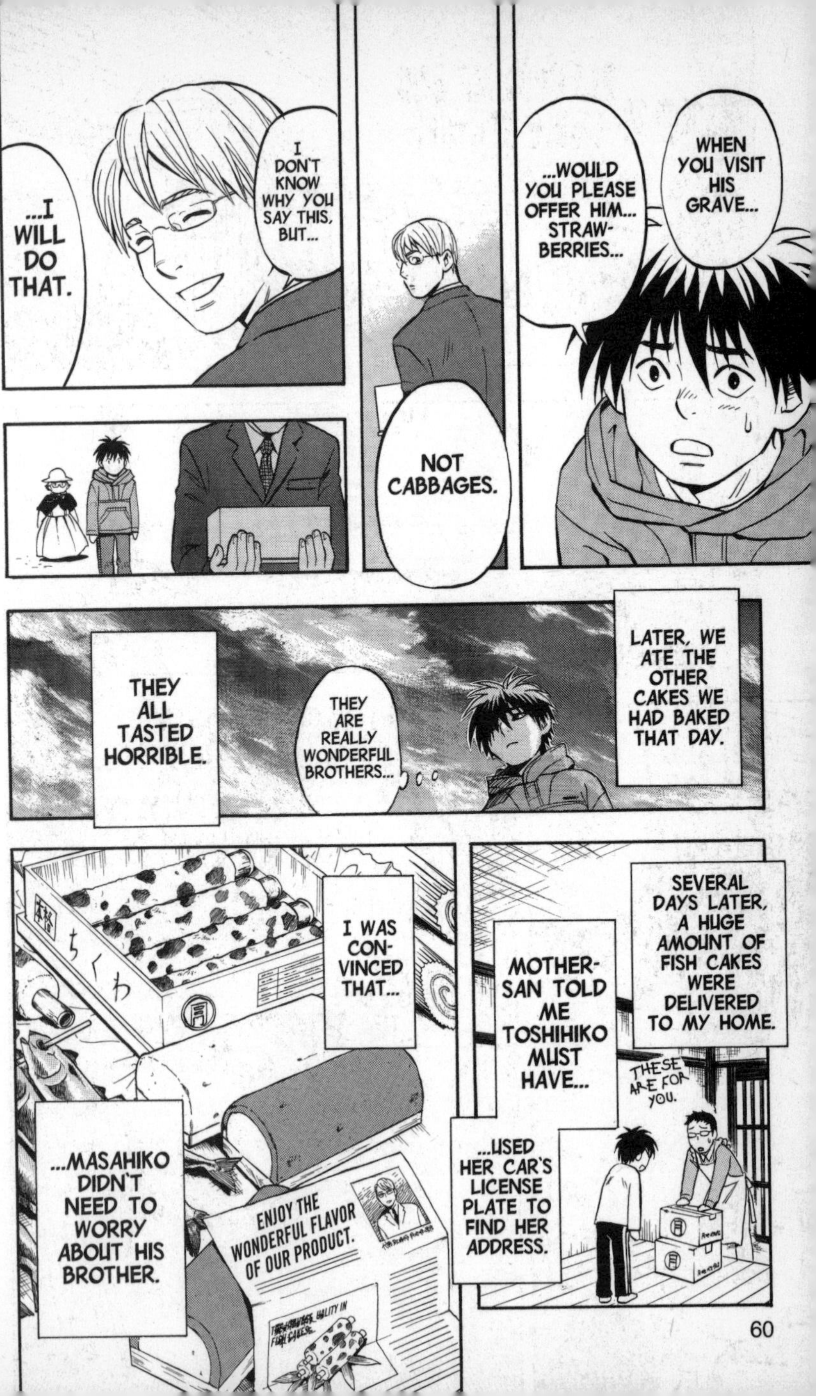
WHEN YOU VISIT HIS GRAVE...
...WOULD YOU PLEASE OFFER HIM... STRAW-BERRIES...
NOT CABBAGES.
I DON'T KNOW WHY YOU SAY THIS, BUT...
...I WILL DO THAT.
LATER, WE ATE THE OTHER CAKES WE HAD BAKED THAT DAY.
THEY ARE REALLY WONDERFUL BROTHERS...
THEY ALL TASTED HORRIBLE.
SEVERAL DAYS LATER, A HUGE AMOUNT OF FISH CAKES WERE DELIVERED TO MY HOME.
THESE ARE FOR YOU.
MOTHER-SAN TOLD ME TOSHIHIKO MUST HAVE...
...USED HER CAR'S LICENSE PLATE TO FIND HER ADDRESS.
I WAS CON-VINCED THAT...
...MASAHIKO DIDN'T NEED TO WORRY ABOUT HIS BROTHER.
ENJOY THE WONDERFUL FLAVOR OF OUR PRODUCT.

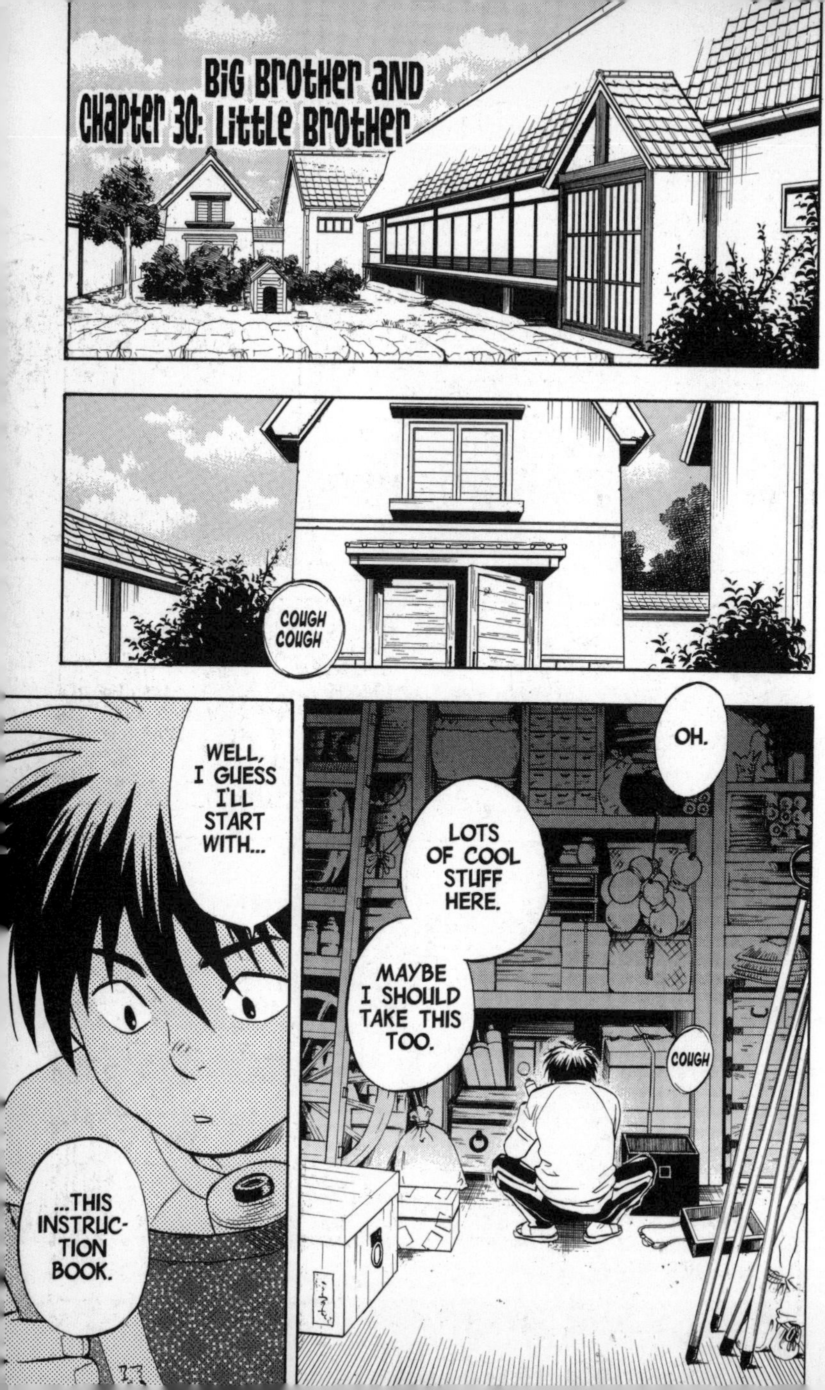
Chapter 30: Big Brother and Little Brother
COUGH COUGH
OH.
LOTS OF COOL STUFF HERE.
MAYBE I SHOULD TAKE THIS TOO.
COUGH
WELL, I GUESS I'LL START WITH...
...THIS INSTRUCTION BOOK.

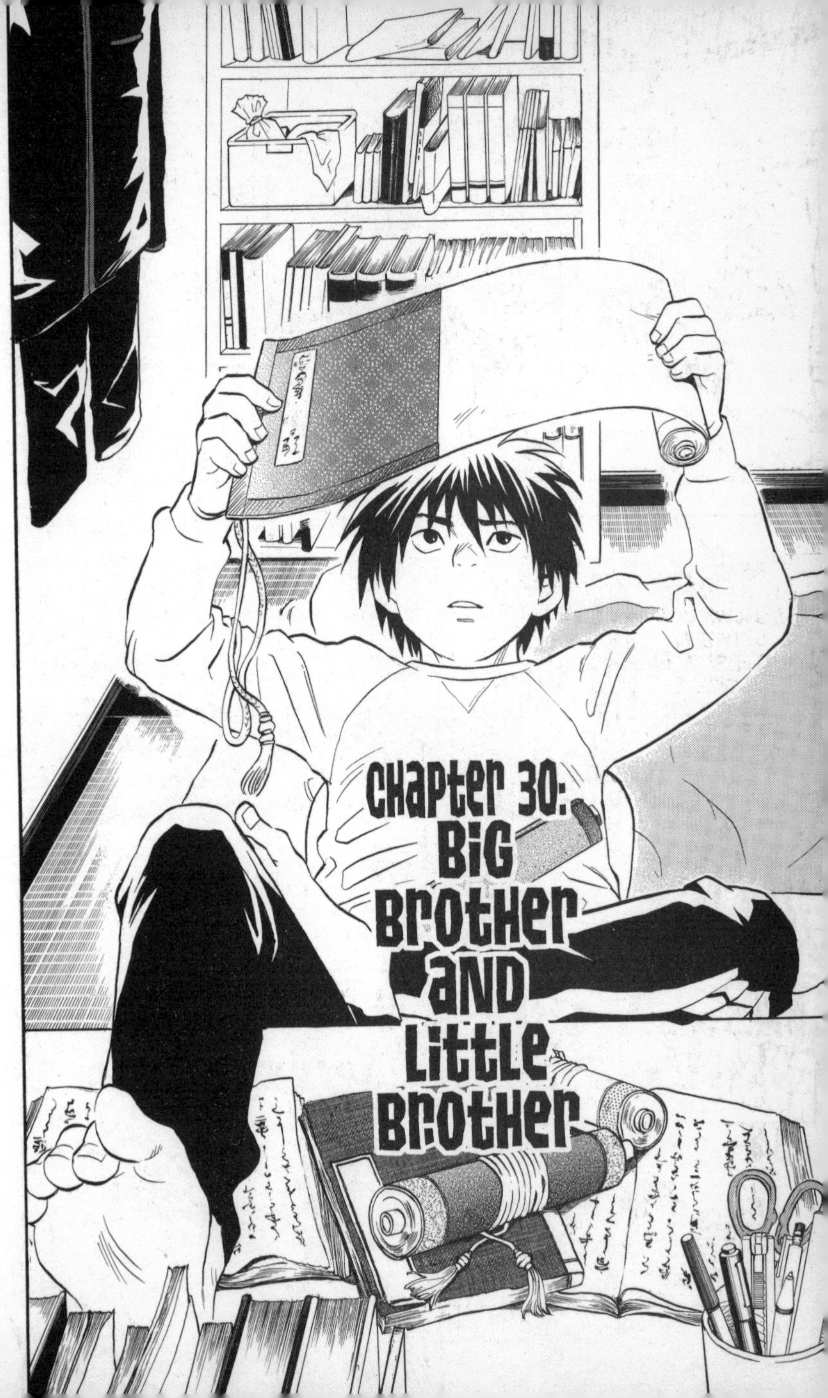
Chapter 30:
Big Brother and Little Brother

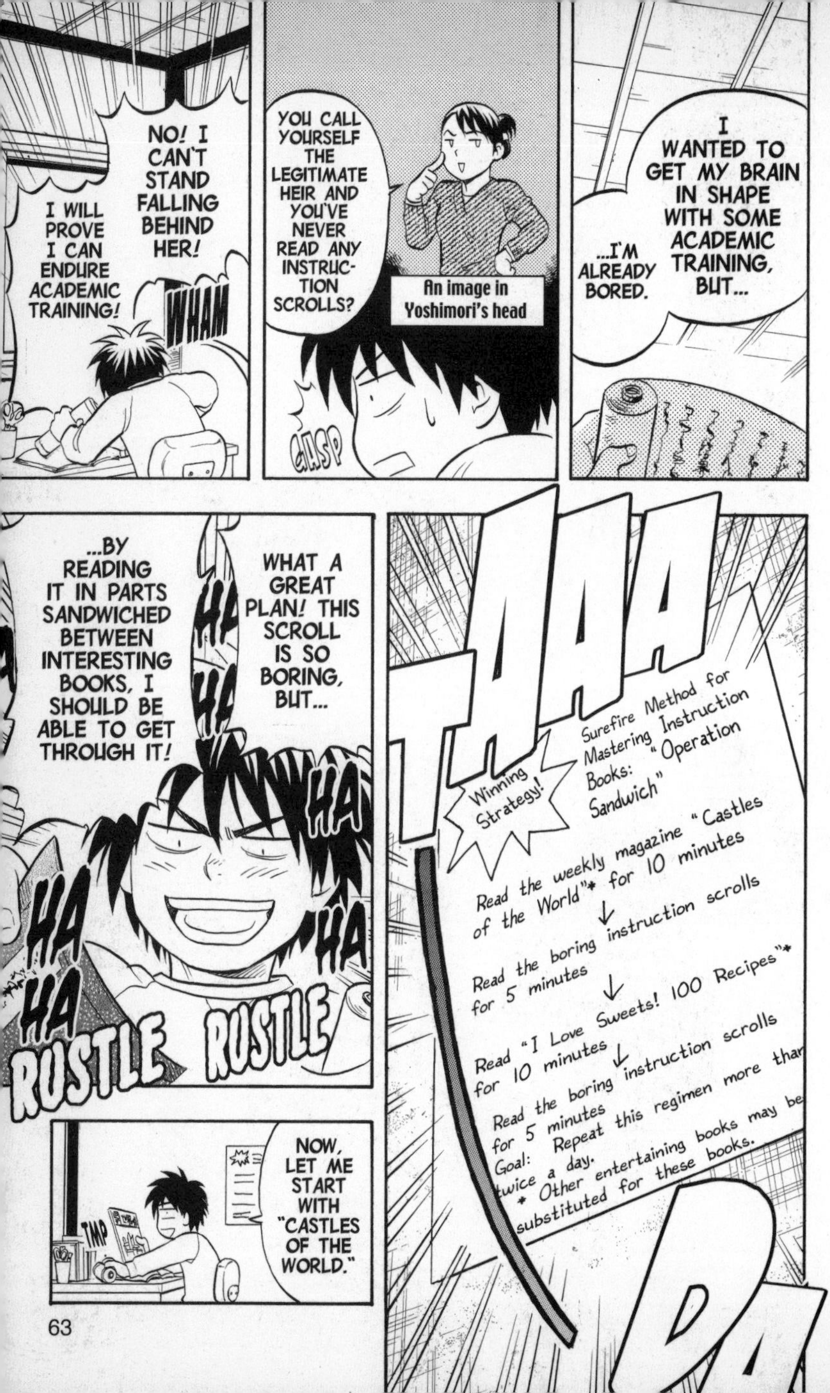

I WANTED TO GET MY BRAIN IN SHAPE WITH SOME ACADEMIC TRAINING, BUT...
...I'M ALREADY BORED.
YOU CALL YOURSELF THE LEGITIMATE HEIR AND YOU'VE NEVER READ ANY INSTRUCTION SCROLLS?
An image in Yoshimori's head
GASP
NO! I CAN'T STAND FALLING BEHIND HER!
I WILL PROVE I CAN ENDURE ACADEMIC TRAINING!
WHAM
TAAA
Winning Strategy!
Surefire Method for Mastering Instruction Books: "Operation Sandwich"
Read the weekly magazine "Castles of the World"* for 10 minutes
↓
Read the boring instruction scrolls for 5 minutes
↓
Read "I Love Sweets! 100 Recipes"* for 10 minutes
↓
Read the boring instruction scrolls for 5 minutes
Goal: Repeat this regimen more than twice a day.
* Other entertaining books may be substituted for these books.
DA
WHAT A GREAT PLAN! THIS SCROLL IS SO BORING, BUT...
...BY READING IT IN PARTS SANDWICHED BETWEEN INTERESTING BOOKS, I SHOULD BE ABLE TO GET THROUGH IT!
HA HA HA HA HA HA HA HA
RUSTLE RUSTLE
NOW, LET ME START WITH "CASTLES OF THE WORLD."
TMP

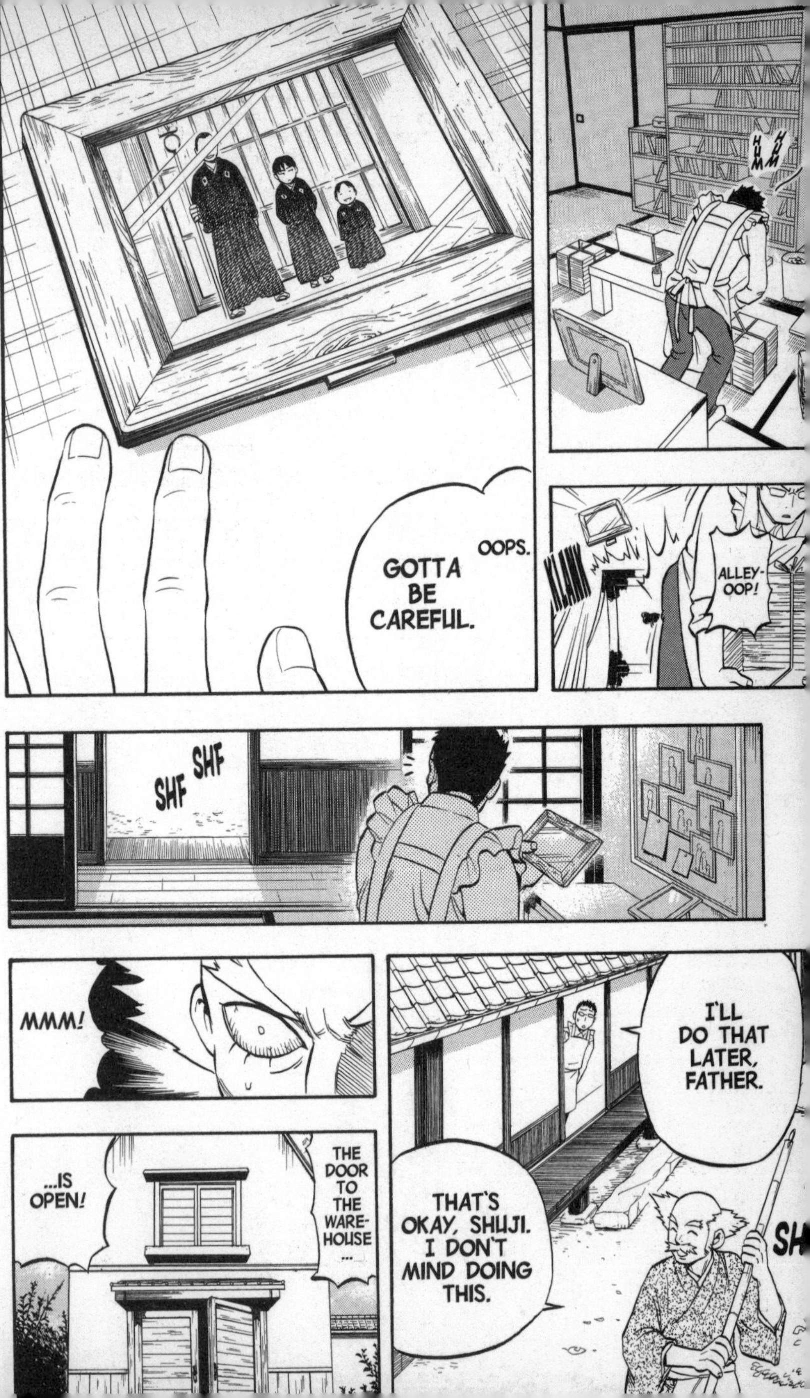
HUM HUM
KLANK
ALLEY-OOP!
OOPS.
GOTTA BE CAREFUL.
SHF SHF
I'LL DO THAT LATER, FATHER.
THAT'S OKAY, SHUJI. I DON'T MIND DOING THIS.
SH
MMM!
THE DOOR TO THE WAREHOUSE...
...IS OPEN!

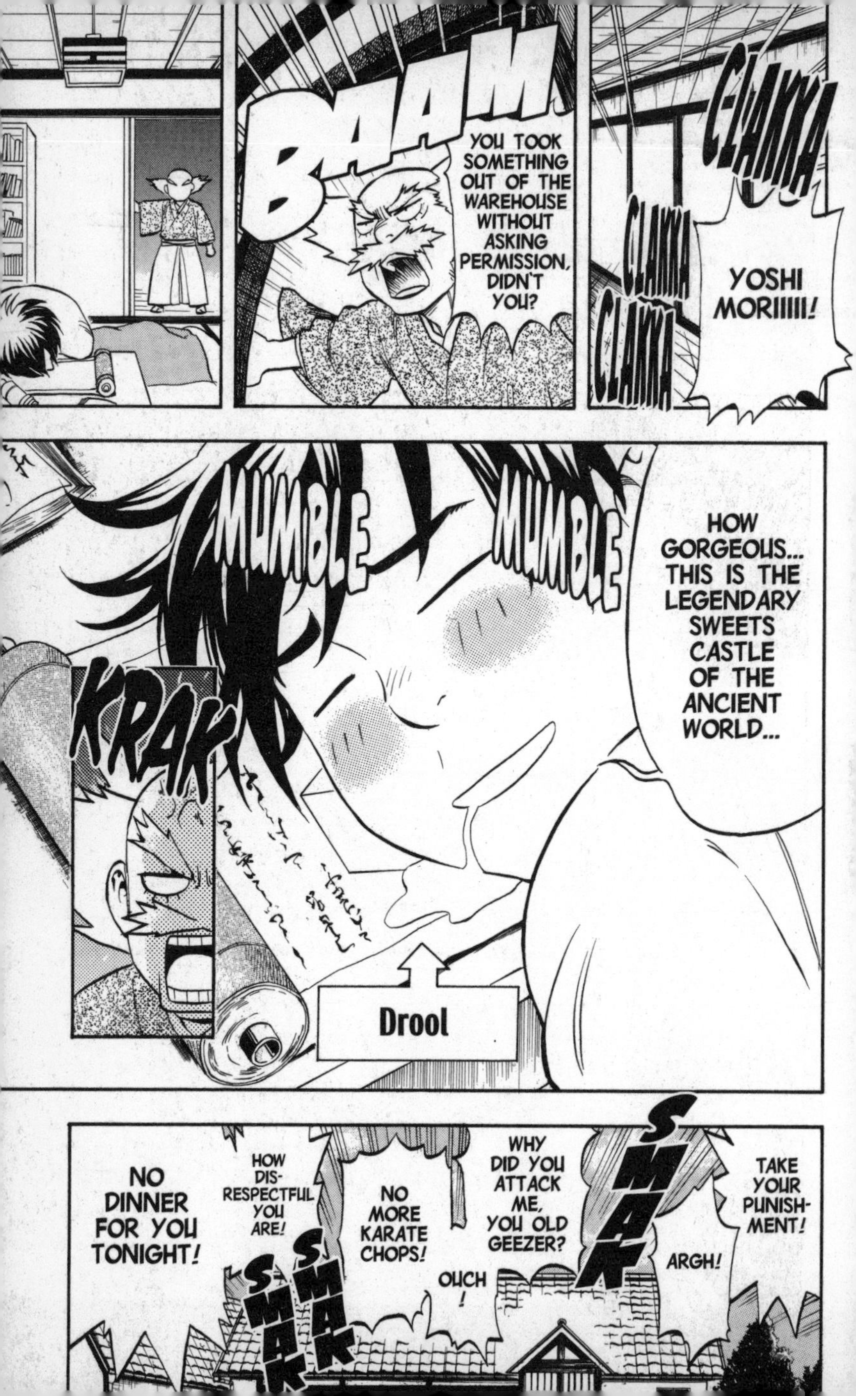
CLAKKA
CLAKKA
CLAKKA
YOSHI MORIIIII!
BAAM
YOU TOOK SOMETHING OUT OF THE WAREHOUSE WITHOUT ASKING PERMISSION, DIDN'T YOU?
MUMBLE
MUMBLE
HOW GORGEOUS... THIS IS THE LEGENDARY SWEETS CASTLE OF THE ANCIENT WORLD...
KRAK
Drool
TAKE YOUR PUNISH-MENT!
SMAK
ARGH!
WHY DID YOU ATTACK ME, YOU OLD GEEZER?
OUCH!
NO MORE KARATE CHOPS!
HOW DIS-RESPECTFUL YOU ARE!
SMAK
SMAK
NO DINNER FOR YOU TONIGHT!

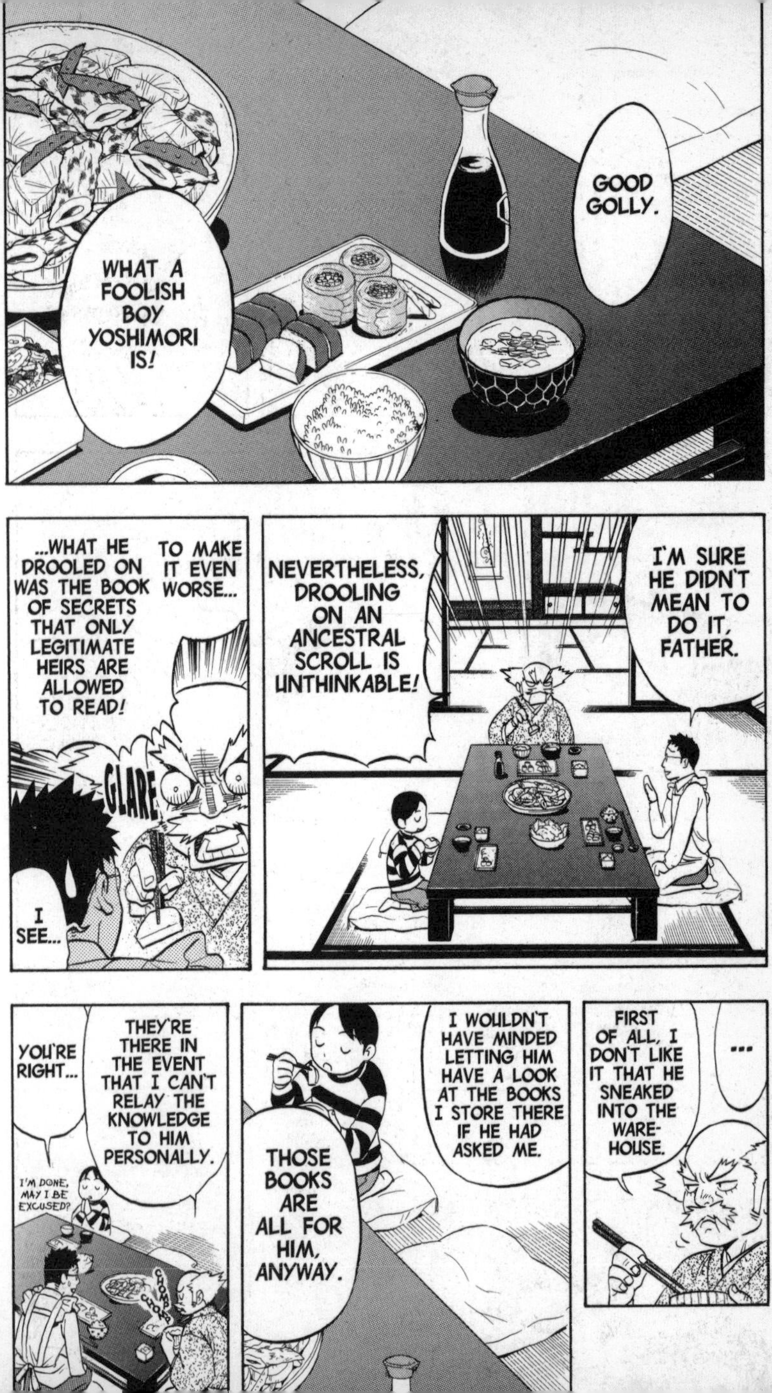

GOOD GOLLY.
WHAT A FOOLISH BOY YOSHIMORI IS!
I'M SURE HE DIDN'T MEAN TO DO IT, FATHER.
NEVERTHELESS, DROOLING ON AN ANCESTRAL SCROLL IS UNTHINKABLE!
TO MAKE IT EVEN WORSE...
...WHAT HE DROOLED ON WAS THE BOOK OF SECRETS THAT ONLY LEGITIMATE HEIRS ARE ALLOWED TO READ!
GLARE
I SEE...
...
FIRST OF ALL, I DON'T LIKE IT THAT HE SNEAKED INTO THE WARE-HOUSE.
I WOULDN'T HAVE MINDED LETTING HIM HAVE A LOOK AT THE BOOKS I STORE THERE IF HE HAD ASKED ME.
THOSE BOOKS ARE ALL FOR HIM, ANYWAY.
THEY'RE THERE IN THE EVENT THAT I CAN'T RELAY THE KNOWLEDGE TO HIM PERSONALLY.
YOU'RE RIGHT...
I'M DONE, MAY I BE EXCUSED?
CHOMP
CHOMP

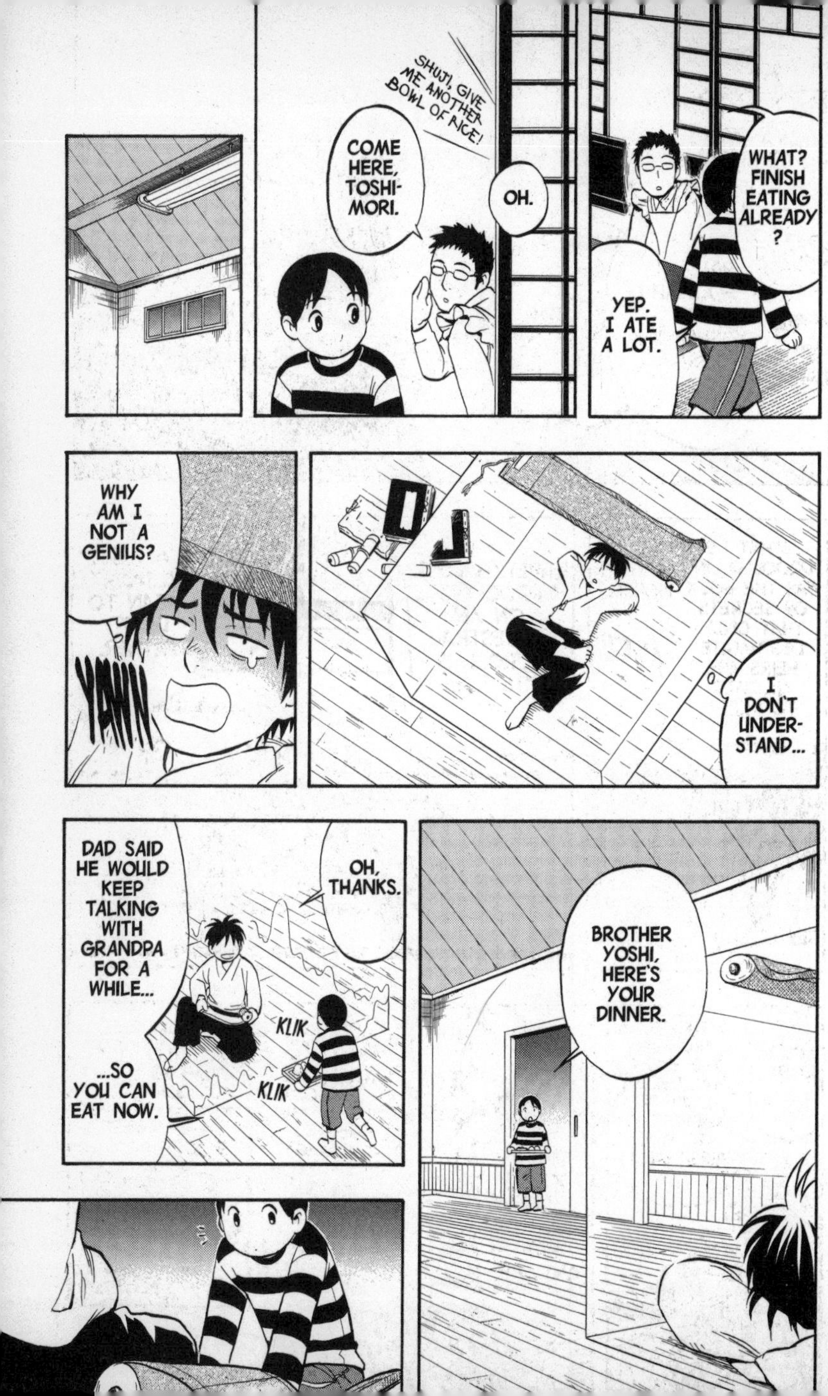
WHAT? FINISH EATING ALREADY?
YEP. I ATE A LOT.
SHUJI, GIVE ME ANOTHER BOWL OF RICE!
OH.
COME HERE, TOSHIMORI.
I DON'T UNDERSTAND...
WHY AM I NOT A GENIUS?
YAWN
BROTHER YOSHI, HERE'S YOUR DINNER.
OH, THANKS.
DAD SAID HE WOULD KEEP TALKING WITH GRANDPA FOR A WHILE...
KLIK
KLIK
...SO YOU CAN EAT NOW.

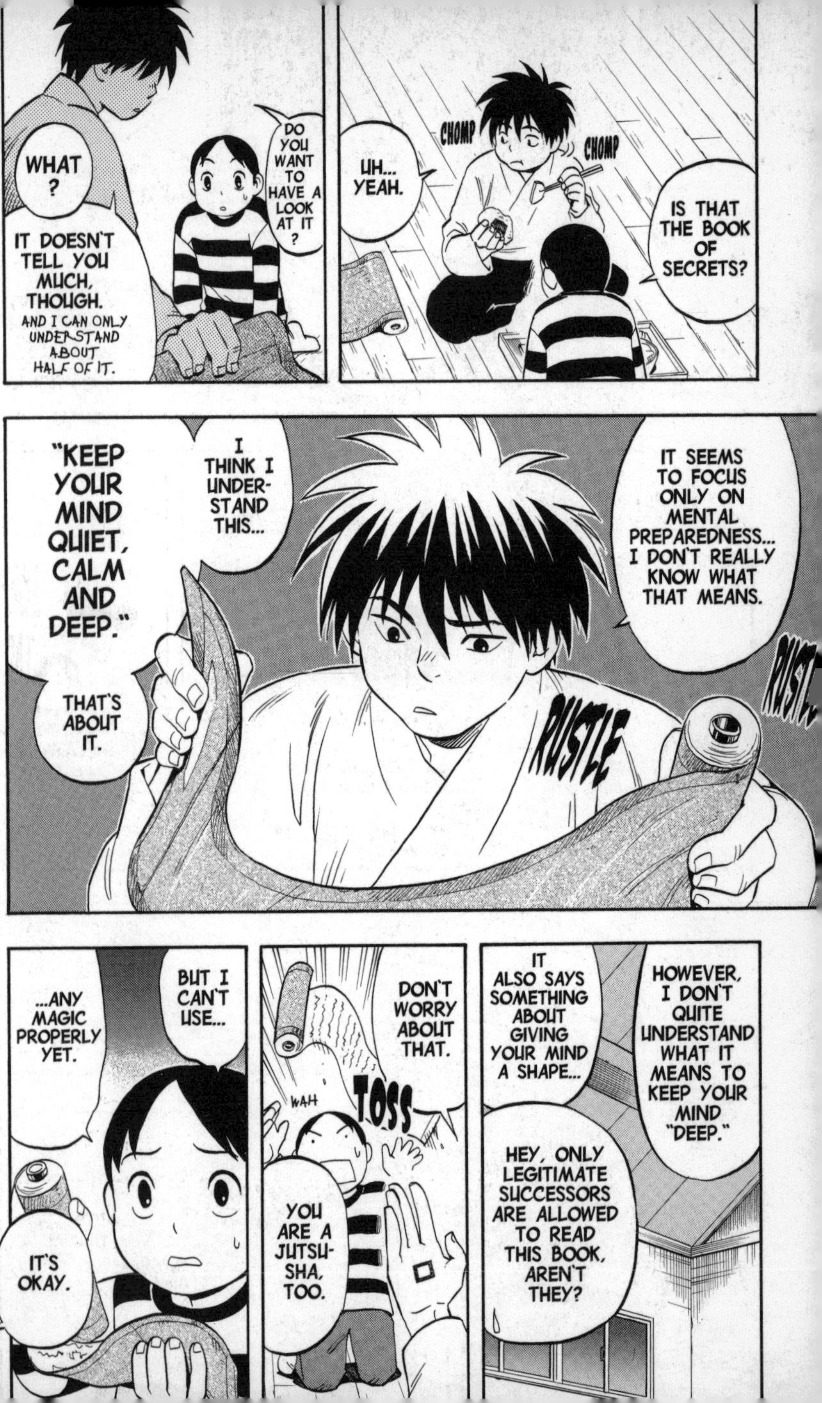
IS THAT THE BOOK OF SECRETS?
CHOMP
CHOMP
UH... YEAH.
DO YOU WANT TO HAVE A LOOK AT IT?
WHAT?
IT DOESN'T TELL YOU MUCH, THOUGH.
AND I CAN ONLY UNDERSTAND ABOUT HALF OF IT.
IT SEEMS TO FOCUS ONLY ON MENTAL PREPAREDNESS... I DON'T REALLY KNOW WHAT THAT MEANS.
RUST
RUSTLE
I THINK I UNDER-STAND THIS...
"KEEP YOUR MIND QUIET, CALM AND DEEP."
THAT'S ABOUT IT.
HOWEVER, I DON'T QUITE UNDERSTAND WHAT IT MEANS TO KEEP YOUR MIND "DEEP."
IT ALSO SAYS SOMETHING ABOUT GIVING YOUR MIND A SHAPE...
HEY, ONLY LEGITIMATE SUCCESSORS ARE ALLOWED TO READ THIS BOOK, AREN'T THEY?
DON'T WORRY ABOUT THAT.
TOSS
WAH
YOU ARE A JUTSU-SHA, TOO.
BUT I CAN'T USE...
...ANY MAGIC PROPERLY YET.
IT'S OKAY.

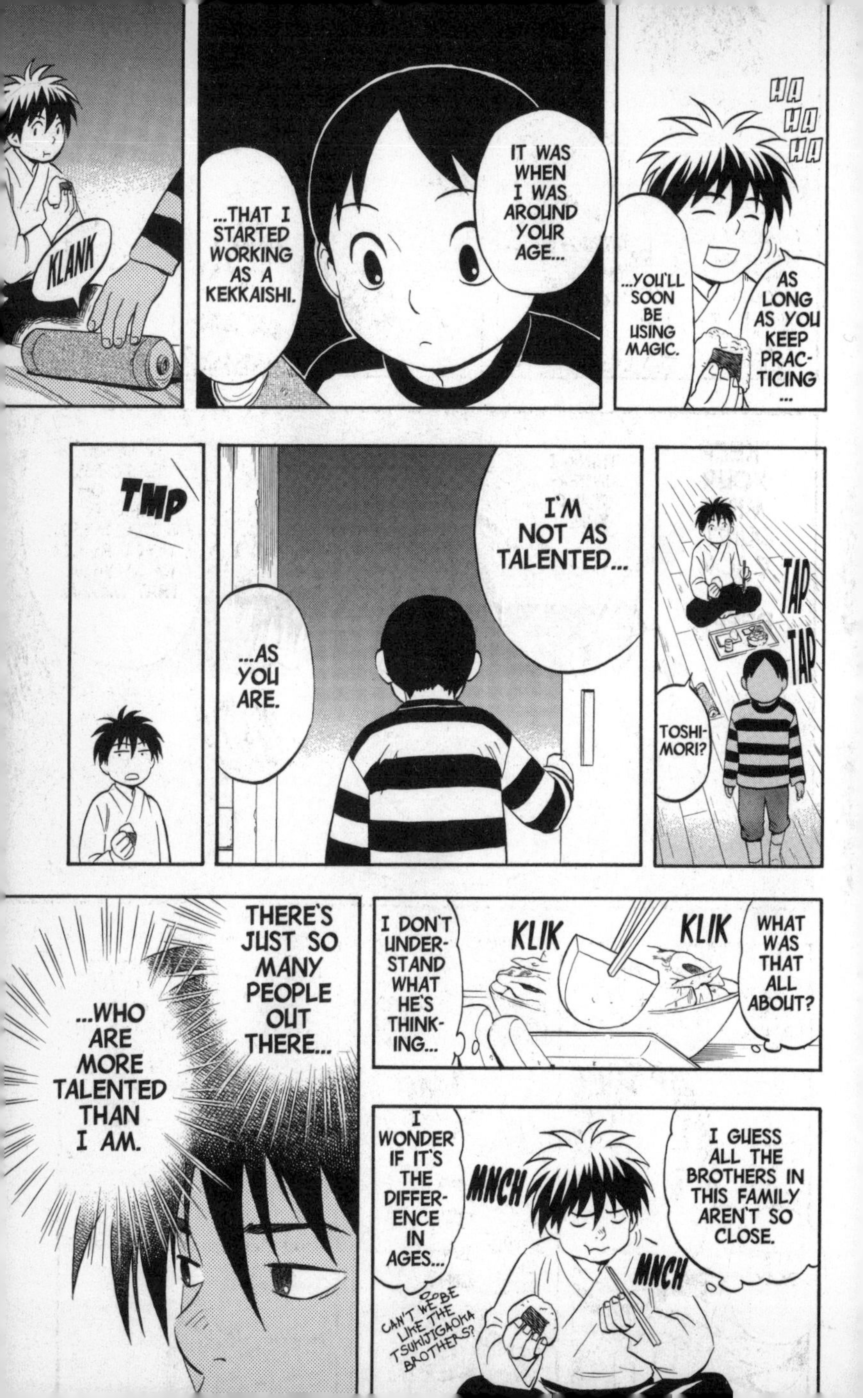
HA HA HA
AS LONG AS YOU KEEP PRACTICING...
...YOU'LL SOON BE USING MAGIC.
IT WAS WHEN I WAS AROUND YOUR AGE...
...THAT I STARTED WORKING AS A KEKKAISHI.
KLANK
TAP TAP
TOSHIMORI?
I'M NOT AS TALENTED...
...AS YOU ARE.
TMP
WHAT WAS THAT ALL ABOUT?
KLIK
KLIK
I DON'T UNDERSTAND WHAT HE'S THINKING...
I GUESS ALL THE BROTHERS IN THIS FAMILY AREN'T SO CLOSE.
MNCH
MNCH
I WONDER IF IT'S THE DIFFERENCE IN AGES...
CAN'T WE BE LIKE THE TSUKIJIGAOKA BROTHERS?
THERE'S JUST SO MANY PEOPLE OUT THERE...
...WHO ARE MORE TALENTED THAN I AM.

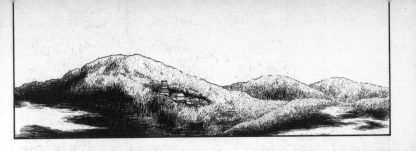

SQUEE EEAK

WELCOME.

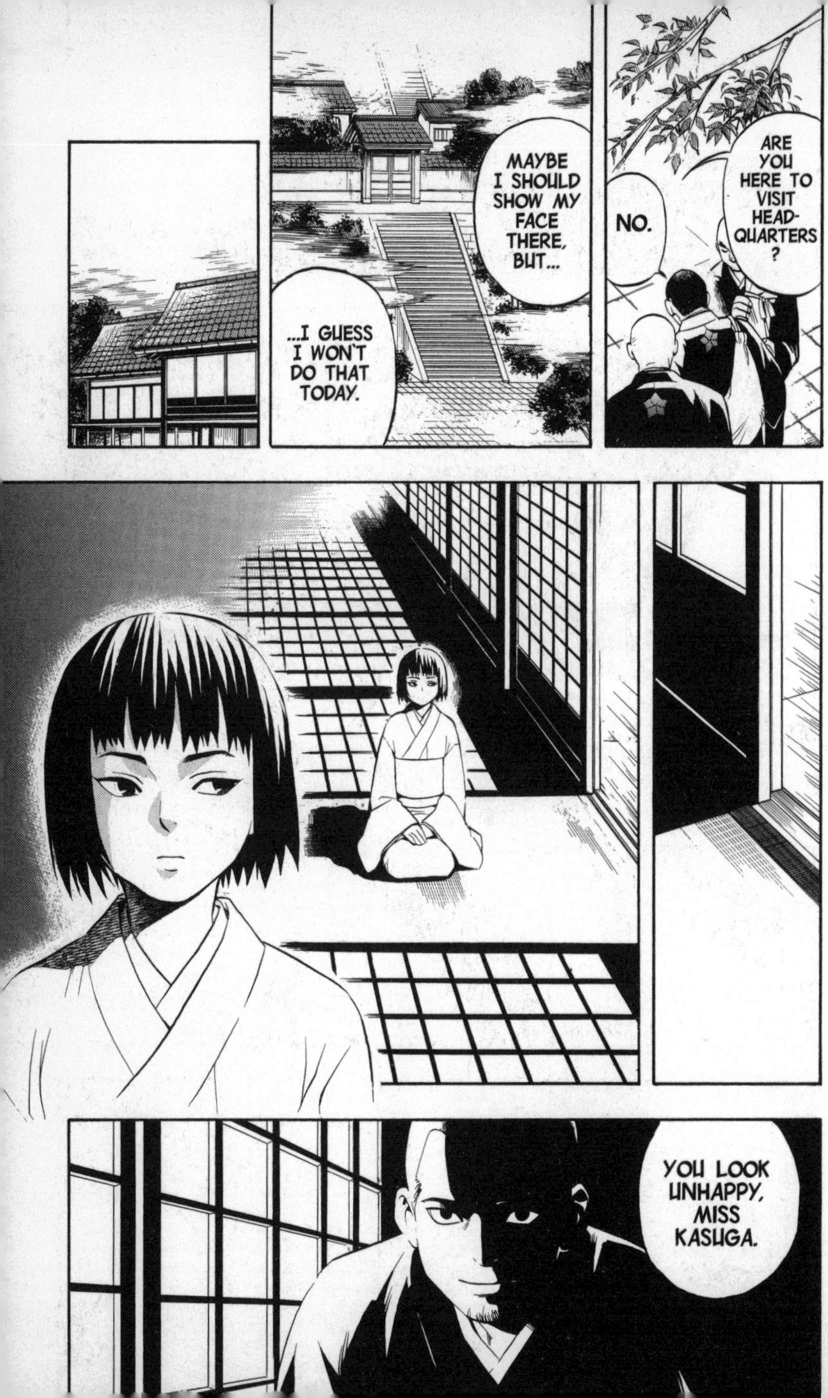
ARE YOU HERE TO VISIT HEAD-QUARTERS?
NO.
MAYBE I SHOULD SHOW MY FACE THERE, BUT...
...I GUESS I WON'T DO THAT TODAY.
YOU LOOK UNHAPPY, MISS KASUGA.

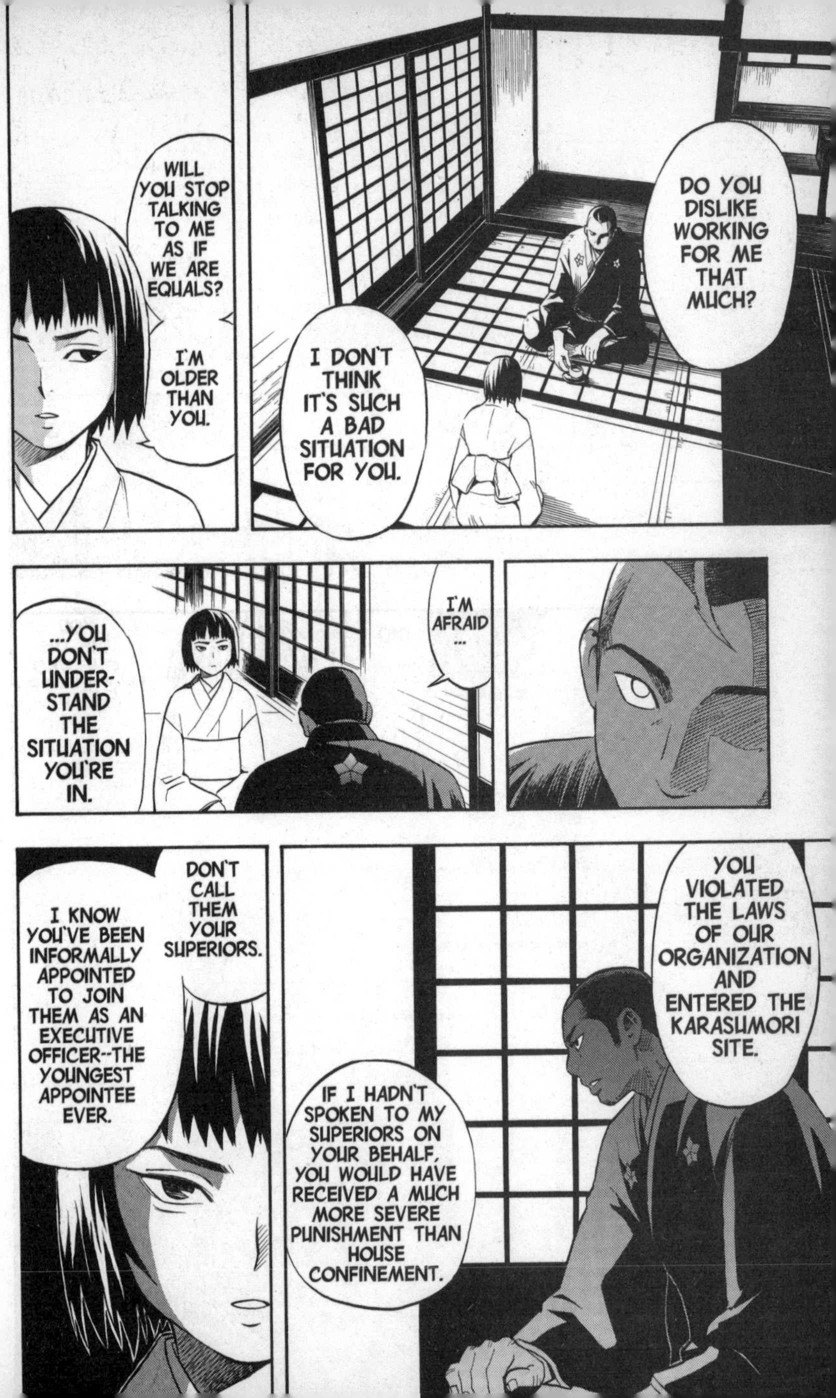
DO YOU DISLIKE WORKING FOR ME THAT MUCH?
I DON'T THINK IT'S SUCH A BAD SITUATION FOR YOU.
WILL YOU STOP TALKING TO ME AS IF WE ARE EQUALS?
I'M OLDER THAN YOU.
I'M AFRAID...
...YOU DON'T UNDER-STAND THE SITUATION YOU'RE IN.
YOU VIOLATED THE LAWS OF OUR ORGANIZATION AND ENTERED THE KARASUMORI SITE.
IF I HADN'T SPOKEN TO MY SUPERIORS ON YOUR BEHALF, YOU WOULD HAVE RECEIVED A MUCH MORE SEVERE PUNISHMENT THAN HOUSE CONFINEMENT.
DON'T CALL THEM YOUR SUPERIORS.
I KNOW YOU'VE BEEN INFORMALLY APPOINTED TO JOIN THEM AS AN EXECUTIVE OFFICER--THE YOUNGEST APPOINTEE EVER.

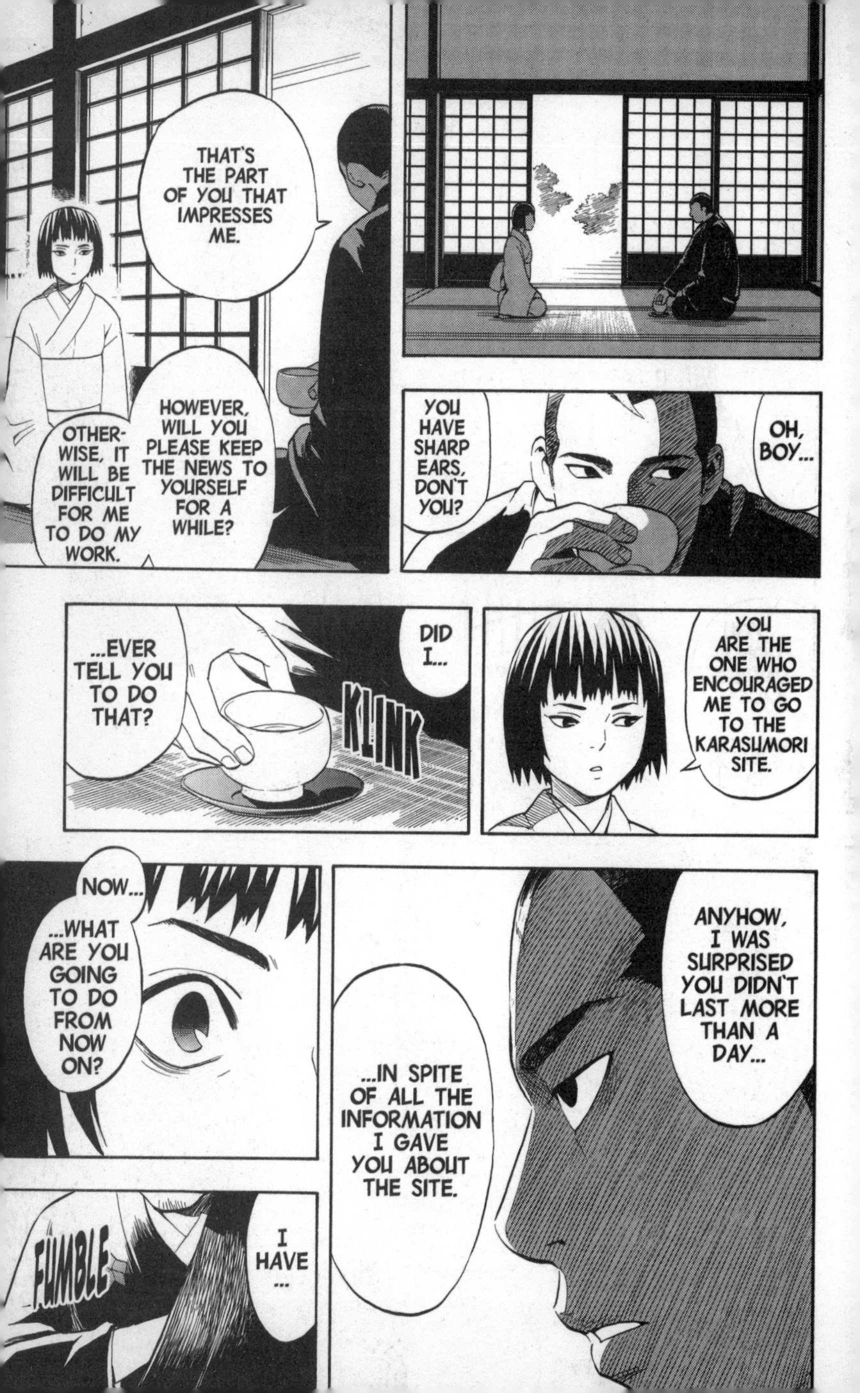
OH, BOY...
YOU HAVE SHARP EARS, DON'T YOU?
THAT'S THE PART OF YOU THAT IMPRESSES ME.
HOWEVER, WILL YOU PLEASE KEEP THE NEWS TO YOURSELF FOR A WHILE?
OTHERWISE, IT WILL BE DIFFICULT FOR ME TO DO MY WORK.
YOU ARE THE ONE WHO ENCOURAGED ME TO GO TO THE KARASUMORI SITE.
DID I...
KLINK
...EVER TELL YOU TO DO THAT?
ANYHOW, I WAS SURPRISED YOU DIDN'T LAST MORE THAN A DAY...
...IN SPITE OF ALL THE INFORMATION I GAVE YOU ABOUT THE SITE.
NOW...
...WHAT ARE YOU GOING TO DO FROM NOW ON?
I HAVE ...
FUMBLE

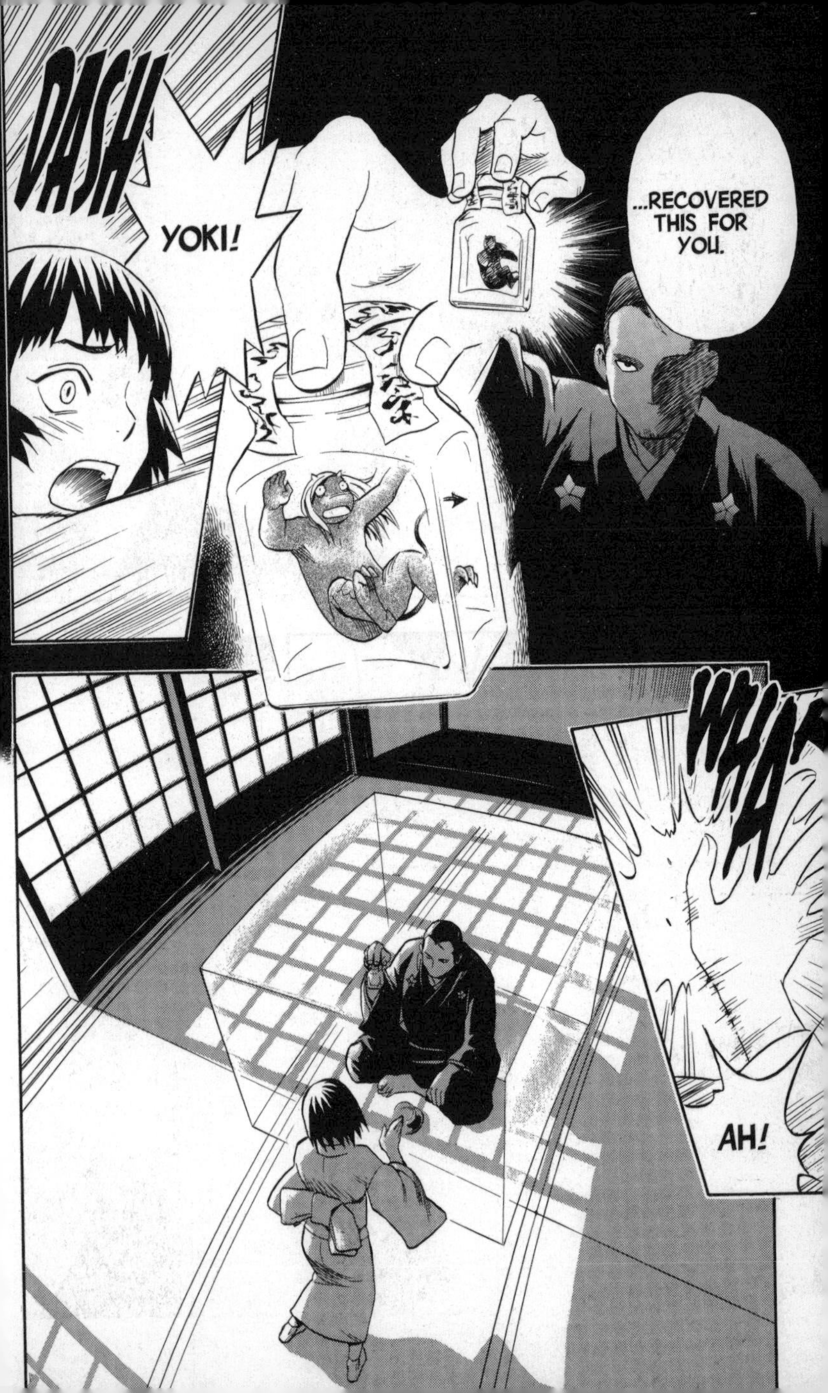
...RECOVERED THIS FOR YOU.
DASH
YOKI!
WHA
AH!

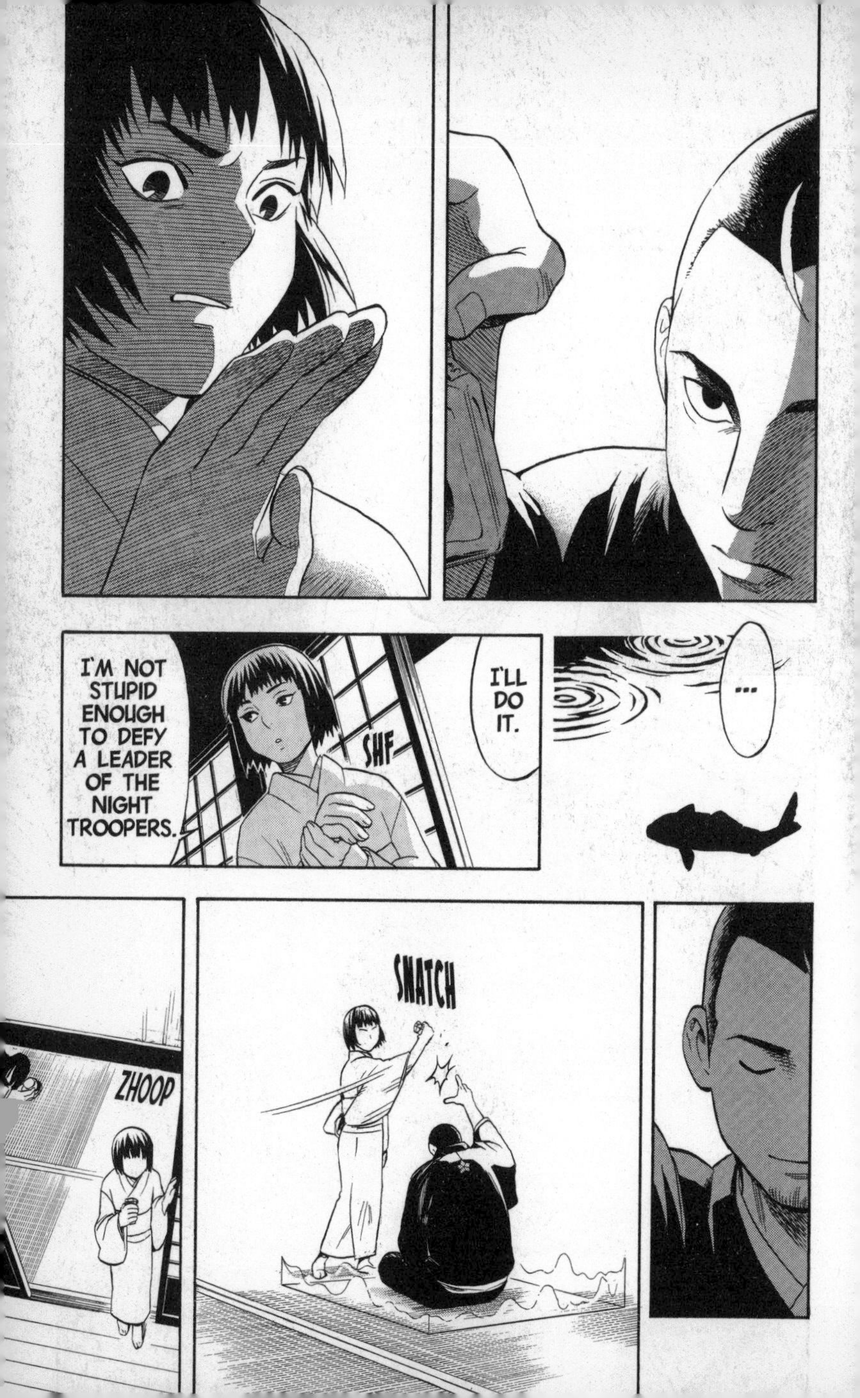
...
I'LL DO IT.
I'M NOT STUPID ENOUGH TO DEFY A LEADER OF THE NIGHT TROOPERS.
SHF
SNATCH
ZHOOP

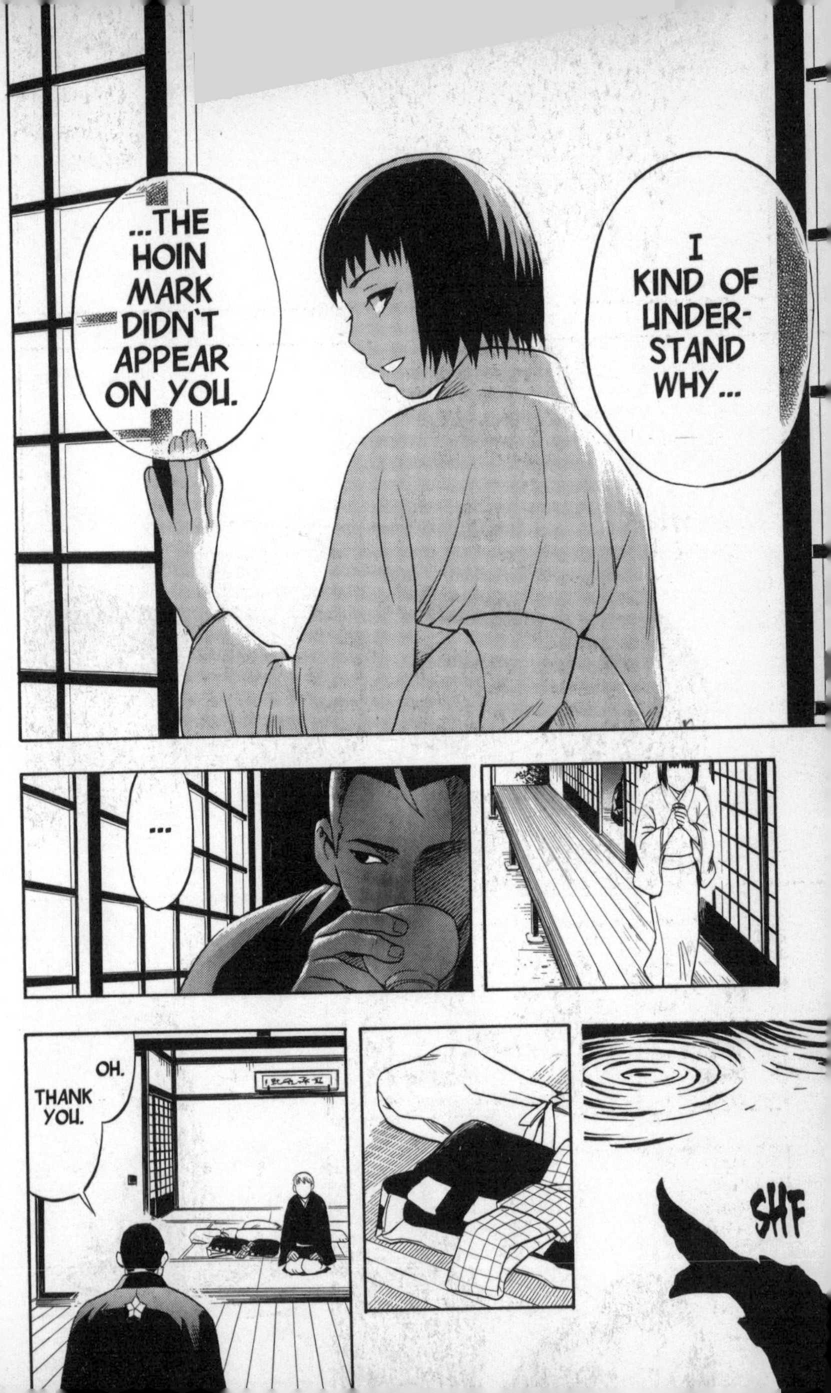
I KIND OF UNDER-STAND WHY...
...THE HOIN MARK DIDN'T APPEAR ON YOU.
...
SHF
OH.
THANK YOU.

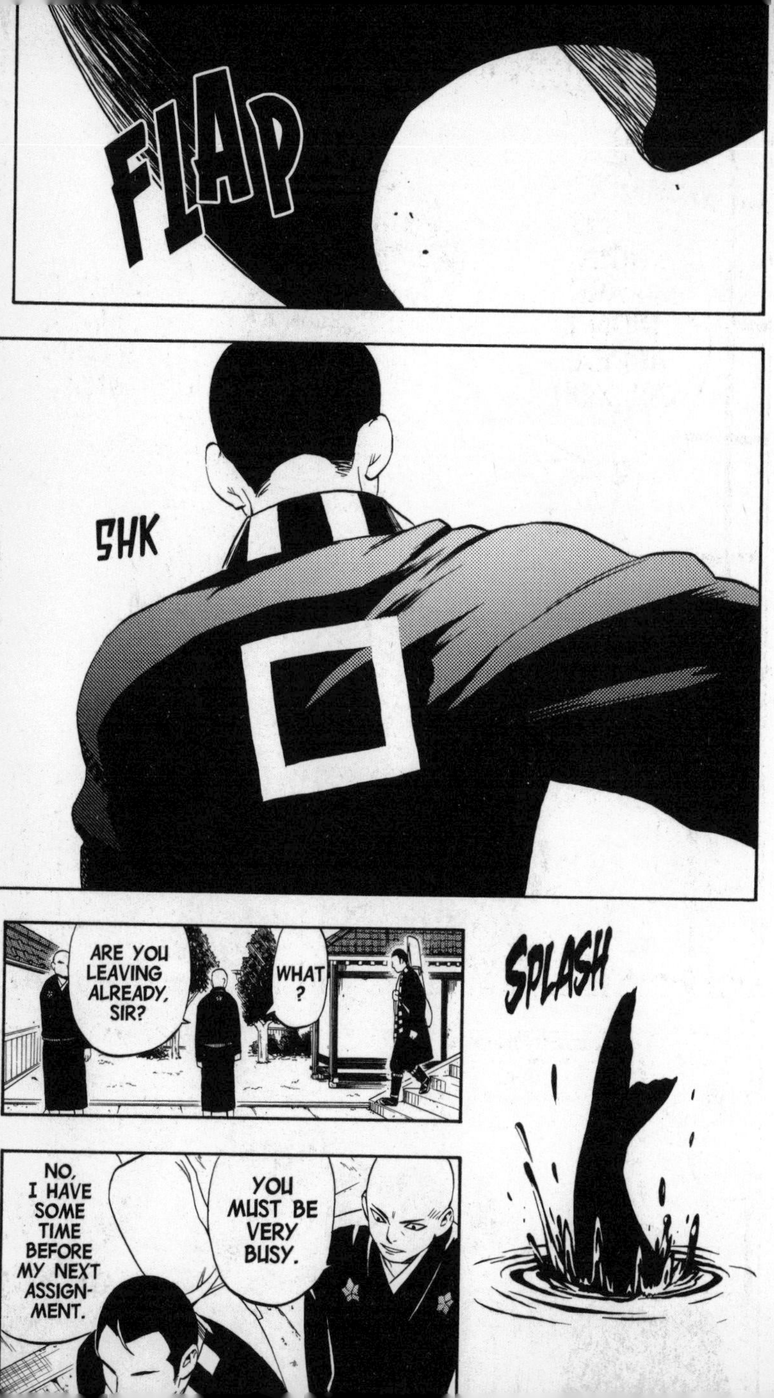
FLAP
SHK
SPLASH
WHAT?
ARE YOU LEAVING ALREADY, SIR?
YOU MUST BE VERY BUSY.
NO, I HAVE SOME TIME BEFORE MY NEXT ASSIGNMENT.

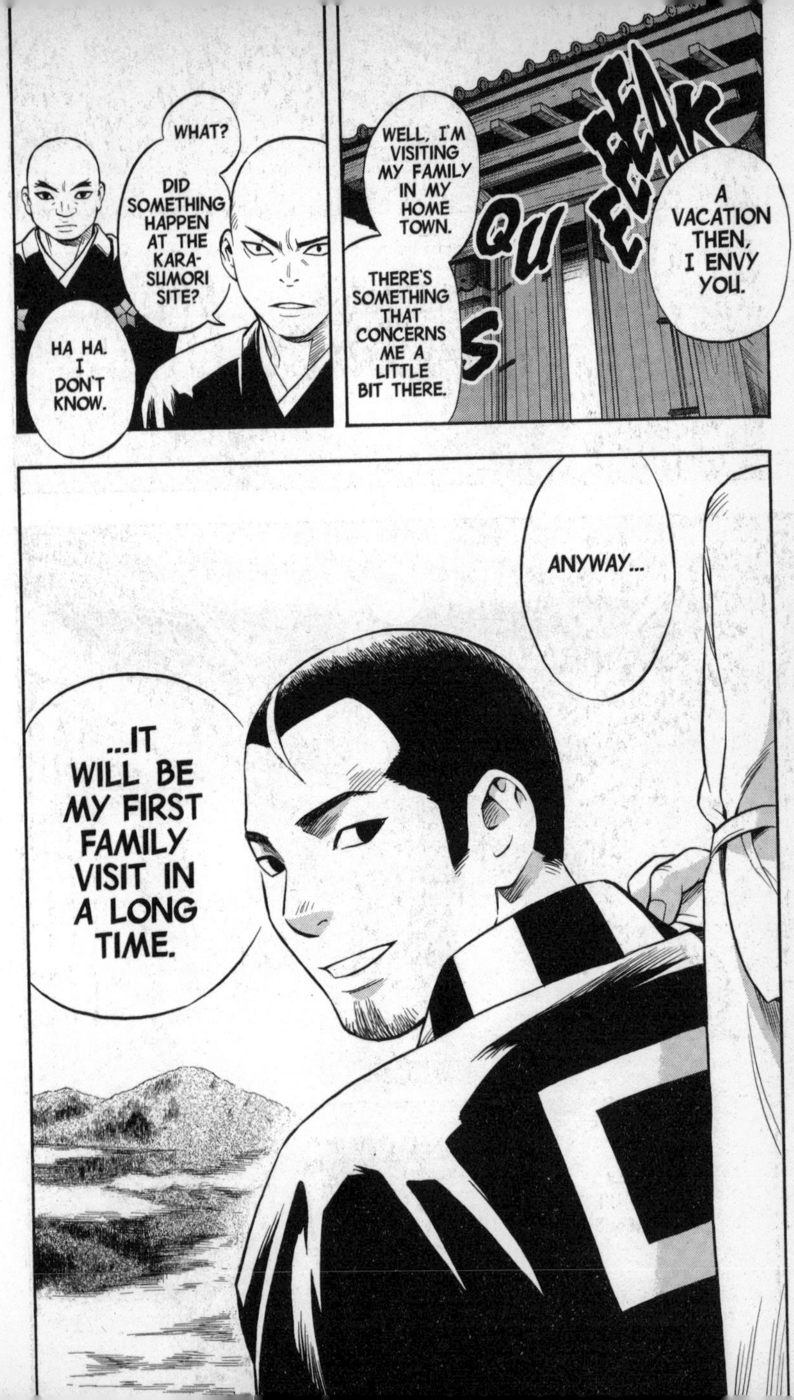
A VACATION THEN, I ENVY YOU.
WELL, I'M VISITING MY FAMILY IN MY HOME TOWN.
THERE'S SOMETHING THAT CONCERNS ME A LITTLE BIT THERE.
WHAT?
DID SOMETHING HAPPEN AT THE KARA-SUMORI SITE?
HA HA. I DON'T KNOW.
ANYWAY...
...IT WILL BE MY FIRST FAMILY VISIT IN A LONG TIME.

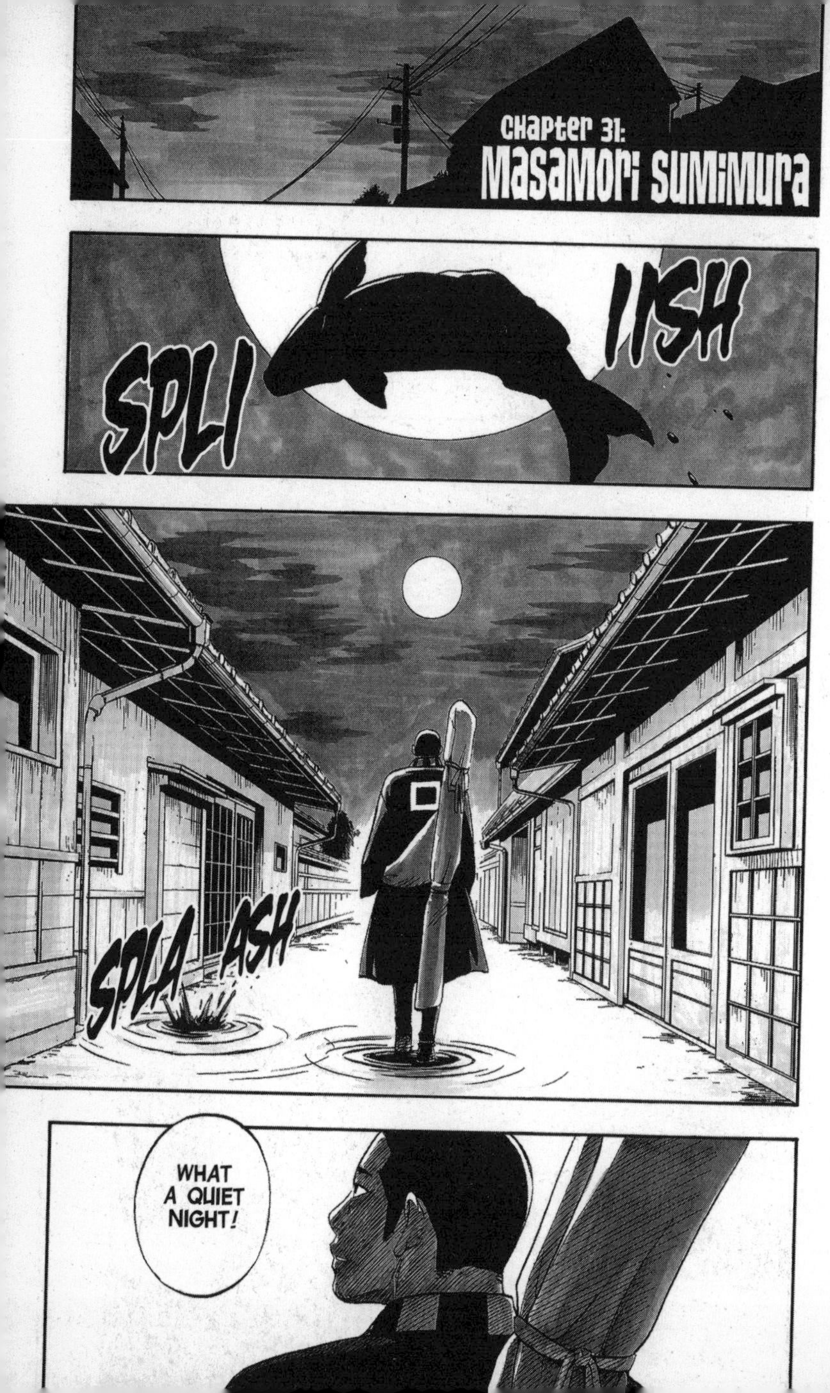

Chapter 31:
Masamori Sumimura
SPLI IISH
SPLA ASH
WHAT A QUIET NIGHT!

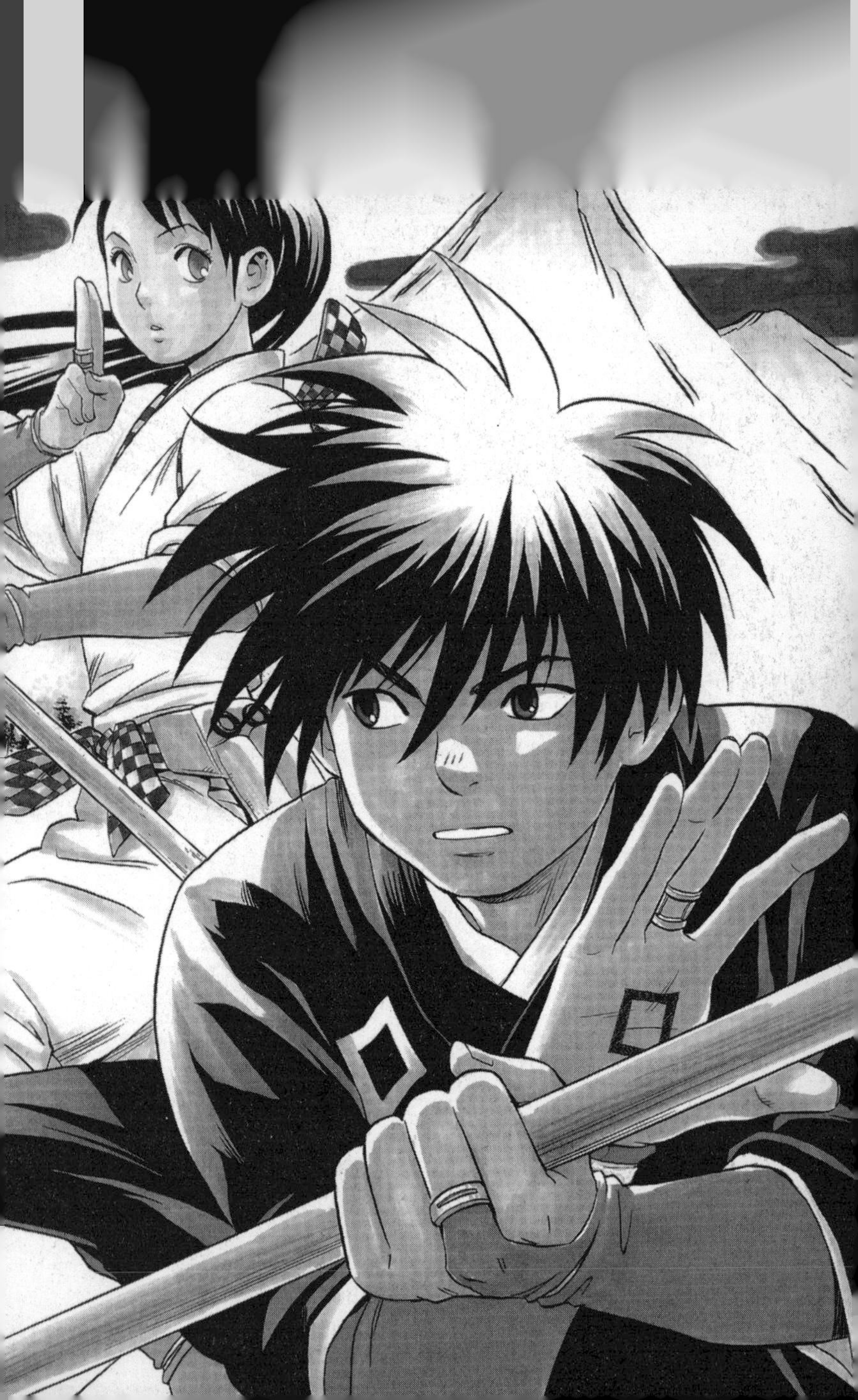

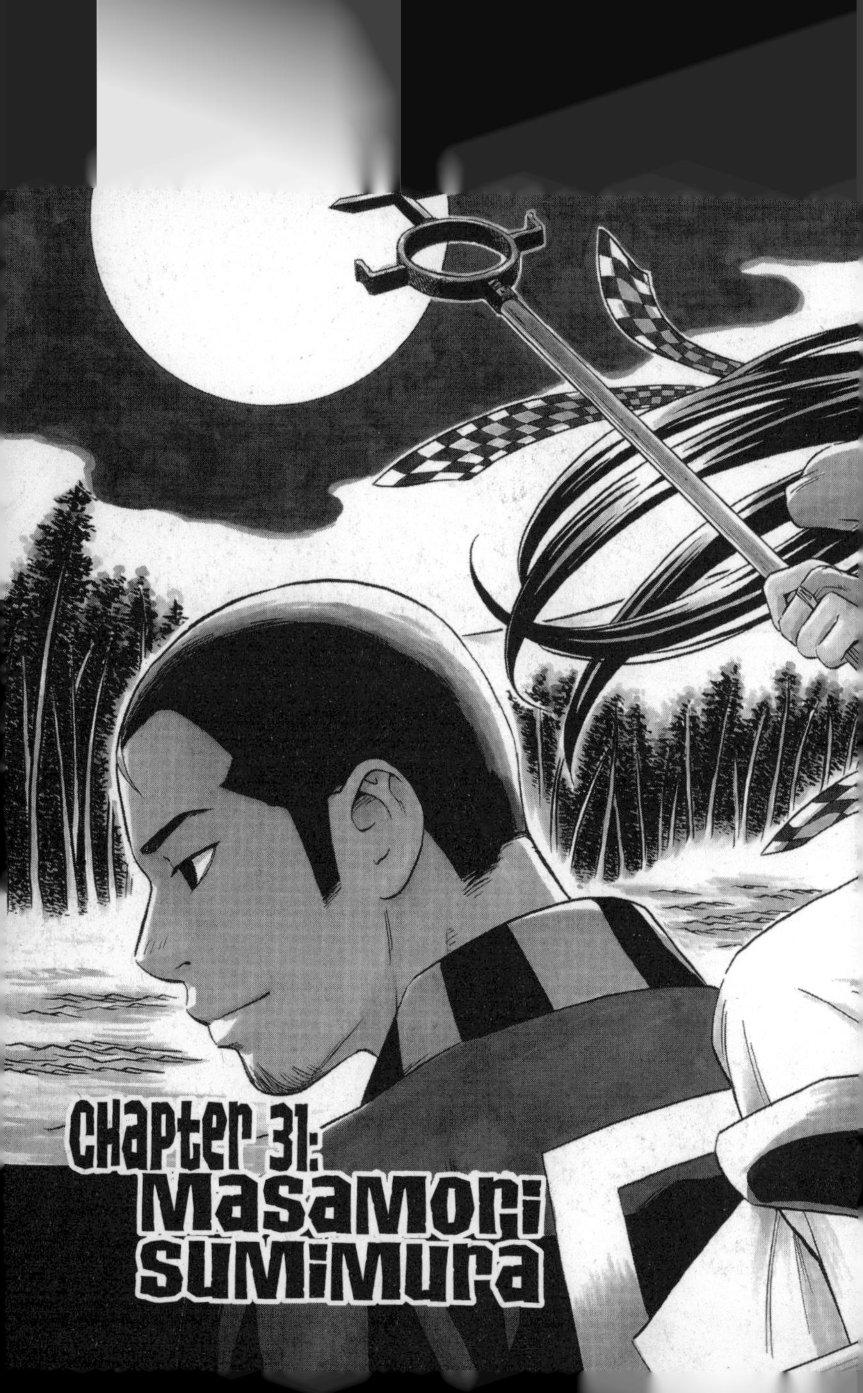
Chapter 31:
Masamori Sumimura

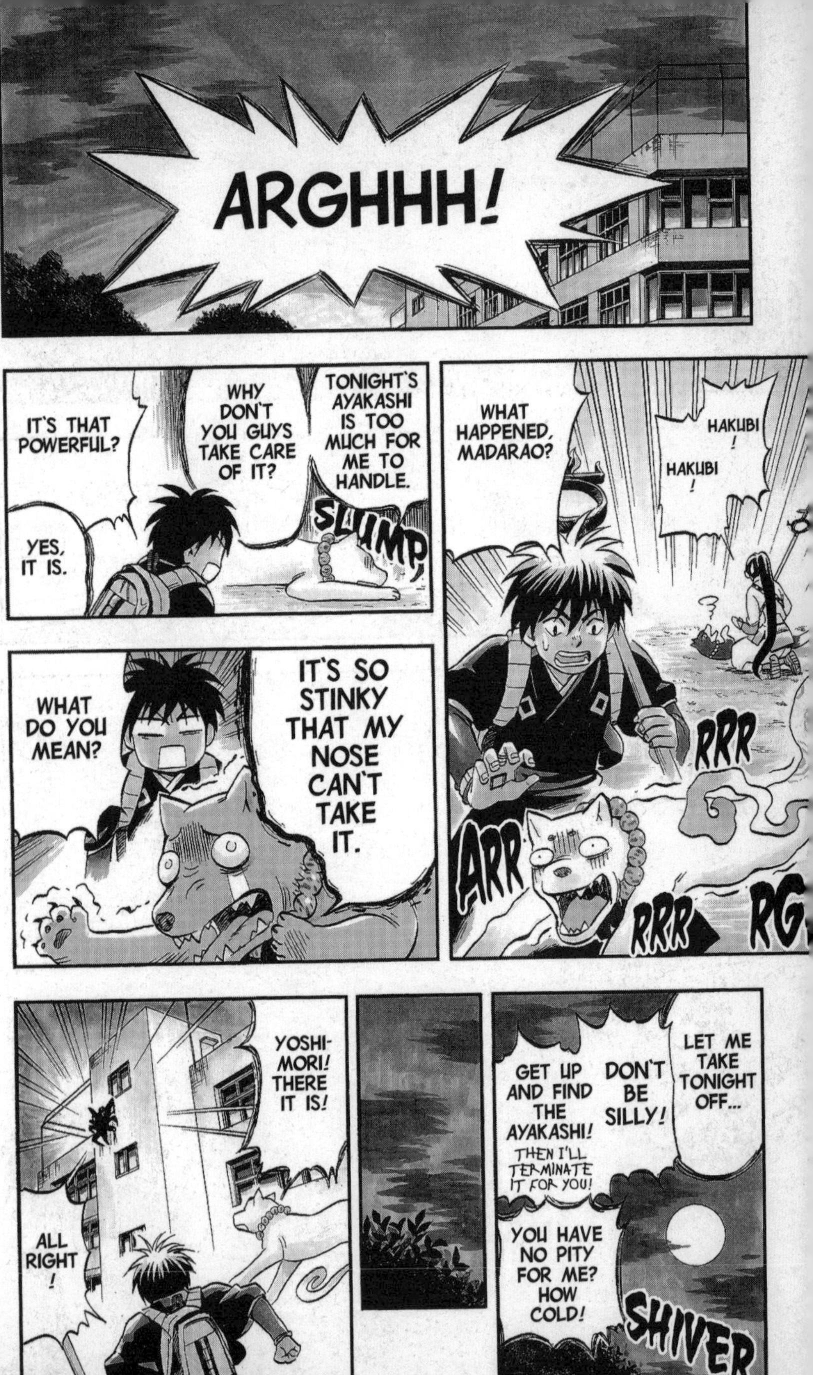
ARGHHH!
HAKUBI! HAKUBI!
WHAT HAPPENED, MADARAO?
RRR
ARR
RRR RG
TONIGHT'S AYAKASHI IS TOO MUCH FOR ME TO HANDLE.
SLUMP
WHY DON'T YOU GUYS TAKE CARE OF IT?
IT'S THAT POWERFUL?
YES, IT IS.
IT'S SO STINKY THAT MY NOSE CAN'T TAKE IT.
WHAT DO YOU MEAN?
LET ME TAKE TONIGHT OFF...
DON'T BE SILLY!
GET UP AND FIND THE AYAKASHI!
THEN I'LL TERMINATE IT FOR YOU!
YOU HAVE NO PITY FOR ME? HOW COLD!
SHIVER
YOSHI-MORI! THERE IT IS!
ALL RIGHT!

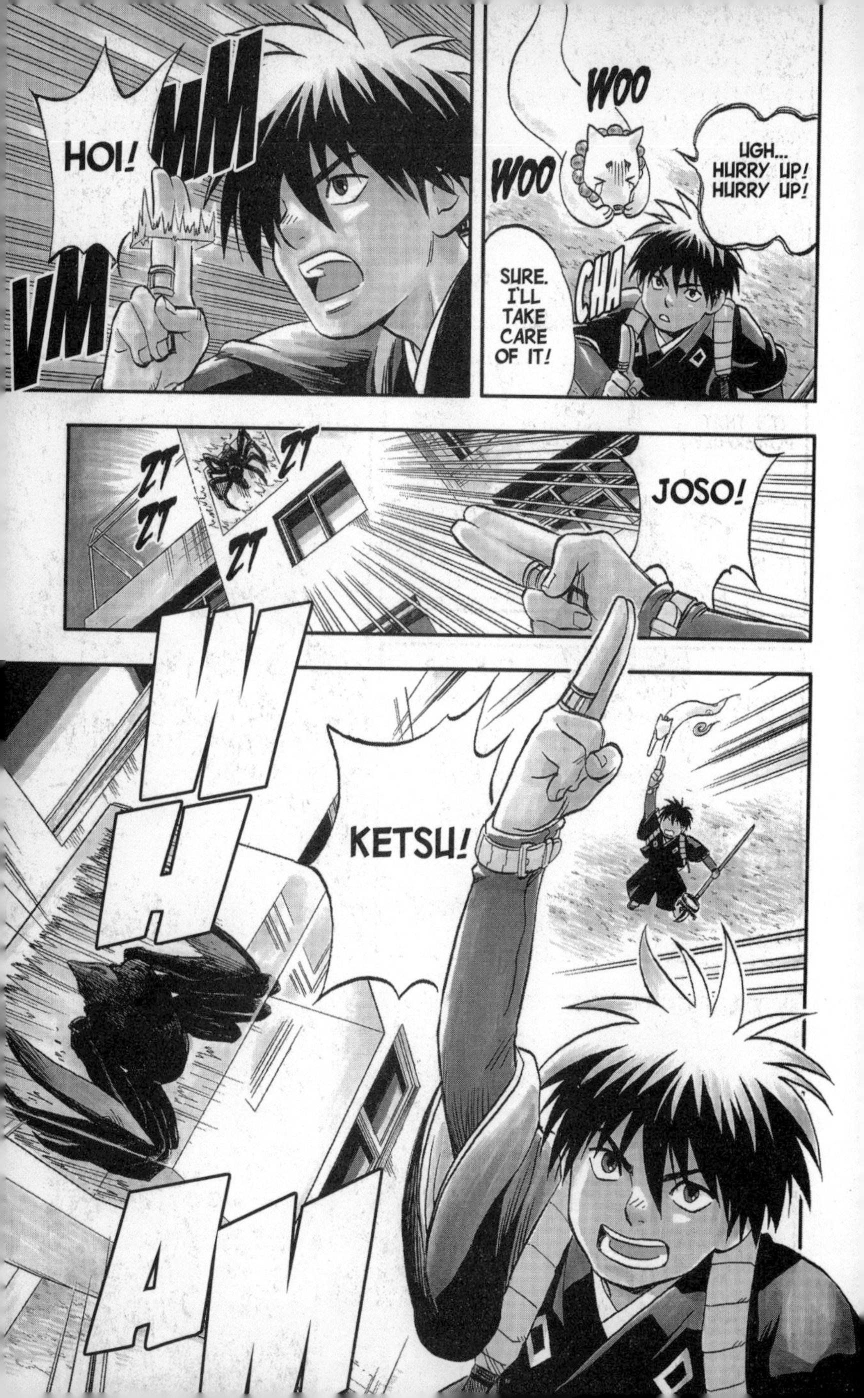
WOO
WOO
UGH... HURRY UP! HURRY UP!
SURE. I'LL TAKE CARE OF IT!
CHA
HOI!
MM
VM
JOSO!
ZT
ZT
ZT
ZT
KETSU!
WHAM

結界師

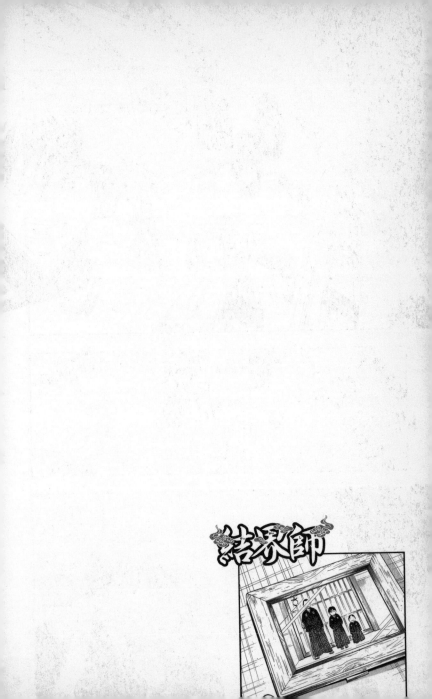

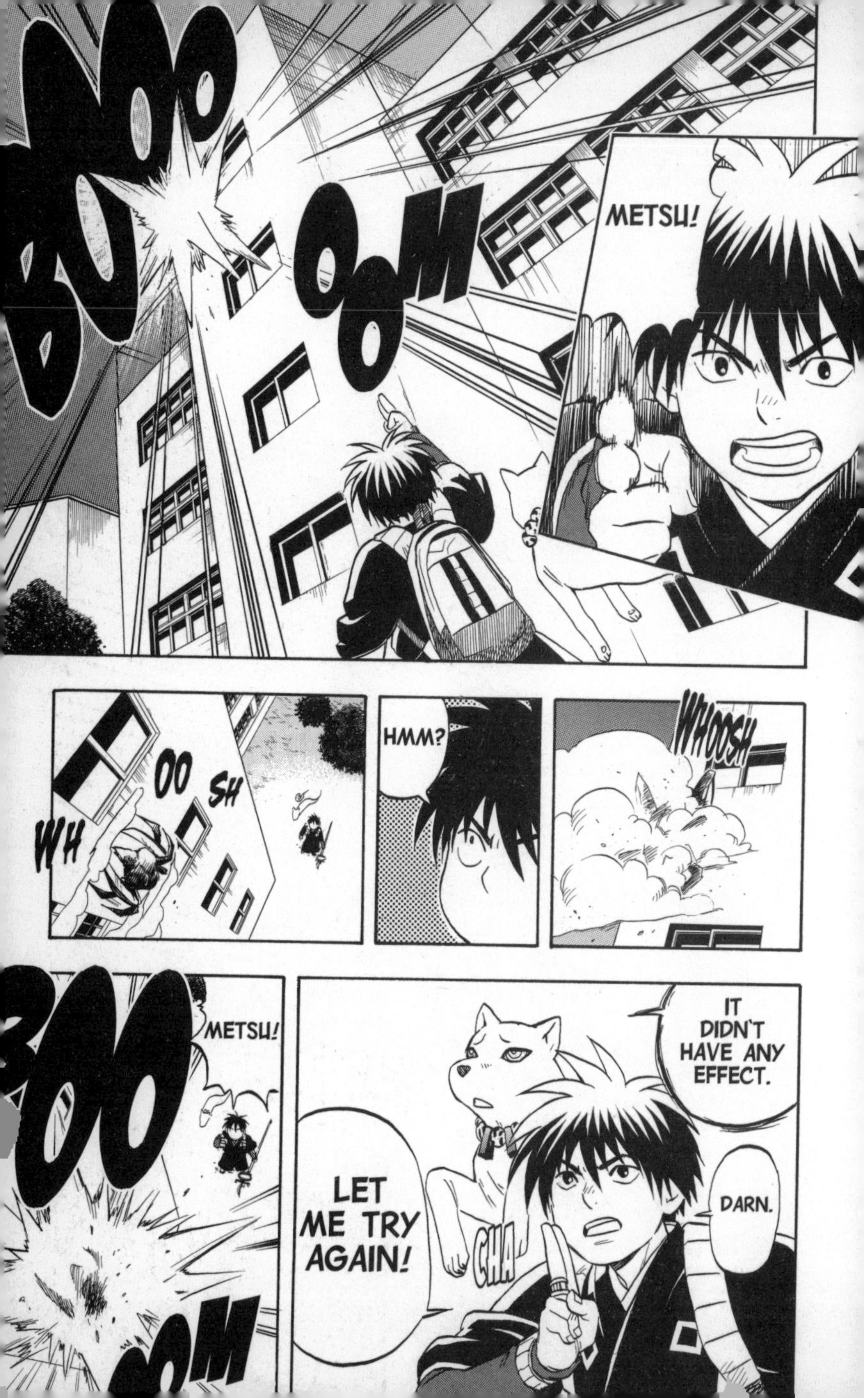
METSU!
BOOOOOOM
WHOOSH
HMM?
WHOOSH
IT DIDN'T HAVE ANY EFFECT.
DARN.
LET ME TRY AGAIN!
CHA
METSU!
BOOOOOM

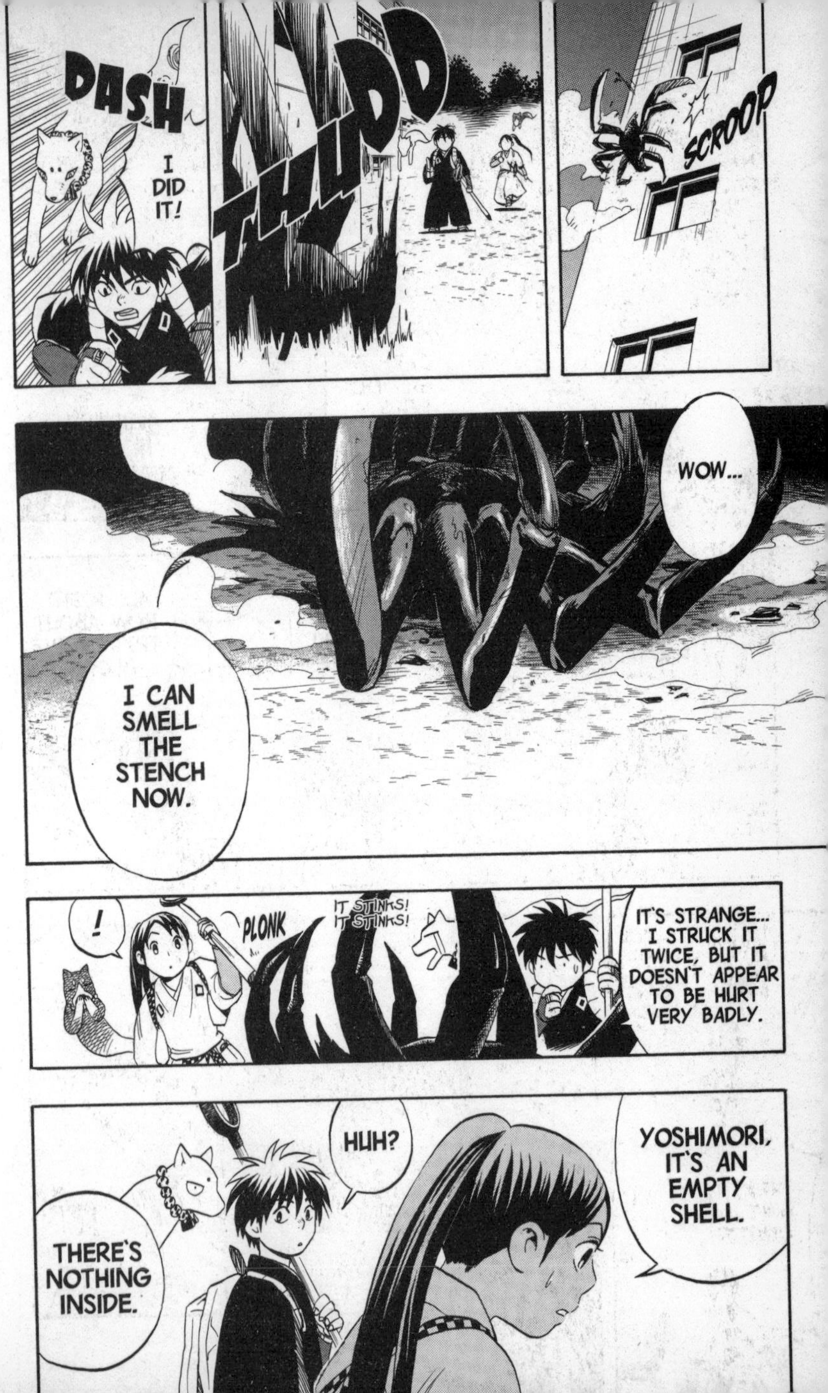
SCROOP
THUDD
DASH
I DID IT!
WOW...
I CAN SMELL THE STENCH NOW.
IT'S STRANGE... I STRUCK IT TWICE, BUT IT DOESN'T APPEAR TO BE HURT VERY BADLY.
IT STINKS! IT STINKS!
PLONK
!
YOSHIMORI, IT'S AN EMPTY SHELL.
HUH?
THERE'S NOTHING INSIDE.

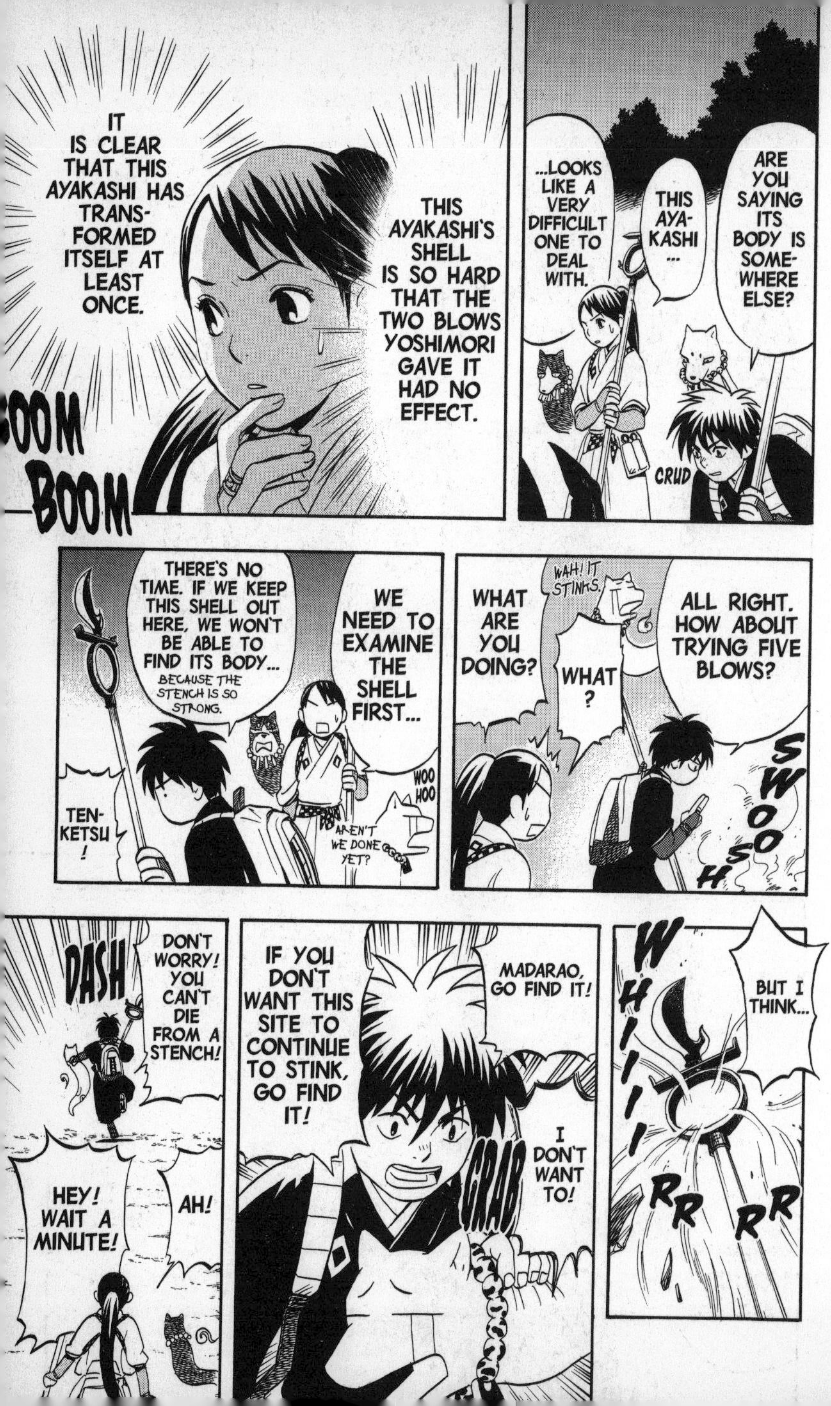
ARE YOU SAYING ITS BODY IS SOMEWHERE ELSE?
THIS AYAKASHI...
...LOOKS LIKE A VERY DIFFICULT ONE TO DEAL WITH.
CRUD
THIS AYAKASHI'S SHELL IS SO HARD THAT THE TWO BLOWS YOSHIMORI GAVE IT HAD NO EFFECT.
IT IS CLEAR THAT THIS AYAKASHI HAS TRANSFORMED ITSELF AT LEAST ONCE.
BOOM BOOM
ALL RIGHT. HOW ABOUT TRYING FIVE BLOWS?
SWOOSH
WAH! IT STINKS.
WHAT?
WHAT ARE YOU DOING?
WE NEED TO EXAMINE THE SHELL FIRST...
THERE'S NO TIME. IF WE KEEP THIS SHELL OUT HERE, WE WON'T BE ABLE TO FIND ITS BODY...
BECAUSE THE STENCH IS SO STRONG.
WOO HOO
AREN'T WE DONE YET?
TENKETSU!
BUT I THINK...
WHIIIIRRRRR
MADARAO, GO FIND IT!
IF YOU DON'T WANT THIS SITE TO CONTINUE TO STINK, GO FIND IT!
I DON'T WANT TO!
GRAB
DON'T WORRY! YOU CAN'T DIE FROM A STENCH!
DASH
AH!
HEY! WAIT A MINUTE!

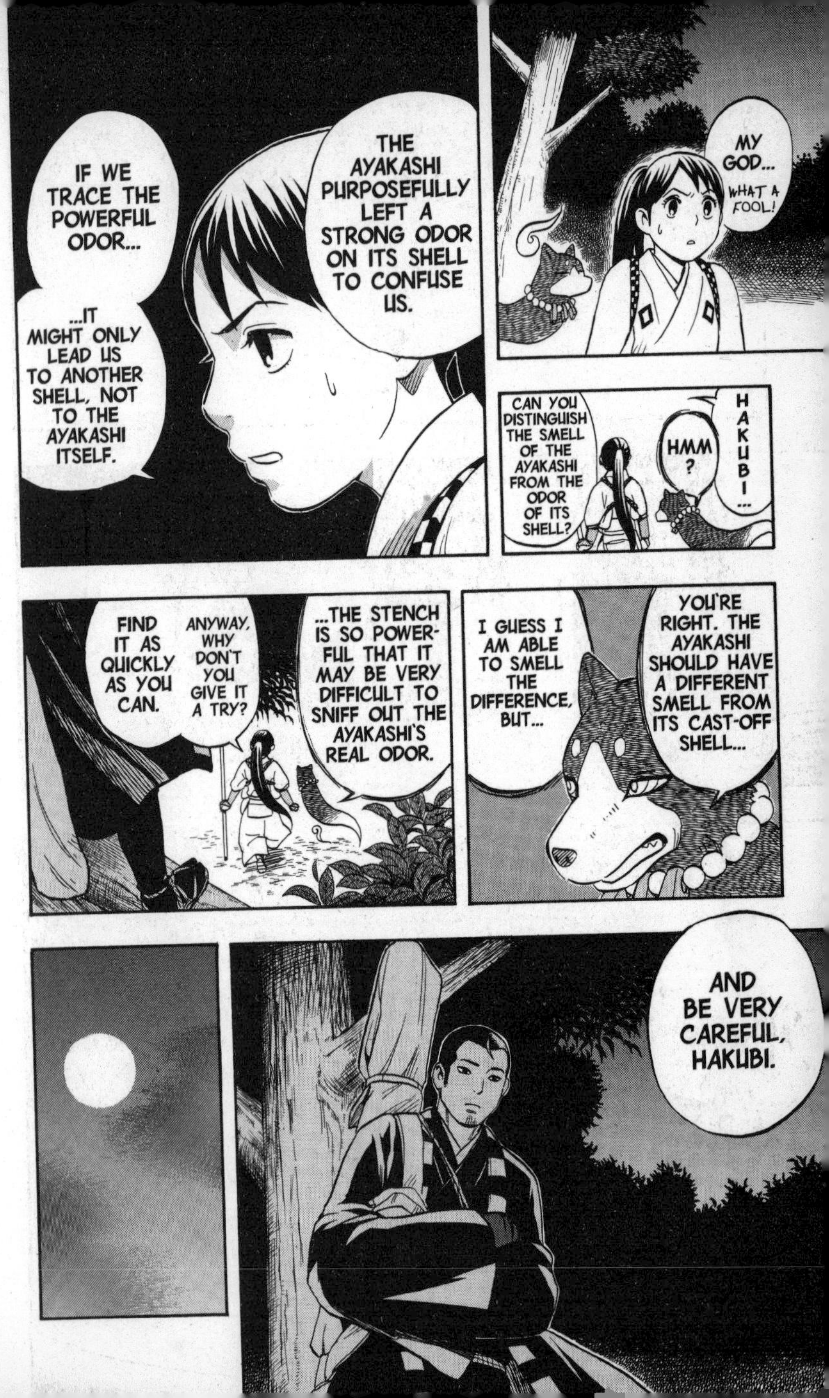
MY GOD...
WHAT A FOOL!
HAKUBI...
HMM?
CAN YOU DISTINGUISH THE SMELL OF THE AYAKASHI FROM THE ODOR OF ITS SHELL?
THE AYAKASHI PURPOSEFULLY LEFT A STRONG ODOR ON ITS SHELL TO CONFUSE US.
IF WE TRACE THE POWERFUL ODOR...
...IT MIGHT ONLY LEAD US TO ANOTHER SHELL, NOT TO THE AYAKASHI ITSELF.
YOU'RE RIGHT. THE AYAKASHI SHOULD HAVE A DIFFERENT SMELL FROM ITS CAST-OFF SHELL...
I GUESS I AM ABLE TO SMELL THE DIFFERENCE, BUT...
...THE STENCH IS SO POWER-FUL THAT IT MAY BE VERY DIFFICULT TO SNIFF OUT THE AYAKASHI'S REAL ODOR.
ANYWAY, WHY DON'T YOU GIVE IT A TRY?
FIND IT AS QUICKLY AS YOU CAN.
AND BE VERY CAREFUL, HAKUBI.

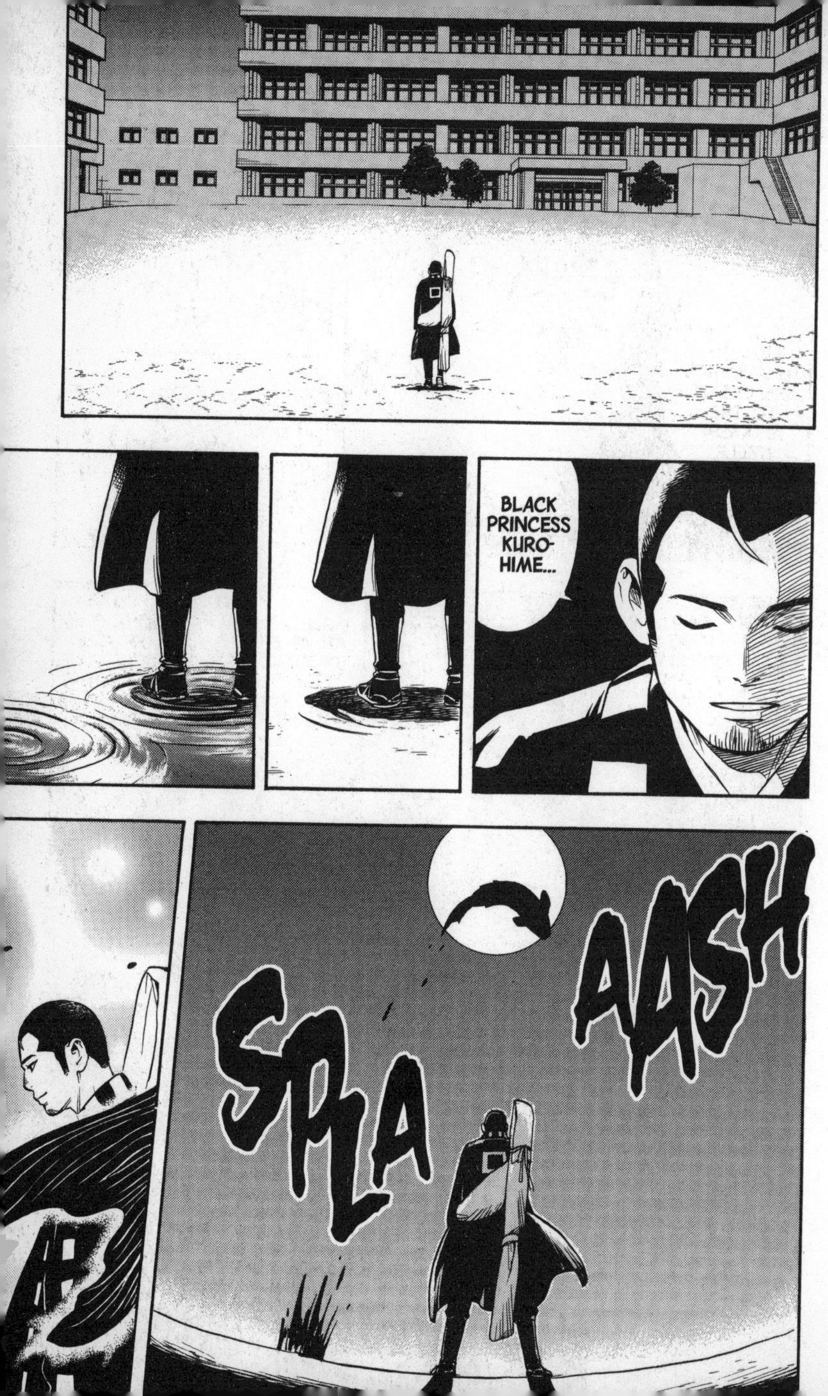
BLACK PRINCESS KURO-HIME...
SPLA
AASH

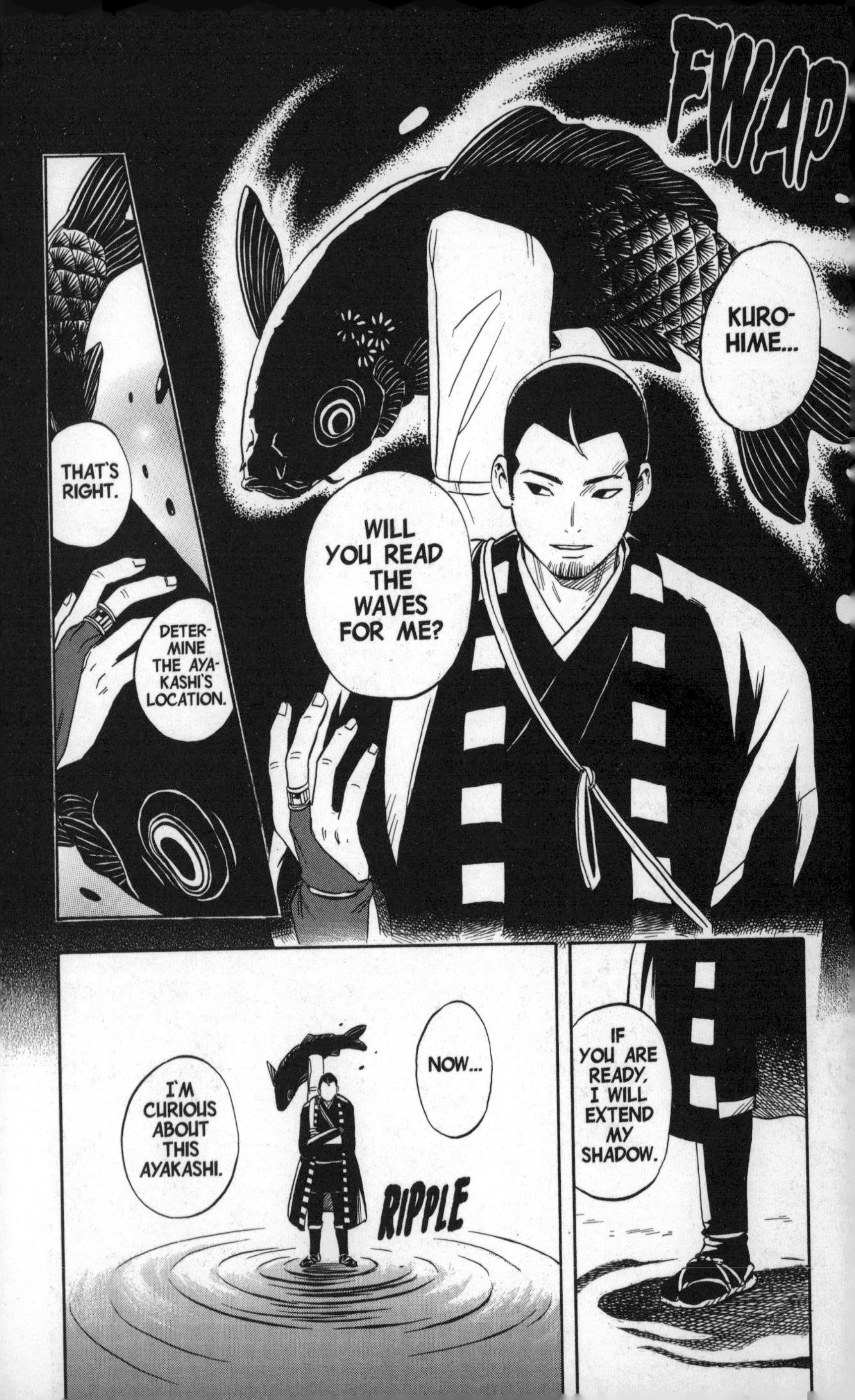
FWAP
KURO-HIME...
WILL YOU READ THE WAVES FOR ME?
THAT'S RIGHT.
DETERMINE THE AYAKASHI'S LOCATION.
IF YOU ARE READY, I WILL EXTEND MY SHADOW.
NOW...
I'M CURIOUS ABOUT THIS AYAKASHI.
RIPPLE

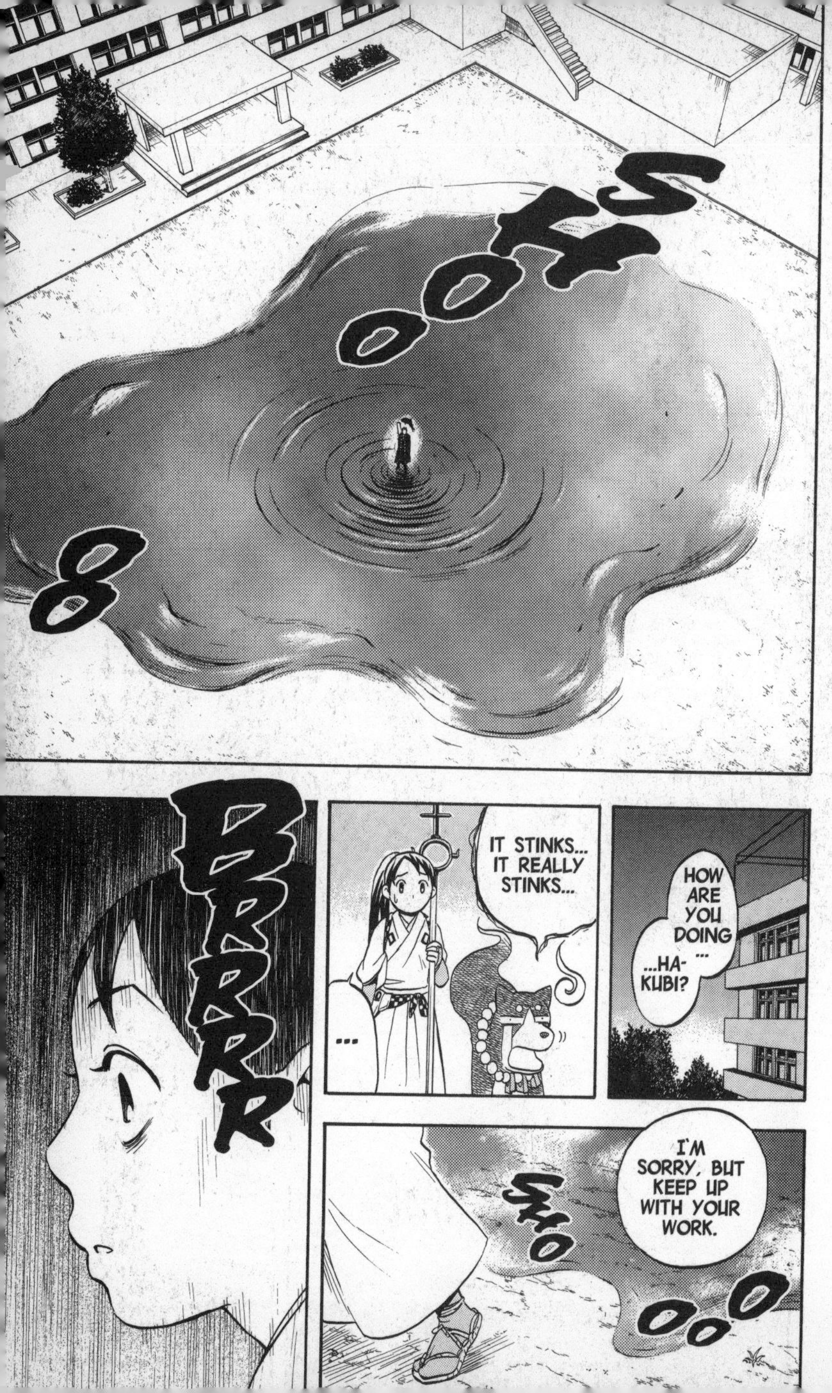

SHOOO
HOW ARE YOU DOING... ...HA-KUBI?
IT STINKS... IT REALLY STINKS...
...
I'M SORRY, BUT KEEP UP WITH YOUR WORK.
SHOOOO
BRRRRR

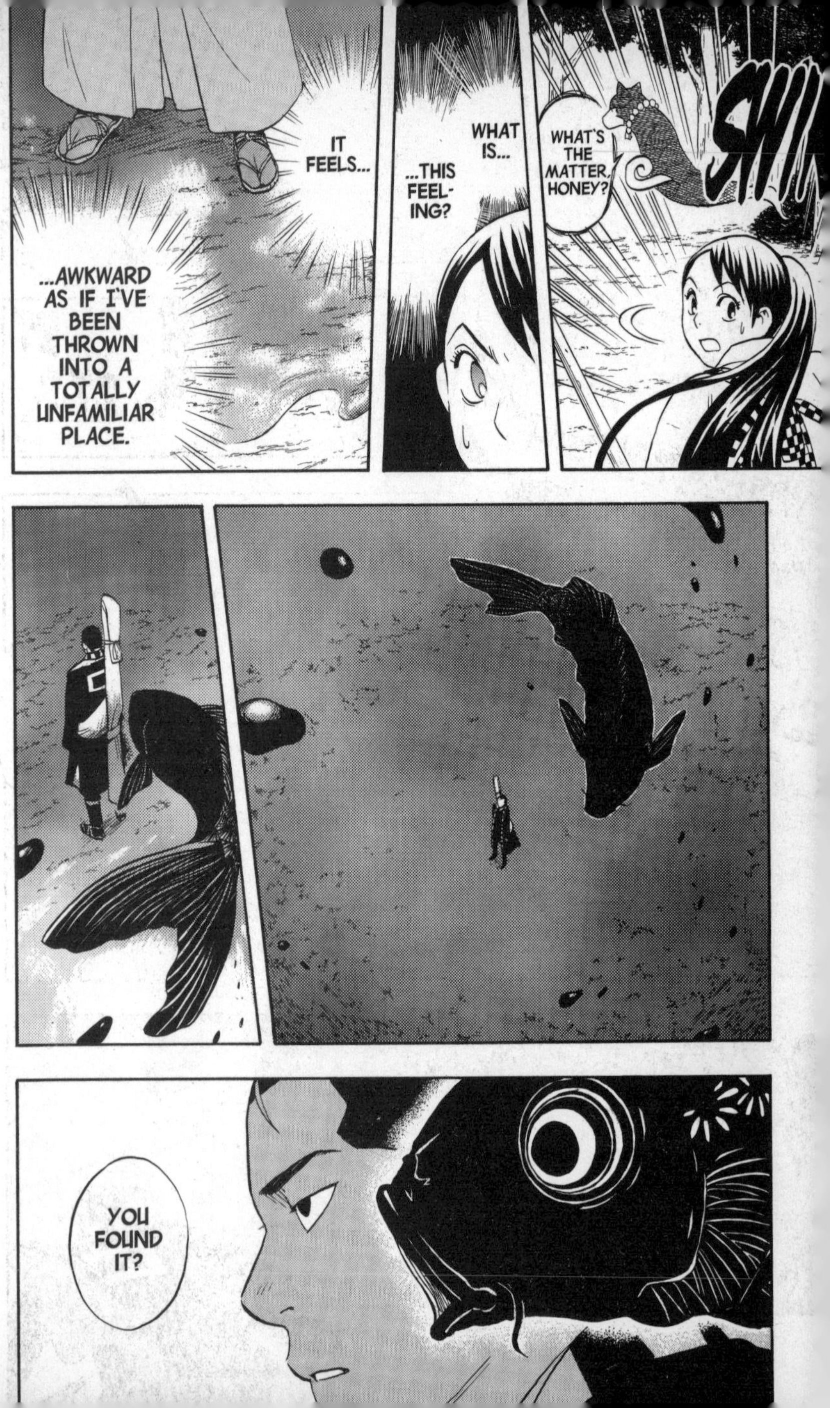
SHU
WHAT'S THE MATTER, HONEY?
WHAT IS...
...THIS FEELING?
IT FEELS...
...AWKWARD AS IF I'VE BEEN THROWN INTO A TOTALLY UNFAMILIAR PLACE.
YOU FOUND IT?

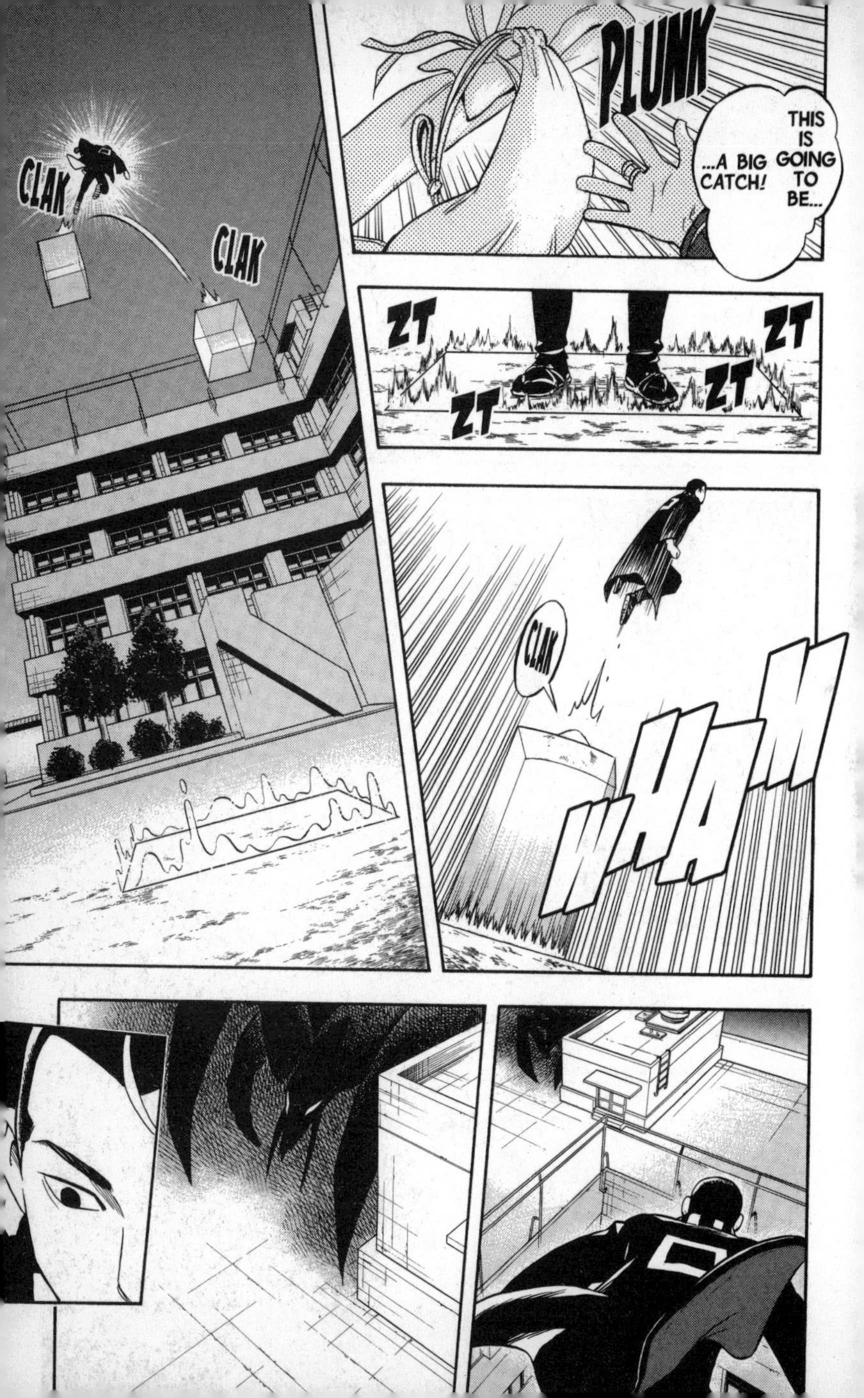
PLUNK
THIS IS GOING TO BE...
...A BIG CATCH!
ZT
ZT
ZT
ZT
CLAK
WHA--M
CLAK
CLAK

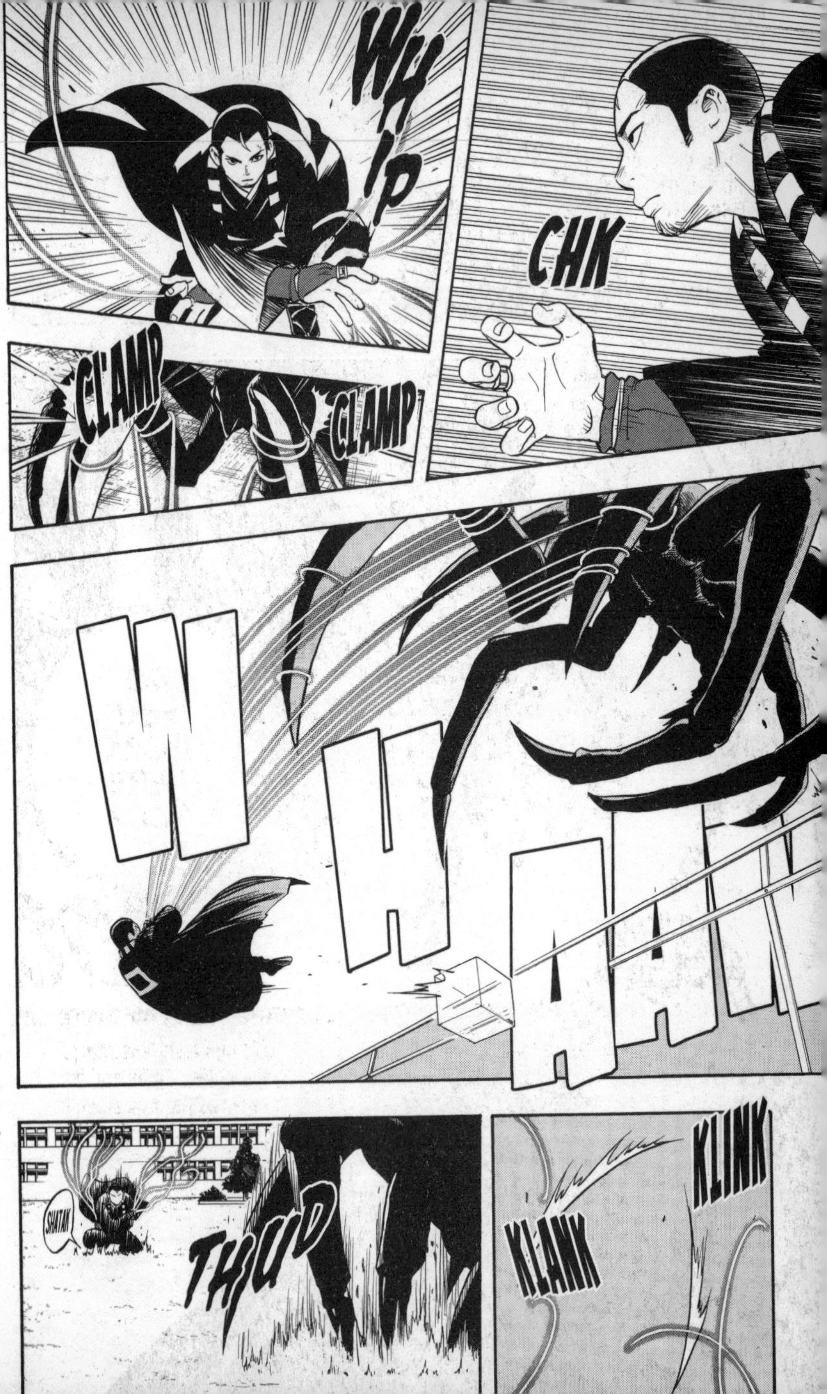
CHK
WHIP
CLAMP
CLAMP
WHA
KLINK
KLANK
THUD
SHATAK

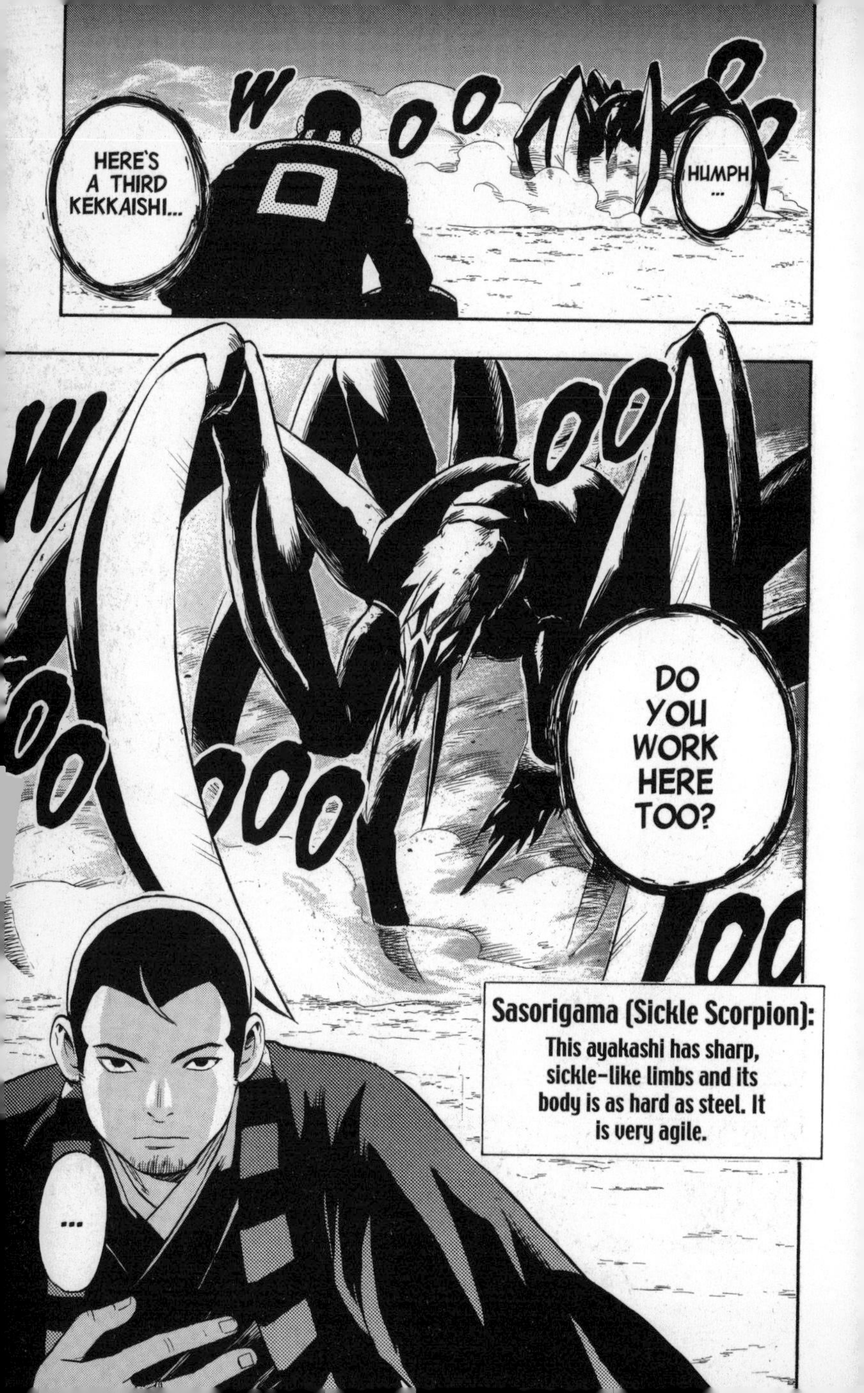
WOOOOO
HUMPH...
HERE'S A THIRD KEKKAISHI...
WOOOOOOOOOO
DO YOU WORK HERE TOO?
Sasorigama (Sickle Scorpion):
This ayakashi has sharp, sickle-like limbs and its body is as hard as steel. It is very agile.
...

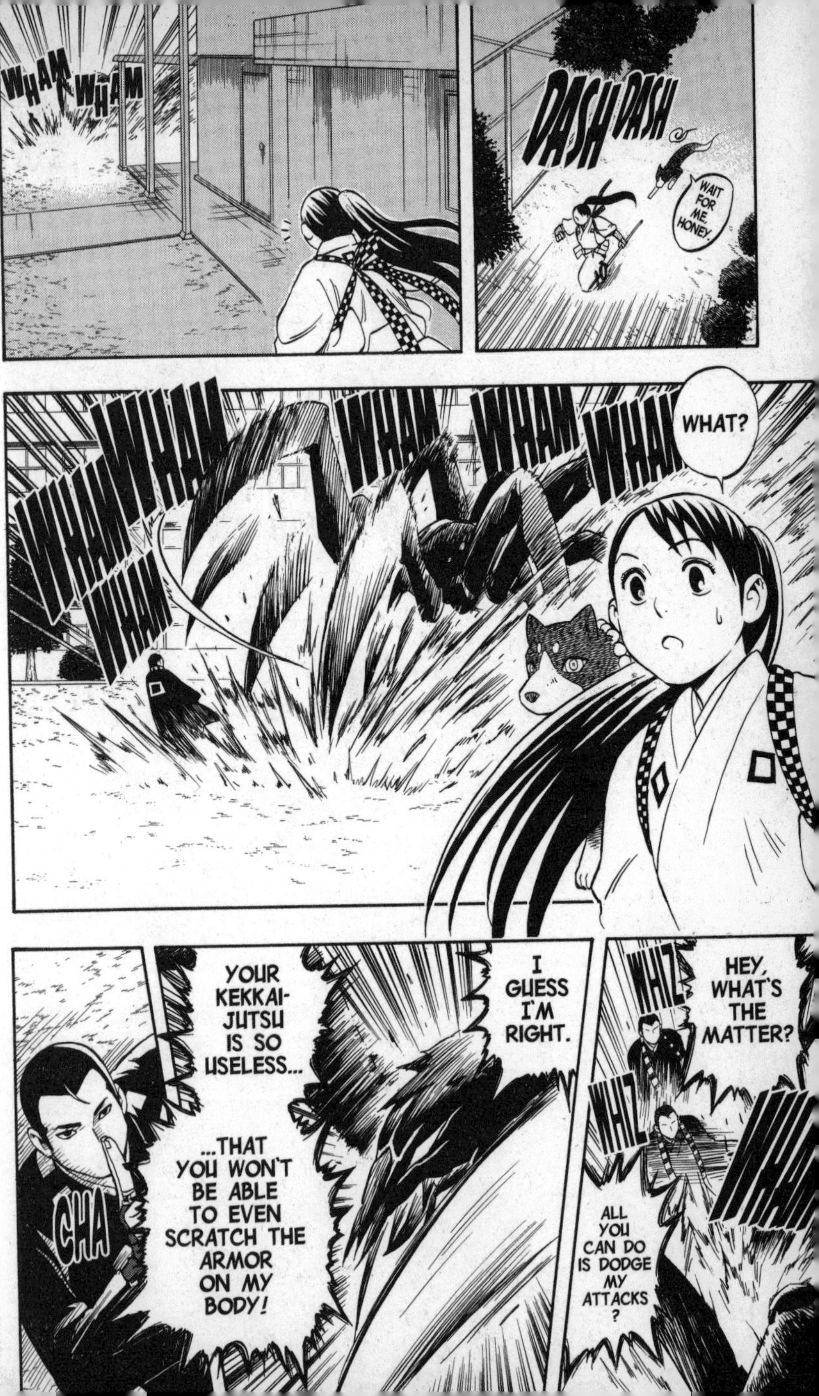
DASH DASH
WAIT FOR ME, HONEY.
WHAM WHAM
WHAT?
WHAM WHAM WHAM
WHAM WHAM WHAM WHAM
HEY, WHAT'S THE MATTER?
WHIZ
WHIZ
ALL YOU CAN DO IS DODGE MY ATTACKS?
I GUESS I'M RIGHT.
YOUR KEKKAI-JUTSU IS SO USELESS...
...THAT YOU WON'T BE ABLE TO EVEN SCRATCH THE ARMOR ON MY BODY!
CHA

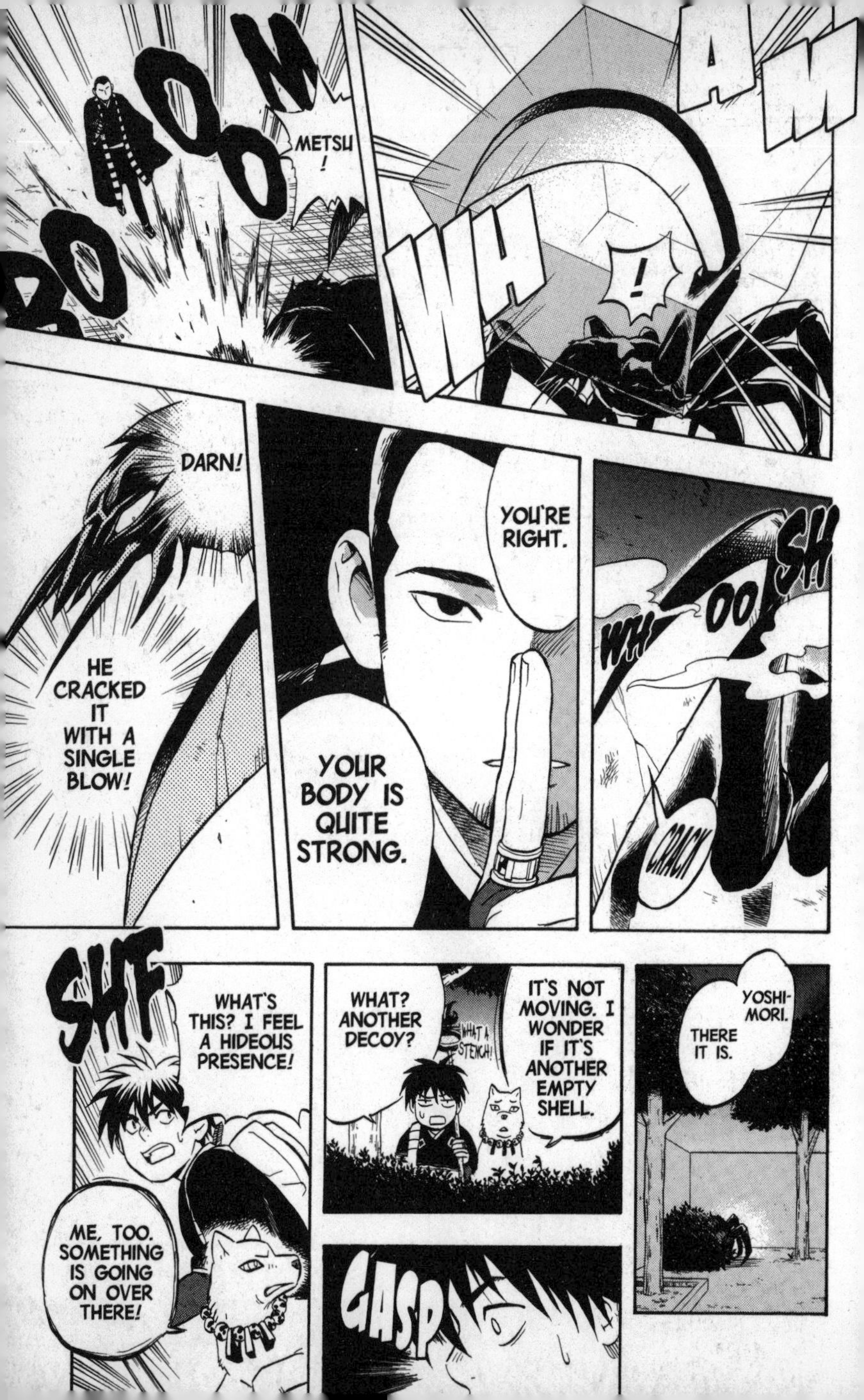
WHAM
!
BOOOOM
METSU!
WHOOSH
CRACK
YOU'RE RIGHT.
YOUR BODY IS QUITE STRONG.
DARN!
HE CRACKED IT WITH A SINGLE BLOW!
YOSHIMORI.
THERE IT IS.
IT'S NOT MOVING. I WONDER IF IT'S ANOTHER EMPTY SHELL.
WHAT? ANOTHER DECOY?
WHAT A STENCH!
GASP
SHF
WHAT'S THIS? I FEEL A HIDEOUS PRESENCE!
ME, TOO. SOMETHING IS GOING ON OVER THERE!

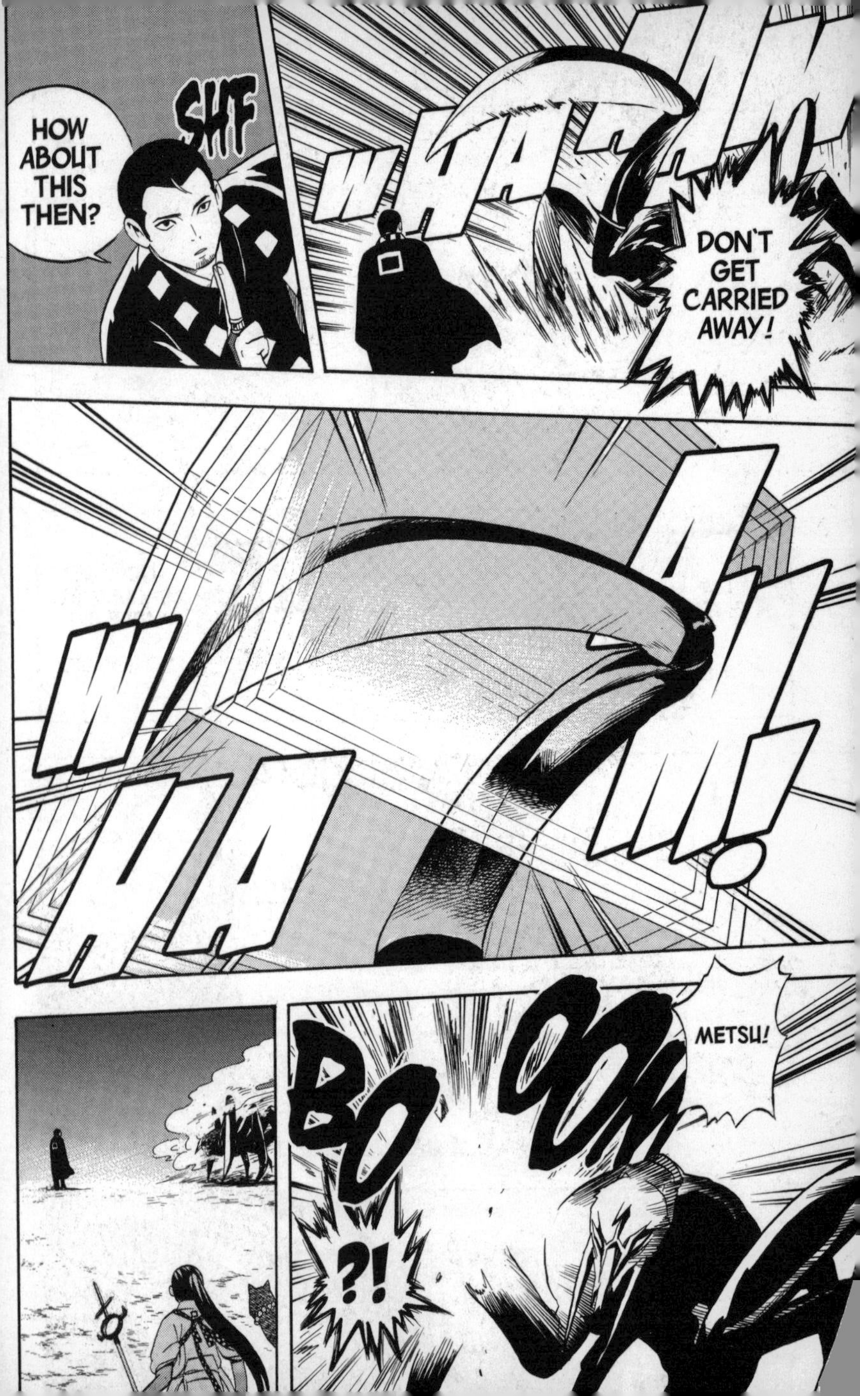
WHA
DON'T GET CARRIED AWAY!
SHF
HOW ABOUT THIS THEN?
WHAAM!
METSU!
BOOOM
?!

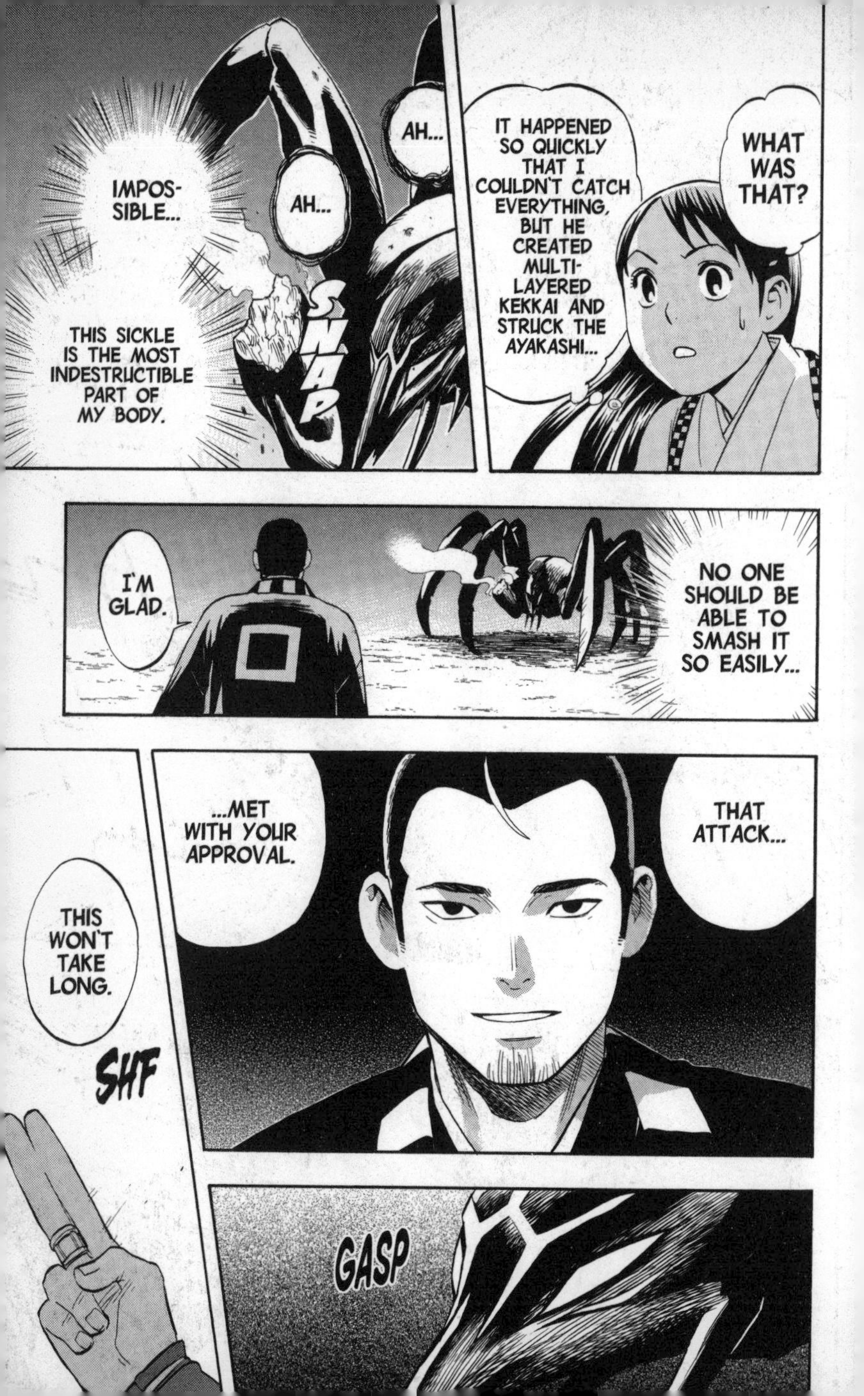
WHAT WAS THAT?
IT HAPPENED SO QUICKLY THAT I COULDN'T CATCH EVERYTHING, BUT HE CREATED MULTI-LAYERED KEKKAI AND STRUCK THE AYAKASHI...
AH...
AH...
IMPOSSIBLE...
SNAP
THIS SICKLE IS THE MOST INDESTRUCTIBLE PART OF MY BODY.
NO ONE SHOULD BE ABLE TO SMASH IT SO EASILY...
I'M GLAD.
THAT ATTACK...
...MET WITH YOUR APPROVAL.
THIS WON'T TAKE LONG.
SHF
GASP

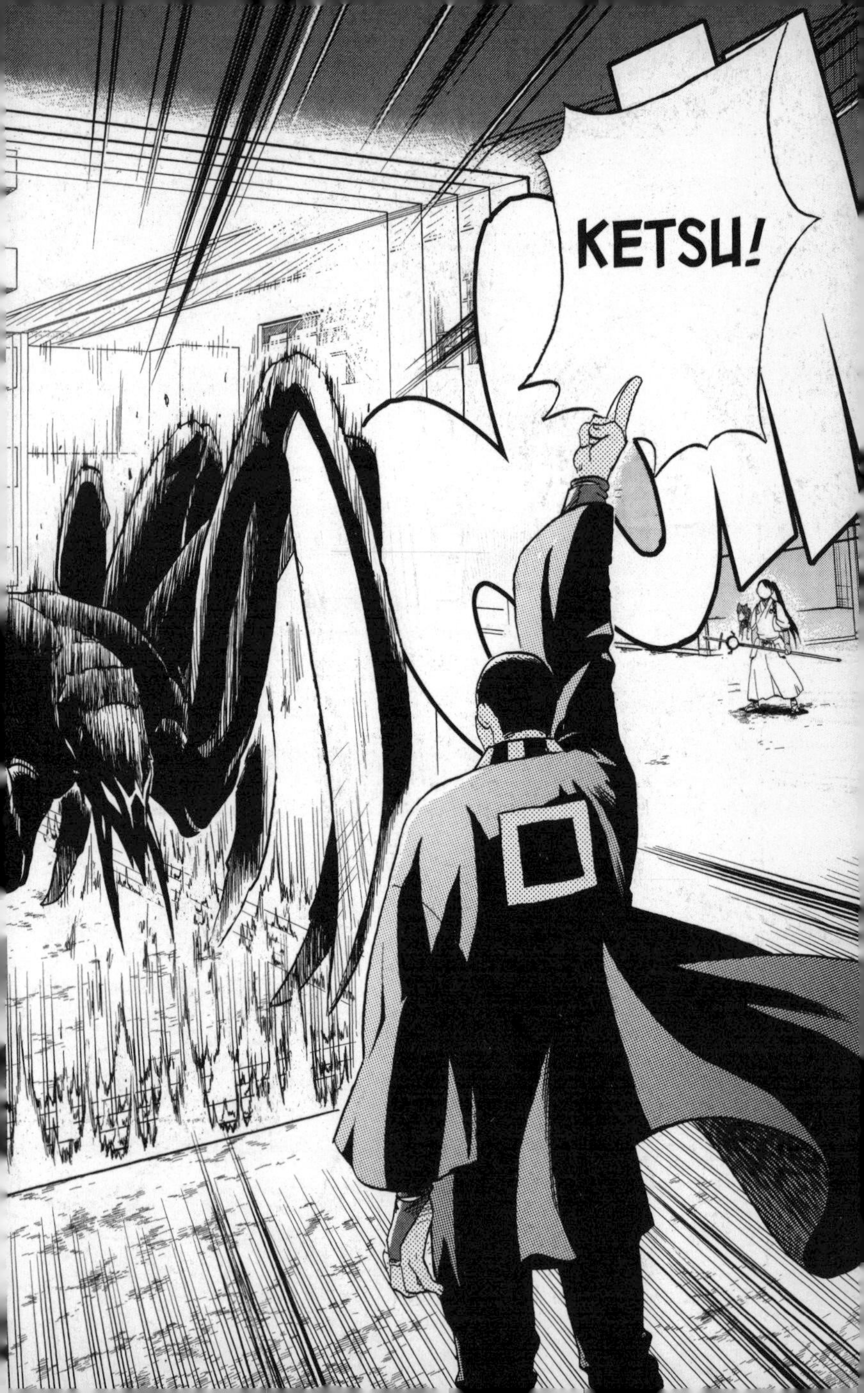
KETSU!

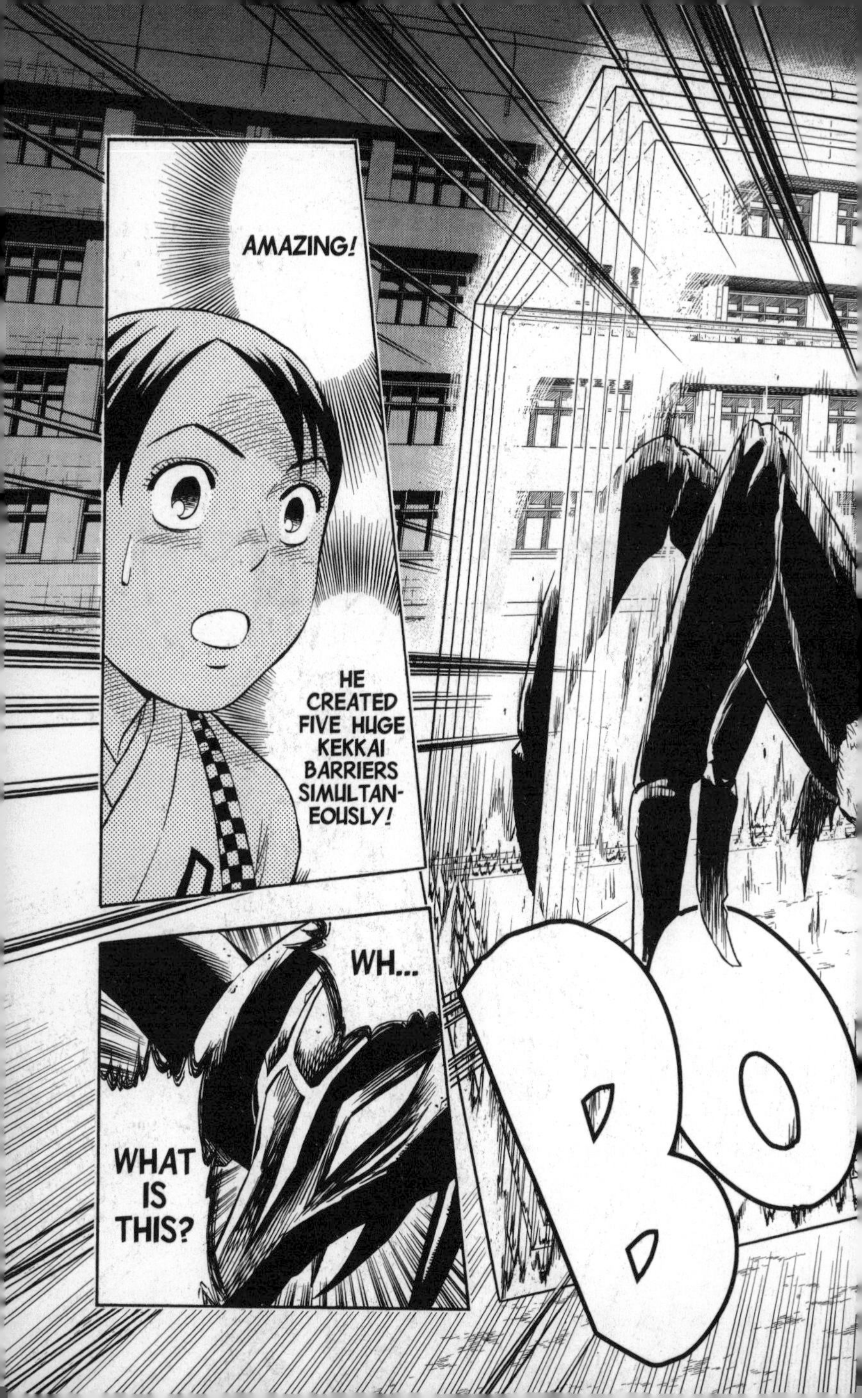
BO
AMAZING!
HE CREATED FIVE HUGE KEKKAI BARRIERS SIMULTAN-EOUSLY!
WH...
WHAT IS THIS?

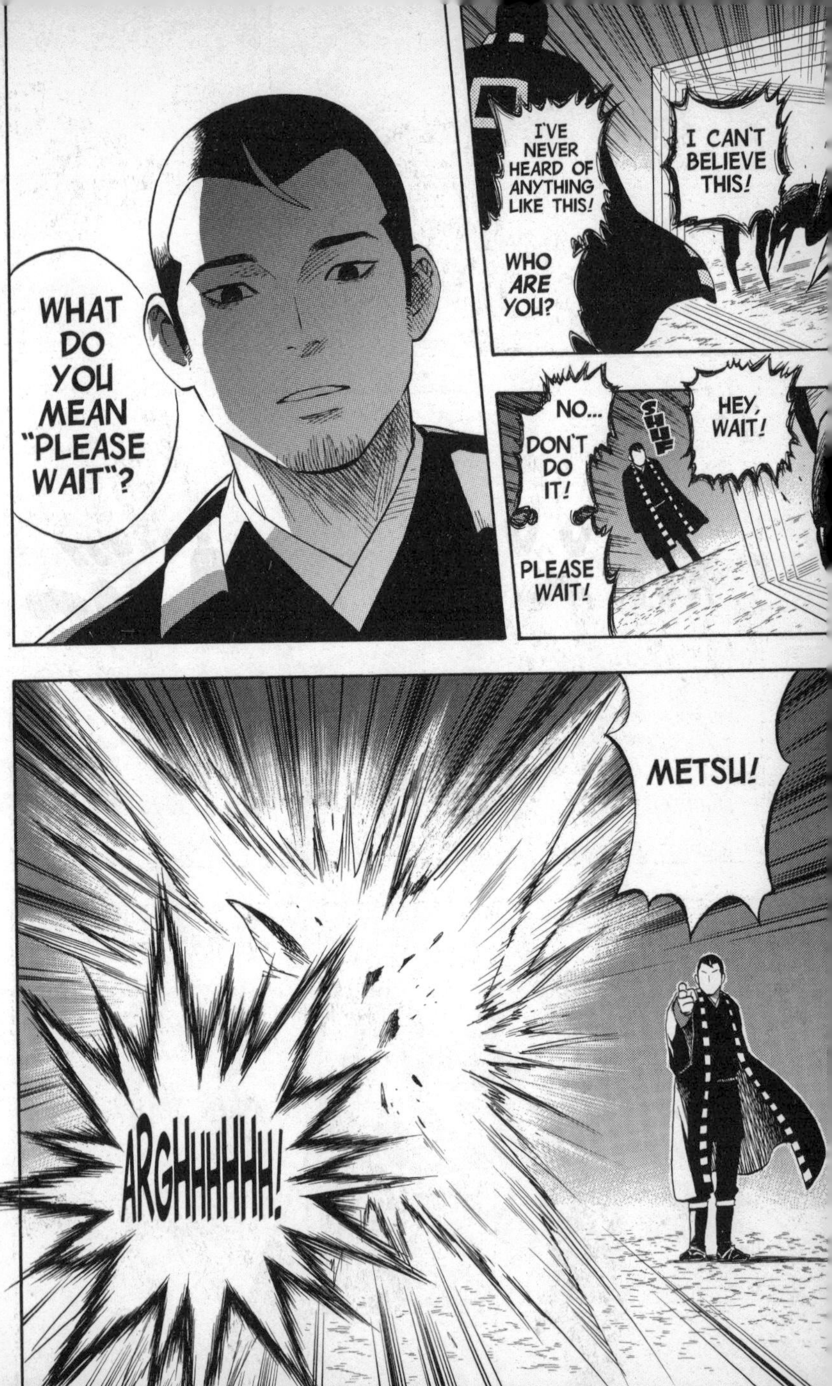
I CAN'T BELIEVE THIS!
I'VE NEVER HEARD OF ANYTHING LIKE THIS!
WHO ARE YOU?
HEY, WAIT!
SHUF
NO... DON'T DO IT!
PLEASE WAIT!
WHAT DO YOU MEAN "PLEASE WAIT"?
METSU!
ARGHHHHHH!

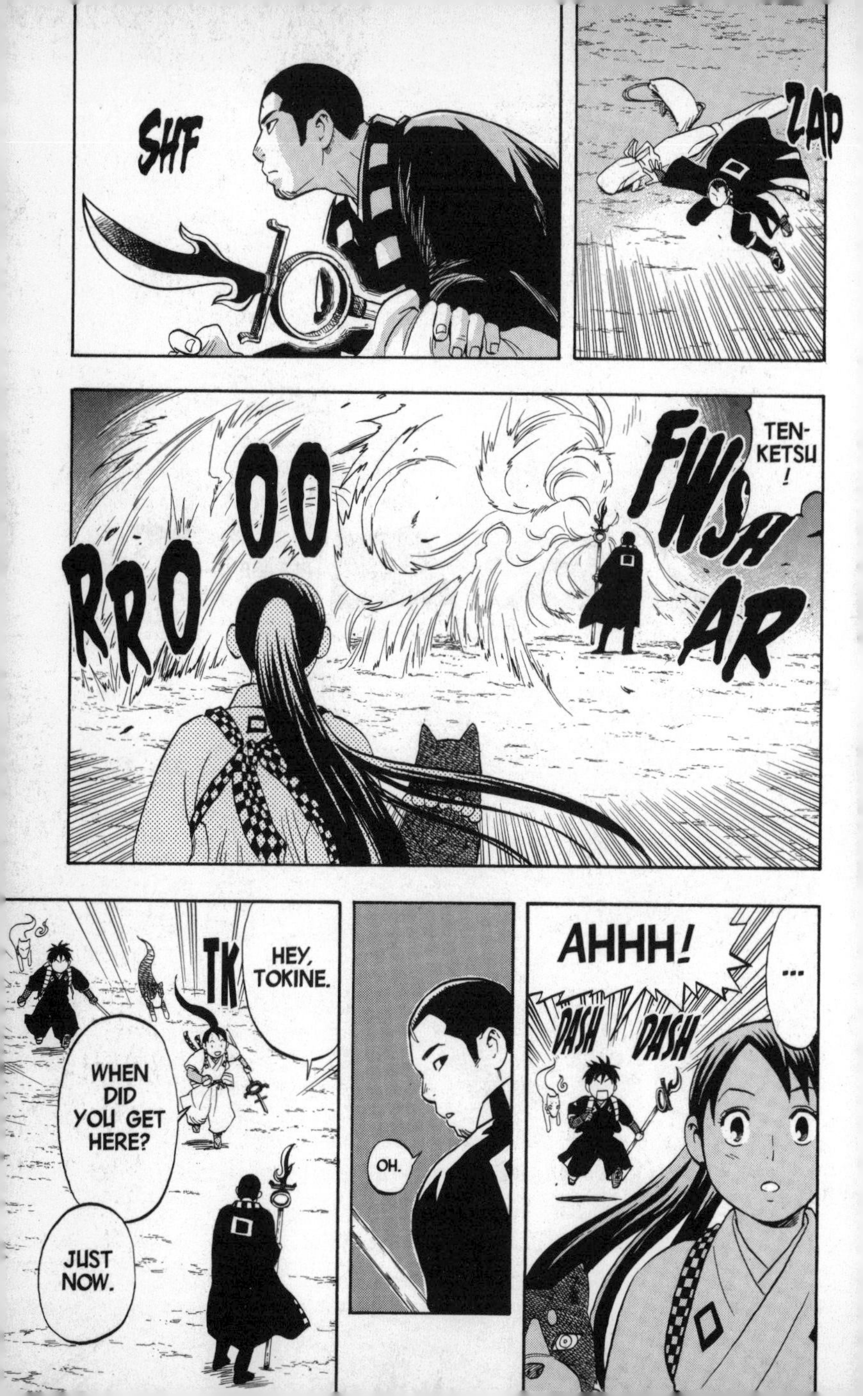
ZAP
SHF
TEN-KETSU!
FWSHAR
RROOOO
...
AHHH!
DASH DASH
OH.
HEY, TOKINE.
TK
WHEN DID YOU GET HERE?
JUST NOW.

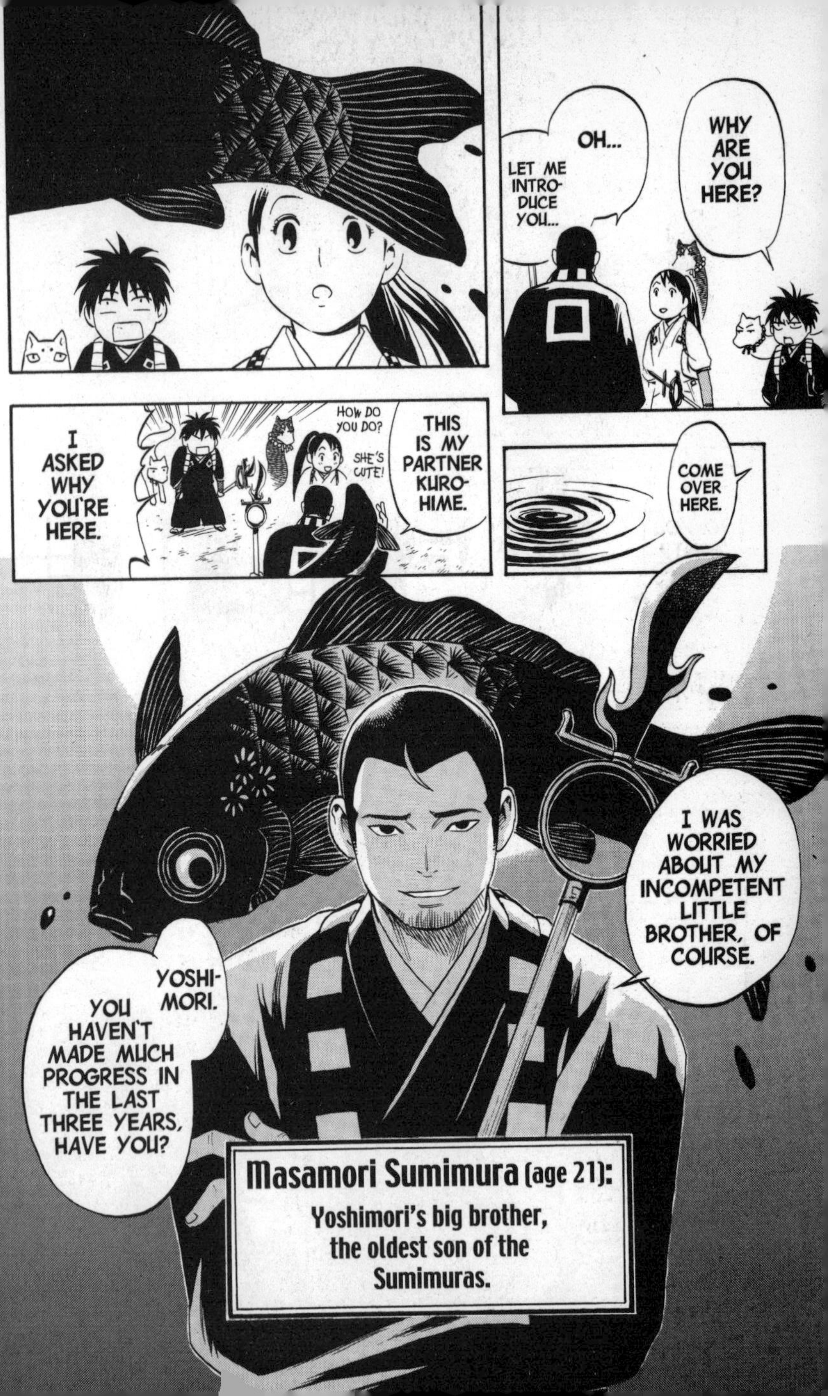
WHY ARE YOU HERE?
OH...
LET ME INTRODUCE YOU...
THIS IS MY PARTNER KUROHIME.
HOW DO YOU DO?
SHE'S CUTE!
I ASKED WHY YOU'RE HERE.
COME OVER HERE.
I WAS WORRIED ABOUT MY INCOMPETENT LITTLE BROTHER, OF COURSE.
YOSHIMORI.
YOU HAVEN'T MADE MUCH PROGRESS IN THE LAST THREE YEARS, HAVE YOU?
Masamori Sumimura (age 21):
Yoshimori's big brother, the oldest son of the Sumimuras.

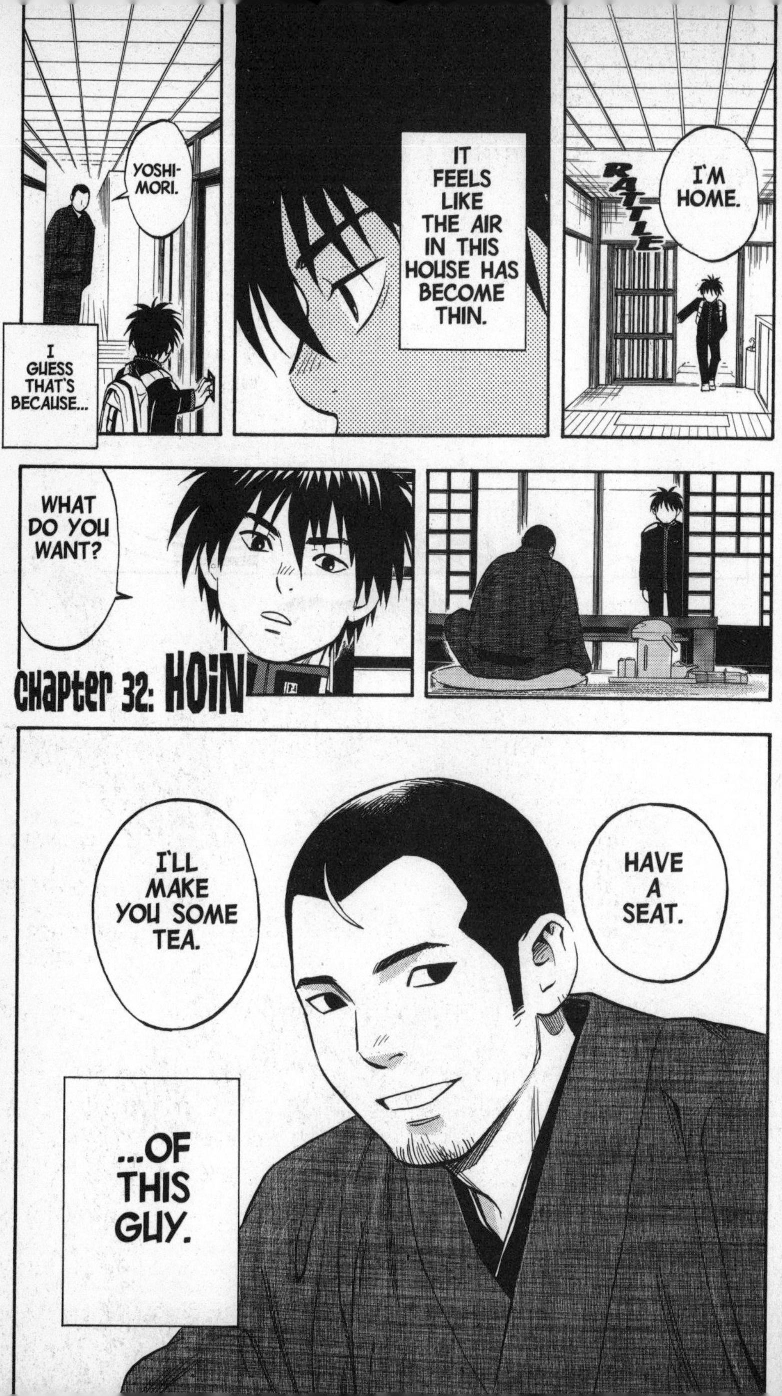
RATTLE
I'M HOME.
IT FEELS LIKE THE AIR IN THIS HOUSE HAS BECOME THIN.
YOSHI-MORI.
I GUESS THAT'S BECAUSE...
WHAT DO YOU WANT?
Chapter 32: HOIN
HAVE A SEAT.
I'LL MAKE YOU SOME TEA.
...OF THIS GUY.

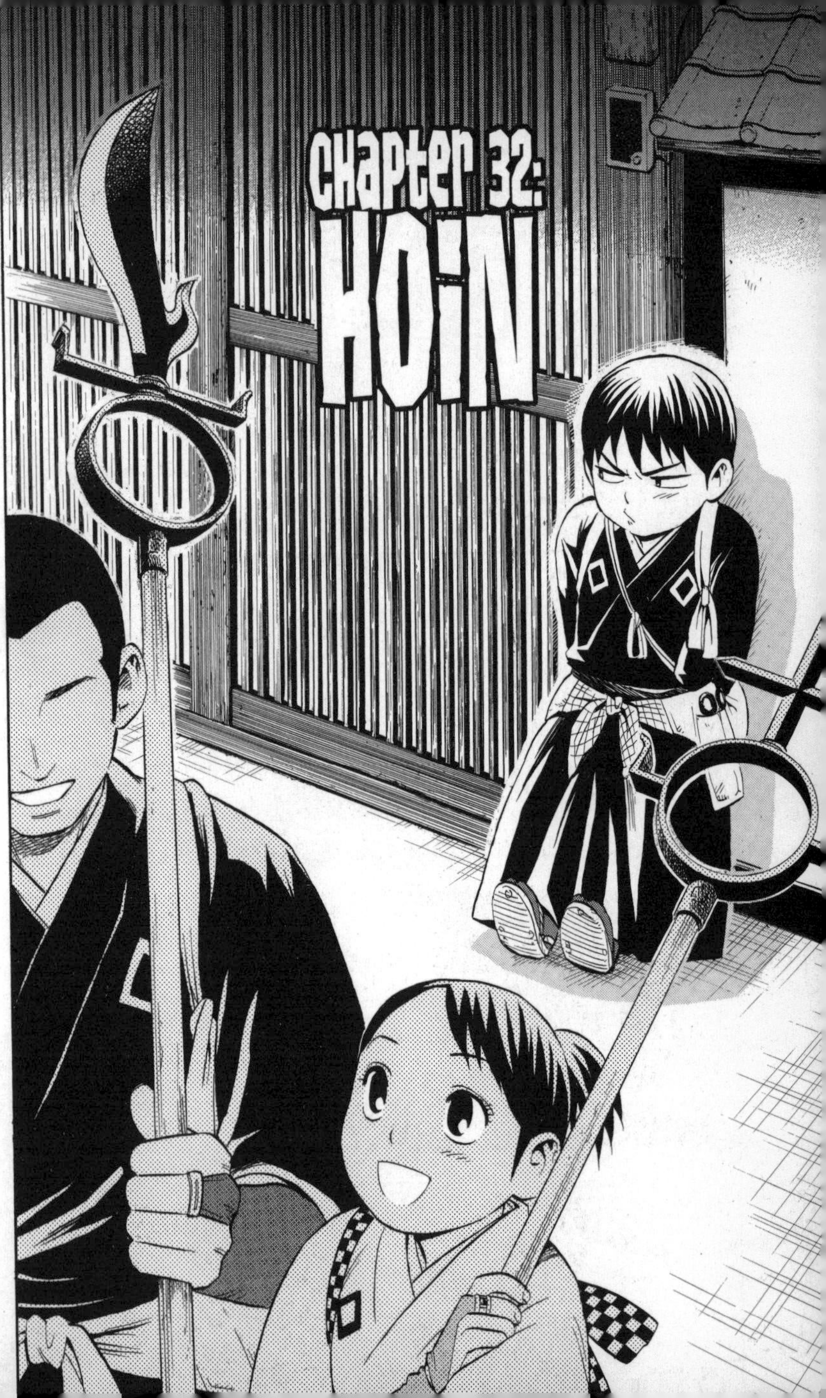

Chapter 32:
HOIN

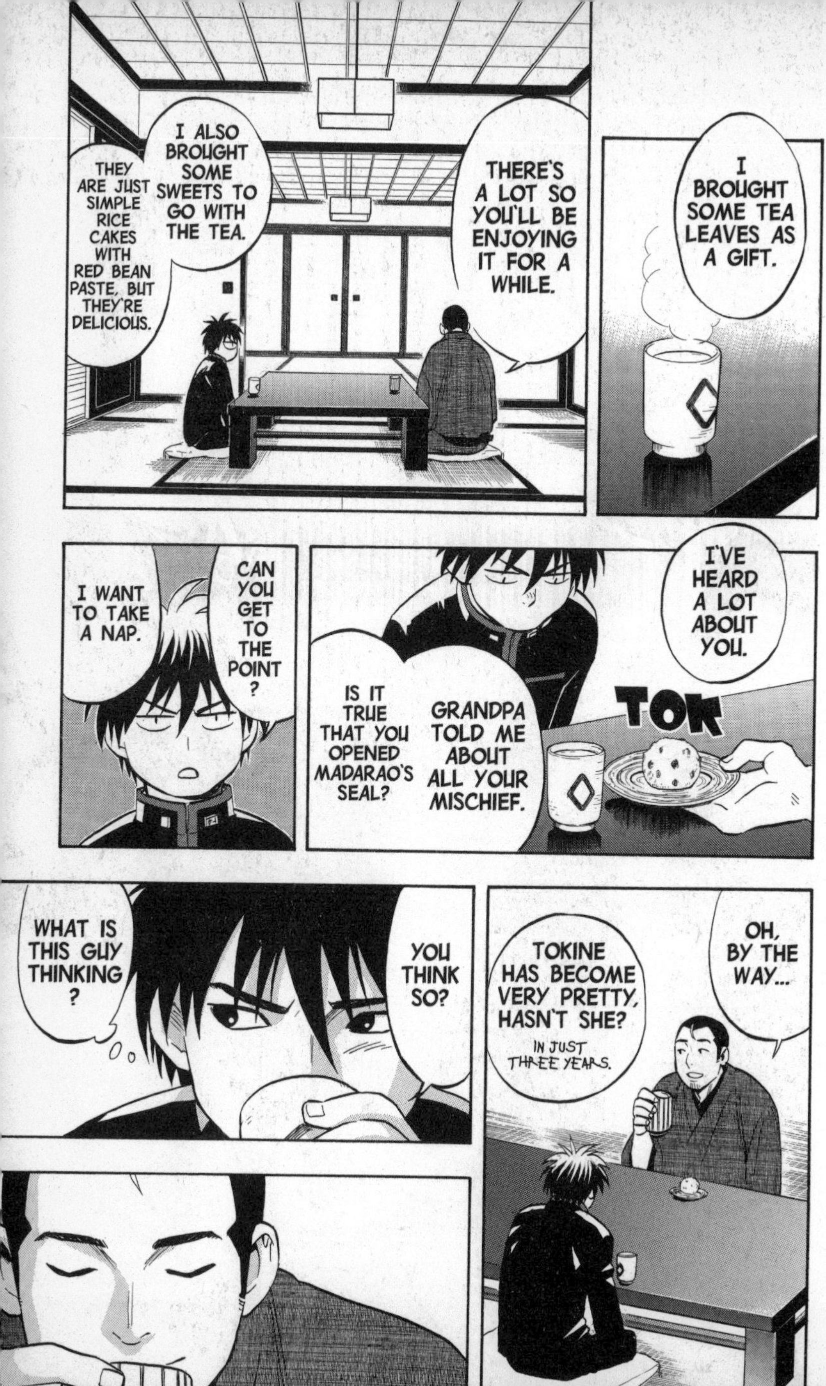
I BROUGHT SOME TEA LEAVES AS A GIFT.
THERE'S A LOT SO YOU'LL BE ENJOYING IT FOR A WHILE.
I ALSO BROUGHT SOME SWEETS TO GO WITH THE TEA.
THEY ARE JUST SIMPLE RICE CAKES WITH RED BEAN PASTE, BUT THEY'RE DELICIOUS.
I'VE HEARD A LOT ABOUT YOU.
TOK
GRANDPA TOLD ME ABOUT ALL YOUR MISCHIEF.
IS IT TRUE THAT YOU OPENED MADARAO'S SEAL?
CAN YOU GET TO THE POINT?
I WANT TO TAKE A NAP.
OH, BY THE WAY...
TOKINE HAS BECOME VERY PRETTY, HASN'T SHE?
IN JUST THREE YEARS.
YOU THINK SO?
WHAT IS THIS GUY THINKING?

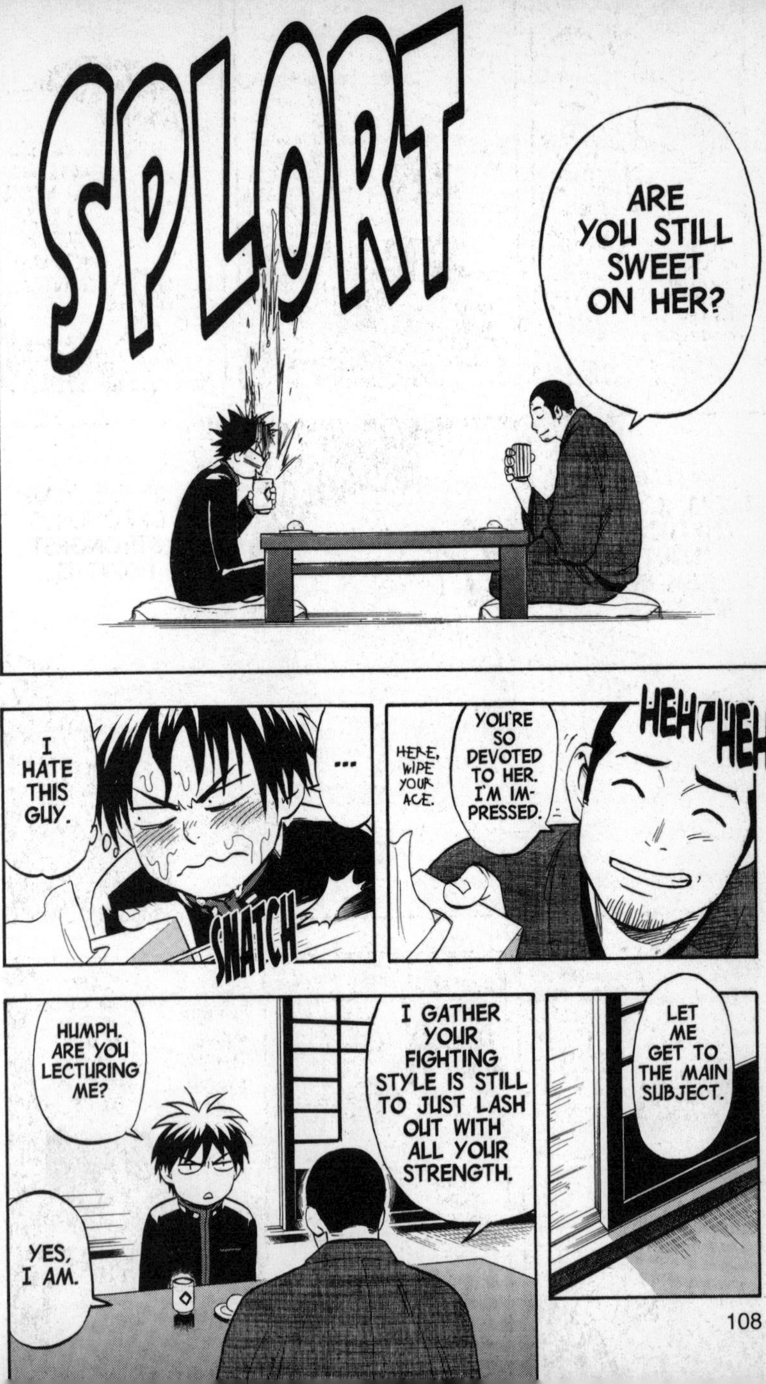
ARE YOU STILL SWEET ON HER?
SPLORT
HEH HEH
YOU'RE SO DEVOTED TO HER. I'M IM-PRESSED.
HERE, WIPE YOUR ACE.
...
I HATE THIS GUY.
SNATCH
LET ME GET TO THE MAIN SUBJECT.
I GATHER YOUR FIGHTING STYLE IS STILL TO JUST LASH OUT WITH ALL YOUR STRENGTH.
HUMPH. ARE YOU LECTURING ME?
YES, I AM.

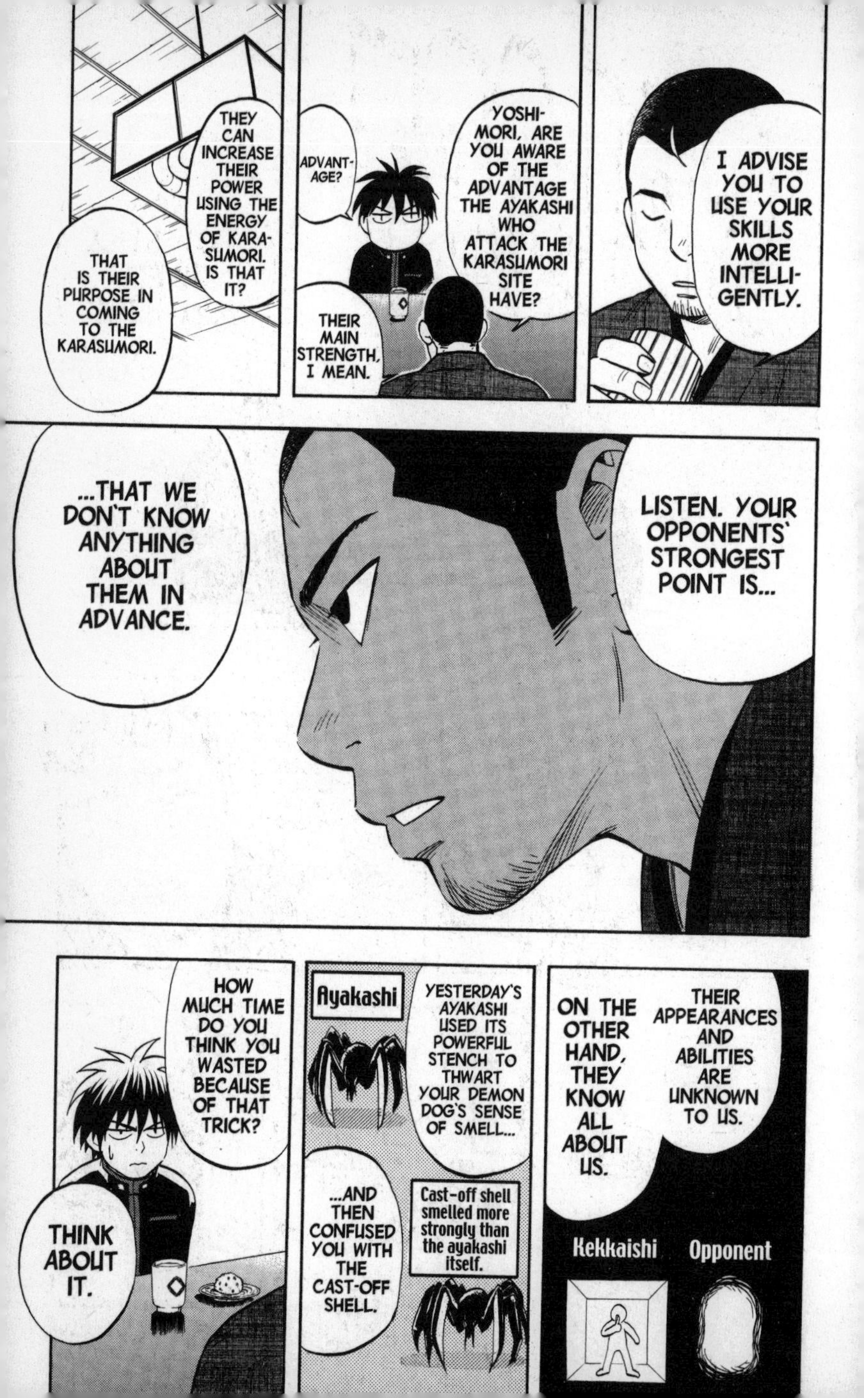
I ADVISE YOU TO USE YOUR SKILLS MORE INTELLIGENTLY.
YOSHIMORI, ARE YOU AWARE OF THE ADVANTAGE THE AYAKASHI WHO ATTACK THE KARASUMORI SITE HAVE?
ADVANTAGE?
THEIR MAIN STRENGTH, I MEAN.
THEY CAN INCREASE THEIR POWER USING THE ENERGY OF KARASUMORI. IS THAT IT?
THAT IS THEIR PURPOSE IN COMING TO THE KARASUMORI.
LISTEN. YOUR OPPONENTS' STRONGEST POINT IS...
...THAT WE DON'T KNOW ANYTHING ABOUT THEM IN ADVANCE.
THEIR APPEARANCES AND ABILITIES ARE UNKNOWN TO US.
ON THE OTHER HAND, THEY KNOW ALL ABOUT US.
Opponent
Kekkaishi
Ayakashi
YESTERDAY'S AYAKASHI USED ITS POWERFUL STENCH TO THWART YOUR DEMON DOG'S SENSE OF SMELL...
Cast-off shell smelled more strongly than the ayakashi itself.
...AND THEN CONFUSED YOU WITH THE CAST-OFF SHELL.
HOW MUCH TIME DO YOU THINK YOU WASTED BECAUSE OF THAT TRICK?
THINK ABOUT IT.

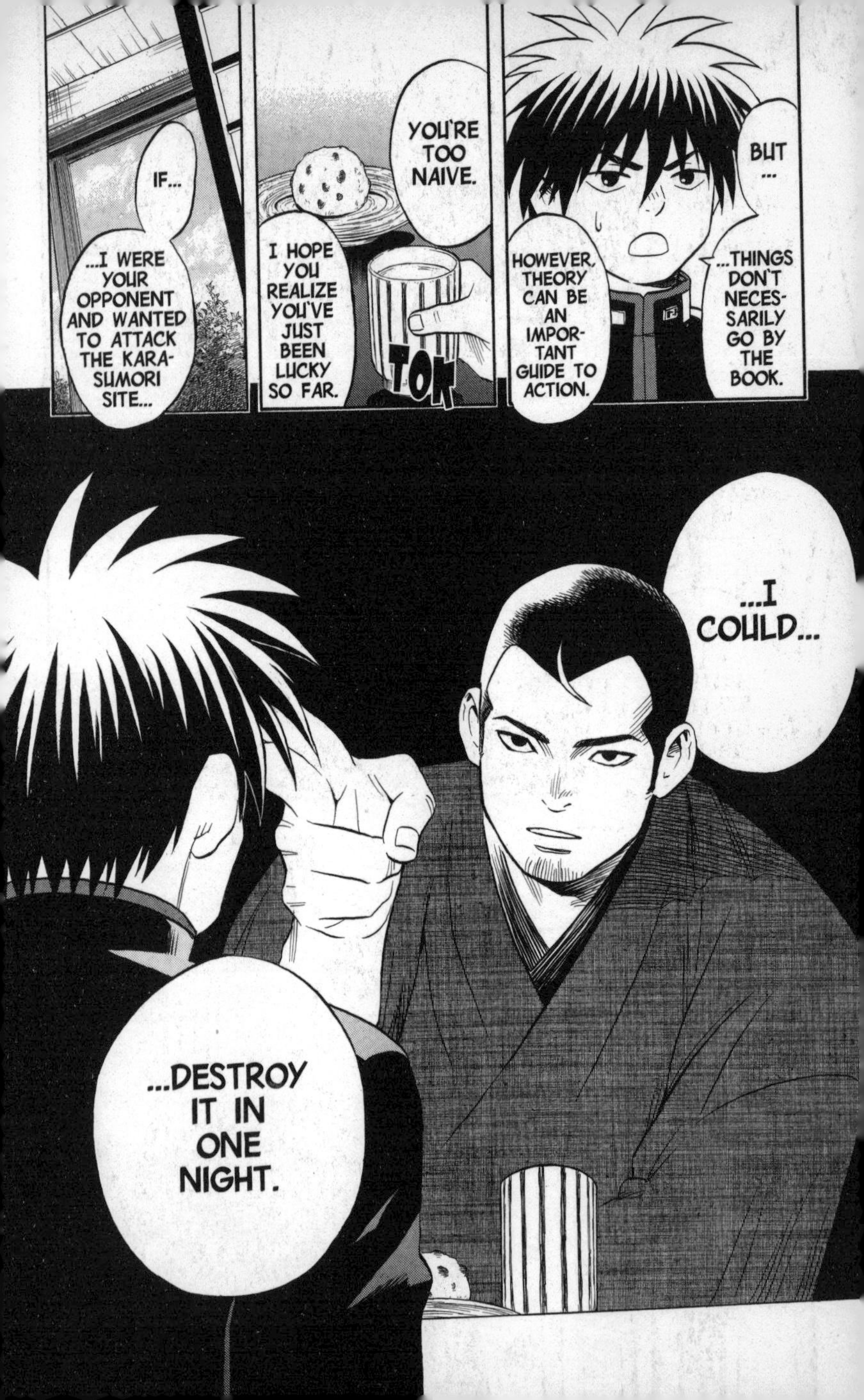
BUT...
...THINGS DON'T NECES-SARILY GO BY THE BOOK.
HOWEVER, THEORY CAN BE AN IMPOR-TANT GUIDE TO ACTION.
YOU'RE TOO NAIVE.
I HOPE YOU REALIZE YOU'VE JUST BEEN LUCKY SO FAR.
TON
IF...
...I WERE YOUR OPPONENT AND WANTED TO ATTACK THE KARA-SUMORI SITE...
...I COULD...
...DESTROY IT IN ONE NIGHT.

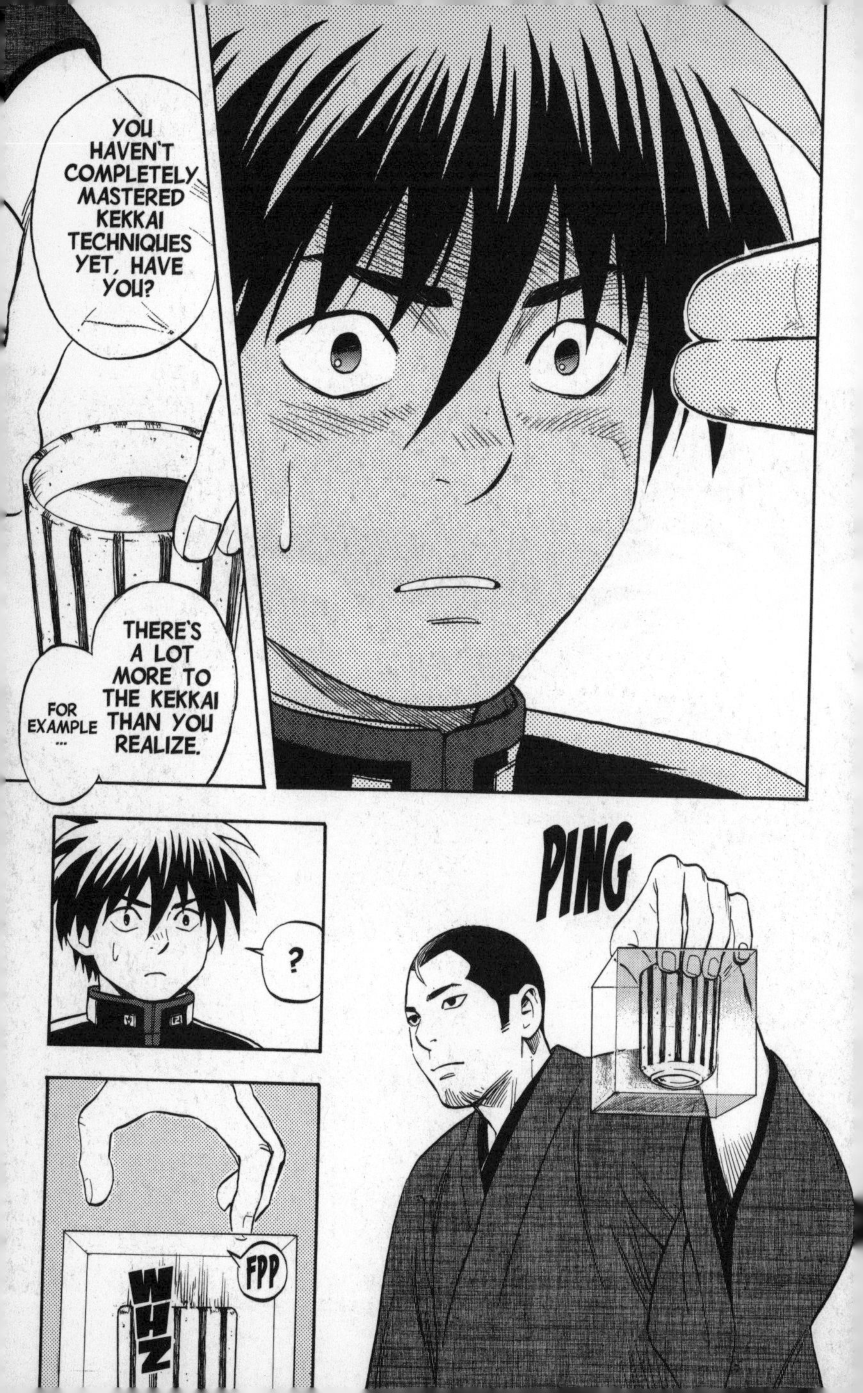
YOU HAVEN'T COMPLETELY MASTERED KEKKAI TECHNIQUES YET, HAVE YOU?
THERE'S A LOT MORE TO THE KEKKAI THAN YOU REALIZE.
FOR EXAMPLE ...
PING
?
FPP
WHZ

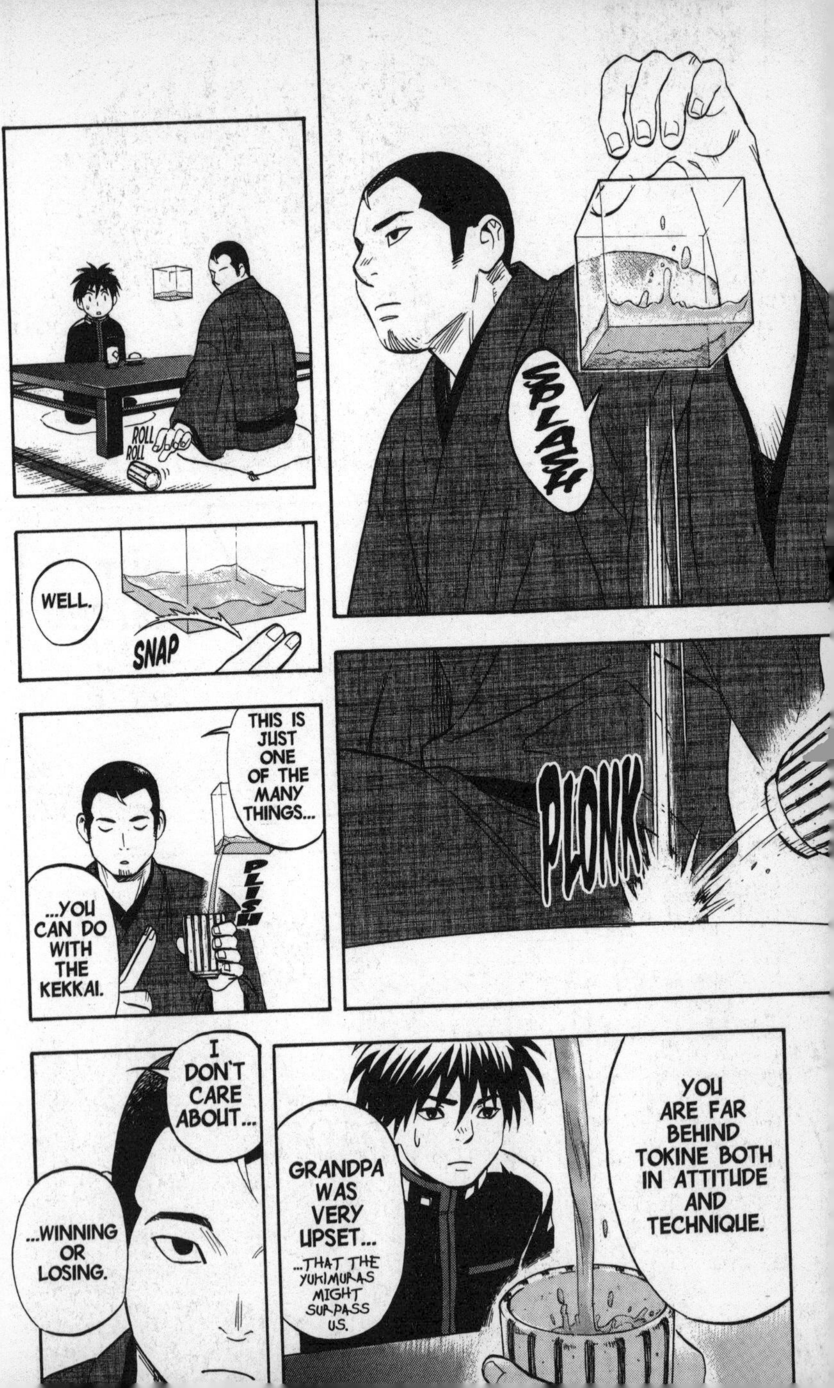
SPLASH
PLONK
ROLL ROLL
WELL.
SNAP
THIS IS JUST ONE OF THE MANY THINGS...
PLISH
...YOU CAN DO WITH THE KEKKAI.
YOU ARE FAR BEHIND TOKINE BOTH IN ATTITUDE AND TECHNIQUE.
GRANDPA WAS VERY UPSET...
...THAT THE YUKIMURAS MIGHT SURPASS US.
I DON'T CARE ABOUT...
...WINNING OR LOSING.

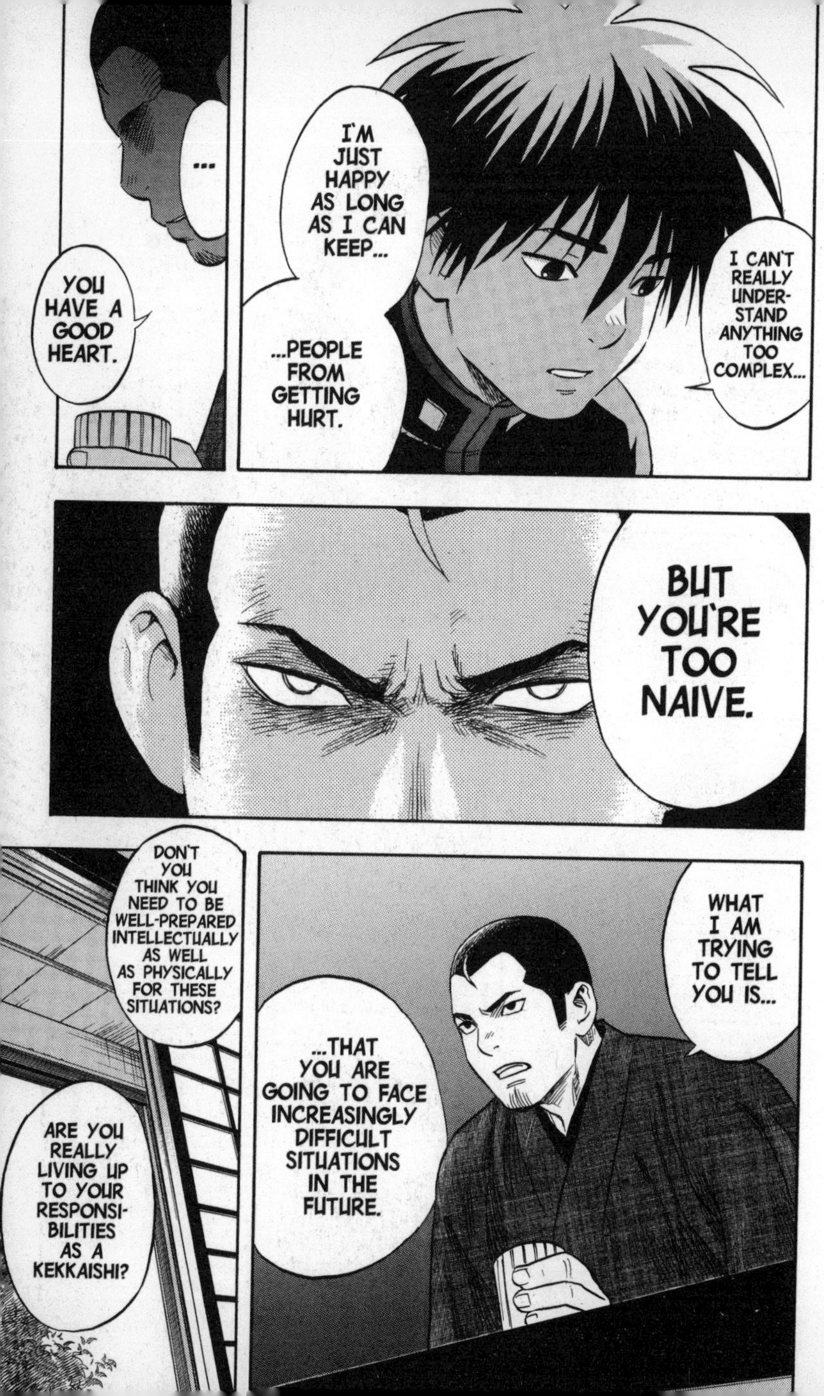
I CAN'T REALLY UNDER-STAND ANYTHING TOO COMPLEX...
I'M JUST HAPPY AS LONG AS I CAN KEEP...
...PEOPLE FROM GETTING HURT.
...
YOU HAVE A GOOD HEART.
BUT YOU'RE TOO NAIVE.
WHAT I AM TRYING TO TELL YOU IS...
...THAT YOU ARE GOING TO FACE INCREASINGLY DIFFICULT SITUATIONS IN THE FUTURE.
DON'T YOU THINK YOU NEED TO BE WELL-PREPARED INTELLECTUALLY AS WELL AS PHYSICALLY FOR THESE SITUATIONS?
ARE YOU REALLY LIVING UP TO YOUR RESPONSI-BILITIES AS A KEKKAISHI?

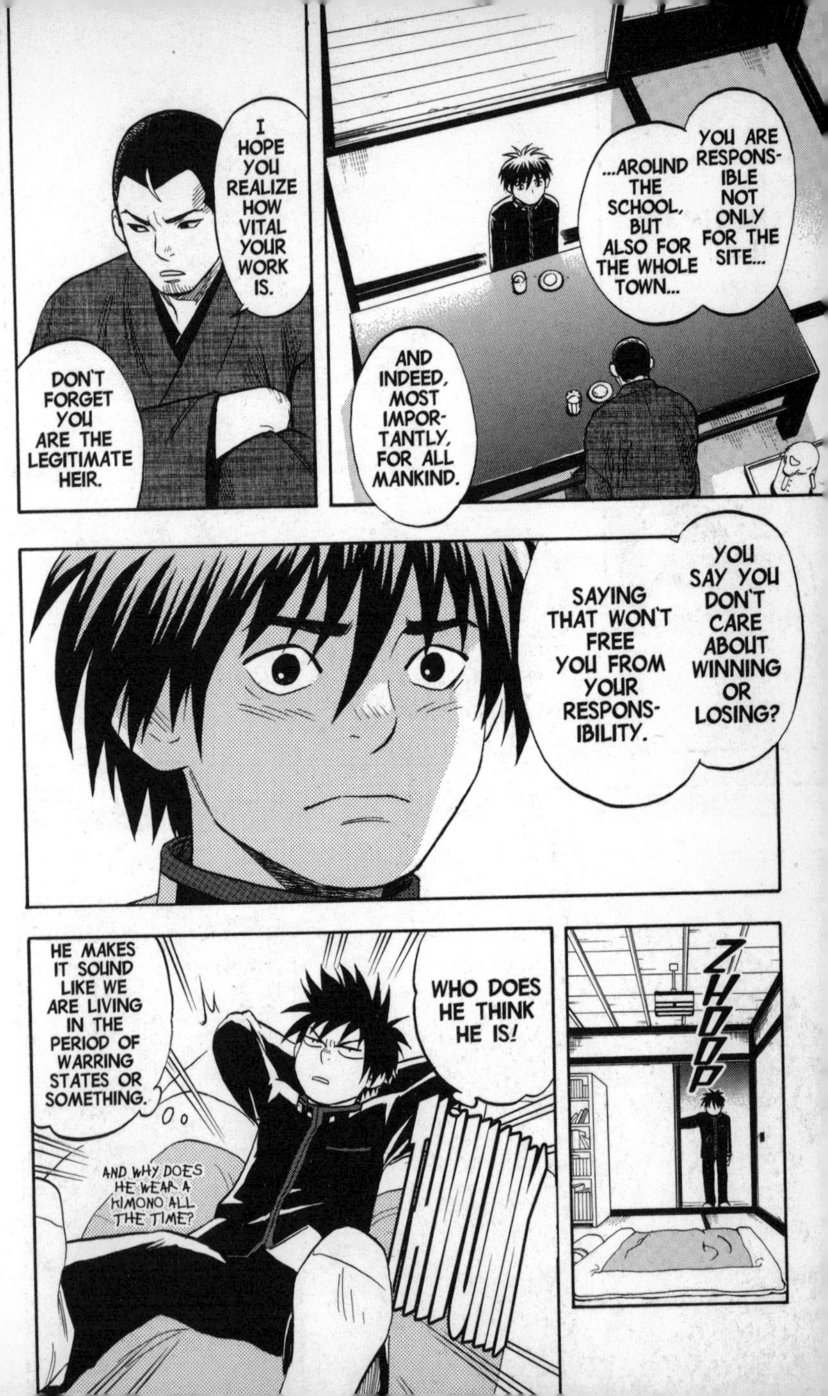
YOU ARE RESPONSIBLE NOT ONLY FOR THE SITE...
...AROUND THE SCHOOL, BUT ALSO FOR THE WHOLE TOWN...
AND INDEED, MOST IMPORTANTLY, FOR ALL MANKIND.
I HOPE YOU REALIZE HOW VITAL YOUR WORK IS.
DON'T FORGET YOU ARE THE LEGITIMATE HEIR.
YOU SAY YOU DON'T CARE ABOUT WINNING OR LOSING?
SAYING THAT WON'T FREE YOU FROM YOUR RESPONSIBILITY.
ZHOOP
WHO DOES HE THINK HE IS!
HE MAKES IT SOUND LIKE WE ARE LIVING IN THE PERIOD OF WARRING STATES OR SOMETHING.
AND WHY DOES HE WEAR A KIMONO ALL THE TIME?

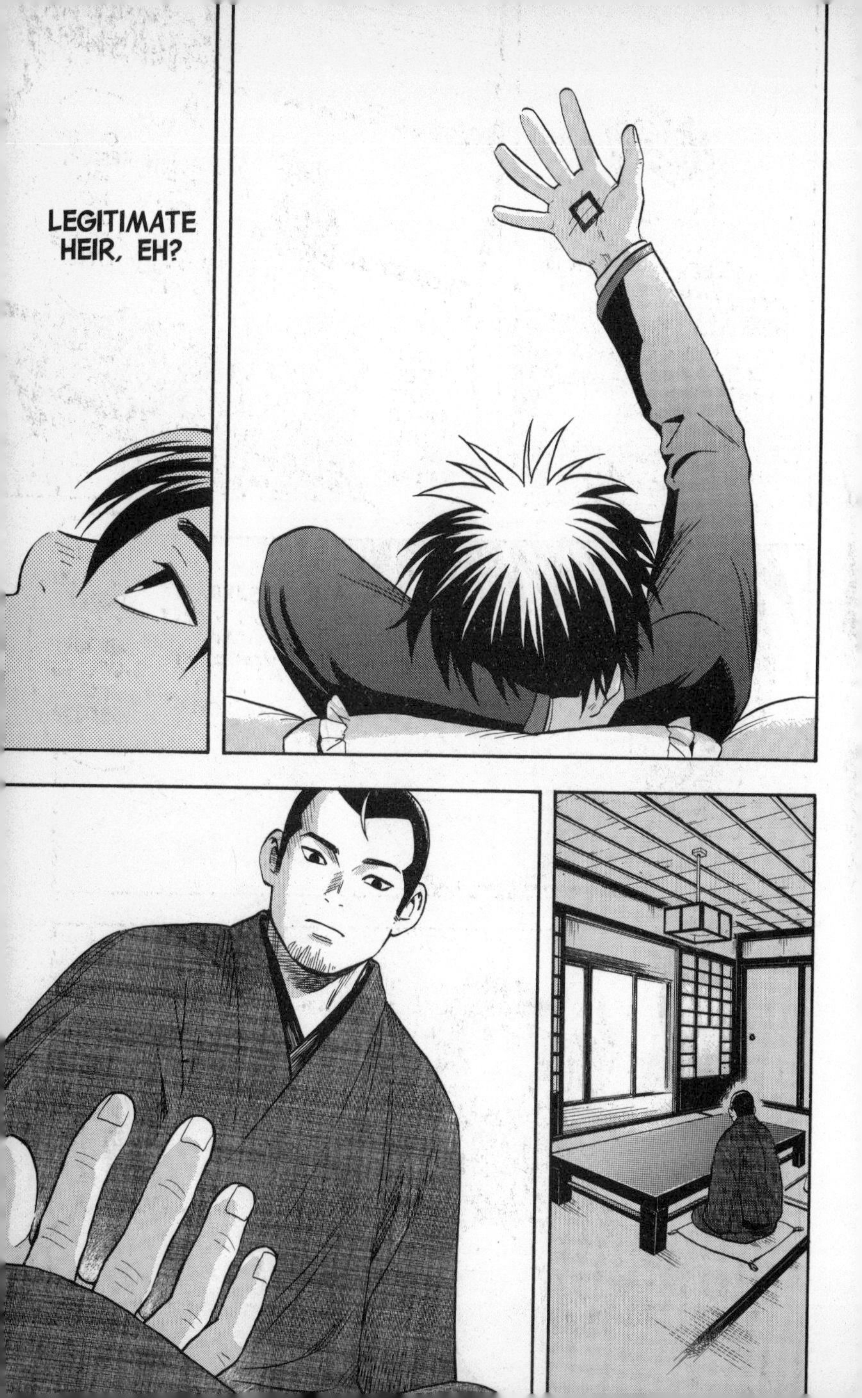
LEGITIMATE HEIR, EH?

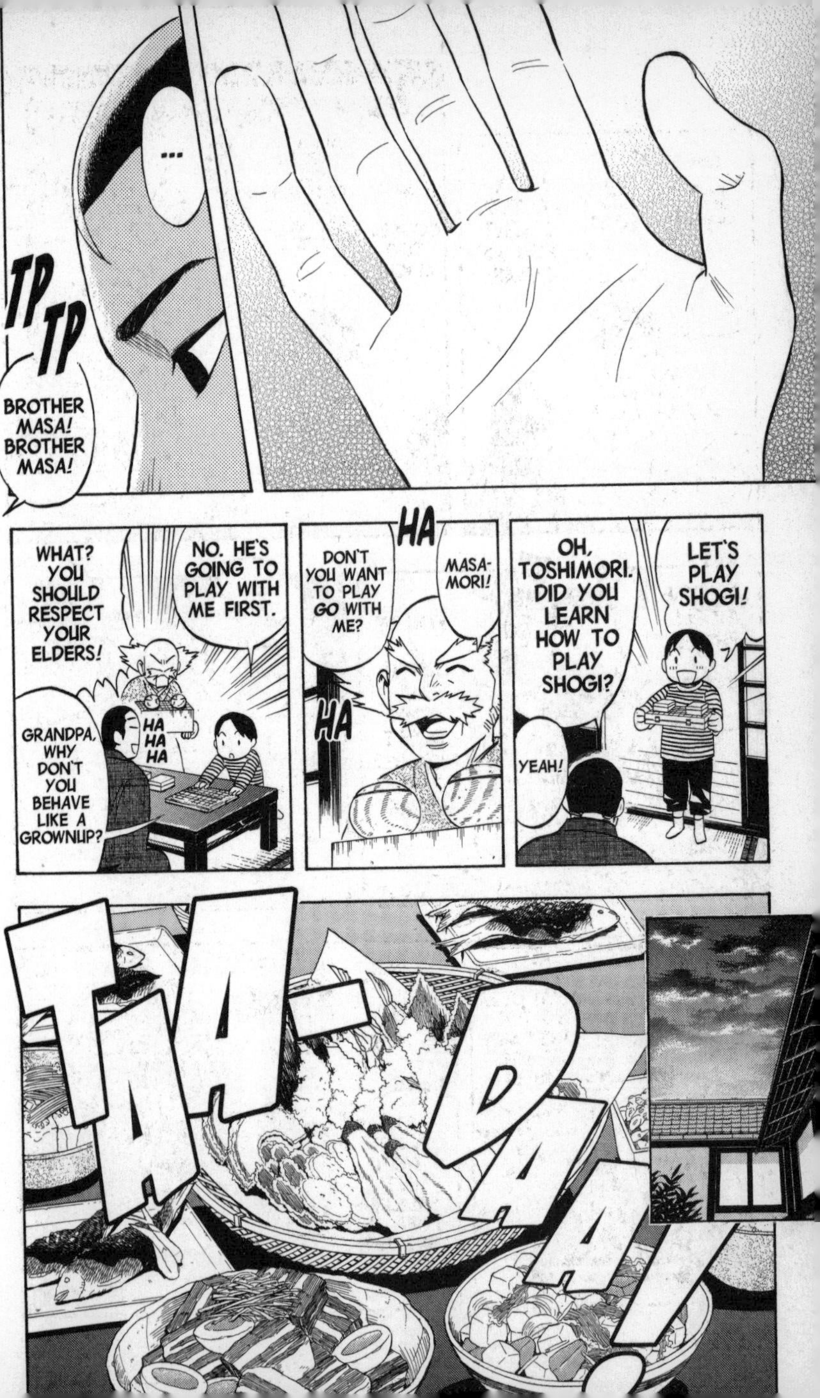
...
TP TP
BROTHER MASA! BROTHER MASA!
LET'S PLAY SHOGI!
OH, TOSHIMORI. DID YOU LEARN HOW TO PLAY SHOGI?
YEAH!
MASA-MORI!
HA
DON'T YOU WANT TO PLAY GO WITH ME?
HA
NO. HE'S GOING TO PLAY WITH ME FIRST.
WHAT? YOU SHOULD RESPECT YOUR ELDERS!
HA HA HA
GRANDPA, WHY DON'T YOU BEHAVE LIKE A GROWNUP?
TA-DA!!

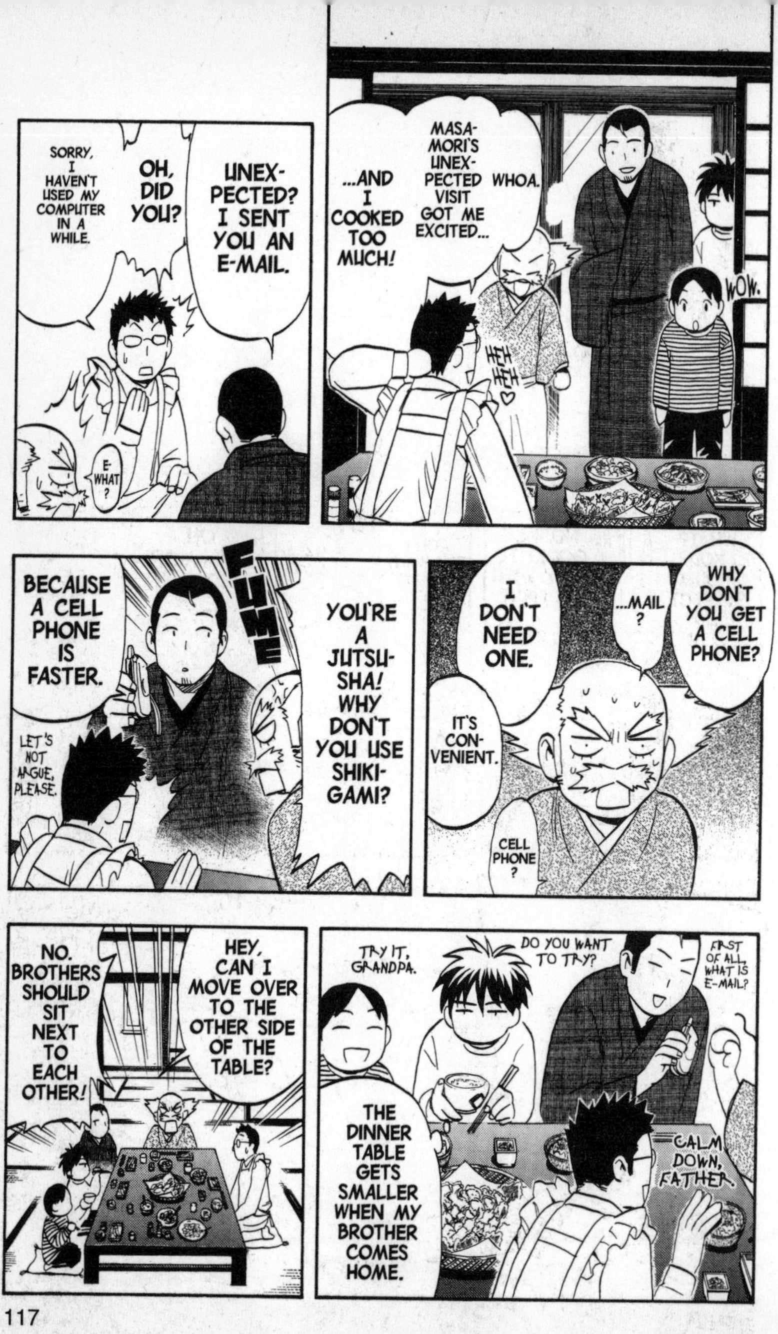
WHOA.
MASA-MORI'S UNEX-PECTED VISIT GOT ME EXCITED...
...AND I COOKED TOO MUCH!
WOW.
HEH HEH ♥
UNEX-PECTED? I SENT YOU AN E-MAIL.
OH, DID YOU?
SORRY, I HAVEN'T USED MY COMPUTER IN A WHILE.
E-WHAT?
WHY DON'T YOU GET A CELL PHONE?
...MAIL?
I DON'T NEED ONE.
IT'S CON-VENIENT.
CELL PHONE?
FUME
YOU'RE A JUTSU-SHA! WHY DON'T YOU USE SHIKI-GAMI?
BECAUSE A CELL PHONE IS FASTER.
LET'S NOT ARGUE, PLEASE.
FIRST OF ALL, WHAT IS E-MAIL?
DO YOU WANT TO TRY?
TRY IT, GRANDPA.
CALM DOWN, FATHER.
THE DINNER TABLE GETS SMALLER WHEN MY BROTHER COMES HOME.
HEY, CAN I MOVE OVER TO THE OTHER SIDE OF THE TABLE?
NO. BROTHERS SHOULD SIT NEXT TO EACH OTHER!

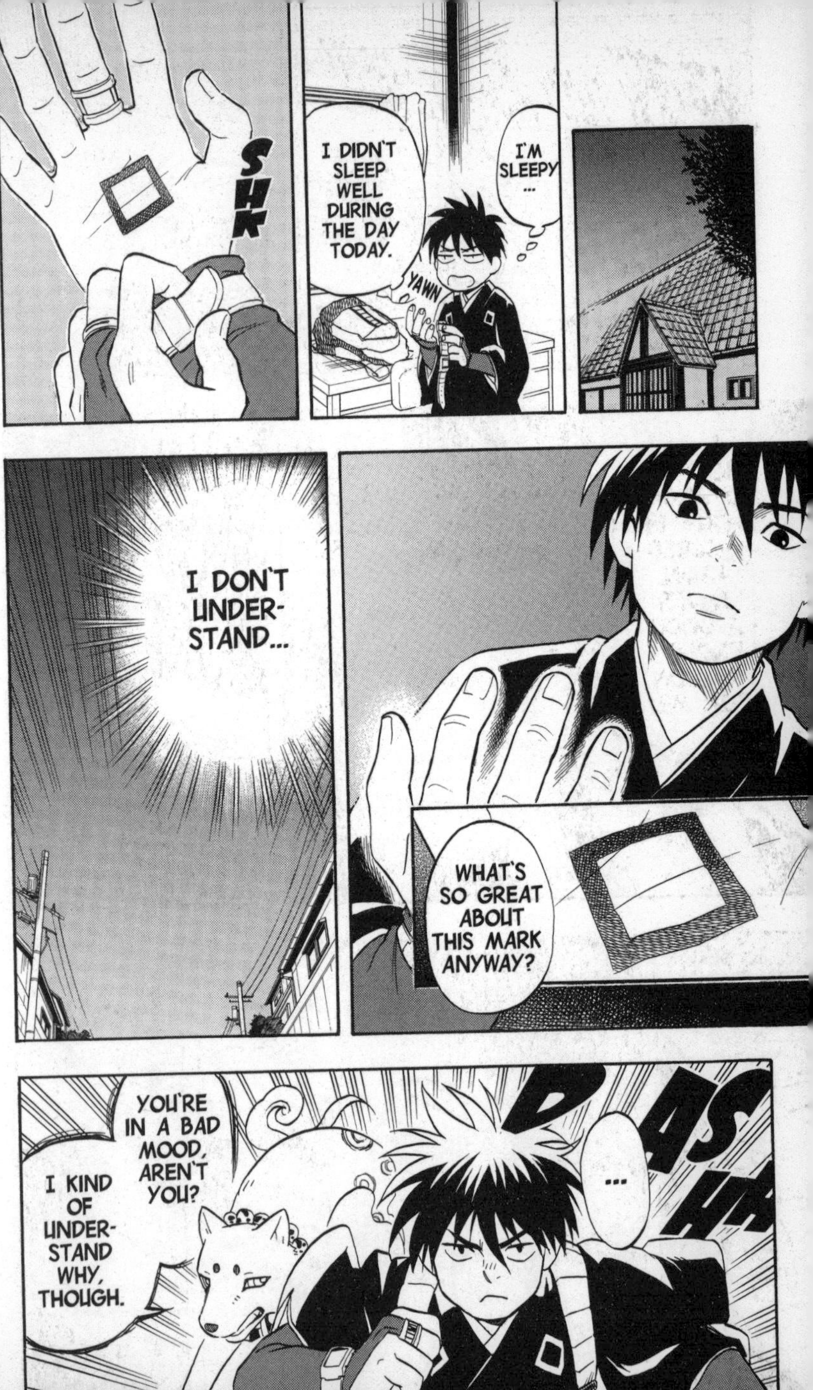
I'M SLEEPY...
I DIDN'T SLEEP WELL DURING THE DAY TODAY.
YAWN
SHK
WHAT'S SO GREAT ABOUT THIS MARK ANYWAY?
I DON'T UNDER-STAND...
DASH
...
YOU'RE IN A BAD MOOD, AREN'T YOU?
I KIND OF UNDER-STAND WHY, THOUGH.

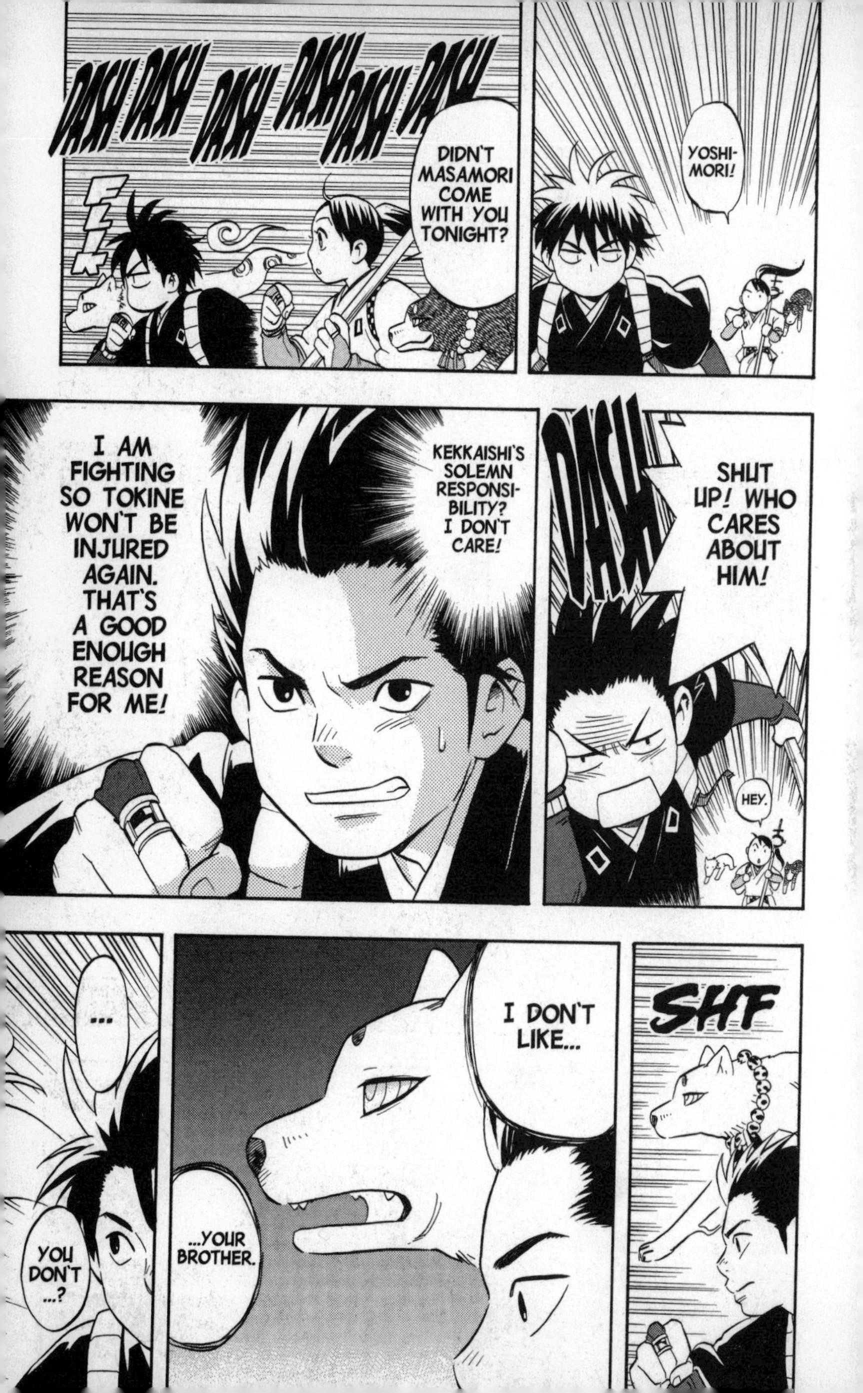
YOSHI-MORI!
DASH DASH DASH DASH DASH DASH
DIDN'T MASAMORI COME WITH YOU TONIGHT?
FLIK
DASH
SHUT UP! WHO CARES ABOUT HIM!
HEY.
KEKKAISHI'S SOLEMN RESPONSI-BILITY? I DON'T CARE!
I AM FIGHTING SO TOKINE WON'T BE INJURED AGAIN. THAT'S A GOOD ENOUGH REASON FOR ME!
SHF
I DON'T LIKE...
...YOUR BROTHER.
...
YOU DON'T ...?

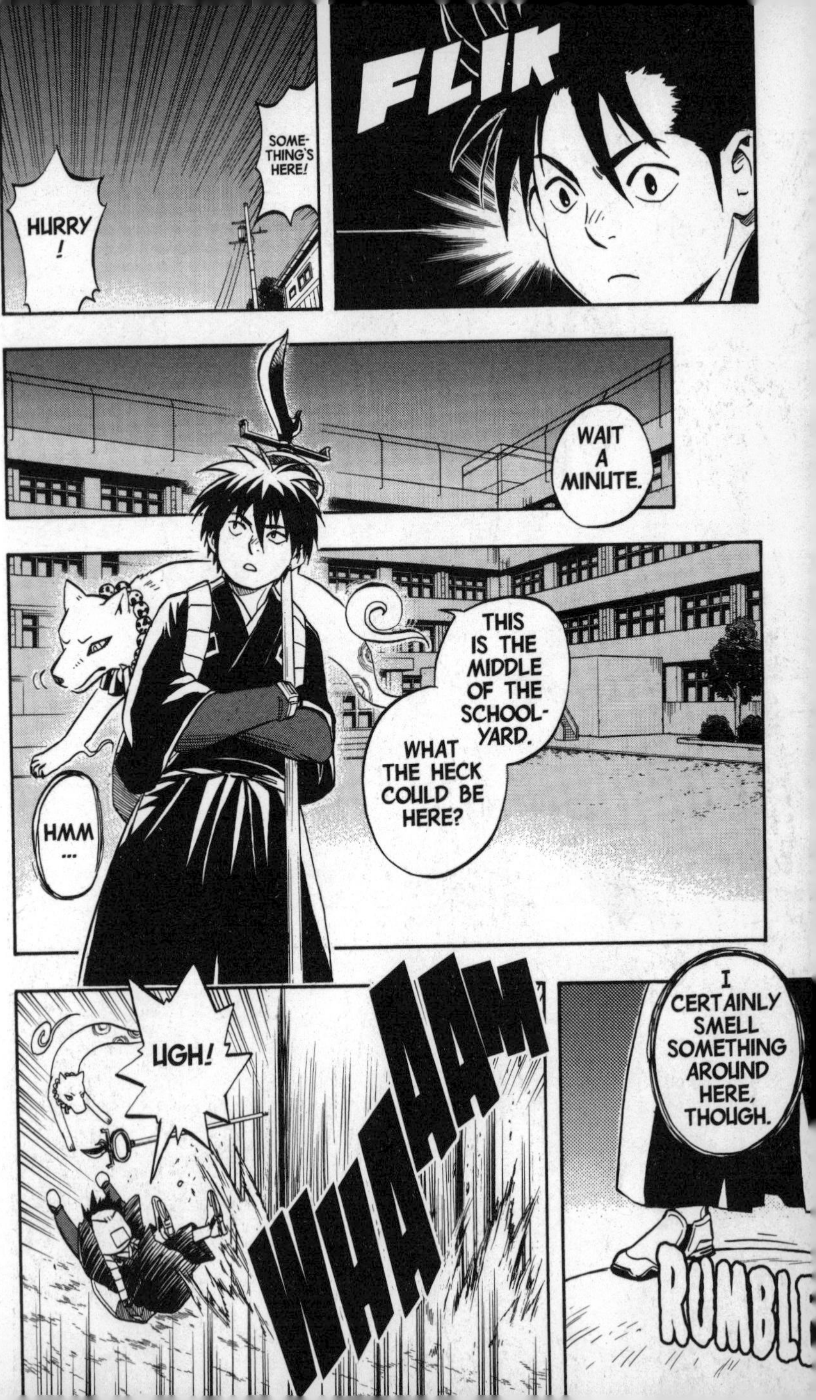
FLIK
SOME-THING'S HERE!
HURRY!
WAIT A MINUTE.
THIS IS THE MIDDLE OF THE SCHOOL-YARD. WHAT THE HECK COULD BE HERE?
HMM...
I CERTAINLY SMELL SOMETHING AROUND HERE, THOUGH.
RUMBL
WHAAAAM
UGH!

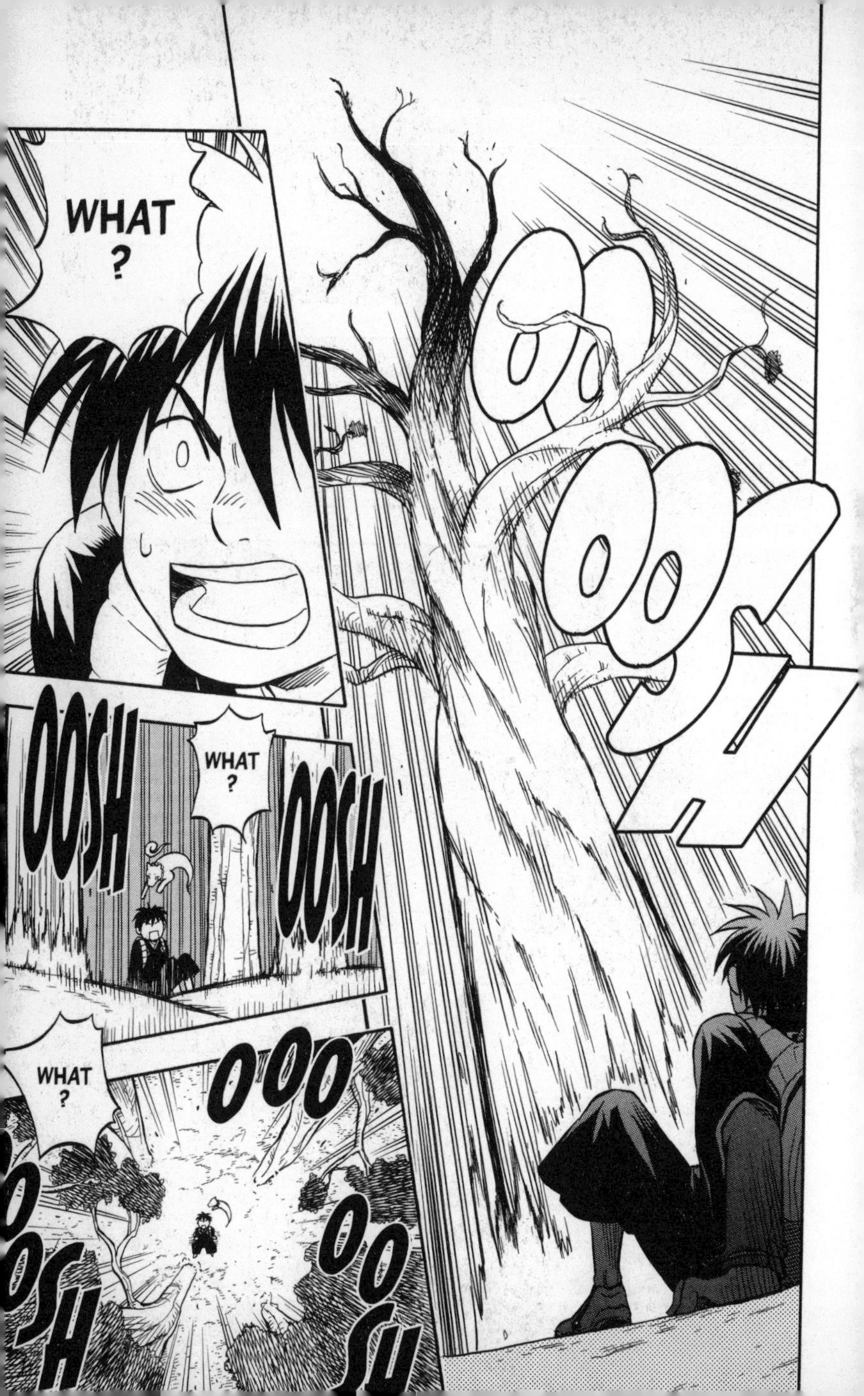
OOOOSH
WHAT ?
OOSH
WHAT ?
OOSH
WHAT ?
OOO
OOSH
OOSH

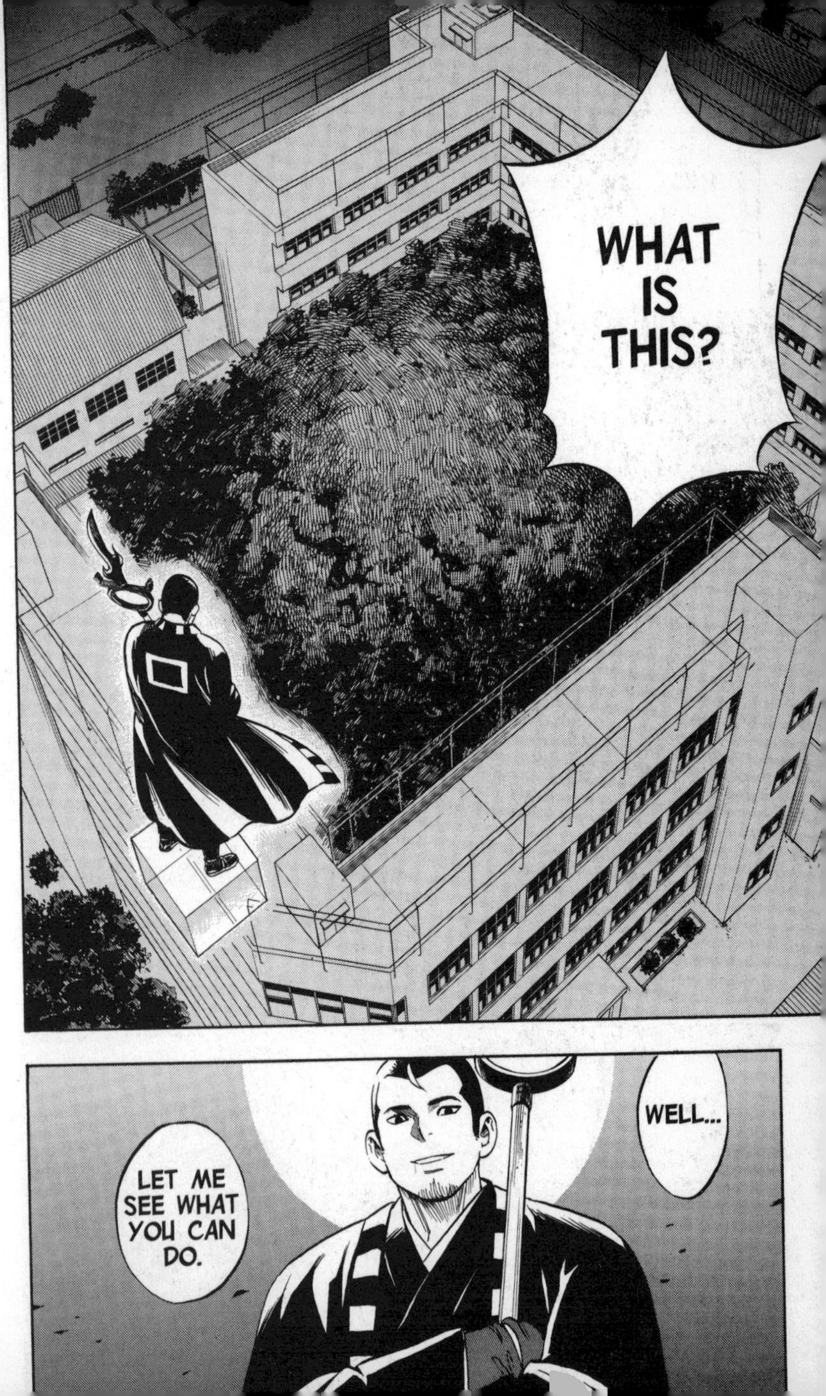
WHAT IS THIS?
WELL...
LET ME SEE WHAT YOU CAN DO.

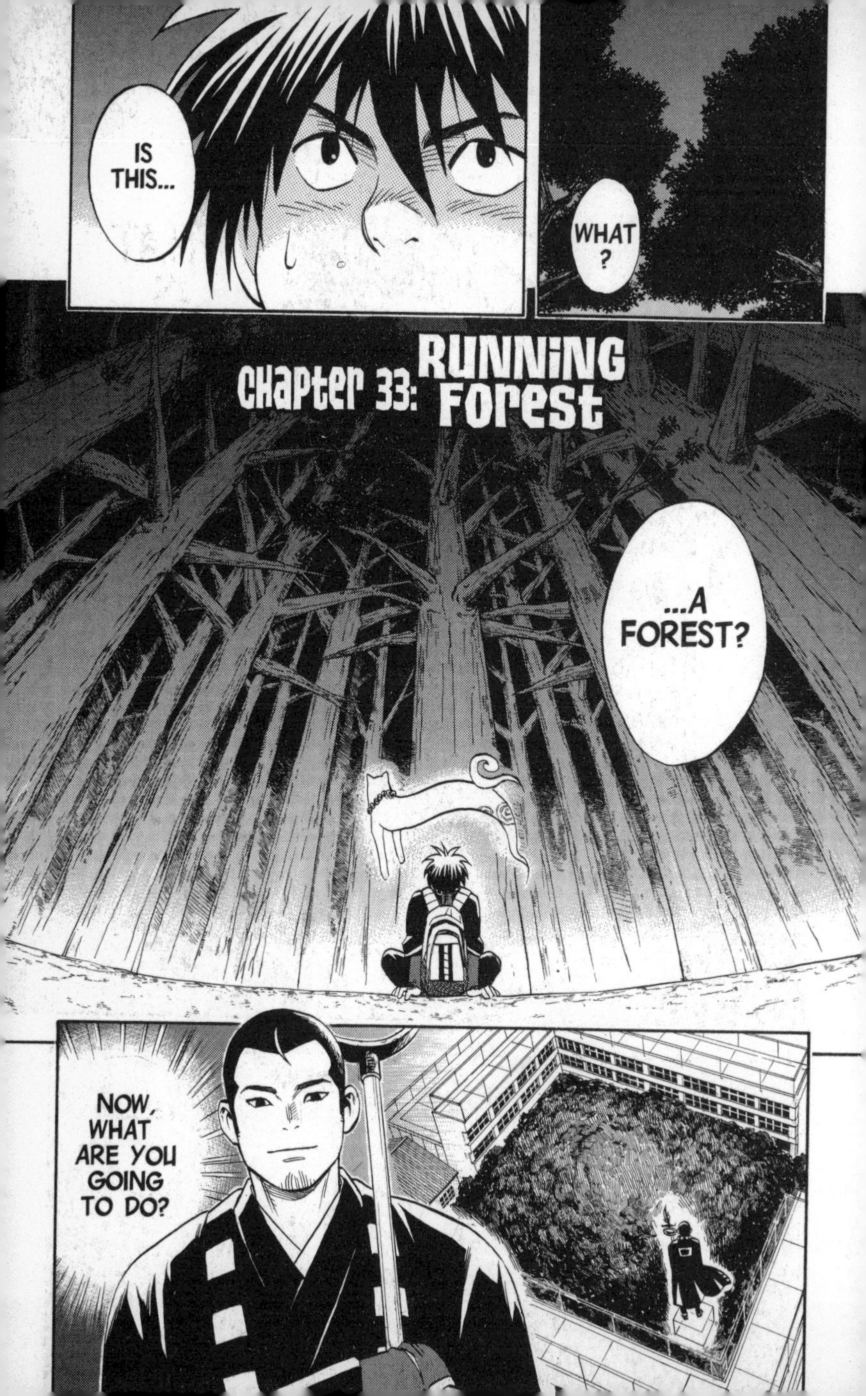
WHAT?
IS THIS...
Chapter 33: RUNNING Forest
...A FOREST?
NOW, WHAT ARE YOU GOING TO DO?

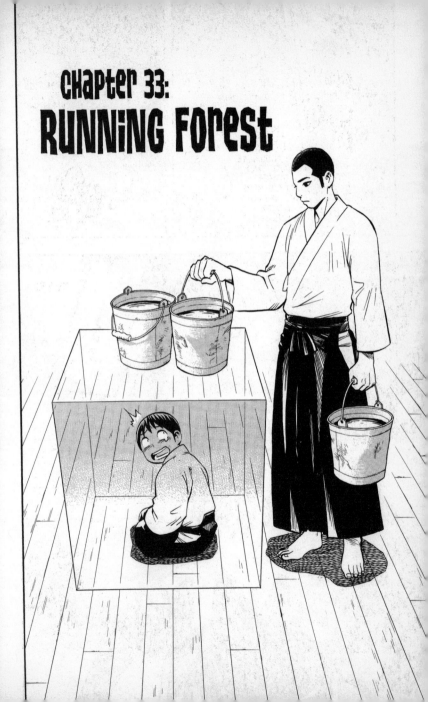

Chapter 33: Running Forest

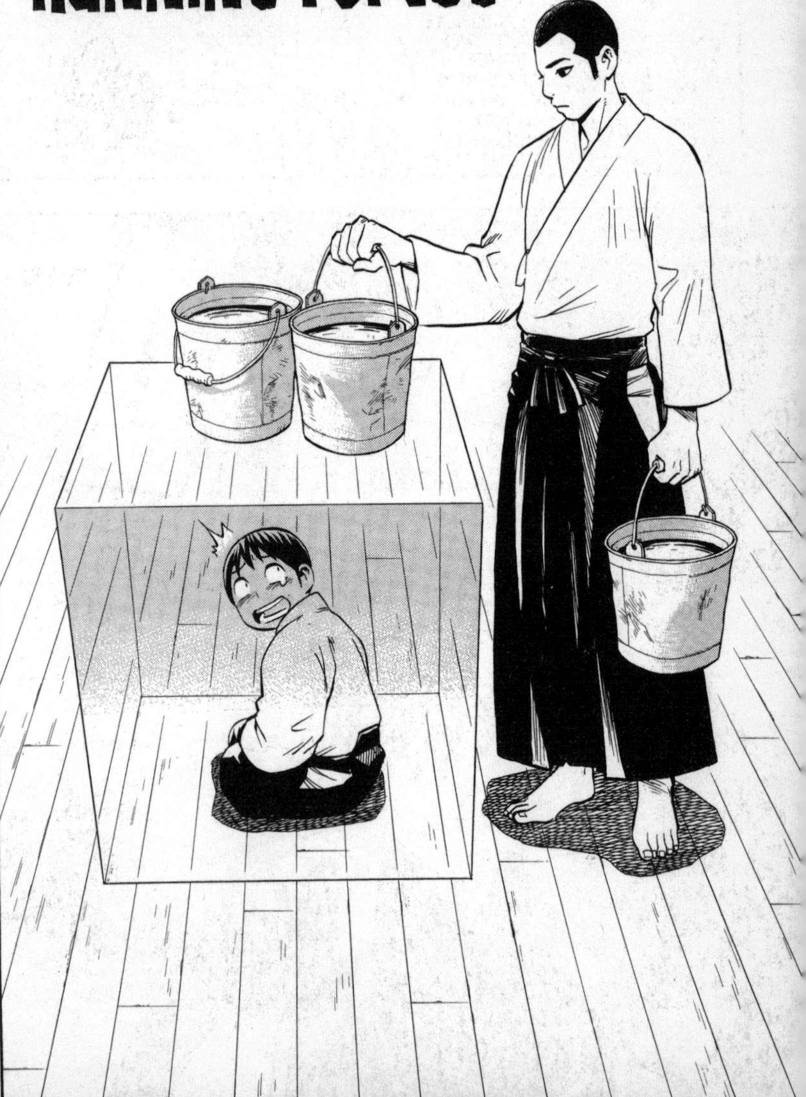

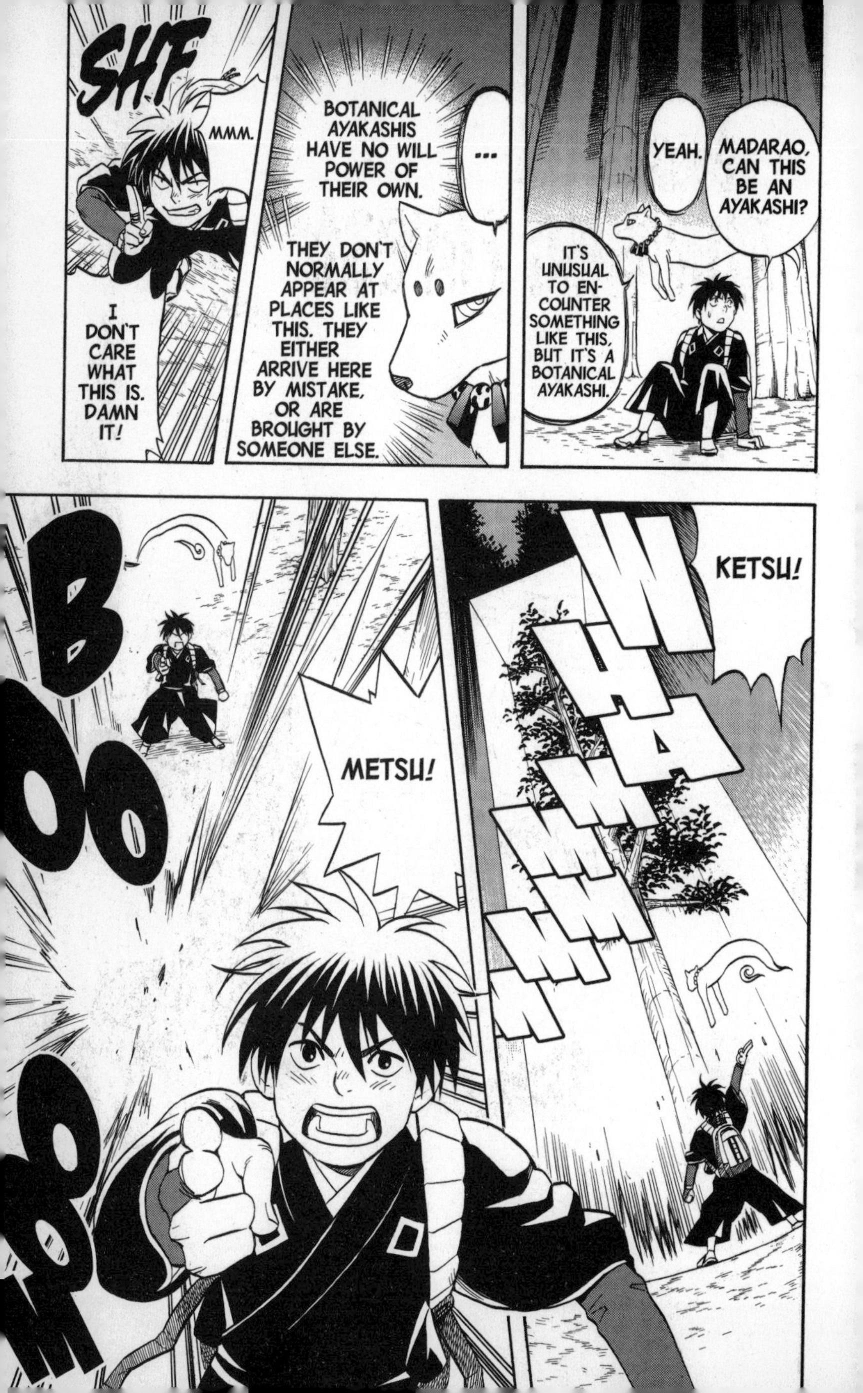
MADARAO, CAN THIS BE AN AYAKASHI?
YEAH.
IT'S UNUSUAL TO EN-COUNTER SOMETHING LIKE THIS, BUT IT'S A BOTANICAL AYAKASHI.
...
BOTANICAL AYAKASHIS HAVE NO WILL POWER OF THEIR OWN.
THEY DON'T NORMALLY APPEAR AT PLACES LIKE THIS. THEY EITHER ARRIVE HERE BY MISTAKE, OR ARE BROUGHT BY SOMEONE ELSE.
SHF
MMM.
I DON'T CARE WHAT THIS IS. DAMN IT!
KETSU!
WHAMMMMM
METSU!
BOOOOM

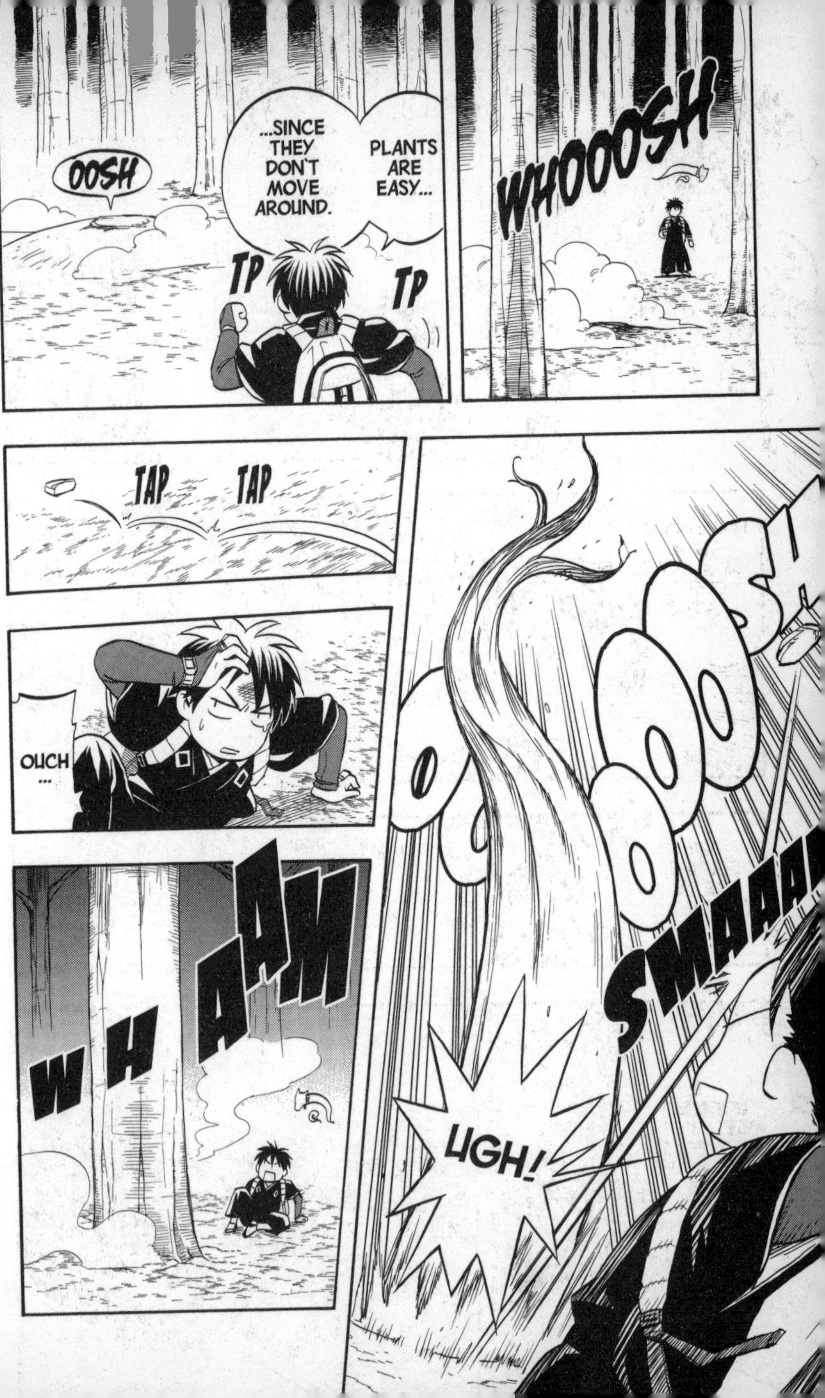
WHOOOSH
PLANTS ARE EASY...
...SINCE THEY DON'T MOVE AROUND.
TP
TP
OOSH
OOOOOSH
SMAAA
UGH!
TAP
TAP
OUCH ...
WHAAM

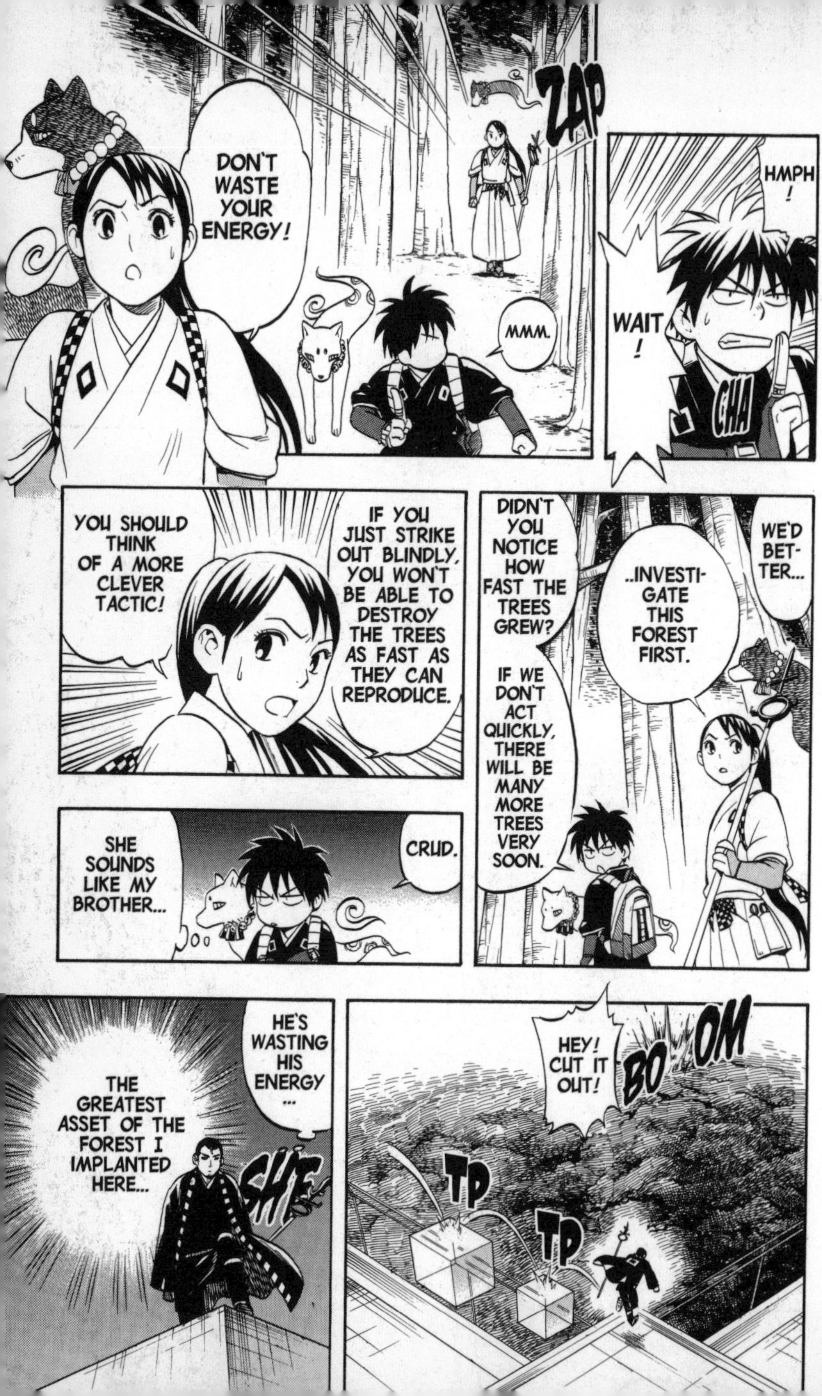
ZAP
DON'T WASTE YOUR ENERGY!
MMM.
HMPH!
WAIT!
CHA
WE'D BET-TER...
..INVESTI-GATE THIS FOREST FIRST.
DIDN'T YOU NOTICE HOW FAST THE TREES GREW?
IF WE DON'T ACT QUICKLY, THERE WILL BE MANY MORE TREES VERY SOON.
IF YOU JUST STRIKE OUT BLINDLY, YOU WON'T BE ABLE TO DESTROY THE TREES AS FAST AS THEY CAN REPRODUCE.
YOU SHOULD THINK OF A MORE CLEVER TACTIC!
CRUD.
SHE SOUNDS LIKE MY BROTHER...
HEY! CUT IT OUT!
BOOM
TP
TP
HE'S WASTING HIS ENERGY...
THE GREATEST ASSET OF THE FOREST I IMPLANTED HERE...
SHF

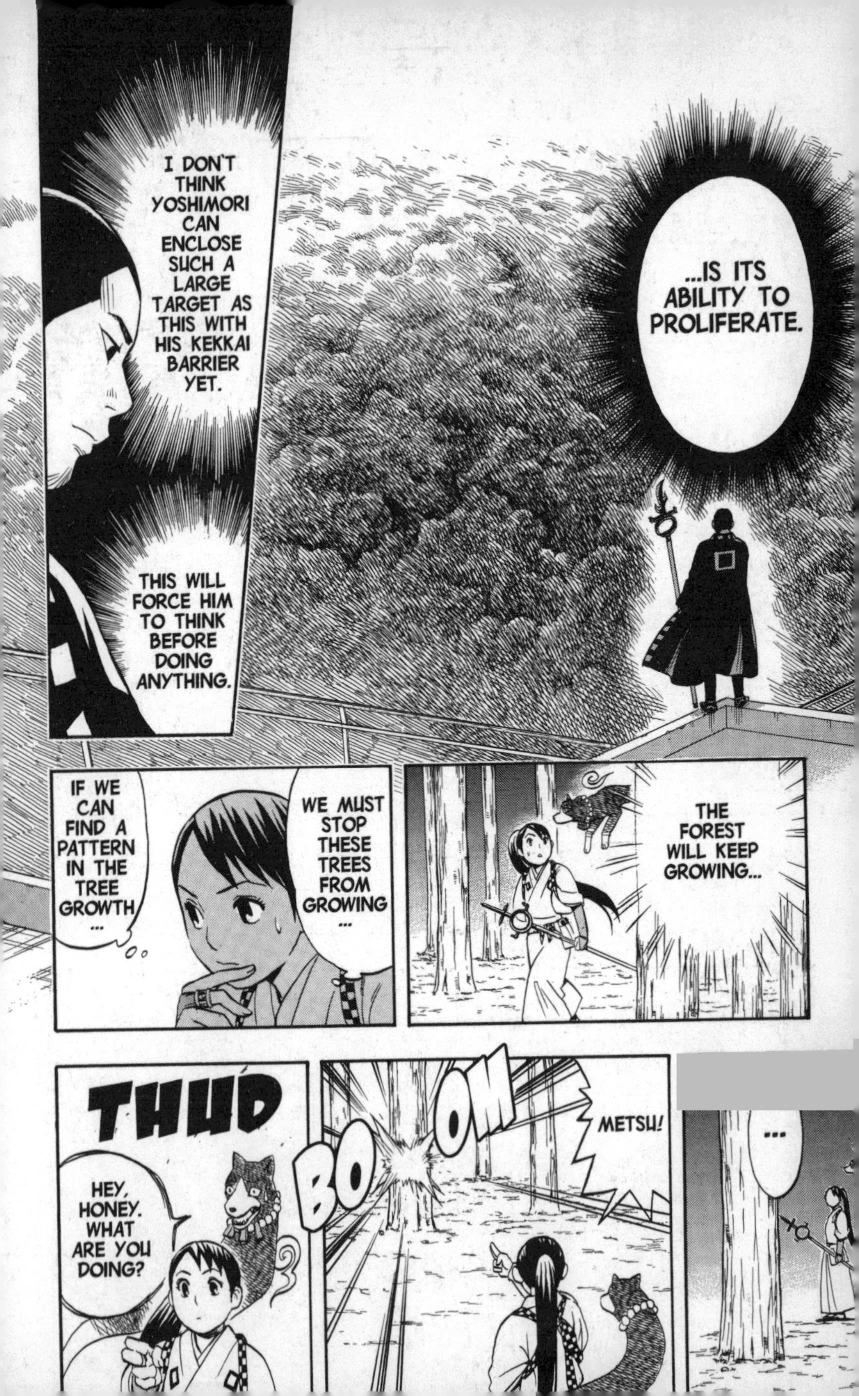
...IS ITS ABILITY TO PROLIFERATE.
I DON'T THINK YOSHIMORI CAN ENCLOSE SUCH A LARGE TARGET AS THIS WITH HIS KEKKAI BARRIER YET.
THIS WILL FORCE HIM TO THINK BEFORE DOING ANYTHING.
THE FOREST WILL KEEP GROWING...
WE MUST STOP THESE TREES FROM GROWING...
IF WE CAN FIND A PATTERN IN THE TREE GROWTH...
...
METSU!
BOOM
THUD
HEY, HONEY. WHAT ARE YOU DOING?

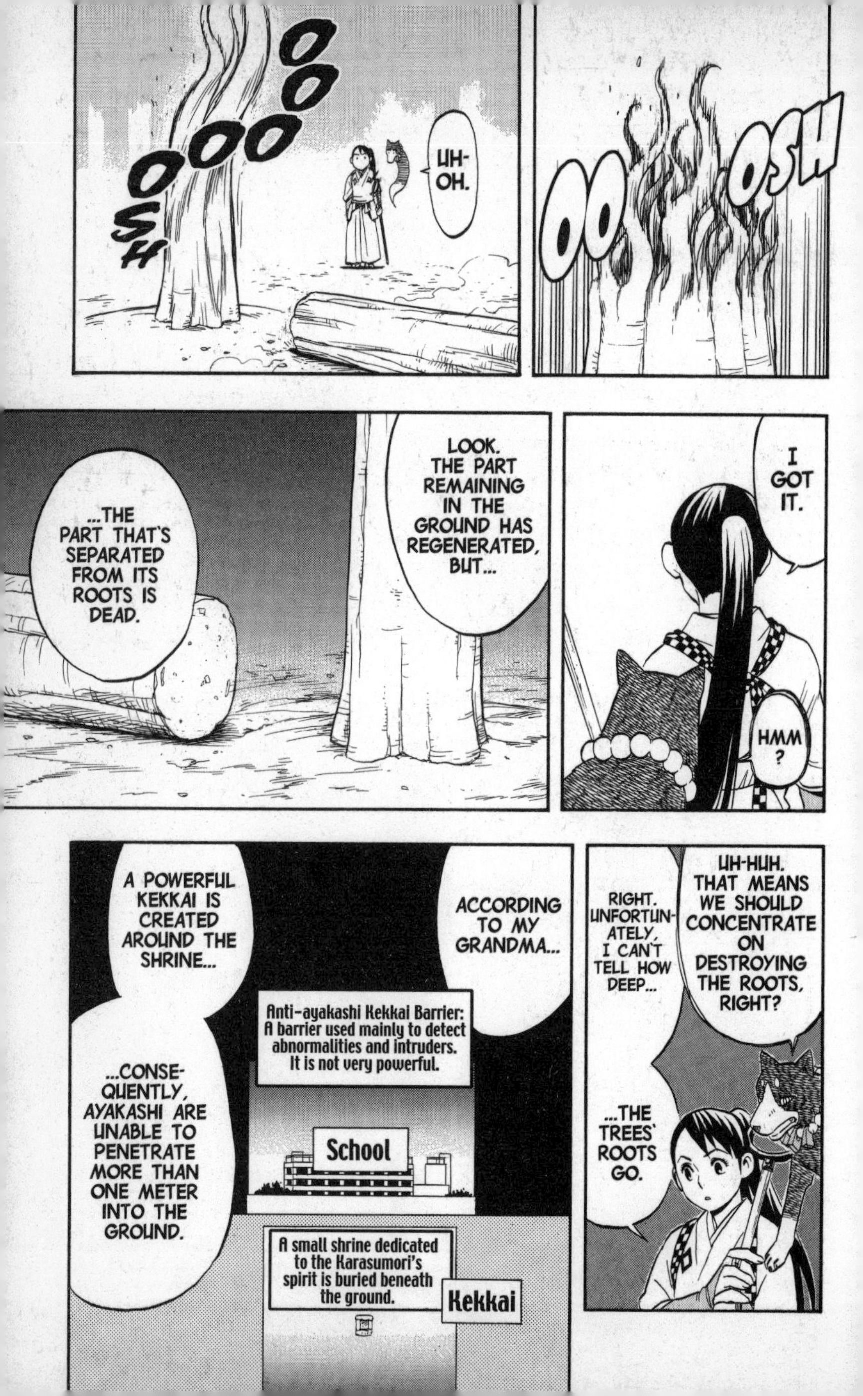
OO OSH
OOOOOOOSH
UH-OH.
I GOT IT.
HMM?
LOOK. THE PART REMAINING IN THE GROUND HAS REGENERATED, BUT...
...THE PART THAT'S SEPARATED FROM ITS ROOTS IS DEAD.
UH-HUH. THAT MEANS WE SHOULD CONCENTRATE ON DESTROYING THE ROOTS, RIGHT?
RIGHT. UNFORTUN-ATELY, I CAN'T TELL HOW DEEP...
...THE TREES' ROOTS GO.
ACCORDING TO MY GRANDMA...
A POWERFUL KEKKAI IS CREATED AROUND THE SHRINE...
Anti-ayakashi Kekkai Barrier: A barrier used mainly to detect abnormalities and intruders. It is not very powerful.
...CONSE-QUENTLY, AYAKASHI ARE UNABLE TO PENETRATE MORE THAN ONE METER INTO THE GROUND.
School
A small shrine dedicated to the Karasumori's spirit is buried beneath the ground.
Kekkai

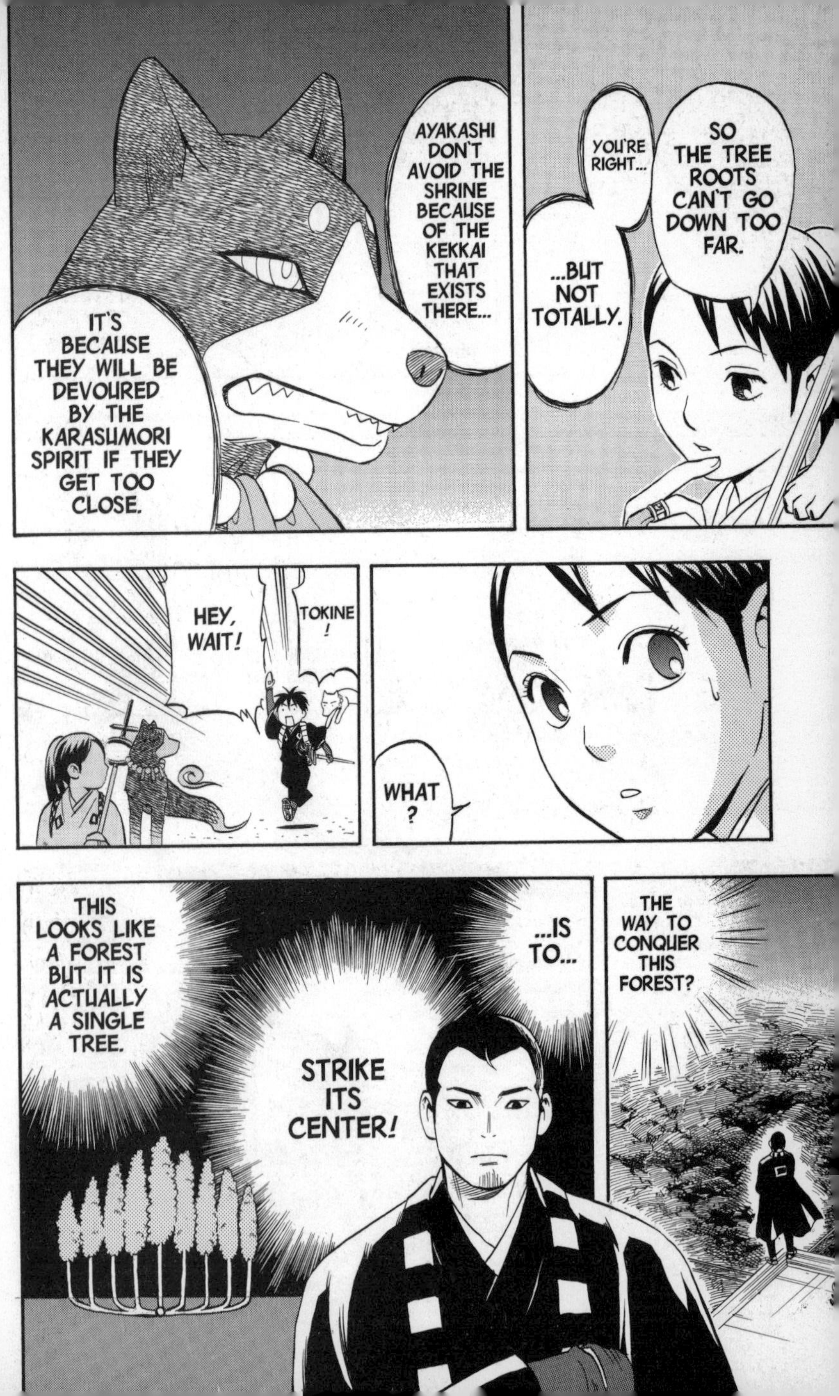
SO THE TREE ROOTS CAN'T GO DOWN TOO FAR.
YOU'RE RIGHT...
...BUT NOT TOTALLY.
AYAKASHI DON'T AVOID THE SHRINE BECAUSE OF THE KEKKAI THAT EXISTS THERE...
IT'S BECAUSE THEY WILL BE DEVOURED BY THE KARASUMORI SPIRIT IF THEY GET TOO CLOSE.
WHAT?
TOKINE!
HEY, WAIT!
THE WAY TO CONQUER THIS FOREST?
...IS TO...
THIS LOOKS LIKE A FOREST BUT IT IS ACTUALLY A SINGLE TREE.
STRIKE ITS CENTER!

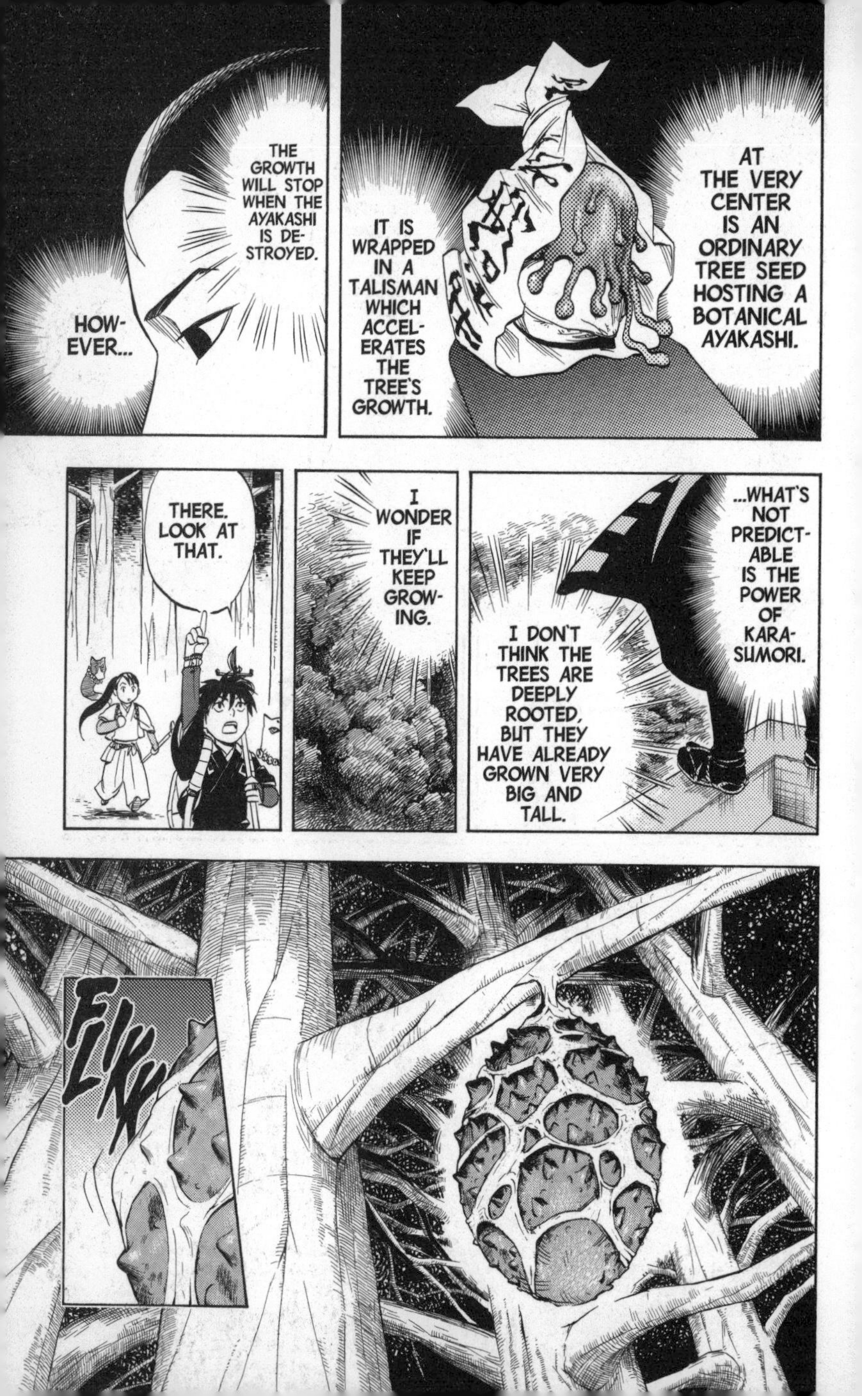
AT THE VERY CENTER IS AN ORDINARY TREE SEED HOSTING A BOTANICAL AYAKASHI.
IT IS WRAPPED IN A TALISMAN WHICH ACCELERATES THE TREE'S GROWTH.
THE GROWTH WILL STOP WHEN THE AYAKASHI IS DESTROYED.
HOWEVER...
...WHAT'S NOT PREDICTABLE IS THE POWER OF KARASUMORI.
I DON'T THINK THE TREES ARE DEEPLY ROOTED, BUT THEY HAVE ALREADY GROWN VERY BIG AND TALL.
I WONDER IF THEY'LL KEEP GROWING.
THERE. LOOK AT THAT.

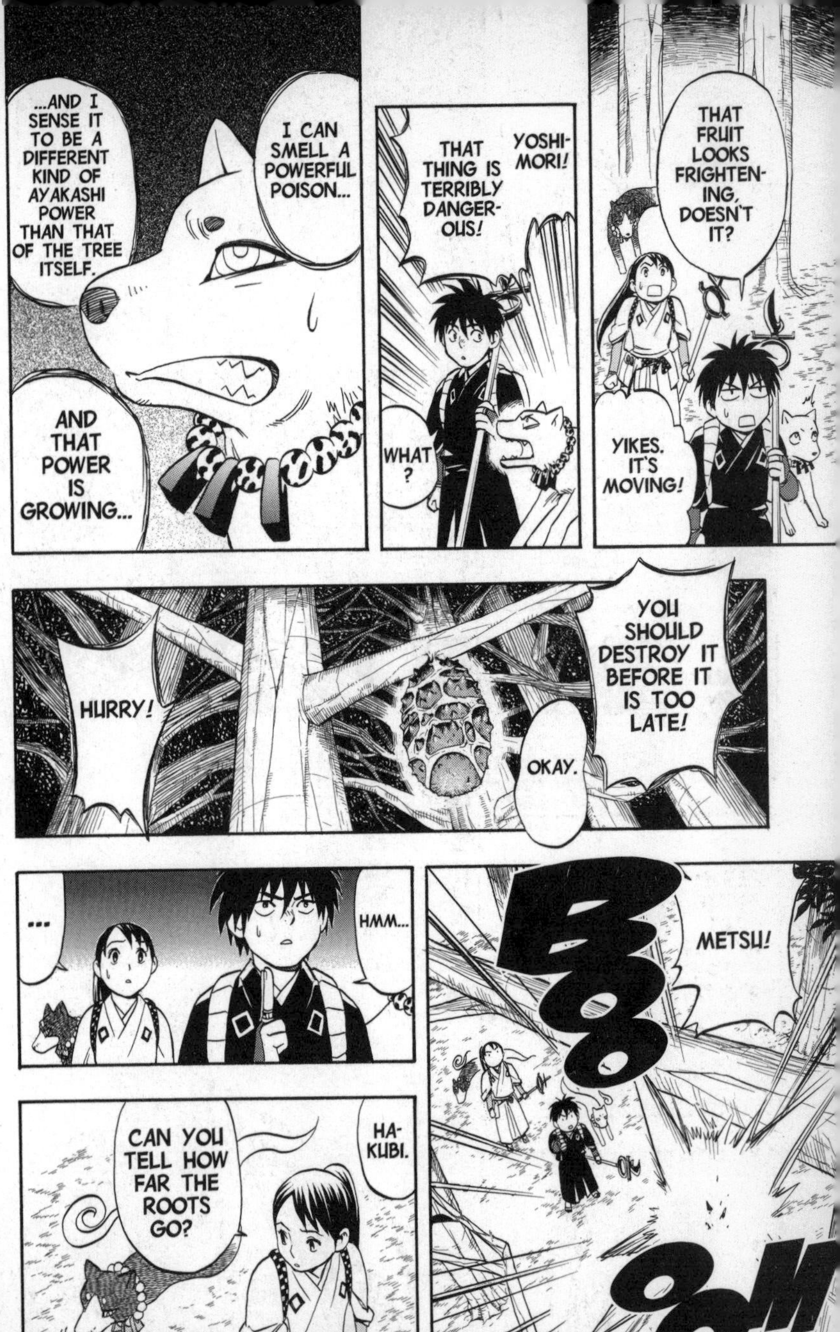

THAT FRUIT LOOKS FRIGHTEN-ING, DOESN'T IT?
YIKES. IT'S MOVING!
YOSHI-MORI!
THAT THING IS TERRIBLY DANGER-OUS!
WHAT?
I CAN SMELL A POWERFUL POISON...
...AND I SENSE IT TO BE A DIFFERENT KIND OF AYAKASHI POWER THAN THAT OF THE TREE ITSELF.
AND THAT POWER IS GROWING...
YOU SHOULD DESTROY IT BEFORE IT IS TOO LATE!
OKAY.
HURRY!
METSU!
BOO
OOM
HMM...
...
HA-KUBI.
CAN YOU TELL HOW FAR THE ROOTS GO?

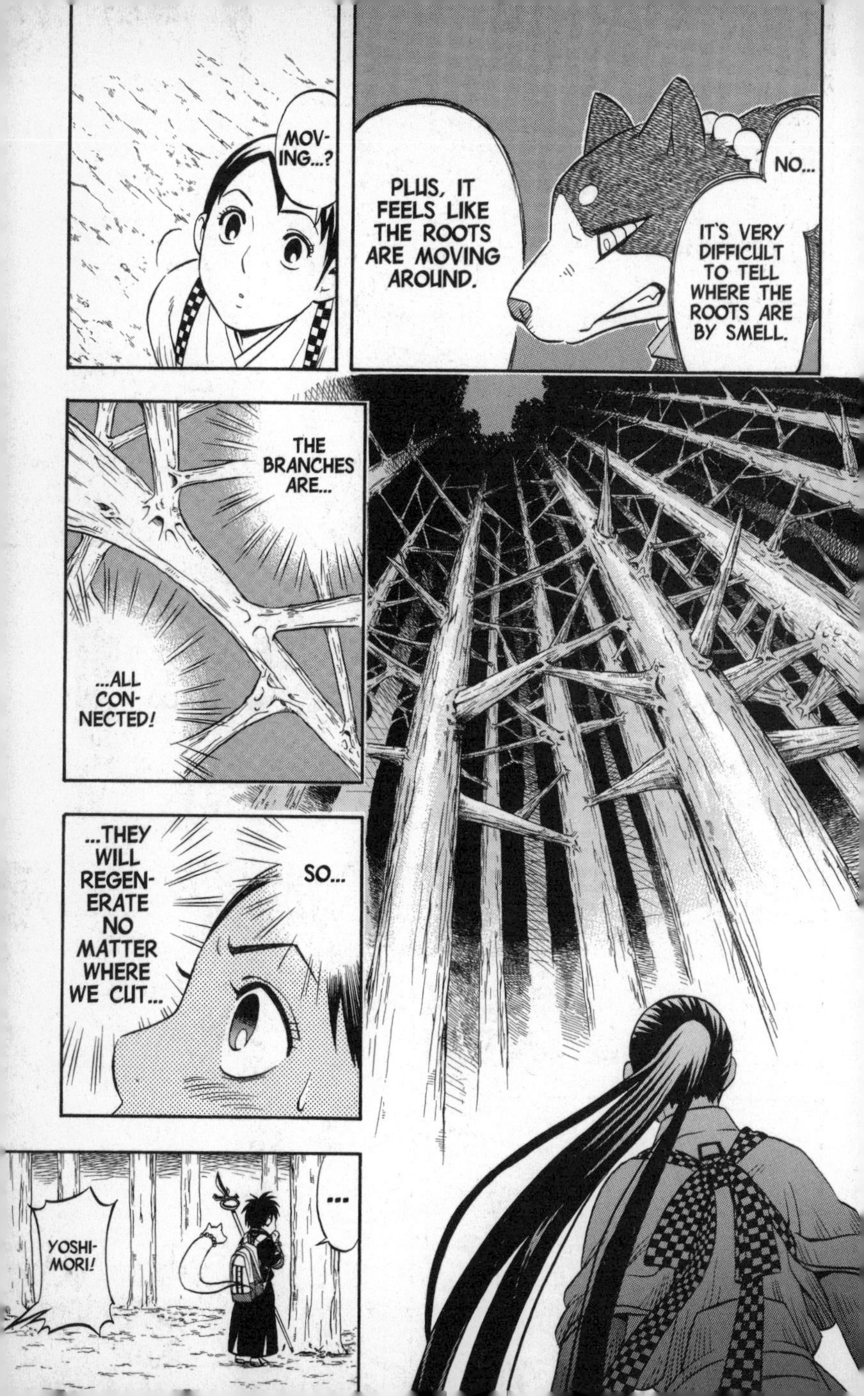
NO...
IT'S VERY DIFFICULT TO TELL WHERE THE ROOTS ARE BY SMELL.
PLUS, IT FEELS LIKE THE ROOTS ARE MOVING AROUND.
MOV-ING...?
THE BRANCHES ARE...
...ALL CON-NECTED!
SO...
...THEY WILL REGEN-ERATE NO MATTER WHERE WE CUT...
...
YOSHI-MORI!

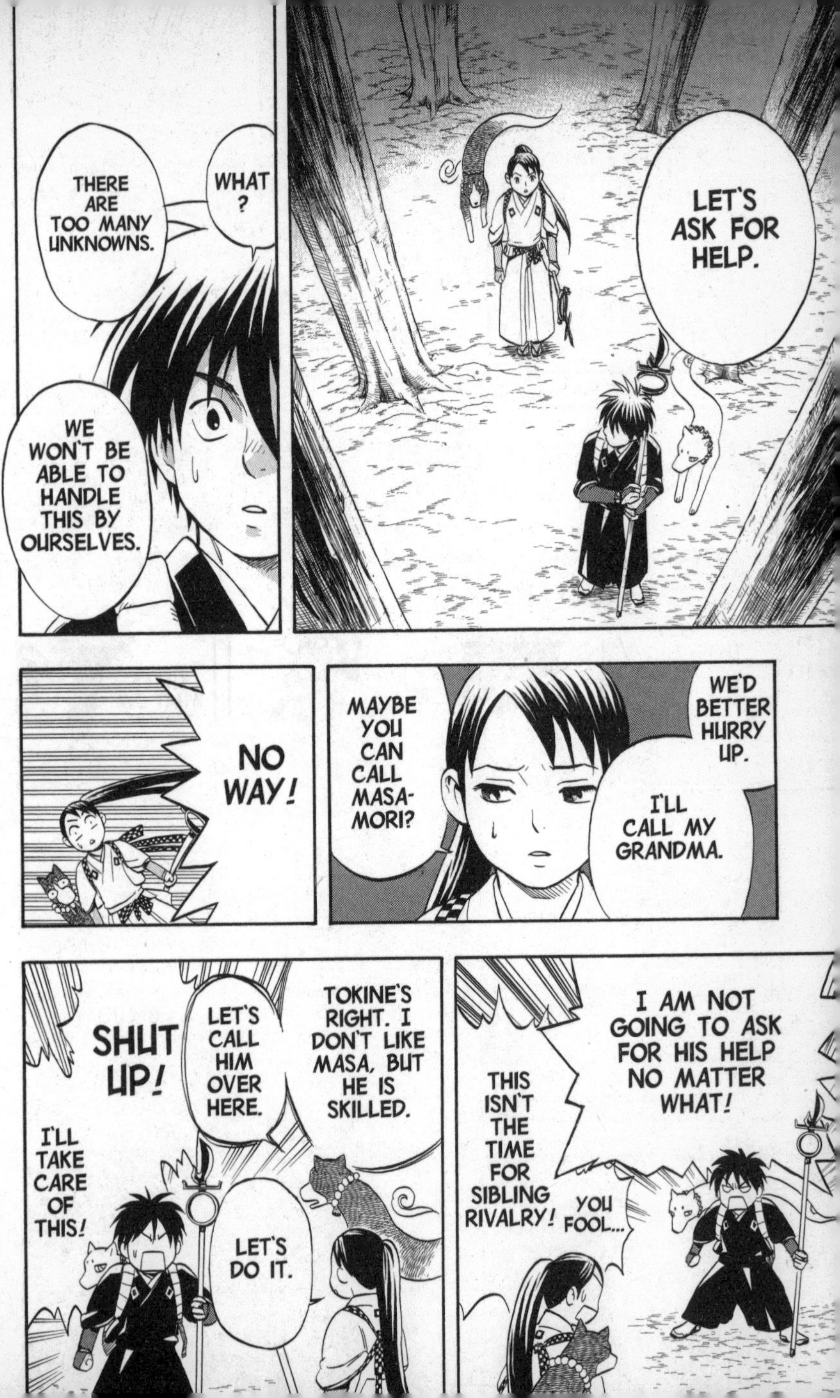

LET'S ASK FOR HELP.
WHAT?
THERE ARE TOO MANY UNKNOWNS.
WE WON'T BE ABLE TO HANDLE THIS BY OURSELVES.
WE'D BETTER HURRY UP.
I'LL CALL MY GRANDMA.
MAYBE YOU CAN CALL MASA-MORI?
NO WAY!
I AM NOT GOING TO ASK FOR HIS HELP NO MATTER WHAT!
THIS ISN'T THE TIME FOR SIBLING RIVALRY!
YOU FOOL...
TOKINE'S RIGHT. I DON'T LIKE MASA, BUT HE IS SKILLED.
LET'S CALL HIM OVER HERE.
SHUT UP!
LET'S DO IT.
I'LL TAKE CARE OF THIS!

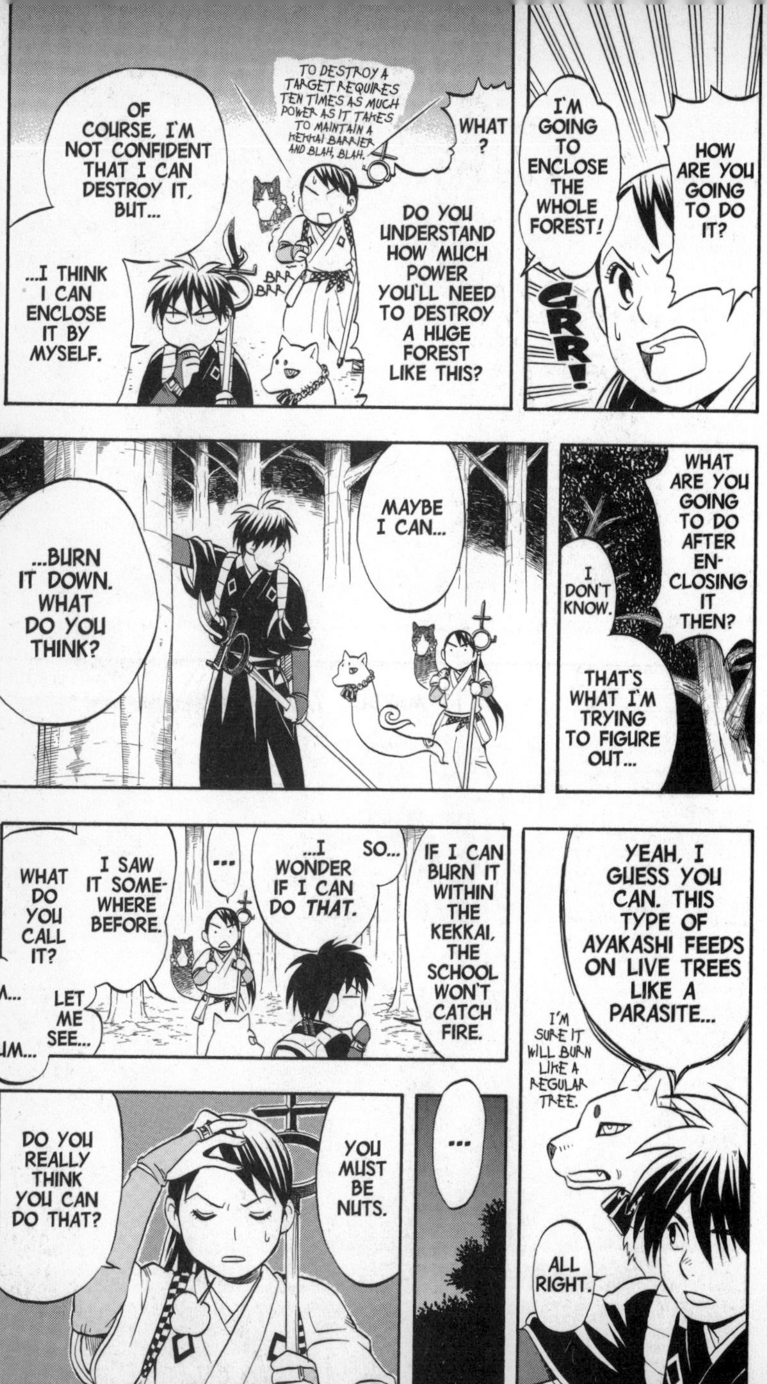
HOW ARE YOU GOING TO DO IT?
I'M GOING TO ENCLOSE THE WHOLE FOREST!
GRR!
WHAT?
DO YOU UNDERSTAND HOW MUCH POWER YOU'LL NEED TO DESTROY A HUGE FOREST LIKE THIS?
TO DESTROY A TARGET REQUIRES TEN TIMES AS MUCH POWER AS IT TAKES TO MAINTAIN A KEKKAI BARRIER AND BLAH, BLAH.
OF COURSE, I'M NOT CONFIDENT THAT I CAN DESTROY IT, BUT...
...I THINK I CAN ENCLOSE IT BY MYSELF.
BRR BRR
WHAT ARE YOU GOING TO DO AFTER EN-CLOSING IT THEN?
I DON'T KNOW.
THAT'S WHAT I'M TRYING TO FIGURE OUT...
MAYBE I CAN...
...BURN IT DOWN. WHAT DO YOU THINK?
YEAH, I GUESS YOU CAN. THIS TYPE OF AYAKASHI FEEDS ON LIVE TREES LIKE A PARASITE...
I'M SURE IT WILL BURN LIKE A REGULAR TREE.
ALL RIGHT.
IF I CAN BURN IT WITHIN THE KEKKAI, THE SCHOOL WON'T CATCH FIRE.
SO...
...I WONDER IF I CAN DO THAT.
...
I SAW IT SOME-WHERE BEFORE.
WHAT DO YOU CALL IT?
UM...
LET ME SEE...
UM...
...
YOU MUST BE NUTS.
DO YOU REALLY THINK YOU CAN DO THAT?

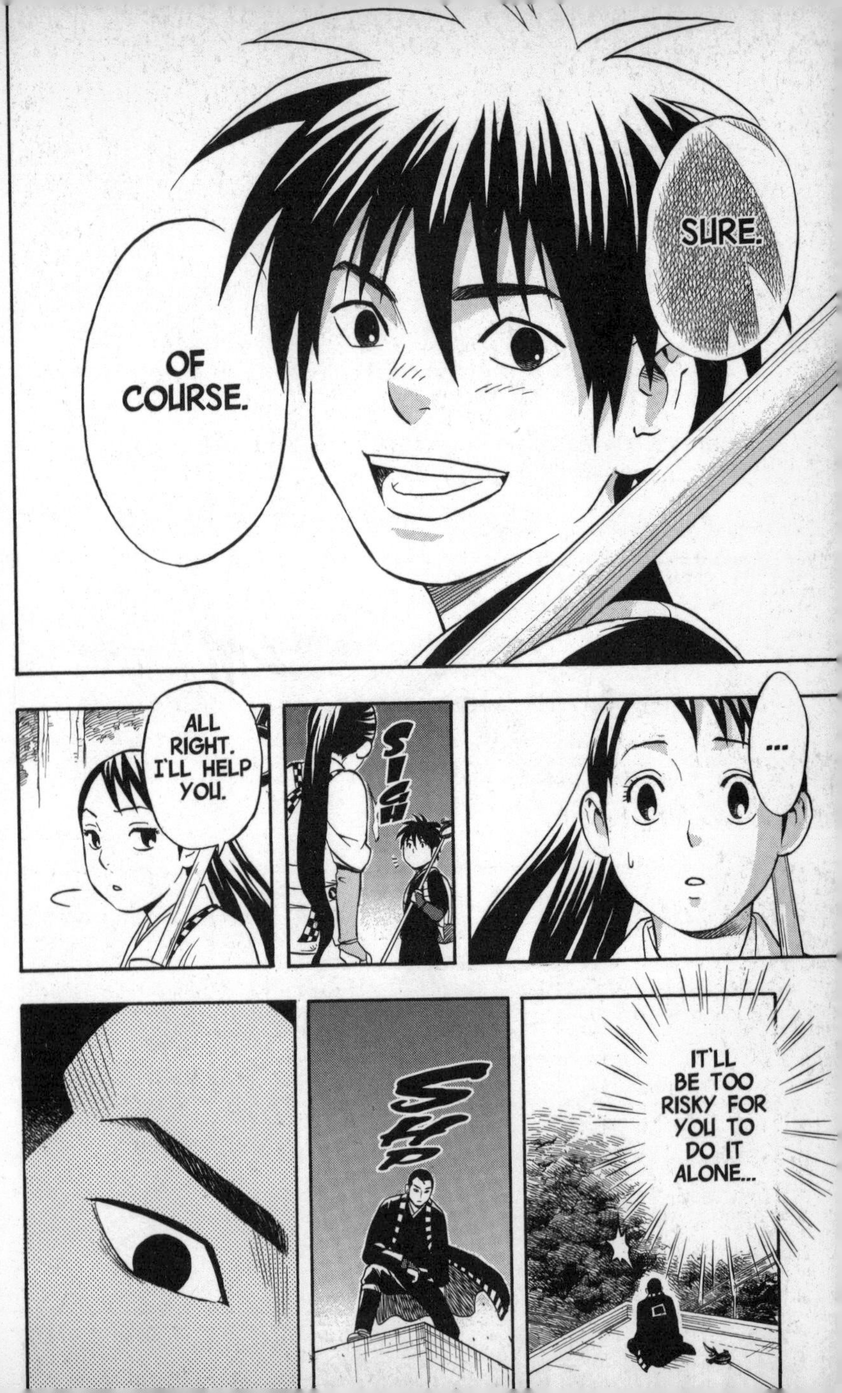
SURE.
OF COURSE.
...
SIGH
ALL RIGHT. I'LL HELP YOU.
IT'LL BE TOO RISKY FOR YOU TO DO IT ALONE...
SHP

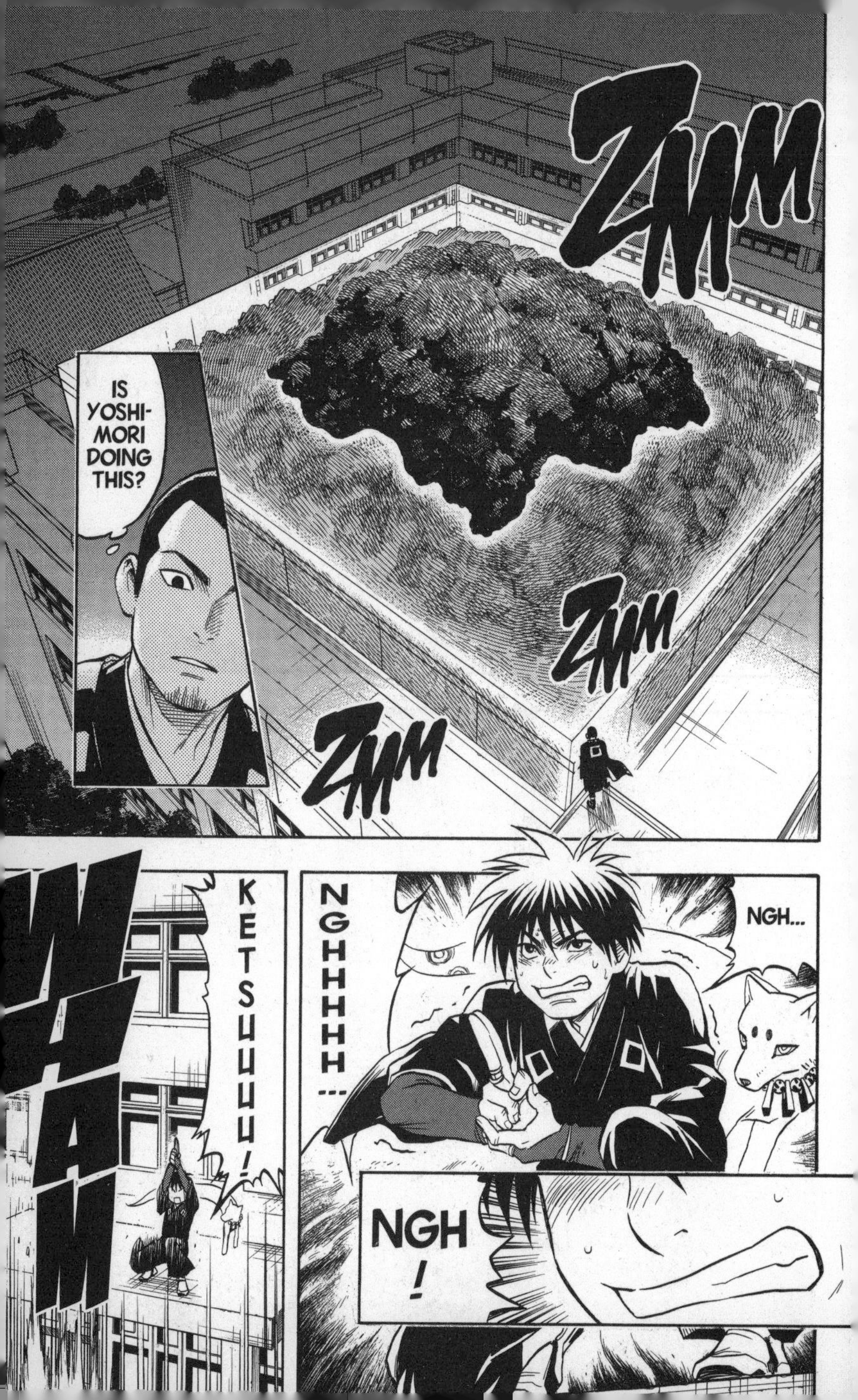
ZMM
IS YOSHIMORI DOING THIS?
ZMM
ZMM
NGH...
NGHHHHHH...
NGH!
KETSUUUUU!
WHAM

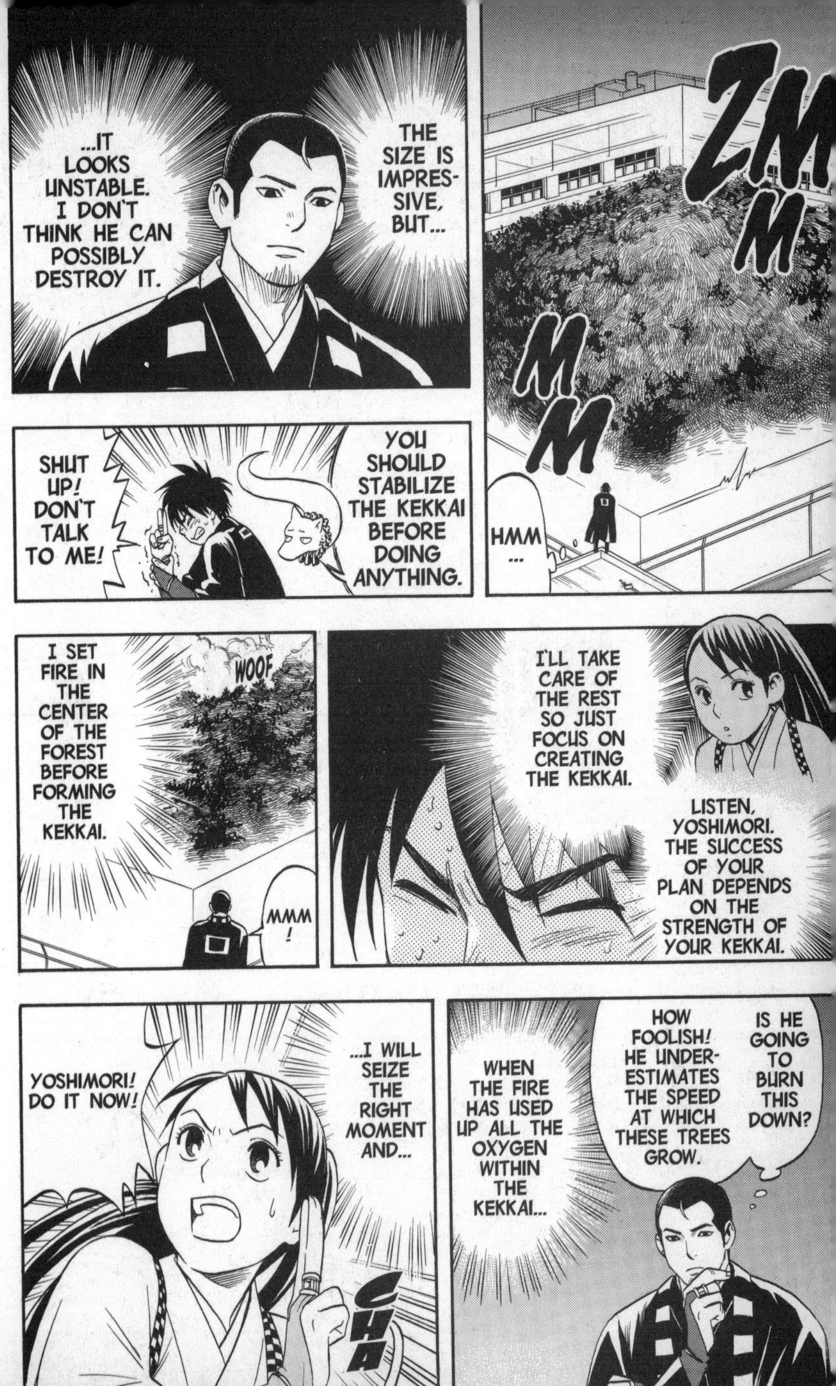
ZMMMM
HMM...
THE SIZE IS IMPRESSIVE, BUT...
...IT LOOKS UNSTABLE. I DON'T THINK HE CAN POSSIBLY DESTROY IT.
YOU SHOULD STABILIZE THE KEKKAI BEFORE DOING ANYTHING.
SHUT UP! DON'T TALK TO ME!
I'LL TAKE CARE OF THE REST SO JUST FOCUS ON CREATING THE KEKKAI.
LISTEN, YOSHIMORI. THE SUCCESS OF YOUR PLAN DEPENDS ON THE STRENGTH OF YOUR KEKKAI.
WOOF
I SET FIRE IN THE CENTER OF THE FOREST BEFORE FORMING THE KEKKAI.
MMM!
IS HE GOING TO BURN THIS DOWN?
HOW FOOLISH! HE UNDER-ESTIMATES THE SPEED AT WHICH THESE TREES GROW.
WHEN THE FIRE HAS USED UP ALL THE OXYGEN WITHIN THE KEKKAI...
...I WILL SEIZE THE RIGHT MOMENT AND...
YOSHIMORI! DO IT NOW!
CHA

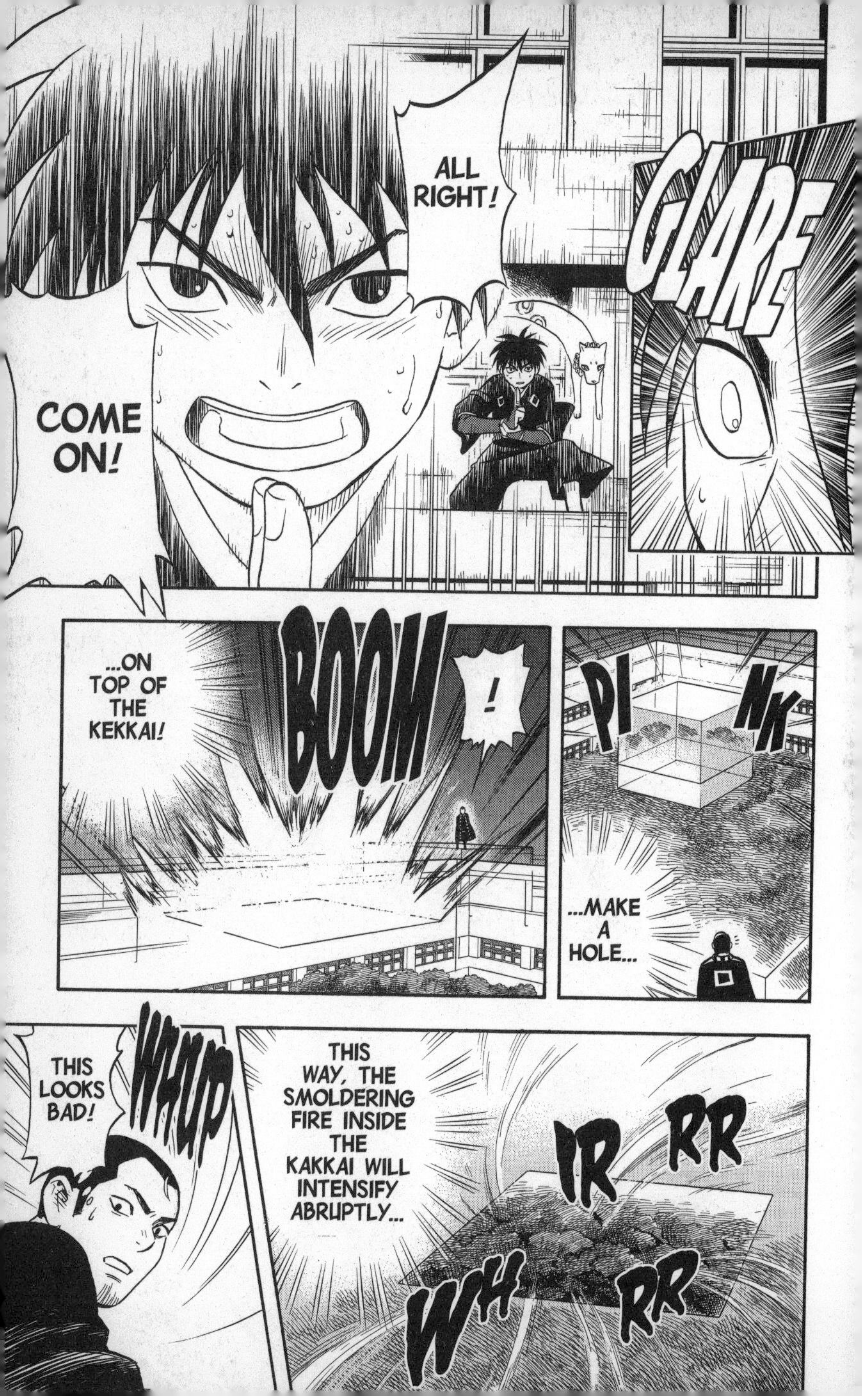
GLARE
ALL RIGHT!
COME ON!
PINK
...MAKE A HOLE...
BOOM
!
...ON TOP OF THE KEKKAI!
THIS WAY, THE SMOLDERING FIRE INSIDE THE KAKKAI WILL INTENSIFY ABRUPTLY...
IR RR
WH RR
WHUP
THIS LOOKS BAD!

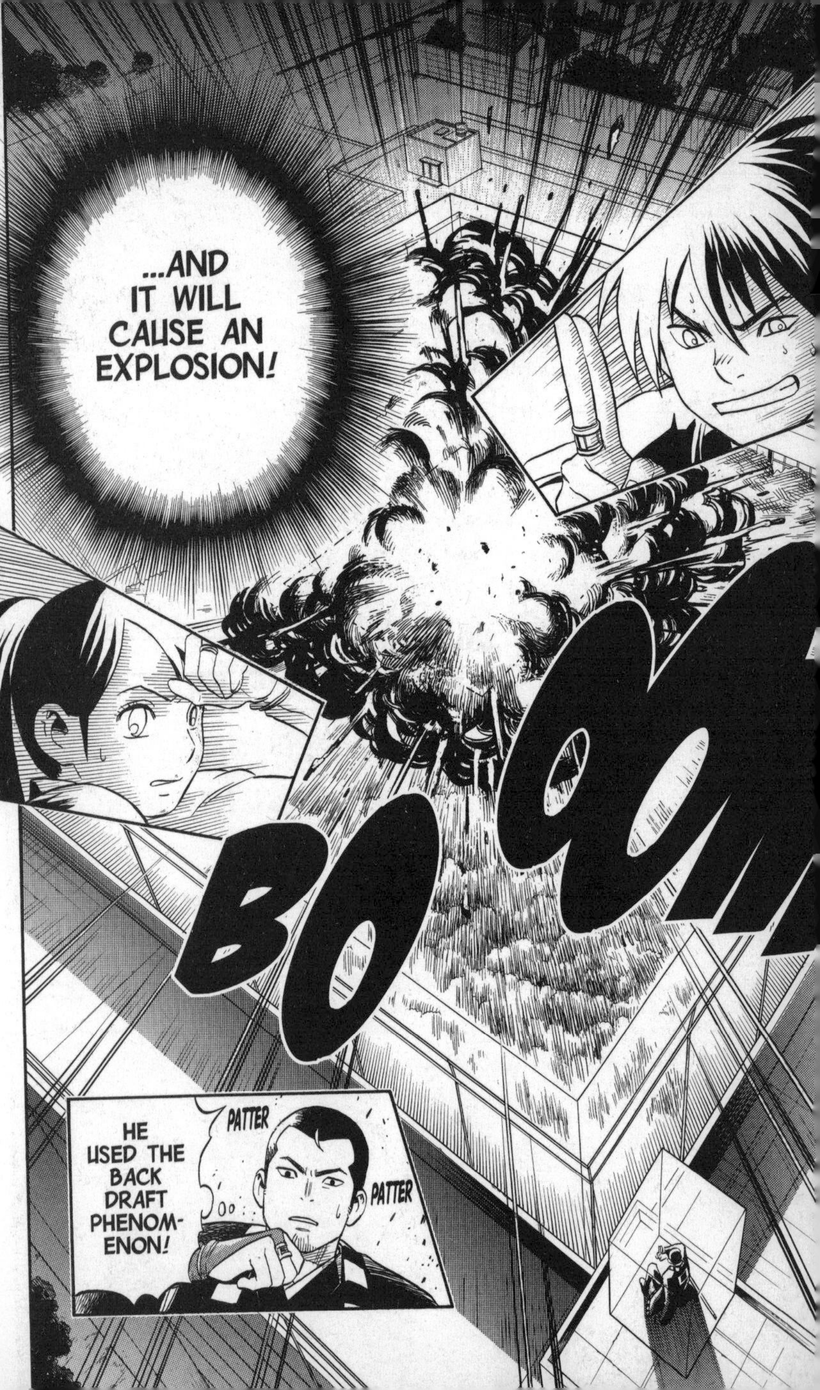
...AND IT WILL CAUSE AN EXPLOSION!
BOOOM
PATTER
PATTER
HE USED THE BACK DRAFT PHENOM-ENON!

Chapter 34: Over the Sky

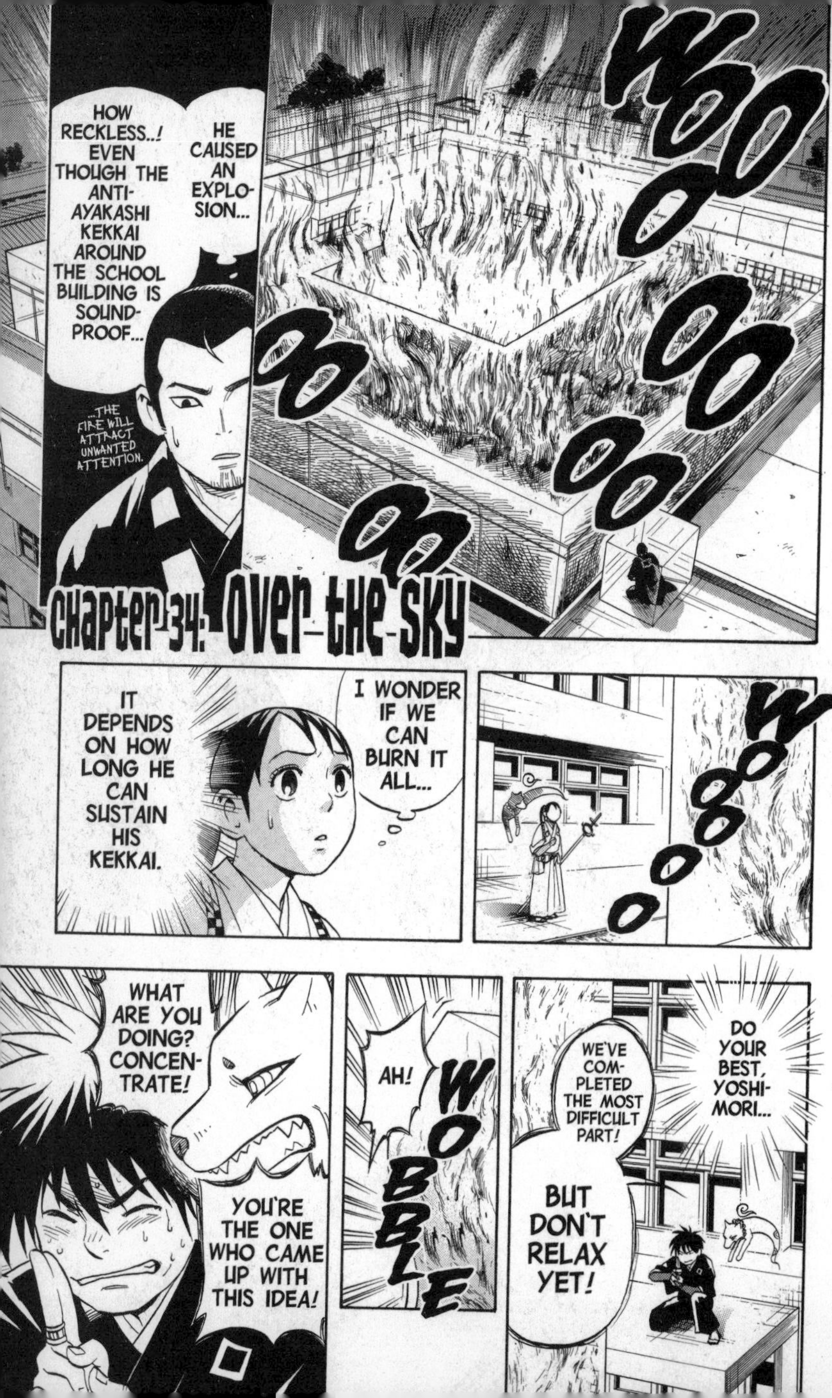
WOOOOOOOOOOO
HE CAUSED AN EXPLOSION...
HOW RECKLESS..! EVEN THOUGH THE ANTI-AYAKASHI KEKKAI AROUND THE SCHOOL BUILDING IS SOUNDPROOF...
...THE FIRE WILL ATTRACT UNWANTED ATTENTION.
WOOOOO
I WONDER IF WE CAN BURN IT ALL...
IT DEPENDS ON HOW LONG HE CAN SUSTAIN HIS KEKKAI.
DO YOUR BEST, YOSHIMORI...
WE'VE COMPLETED THE MOST DIFFICULT PART!
BUT DON'T RELAX YET!
AH!
WOBBLE
WHAT ARE YOU DOING? CONCENTRATE!
YOU'RE THE ONE WHO CAME UP WITH THIS IDEA!

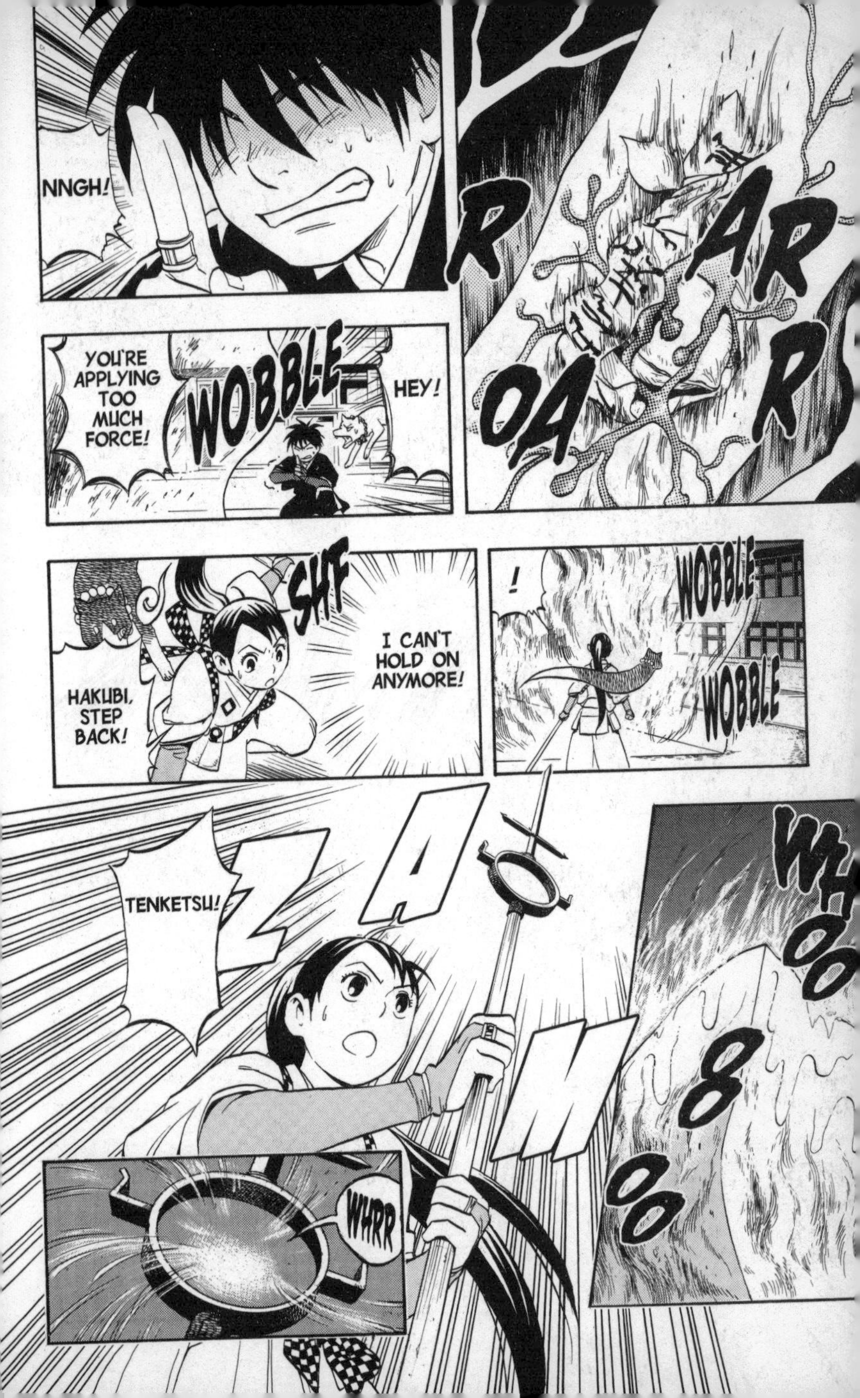
ROAARR
NNGH!
HEY!
WOBBLE
YOU'RE APPLYING TOO MUCH FORCE!
!
WOBBLE
WOBBLE
SHF
I CAN'T HOLD ON ANYMORE!
HAKUBI, STEP BACK!
WHOOOOO
TENKETSU!
ZAM
WHRR

WO

WO

WO

TEN-
KETSU!

'SHOOO

DARN
IT!

GRAB

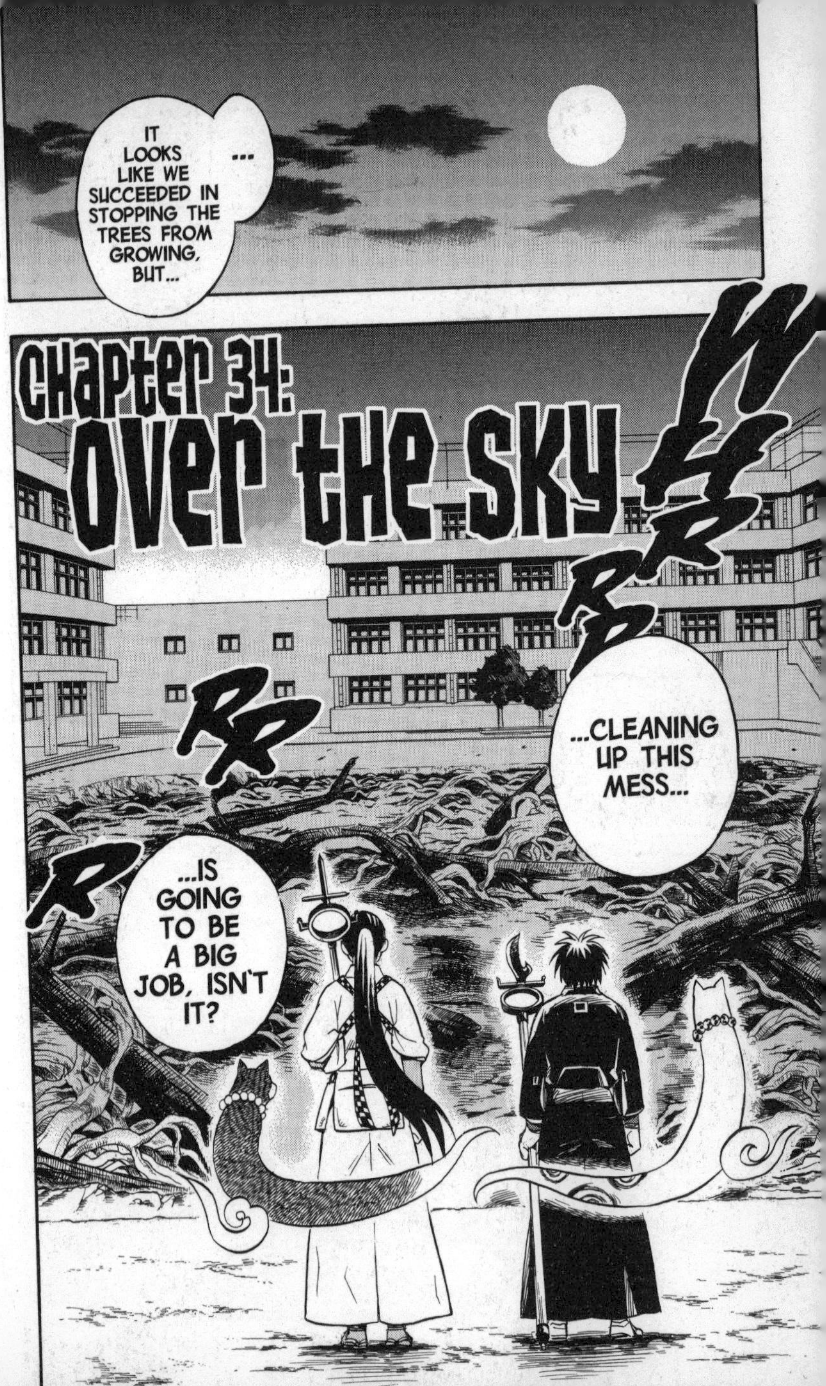
IT LOOKS LIKE WE SUCCEEDED IN STOPPING THE TREES FROM GROWING, BUT... ...
Chapter 34: Over the Sky
...CLEANING UP THIS MESS...
...IS GOING TO BE A BIG JOB, ISN'T IT?

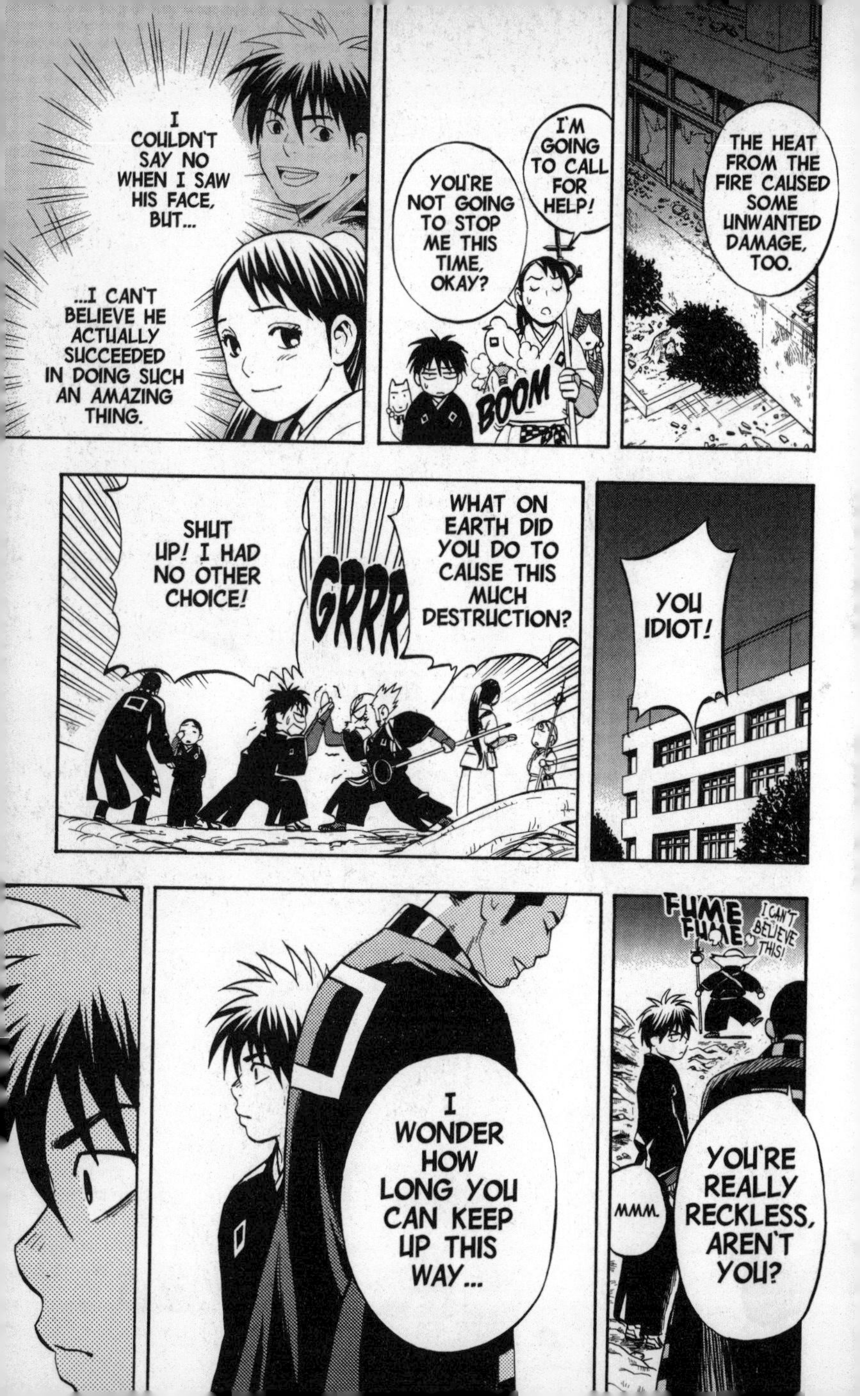
THE HEAT FROM THE FIRE CAUSED SOME UNWANTED DAMAGE, TOO.
I'M GOING TO CALL FOR HELP!
YOU'RE NOT GOING TO STOP ME THIS TIME, OKAY?
BOOM
I COULDN'T SAY NO WHEN I SAW HIS FACE, BUT...
...I CAN'T BELIEVE HE ACTUALLY SUCCEEDED IN DOING SUCH AN AMAZING THING.
YOU IDIOT!
WHAT ON EARTH DID YOU DO TO CAUSE THIS MUCH DESTRUCTION?
GRRR
SHUT UP! I HAD NO OTHER CHOICE!
FUME FUME
I CAN'T BELIEVE THIS!
YOU'RE REALLY RECKLESS, AREN'T YOU?
MMM.
I WONDER HOW LONG YOU CAN KEEP UP THIS WAY...

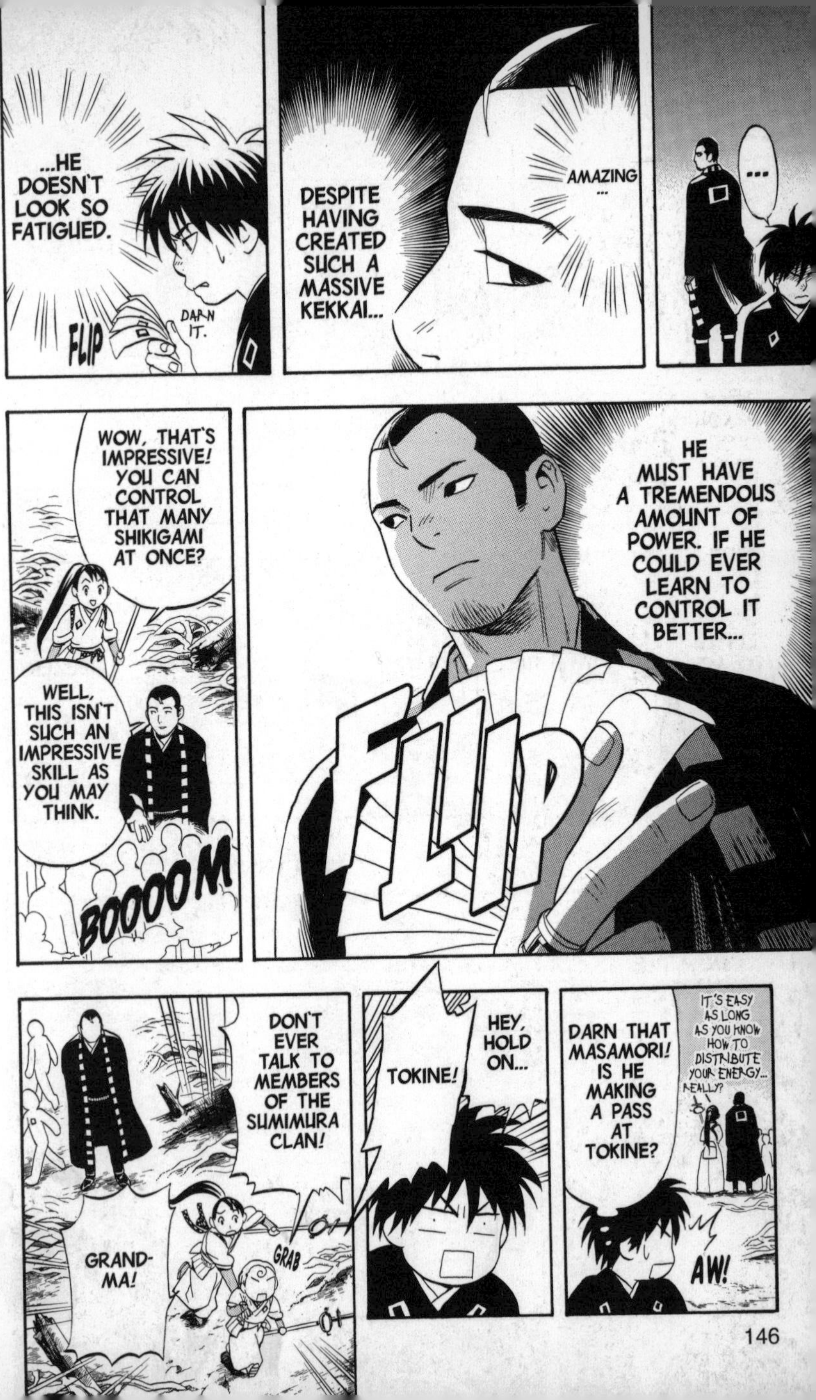
...
AMAZING...
DESPITE HAVING CREATED SUCH A MASSIVE KEKKAI...
...HE DOESN'T LOOK SO FATIGUED.
DARN IT.
FLIP
HE MUST HAVE A TREMENDOUS AMOUNT OF POWER. IF HE COULD EVER LEARN TO CONTROL IT BETTER...
FLIP
WOW, THAT'S IMPRESSIVE! YOU CAN CONTROL THAT MANY SHIKIGAMI AT ONCE?
WELL, THIS ISN'T SUCH AN IMPRESSIVE SKILL AS YOU MAY THINK.
BOOOOM
IT'S EASY AS LONG AS YOU KNOW HOW TO DISTRIBUTE YOUR ENERGY...
REALLY?
DARN THAT MASAMORI! IS HE MAKING A PASS AT TOKINE?
AW!
HEY, HOLD ON...
TOKINE!
DON'T EVER TALK TO MEMBERS OF THE SUMIMURA CLAN!
GRAB
GRAND-MA!

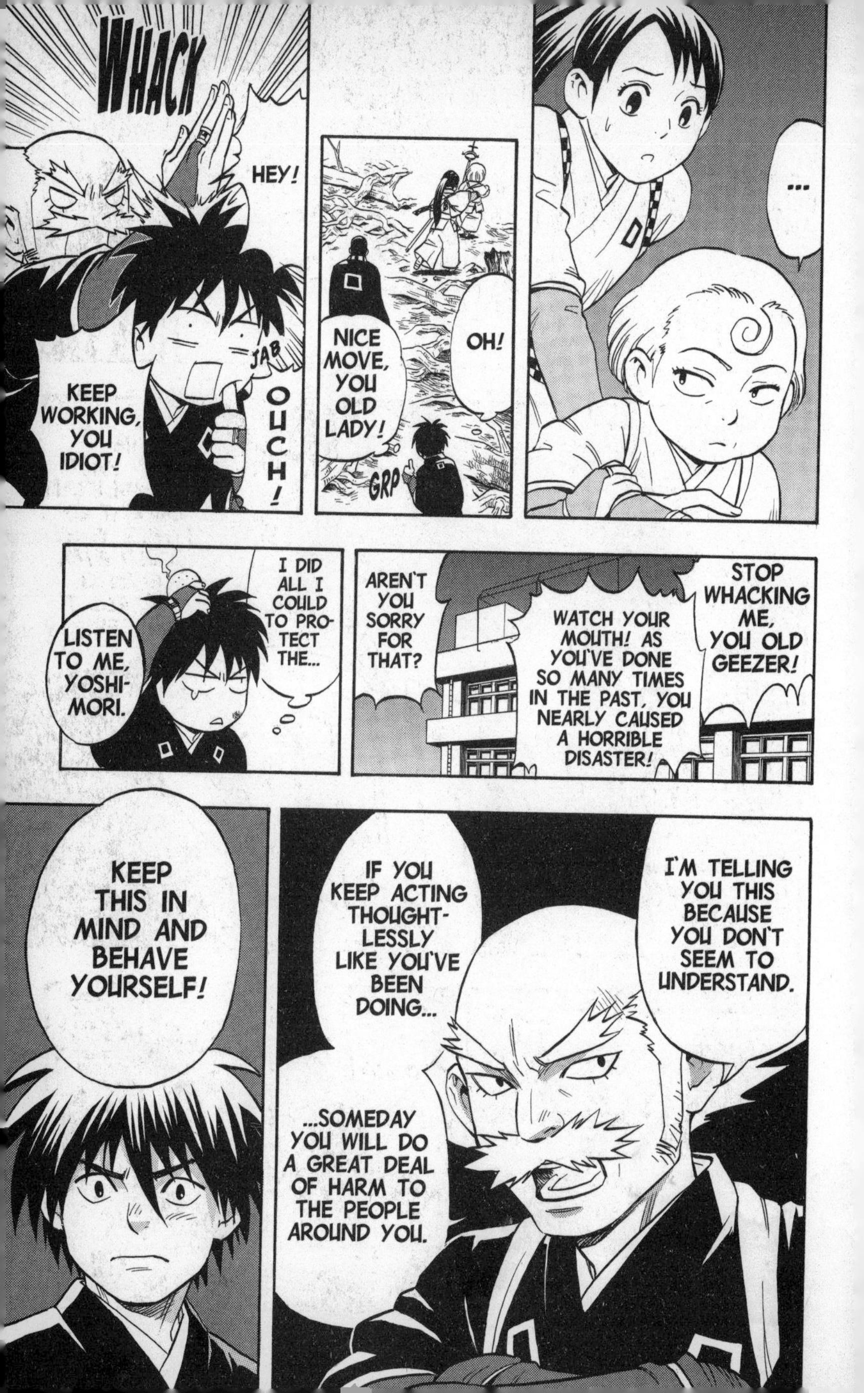
...
OH!
NICE MOVE, YOU OLD LADY!
GRP
WHACK
HEY!
JAB
OUCH!
KEEP WORKING, YOU IDIOT!
STOP WHACKING ME, YOU OLD GEEZER!
WATCH YOUR MOUTH! AS YOU'VE DONE SO MANY TIMES IN THE PAST, YOU NEARLY CAUSED A HORRIBLE DISASTER!
AREN'T YOU SORRY FOR THAT?
I DID ALL I COULD TO PRO-TECT THE...
LISTEN TO ME, YOSHI-MORI.
I'M TELLING YOU THIS BECAUSE YOU DON'T SEEM TO UNDERSTAND.
IF YOU KEEP ACTING THOUGHT-LESSLY LIKE YOU'VE BEEN DOING...
...SOMEDAY YOU WILL DO A GREAT DEAL OF HARM TO THE PEOPLE AROUND YOU.
KEEP THIS IN MIND AND BEHAVE YOURSELF!

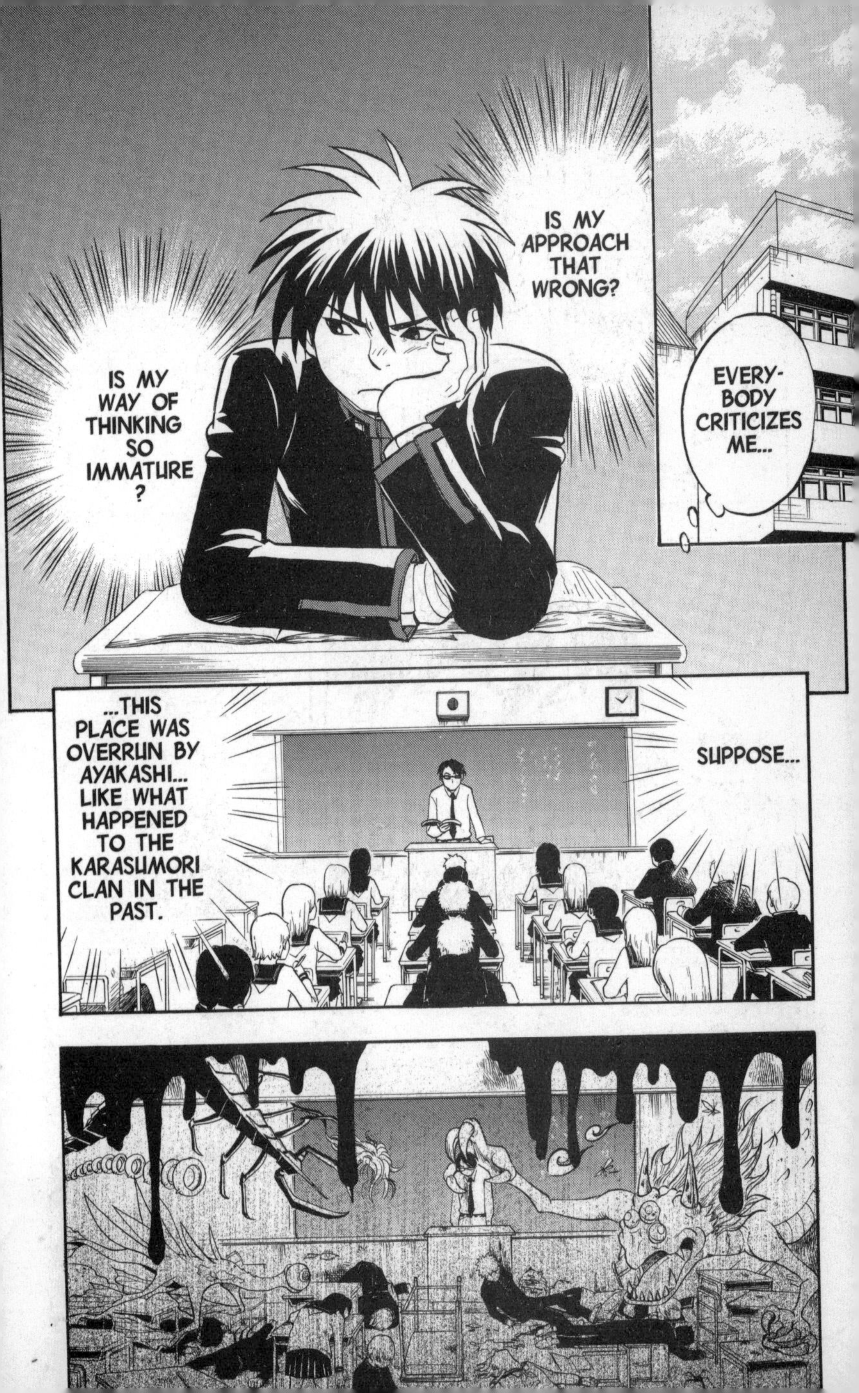
EVERY-BODY CRITICIZES ME...
IS MY APPROACH THAT WRONG?
IS MY WAY OF THINKING SO IMMATURE?
SUPPOSE...
...THIS PLACE WAS OVERRUN BY AYAKASHI... LIKE WHAT HAPPENED TO THE KARASUMORI CLAN IN THE PAST.

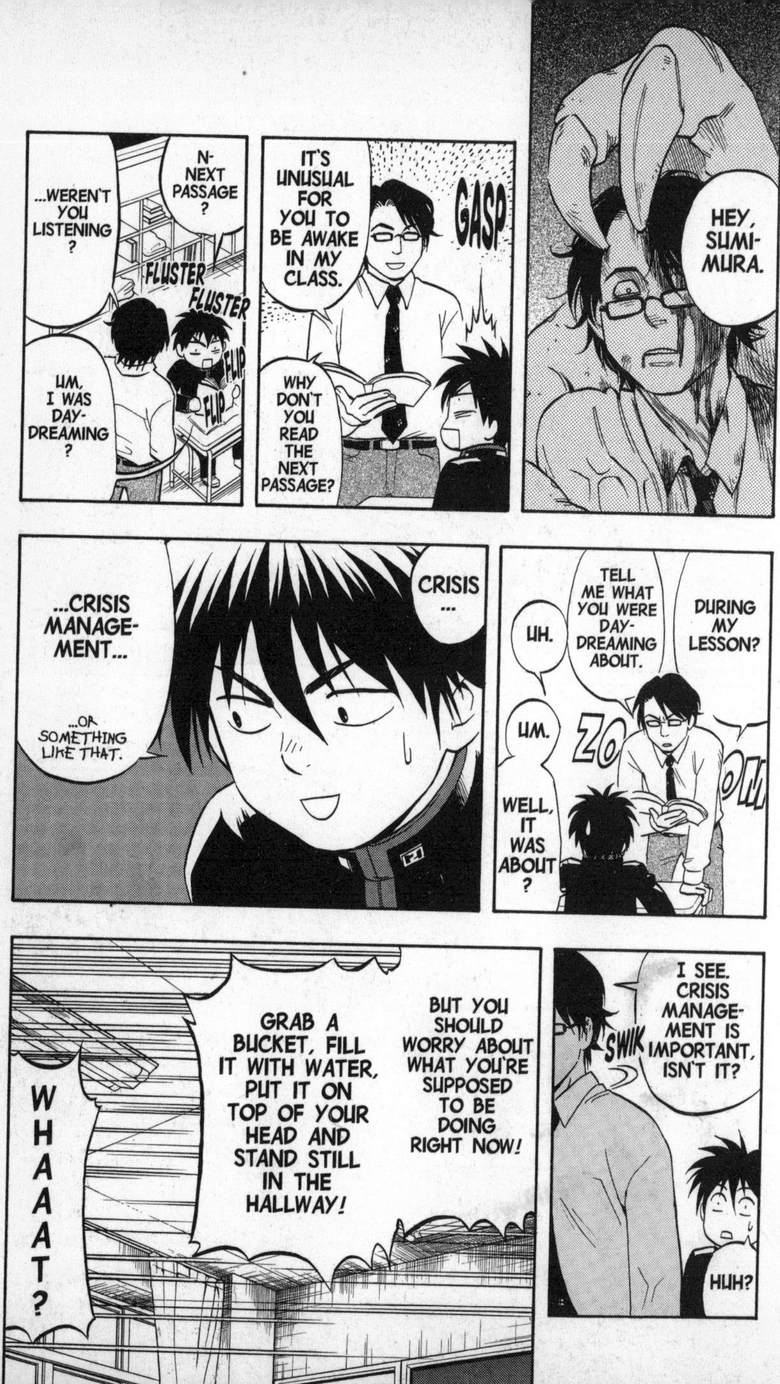
HEY, SUMIMURA.
GASP
IT'S UNUSUAL FOR YOU TO BE AWAKE IN MY CLASS.
WHY DON'T YOU READ THE NEXT PASSAGE?
N-NEXT PASSAGE?
FLUSTER
FLUSTER
...WEREN'T YOU LISTENING?
FLIP
FLIP
UM, I WAS DAY-DREAMING?
DURING MY LESSON?
TELL ME WHAT YOU WERE DAY-DREAMING ABOUT.
UH.
ZOOM
UM.
WELL, IT WAS ABOUT?
CRISIS...
...CRISIS MANAGEMENT...
...OR SOMETHING LIKE THAT.
I SEE. CRISIS MANAGEMENT IS IMPORTANT, ISN'T IT?
SWIK
HUH?
BUT YOU SHOULD WORRY ABOUT WHAT YOU'RE SUPPOSED TO BE DOING RIGHT NOW!
GRAB A BUCKET, FILL IT WITH WATER, PUT IT ON TOP OF YOUR HEAD AND STAND STILL IN THE HALLWAY!
WHAAAT?

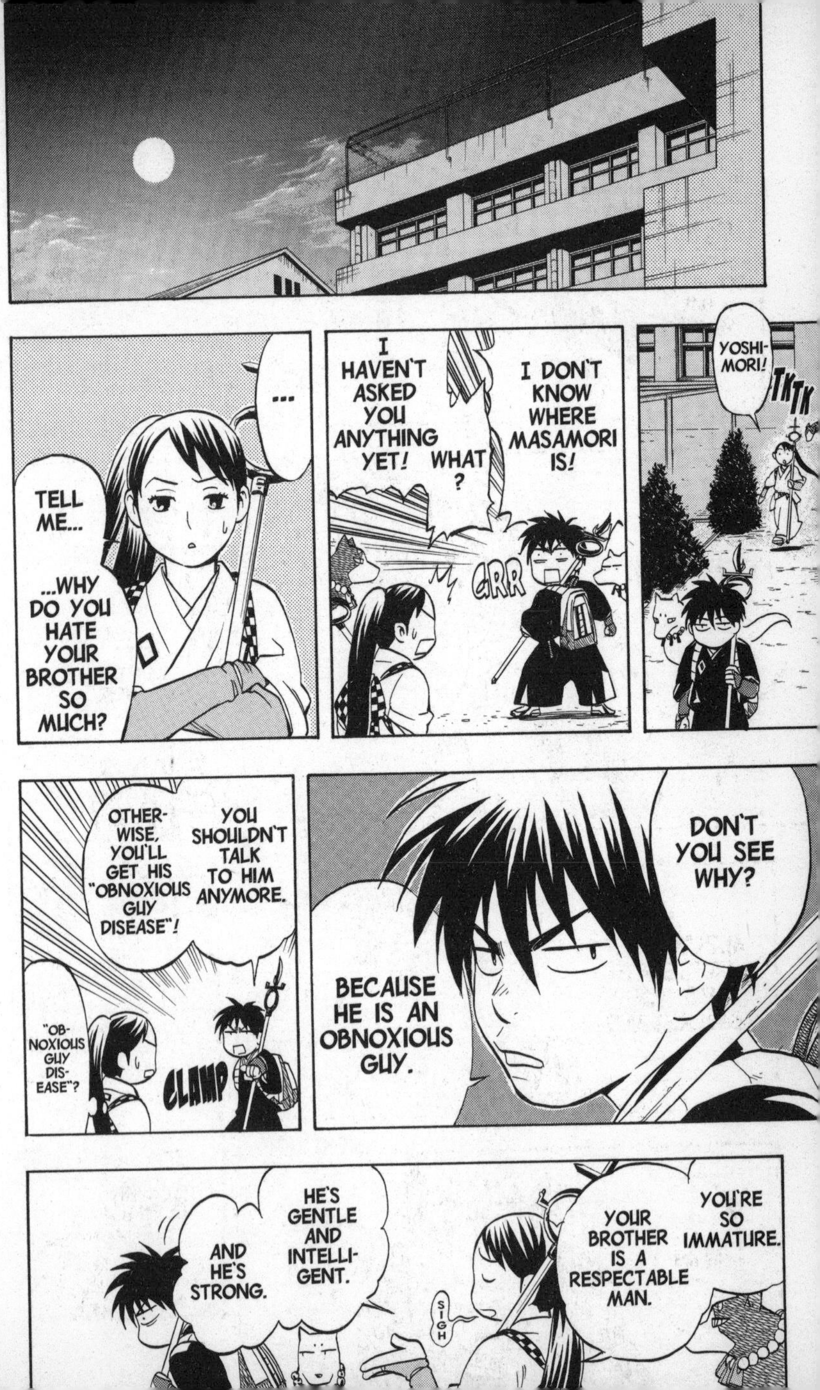
YOSHIMORI!
TKTK
I DON'T KNOW WHERE MASAMORI IS!
WHAT?
I HAVEN'T ASKED YOU ANYTHING YET!
GRR
...
TELL ME...
...WHY DO YOU HATE YOUR BROTHER SO MUCH?
DON'T YOU SEE WHY?
BECAUSE HE IS AN OBNOXIOUS GUY.
YOU SHOULDN'T TALK TO HIM ANYMORE.
OTHERWISE, YOU'LL GET HIS "OBNOXIOUS GUY DISEASE"!
CLAMP
"OBNOXIOUS GUY DISEASE"?
YOU'RE SO IMMATURE.
YOUR BROTHER IS A RESPECTABLE MAN.
SIGH
HE'S GENTLE AND INTELLIGENT.
AND HE'S STRONG.

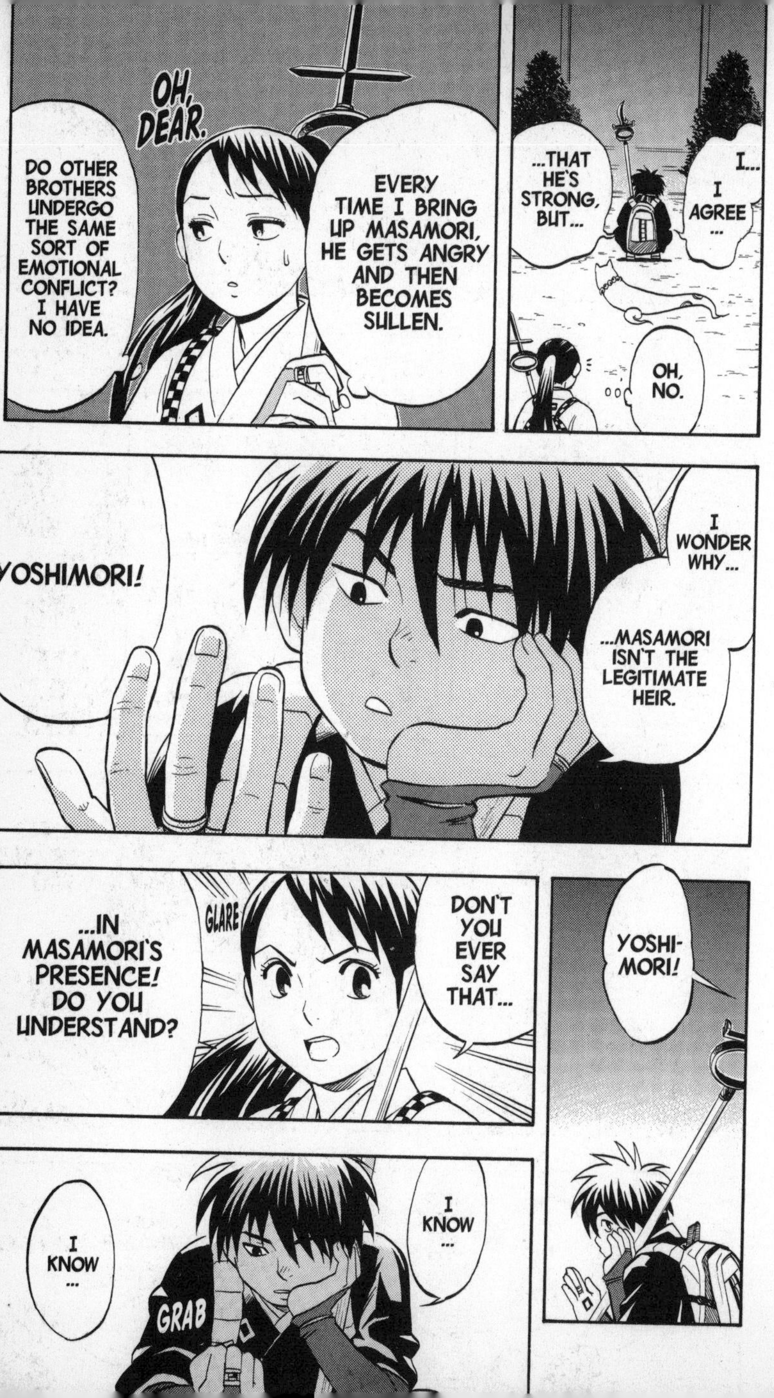
I... I AGREE...
...THAT HE'S STRONG, BUT...
OH, NO.
OH, DEAR.
EVERY TIME I BRING UP MASAMORI, HE GETS ANGRY AND THEN BECOMES SULLEN.
DO OTHER BROTHERS UNDERGO THE SAME SORT OF EMOTIONAL CONFLICT? I HAVE NO IDEA.
I WONDER WHY...
...MASAMORI ISN'T THE LEGITIMATE HEIR.
YOSHIMORI!
YOSHI-MORI!
DON'T YOU EVER SAY THAT...
GLARE
...IN MASAMORI'S PRESENCE! DO YOU UNDERSTAND?
I KNOW...
I KNOW...
GRAB

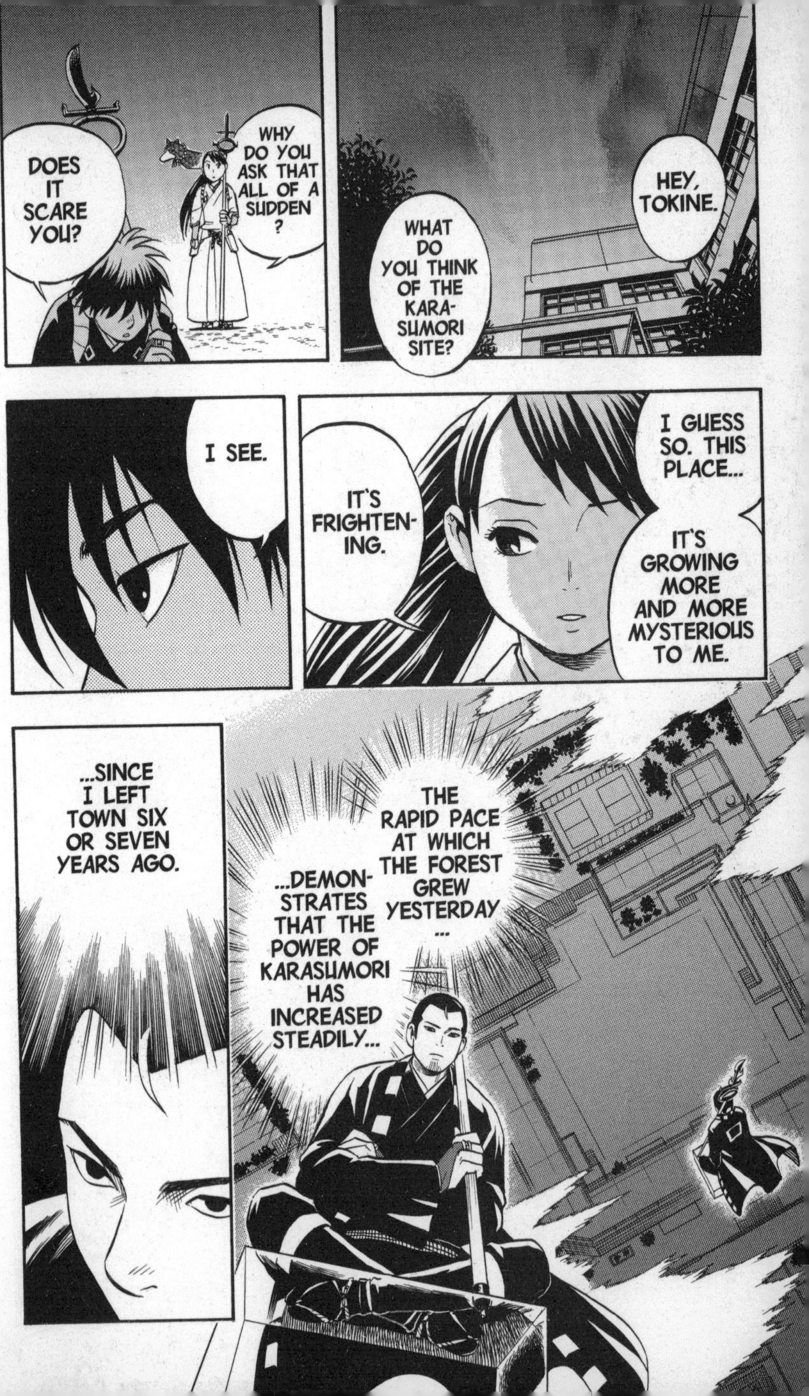
HEY, TOKINE.
WHAT DO YOU THINK OF THE KARA-SUMORI SITE?
WHY DO YOU ASK THAT ALL OF A SUDDEN?
DOES IT SCARE YOU?
I GUESS SO. THIS PLACE...
IT'S GROWING MORE AND MORE MYSTERIOUS TO ME.
IT'S FRIGHTEN-ING.
I SEE.
THE RAPID PACE AT WHICH THE FOREST GREW YESTERDAY...
...DEMON-STRATES THAT THE POWER OF KARASUMORI HAS INCREASED STEADILY...
...SINCE I LEFT TOWN SIX OR SEVEN YEARS AGO.

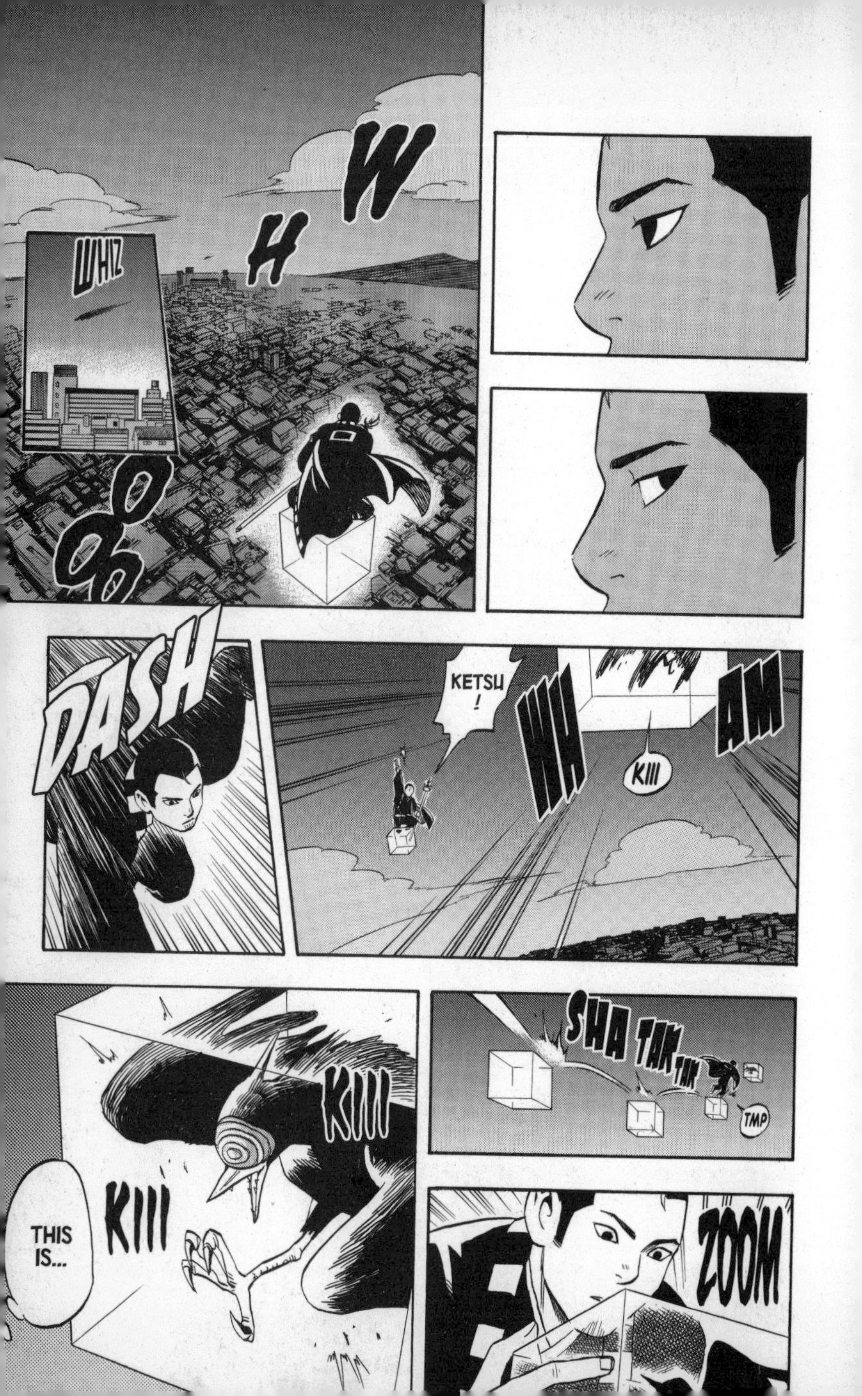

WHOO
WHIZ
KETSU!
WH AM
KIII
DASH
SHA
TAK TAK
TMP
ZOOM
KIII
KIII
THIS IS...

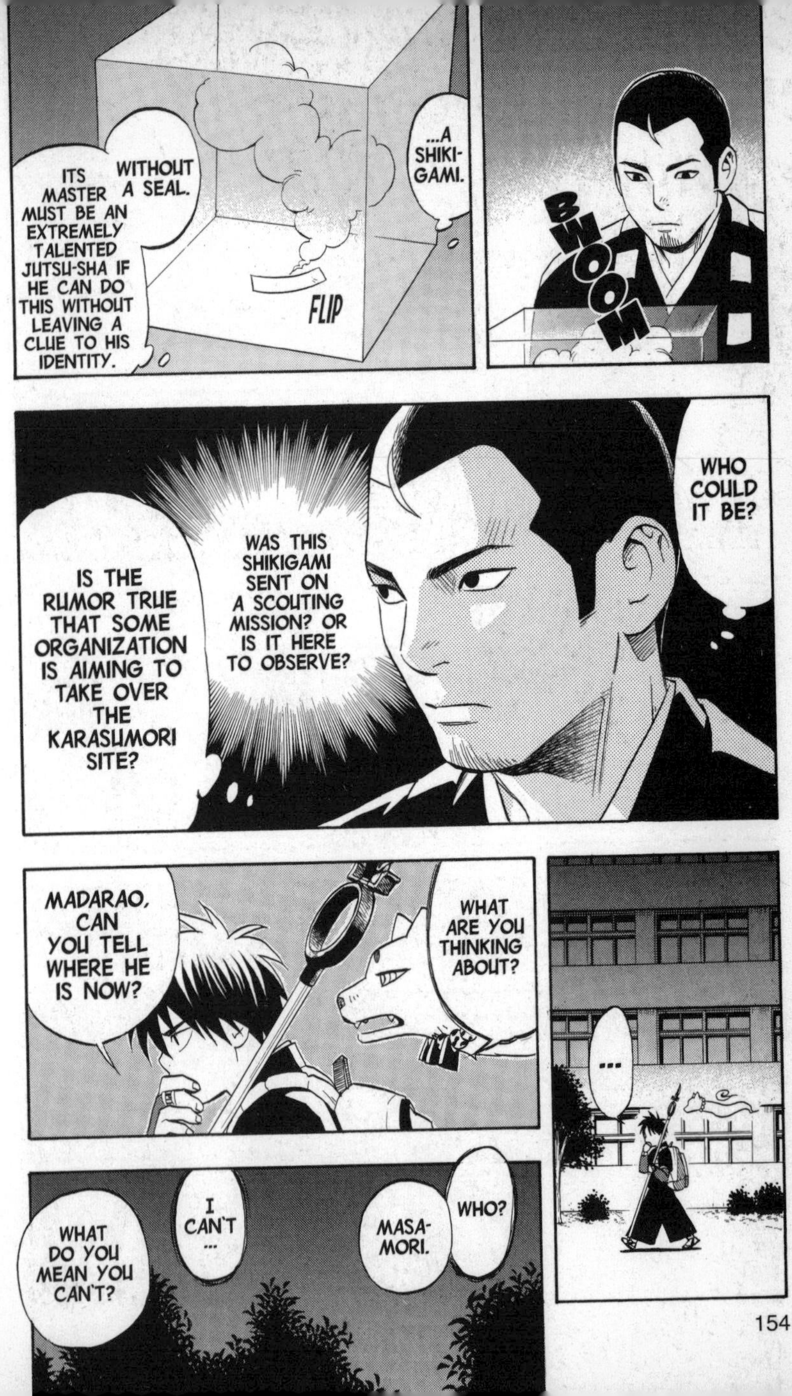
BWOOM
...A SHIKI-GAMI.
WITHOUT A SEAL.
ITS MASTER MUST BE AN EXTREMELY TALENTED JUTSU-SHA IF HE CAN DO THIS WITHOUT LEAVING A CLUE TO HIS IDENTITY.
FLIP
WHO COULD IT BE?
WAS THIS SHIKIGAMI SENT ON A SCOUTING MISSION? OR IS IT HERE TO OBSERVE?
IS THE RUMOR TRUE THAT SOME ORGANIZATION IS AIMING TO TAKE OVER THE KARASUMORI SITE?
...
WHAT ARE YOU THINKING ABOUT?
MADARAO, CAN YOU TELL WHERE HE IS NOW?
WHO?
MASA-MORI.
I CAN'T ...
WHAT DO YOU MEAN YOU CAN'T?

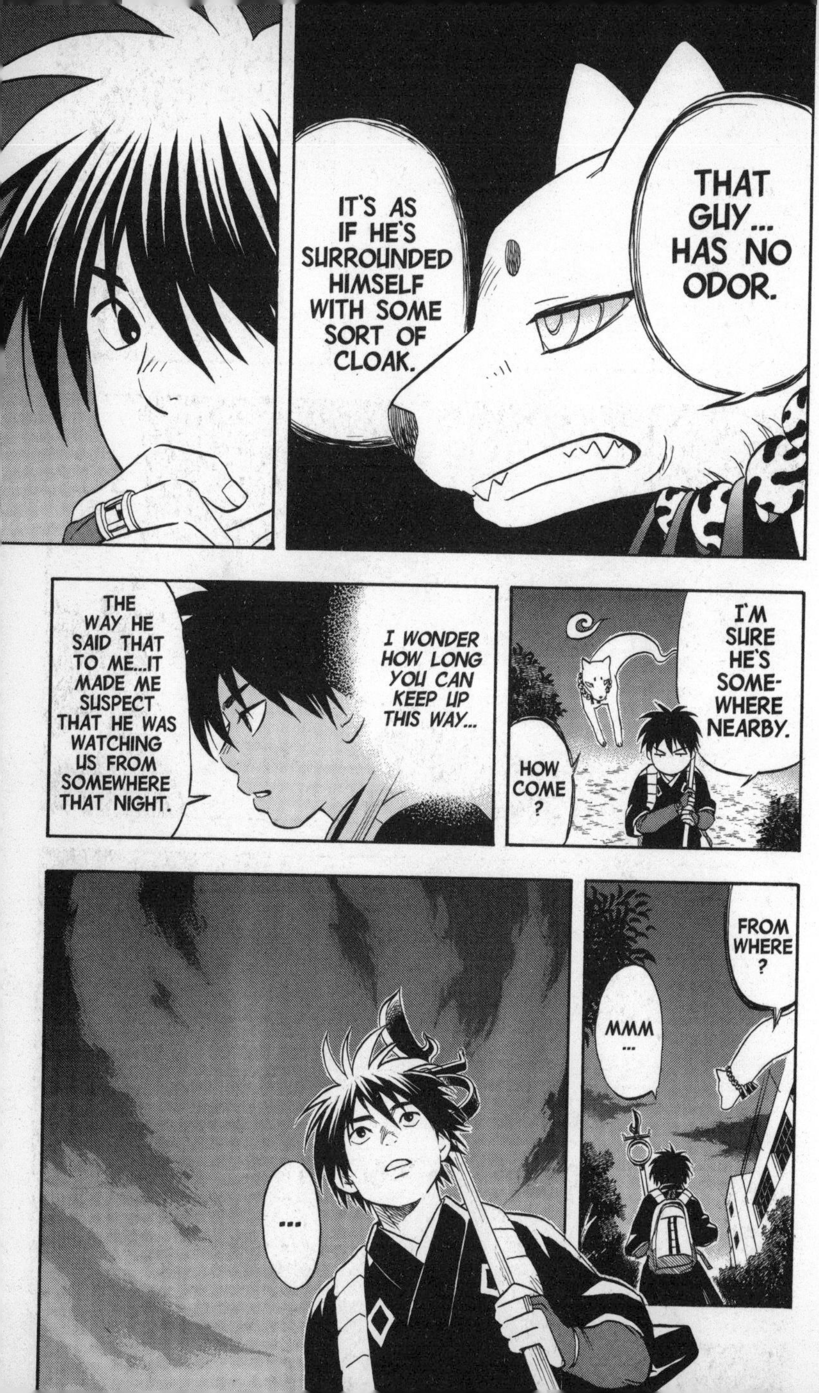
THAT GUY... HAS NO ODOR.
IT'S AS IF HE'S SURROUNDED HIMSELF WITH SOME SORT OF CLOAK.
I'M SURE HE'S SOME-WHERE NEARBY.
HOW COME?
I WONDER HOW LONG YOU CAN KEEP UP THIS WAY...
THE WAY HE SAID THAT TO ME...IT MADE ME SUSPECT THAT HE WAS WATCHING US FROM SOMEWHERE THAT NIGHT.
FROM WHERE?
MMM...
...

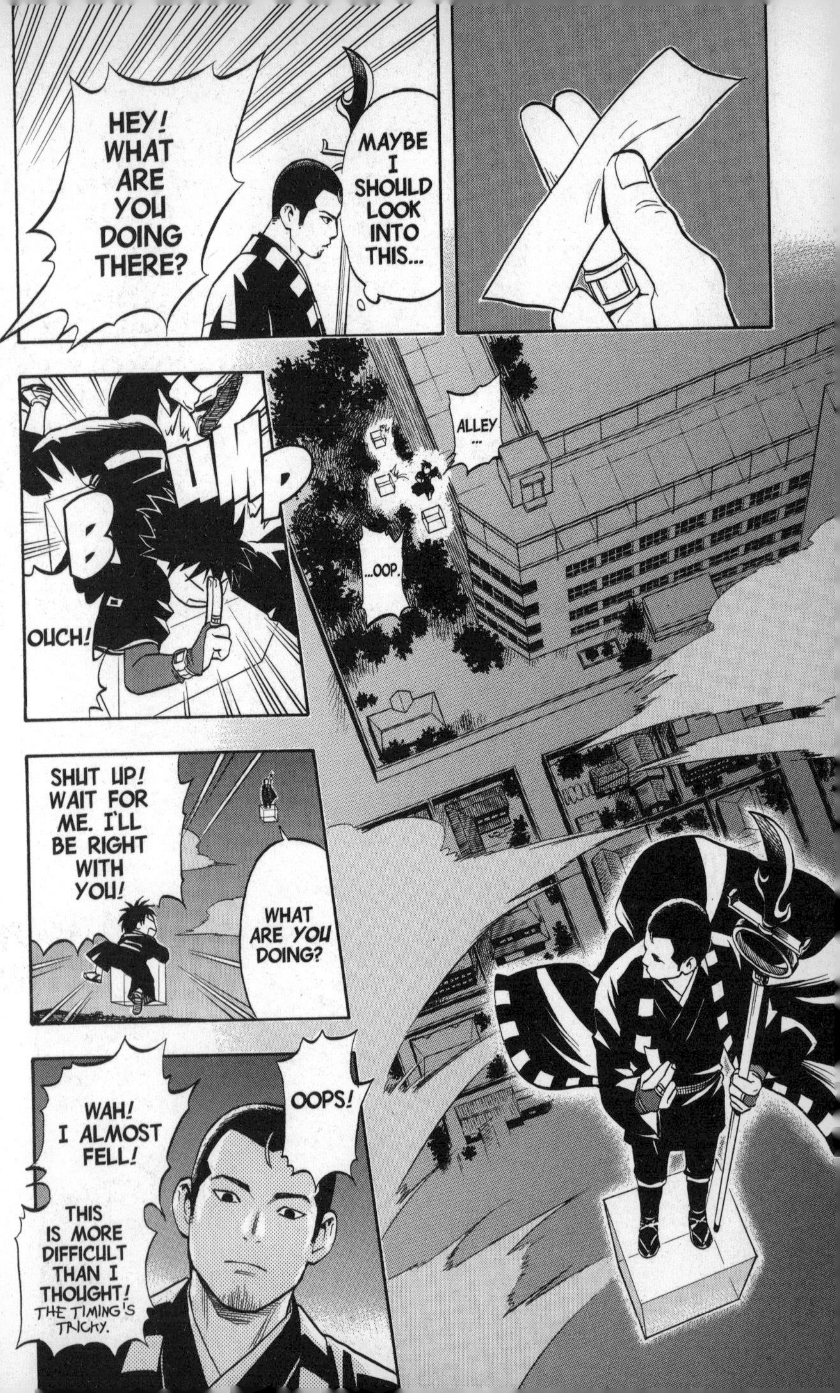
MAYBE I SHOULD LOOK INTO THIS...
HEY! WHAT ARE YOU DOING THERE?
ALLEY ...
...OOP.
BUMP
OUCH!
WHAT ARE YOU DOING?
SHUT UP! WAIT FOR ME. I'LL BE RIGHT WITH YOU!
OOPS!
WAH! I ALMOST FELL!
THIS IS MORE DIFFICULT THAN I THOUGHT!
THE TIMING'S TRICKY.

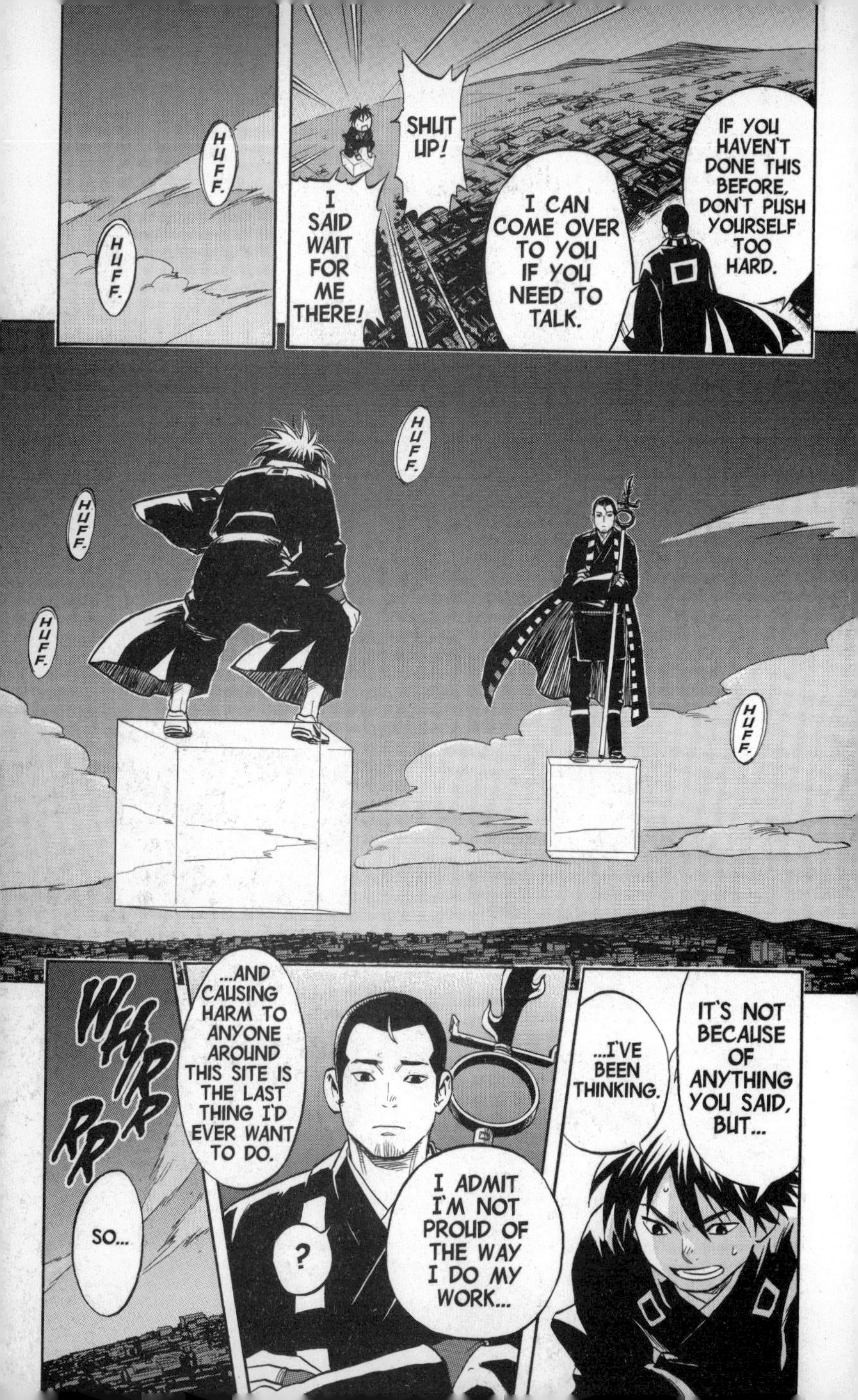
IF YOU HAVEN'T DONE THIS BEFORE, DON'T PUSH YOURSELF TOO HARD.
I CAN COME OVER TO YOU IF YOU NEED TO TALK.
SHUT UP!
I SAID WAIT FOR ME THERE!
HUFF.
HUFF.
HUFF.
HUFF.
HUFF.
HUFF.
IT'S NOT BECAUSE OF ANYTHING YOU SAID, BUT...
...I'VE BEEN THINKING.
I ADMIT I'M NOT PROUD OF THE WAY I DO MY WORK...
...AND CAUSING HARM TO ANYONE AROUND THIS SITE IS THE LAST THING I'D EVER WANT TO DO.
?
WHIRRR
SO...

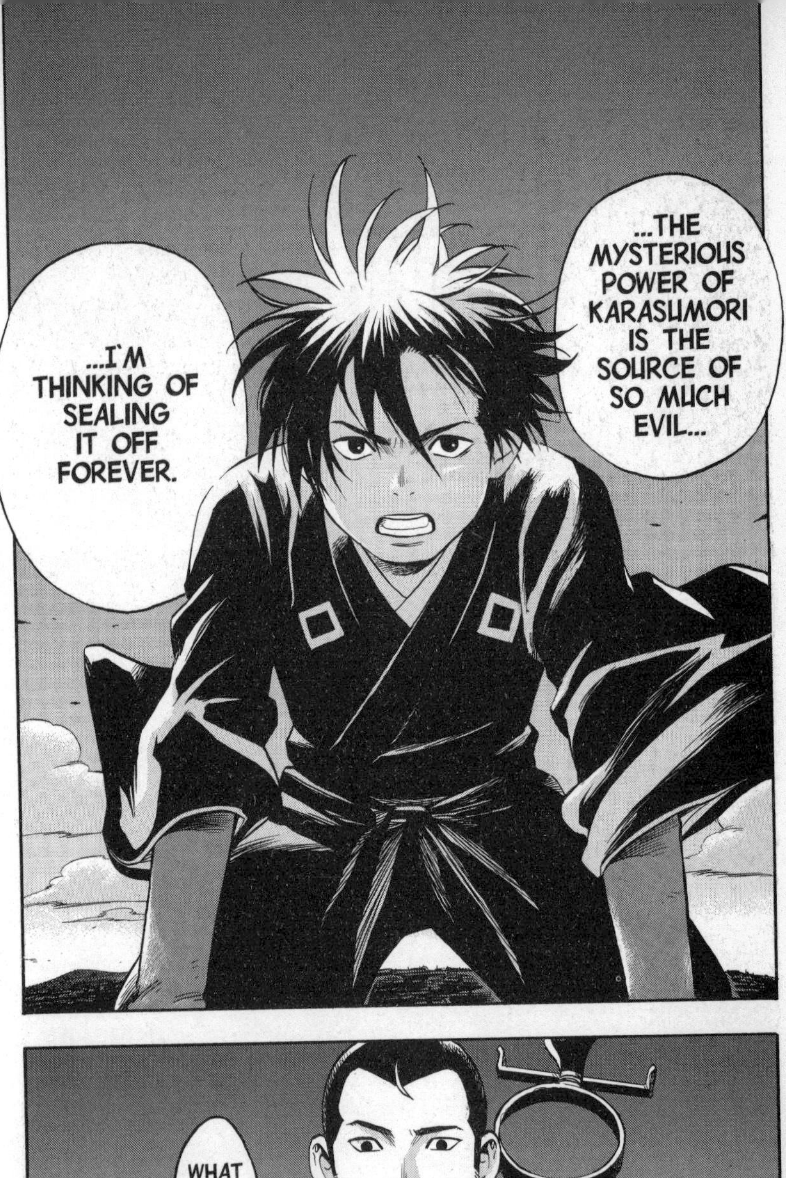
...THE MYSTERIOUS POWER OF KARASUMORI IS THE SOURCE OF SO MUCH EVIL...
...I'M THINKING OF SEALING IT OFF FOREVER.
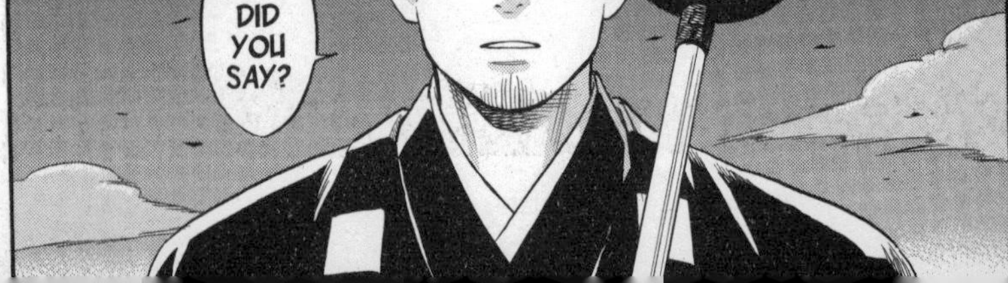
WHAT DID YOU SAY?

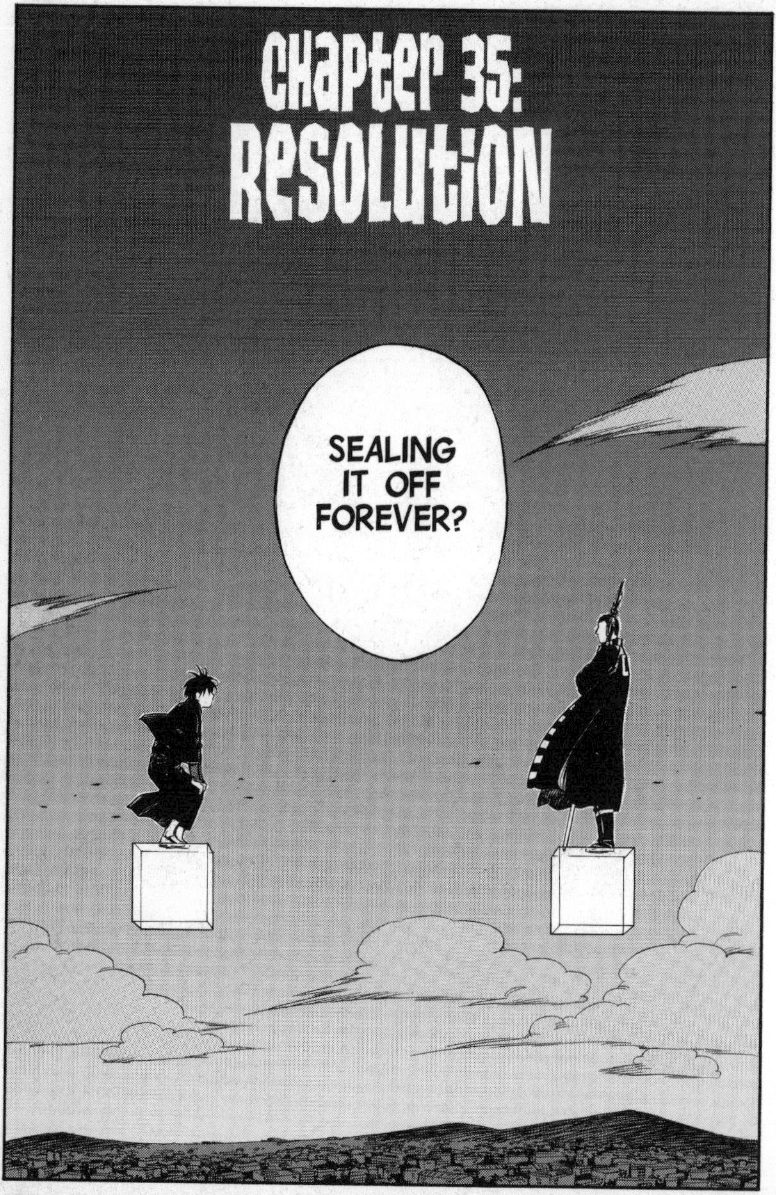
Chapter 35:
Resolution
SEALING IT OFF FOREVER?

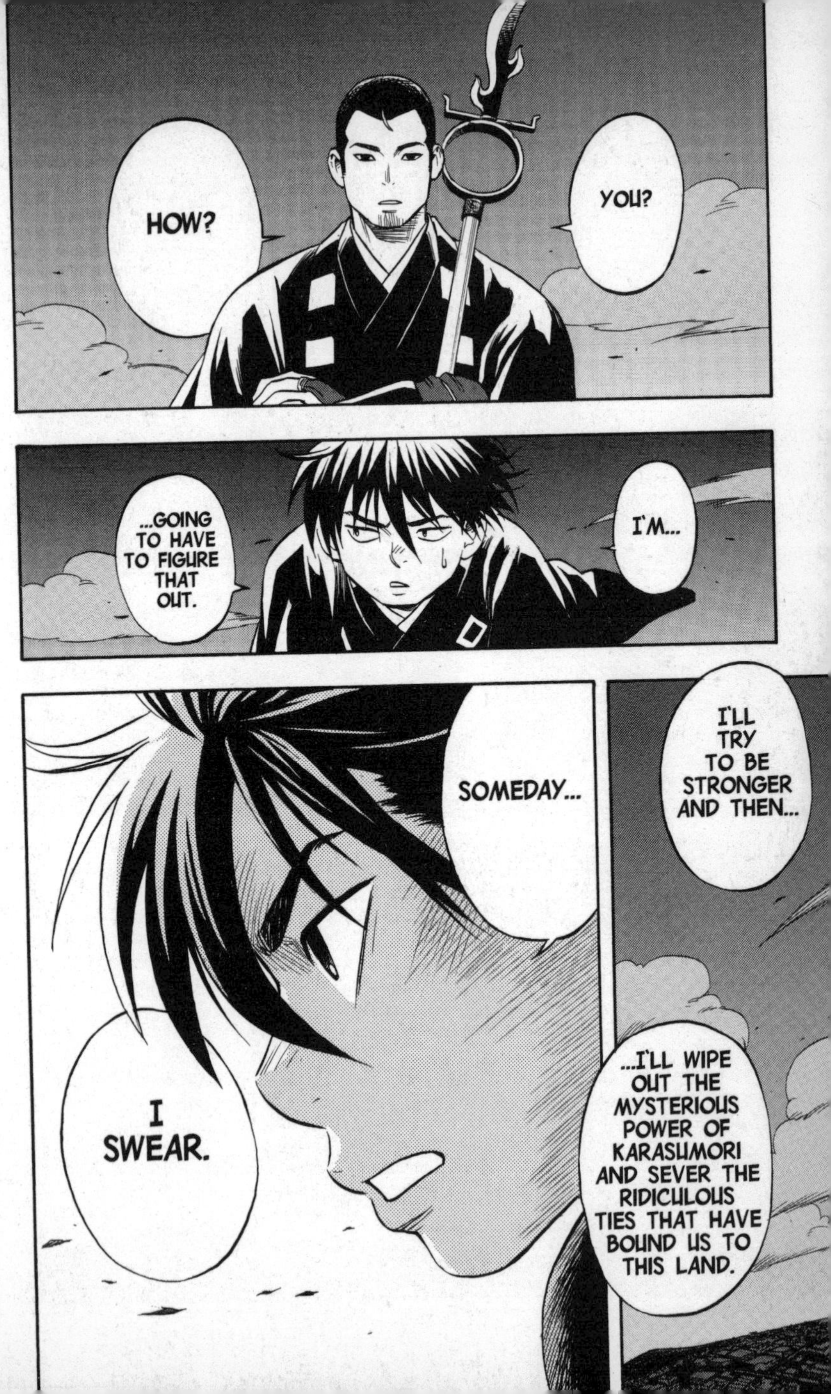
YOU?
HOW?
I'M...
...GOING TO HAVE TO FIGURE THAT OUT.
I'LL TRY TO BE STRONGER AND THEN...
...I'LL WIPE OUT THE MYSTERIOUS POWER OF KARASUMORI AND SEVER THE RIDICULOUS TIES THAT HAVE BOUND US TO THIS LAND.
SOMEDAY...
I SWEAR.

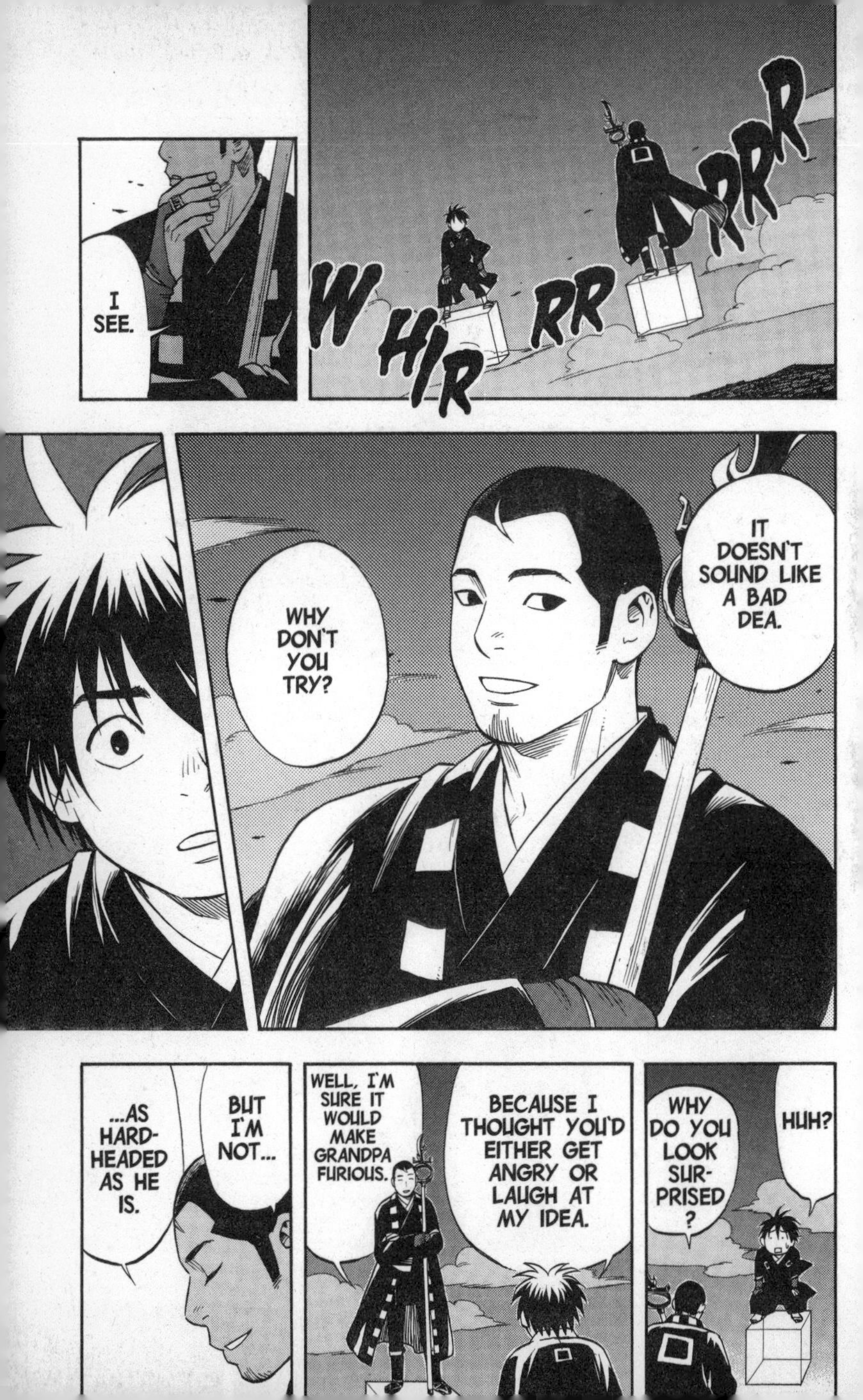
WHIRRRRRR
I SEE.
IT DOESN'T SOUND LIKE A BAD DEA.
WHY DON'T YOU TRY?
HUH?
WHY DO YOU LOOK SUR-PRISED?
BECAUSE I THOUGHT YOU'D EITHER GET ANGRY OR LAUGH AT MY IDEA.
WELL, I'M SURE IT WOULD MAKE GRANDPA FURIOUS.
BUT I'M NOT...
...AS HARD-HEADED AS HE IS.

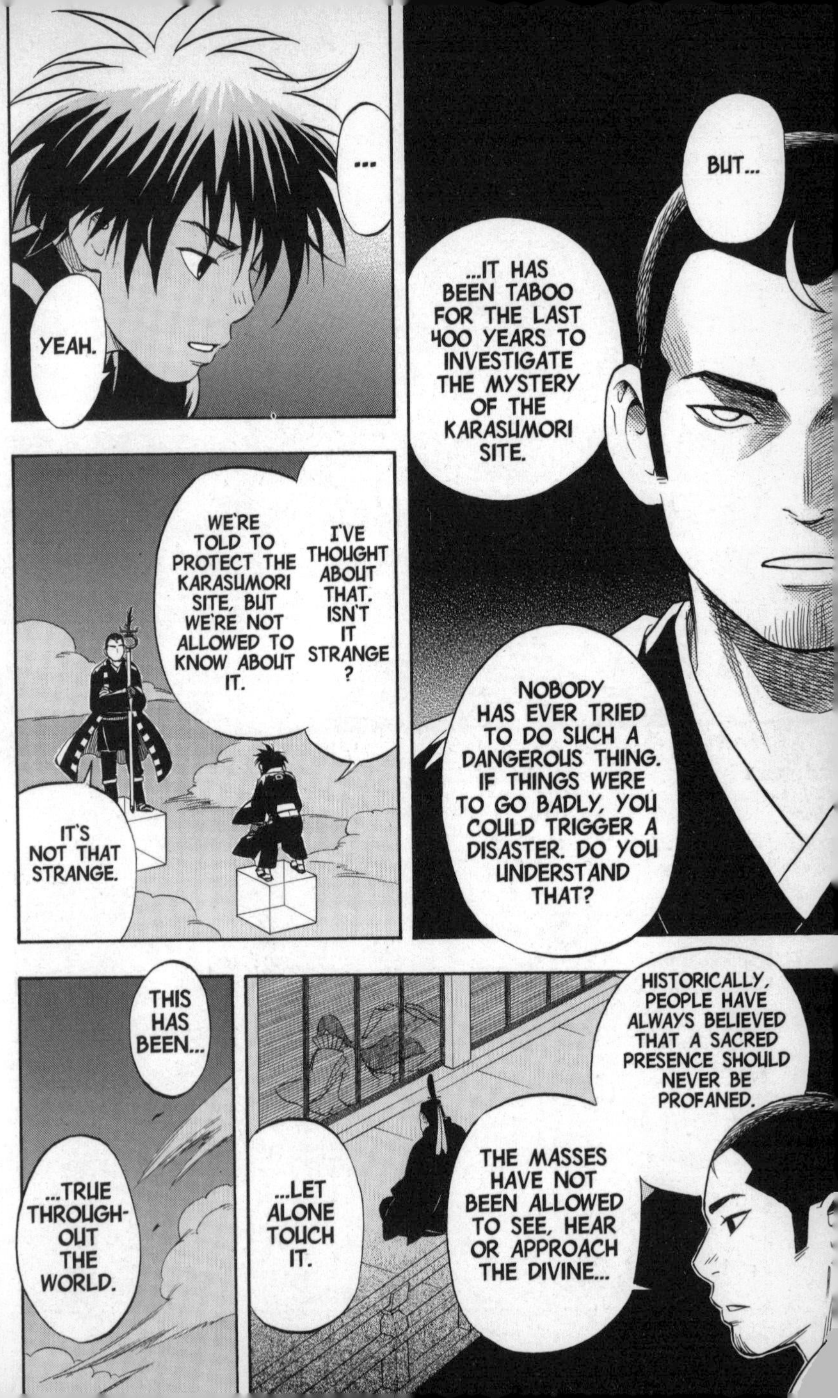
BUT...
...IT HAS BEEN TABOO FOR THE LAST 400 YEARS TO INVESTIGATE THE MYSTERY OF THE KARASUMORI SITE.
NOBODY HAS EVER TRIED TO DO SUCH A DANGEROUS THING. IF THINGS WERE TO GO BADLY, YOU COULD TRIGGER A DISASTER. DO YOU UNDERSTAND THAT?
...
YEAH.
I'VE THOUGHT ABOUT THAT. ISN'T IT STRANGE?
WE'RE TOLD TO PROTECT THE KARASUMORI SITE, BUT WE'RE NOT ALLOWED TO KNOW ABOUT IT.
IT'S NOT THAT STRANGE.
HISTORICALLY, PEOPLE HAVE ALWAYS BELIEVED THAT A SACRED PRESENCE SHOULD NEVER BE PROFANED.
THE MASSES HAVE NOT BEEN ALLOWED TO SEE, HEAR OR APPROACH THE DIVINE...
...LET ALONE TOUCH IT.
THIS HAS BEEN...
...TRUE THROUGHOUT THE WORLD.

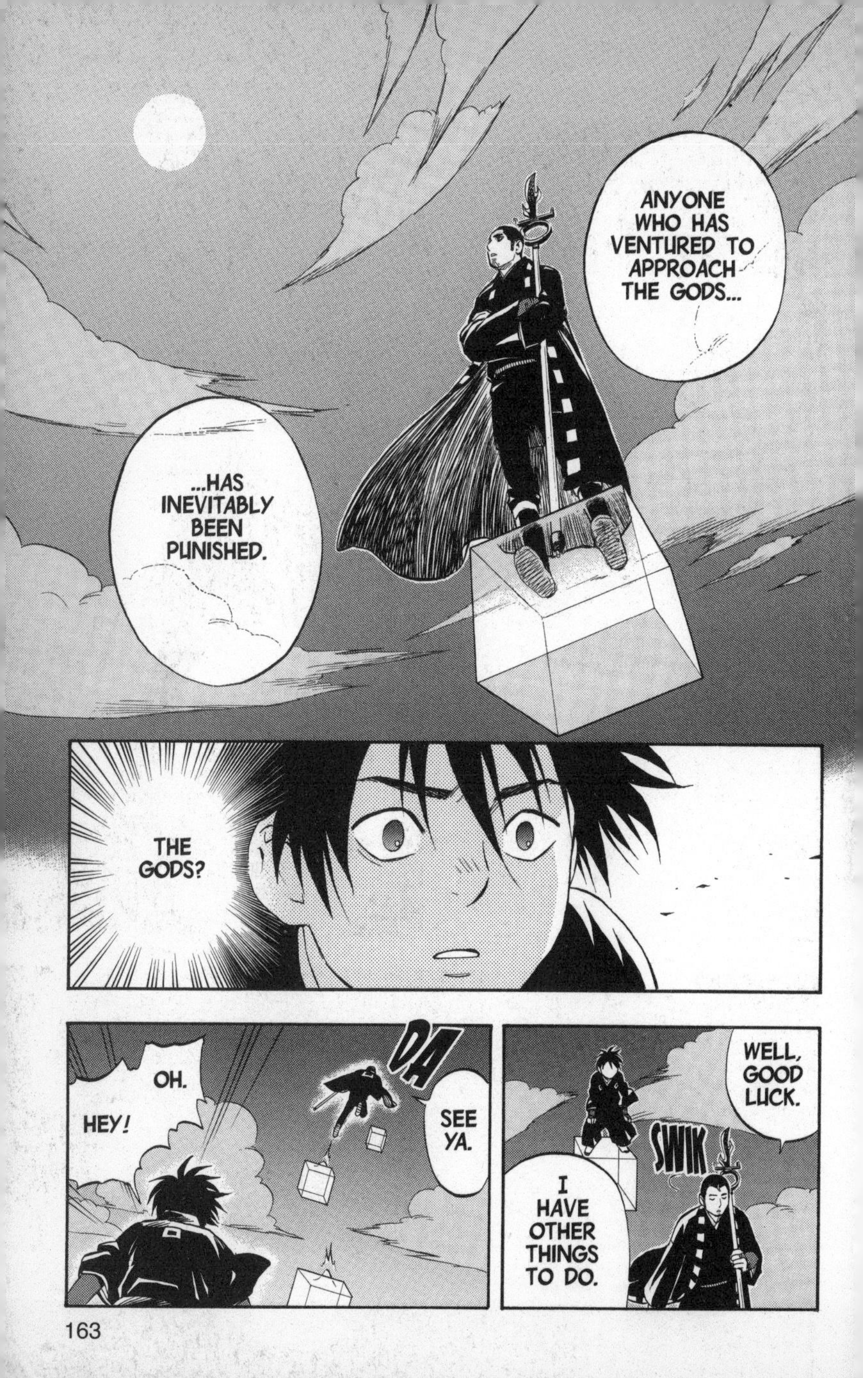
ANYONE WHO HAS VENTURED TO APPROACH THE GODS...
...HAS INEVITABLY BEEN PUNISHED.
THE GODS?
WELL, GOOD LUCK.
SWIK
I HAVE OTHER THINGS TO DO.
DA
SEE YA.
OH.
HEY!

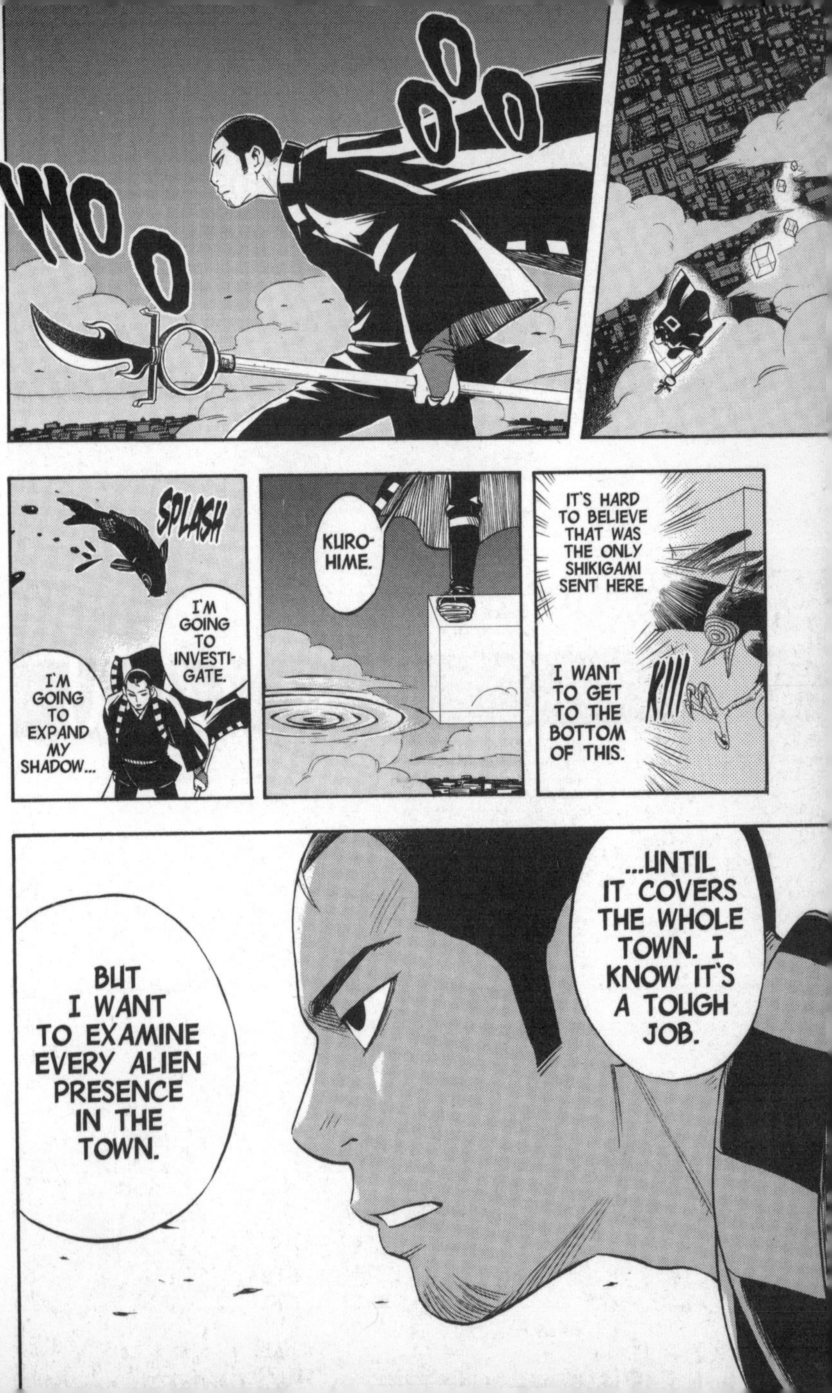
WOOOOOO
IT'S HARD TO BELIEVE THAT WAS THE ONLY SHIKIGAMI SENT HERE.
I WANT TO GET TO THE BOTTOM OF THIS.
KIII
KURO-HIME.
SPLASH
I'M GOING TO INVESTI-GATE.
I'M GOING TO EXPAND MY SHADOW...
...UNTIL IT COVERS THE WHOLE TOWN. I KNOW IT'S A TOUGH JOB.
BUT I WANT TO EXAMINE EVERY ALIEN PRESENCE IN THE TOWN.

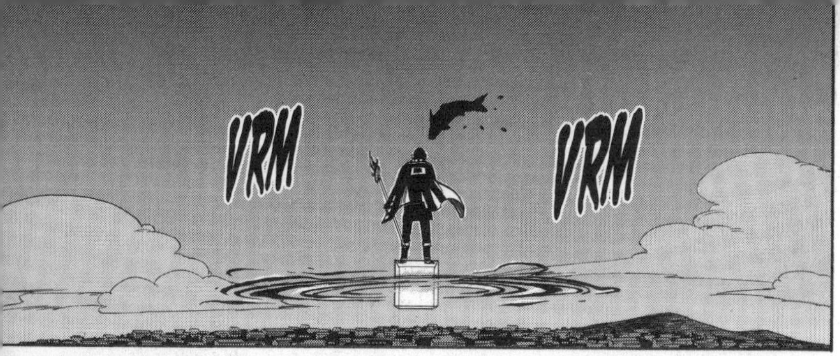
VRM
VRM
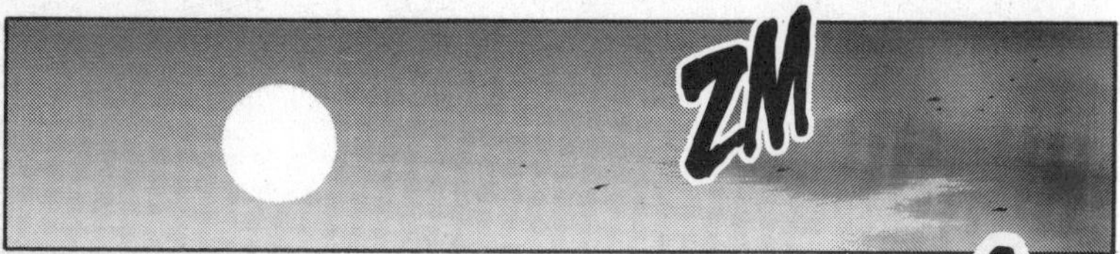
ZM
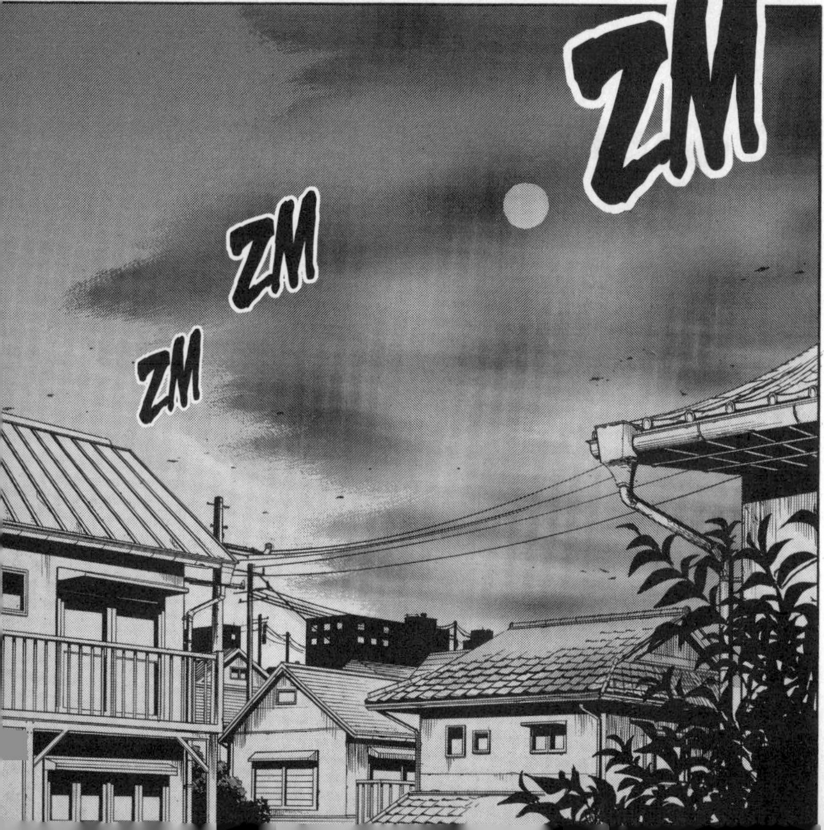
ZM
ZM
ZM

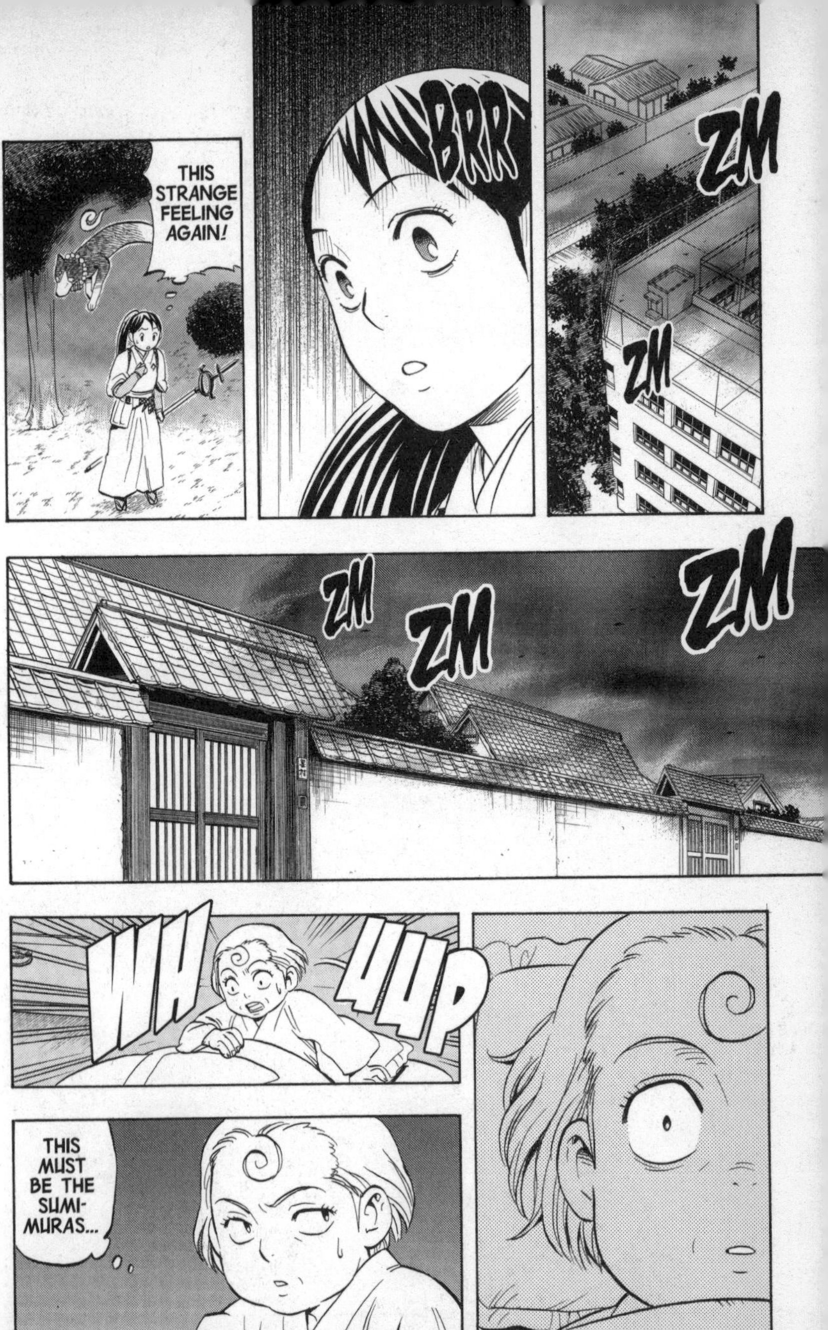
ZM
ZM
BRR
THIS STRANGE FEELING AGAIN!
ZM
ZM
ZM
WH UUP
THIS MUST BE THE SUMI-MURAS...

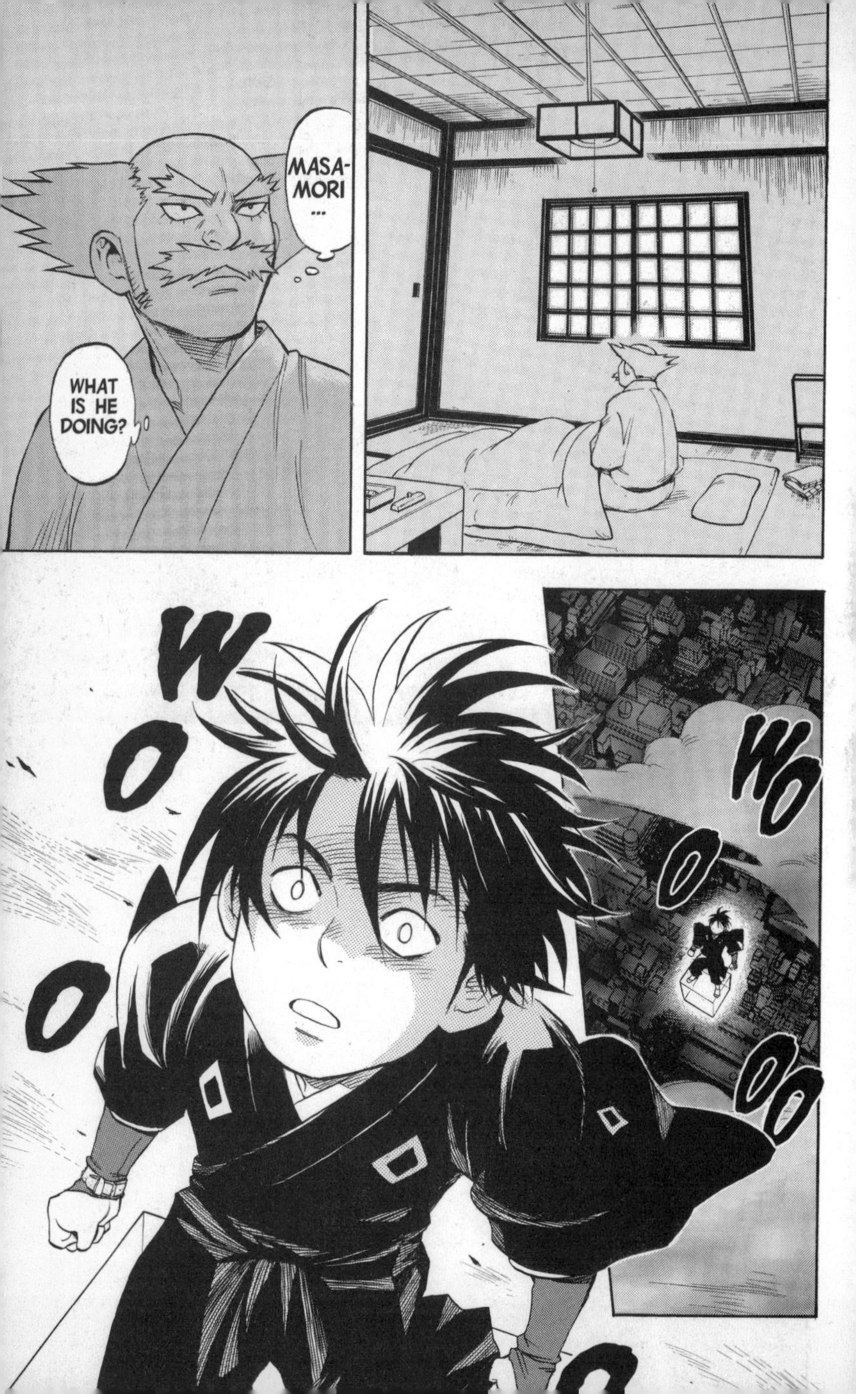
MASA-MORI ...
WHAT IS HE DOING?
WOOOO
WOOO

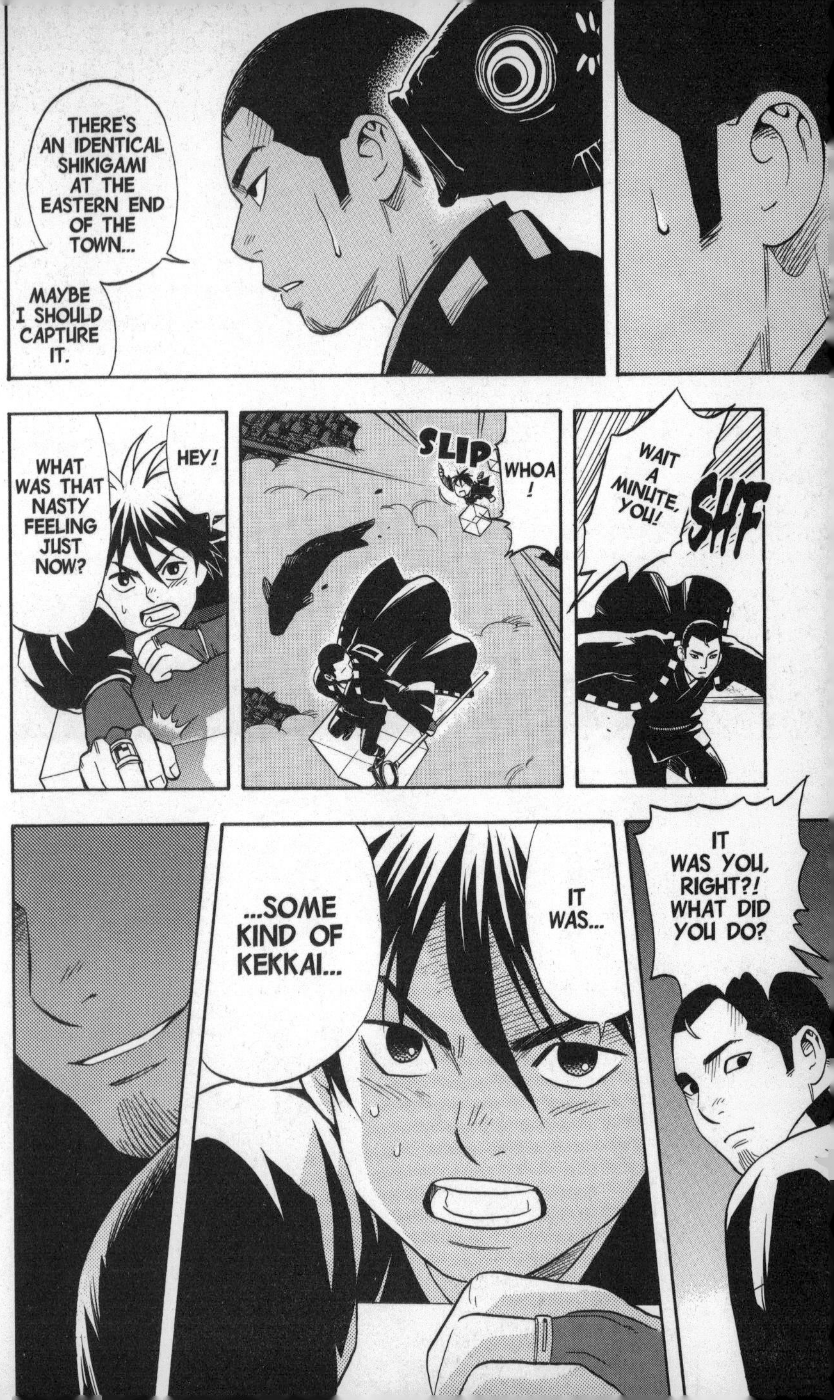
THERE'S AN IDENTICAL SHIKIGAMI AT THE EASTERN END OF THE TOWN...
MAYBE I SHOULD CAPTURE IT.
WAIT A MINUTE, YOU!
SHF
SLIP
WHOA!
HEY!
WHAT WAS THAT NASTY FEELING JUST NOW?
IT WAS YOU, RIGHT?! WHAT DID YOU DO?
IT WAS...
...SOME KIND OF KEKKAI...

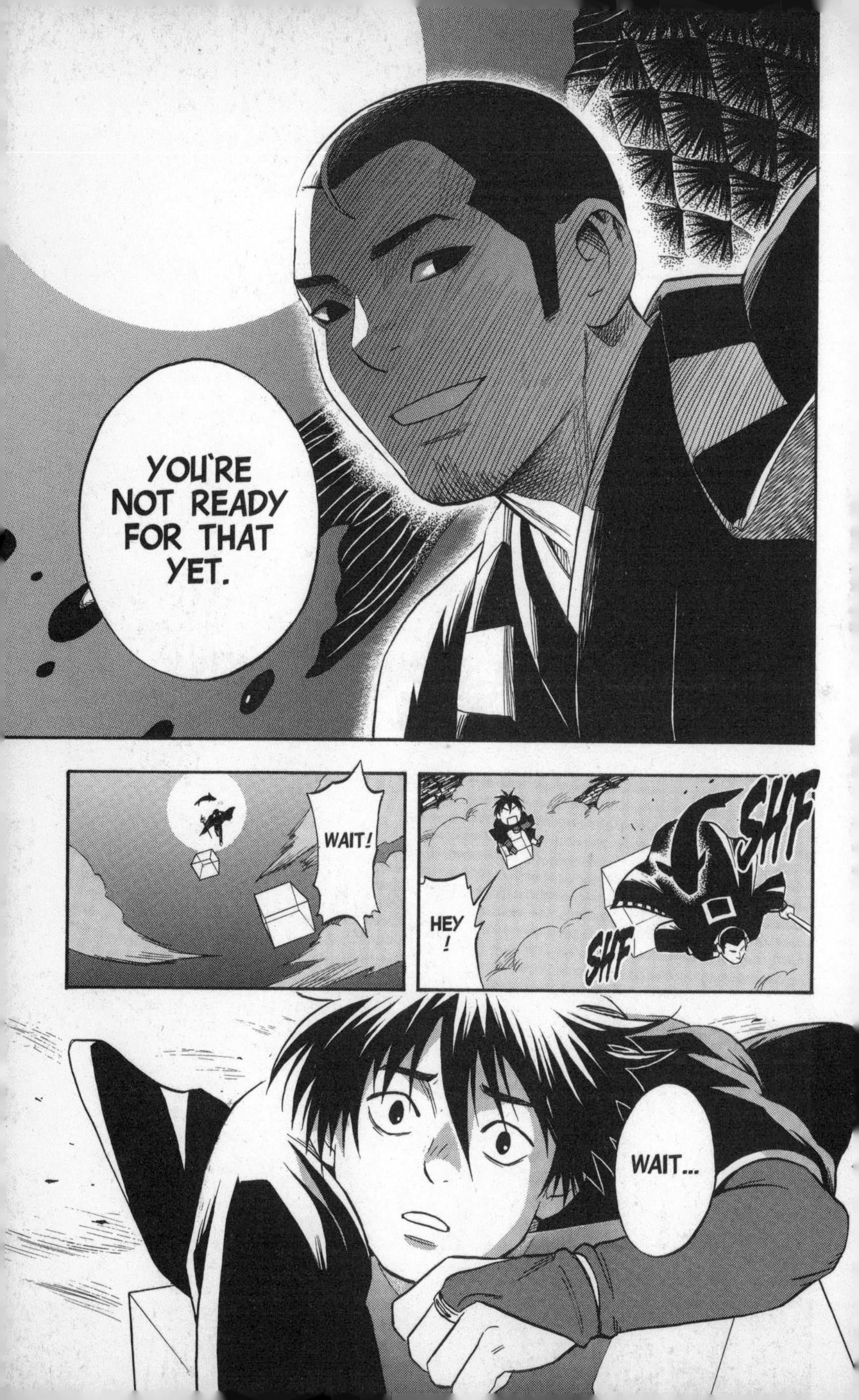
YOU'RE NOT READY FOR THAT YET.
SHF
SHF
HEY!
WAIT!
WAIT...

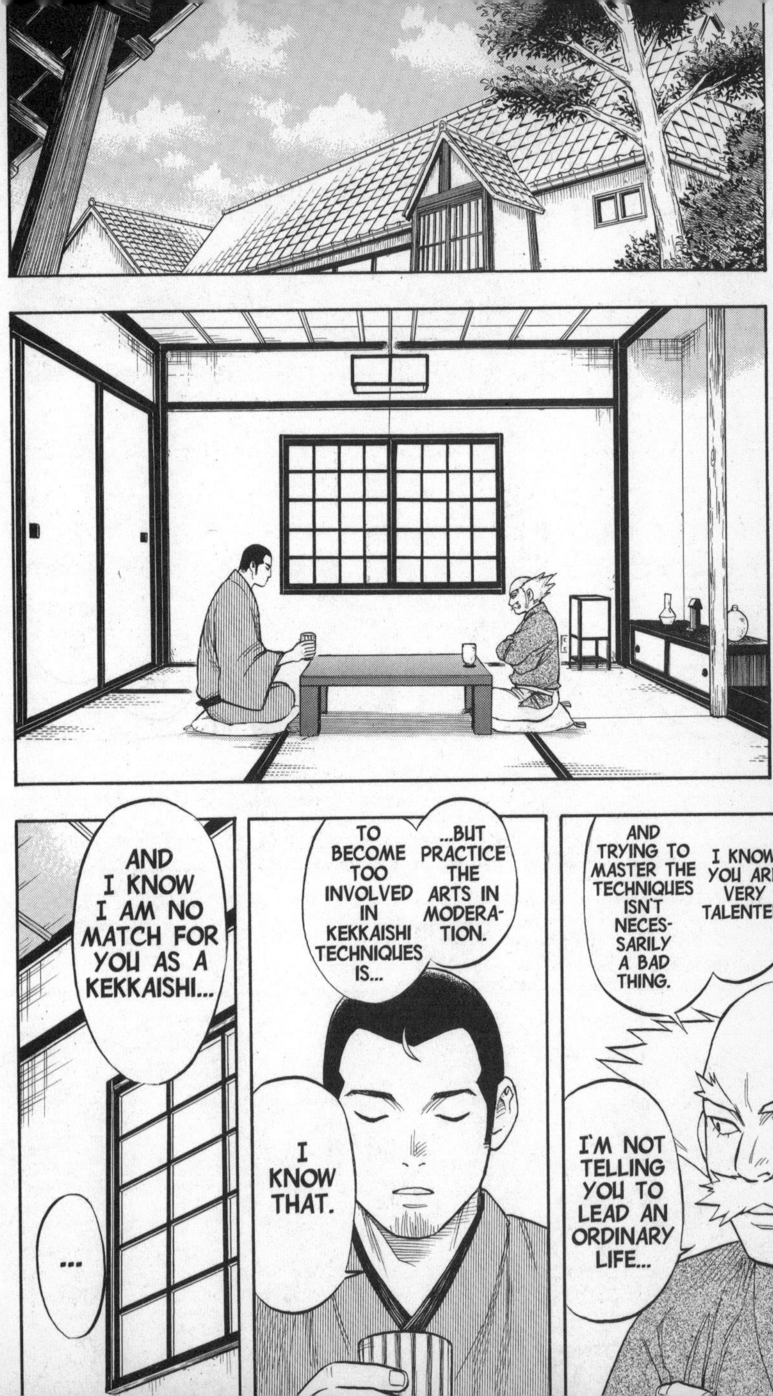
I KNOW YOU ARE VERY TALENTED.
AND TRYING TO MASTER THE TECHNIQUES ISN'T NECES-SARILY A BAD THING.
I'M NOT TELLING YOU TO LEAD AN ORDINARY LIFE...
...BUT PRACTICE THE ARTS IN MODERA-TION.
TO BECOME TOO INVOLVED IN KEKKAISHI TECHNIQUES IS...
I KNOW THAT.
AND I KNOW I AM NO MATCH FOR YOU AS A KEKKAISHI...
...

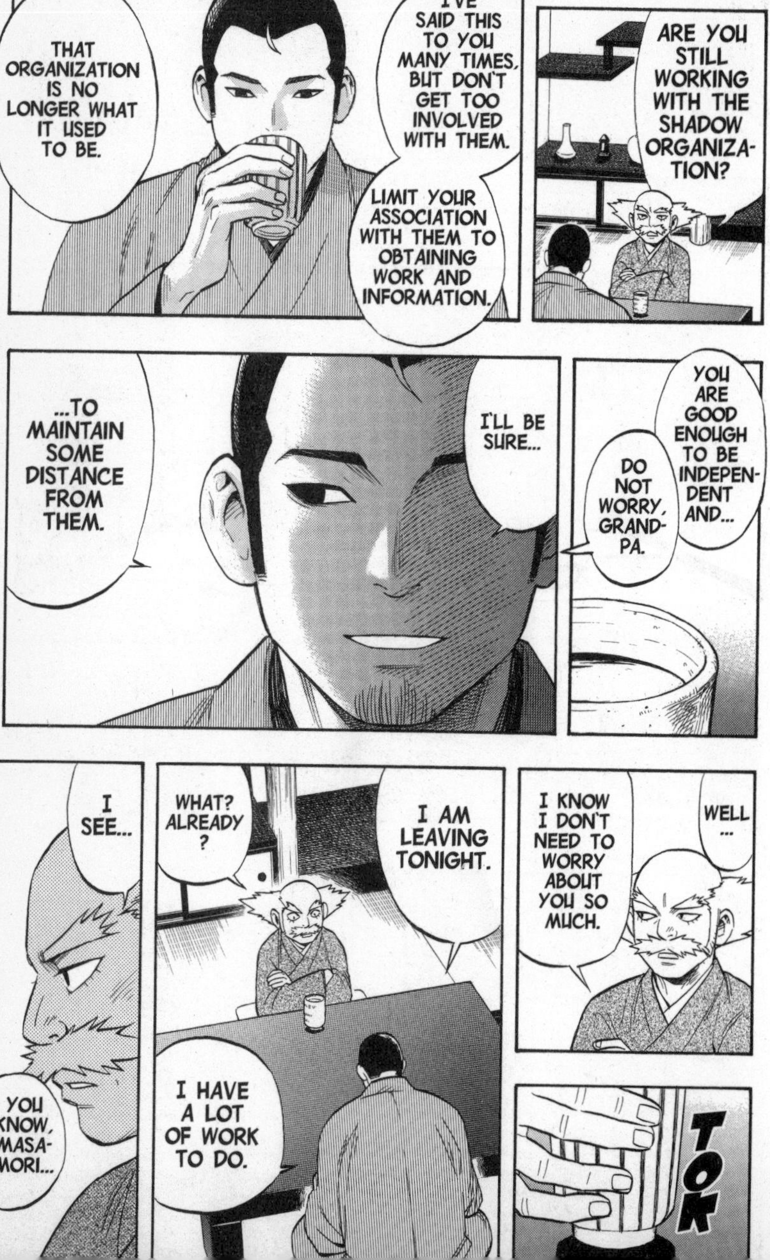
ARE YOU STILL WORKING WITH THE SHADOW ORGANIZATION?
I'VE SAID THIS TO YOU MANY TIMES, BUT DON'T GET TOO INVOLVED WITH THEM.
LIMIT YOUR ASSOCIATION WITH THEM TO OBTAINING WORK AND INFORMATION.
THAT ORGANIZATION IS NO LONGER WHAT IT USED TO BE.
YOU ARE GOOD ENOUGH TO BE INDEPENDENT AND...
DO NOT WORRY, GRANDPA.
I'LL BE SURE...
...TO MAINTAIN SOME DISTANCE FROM THEM.
WELL...
I KNOW I DON'T NEED TO WORRY ABOUT YOU SO MUCH.
TOK
I AM LEAVING TONIGHT.
WHAT? ALREADY?
I HAVE A LOT OF WORK TO DO.
I SEE...
YOU KNOW, MASAMORI...

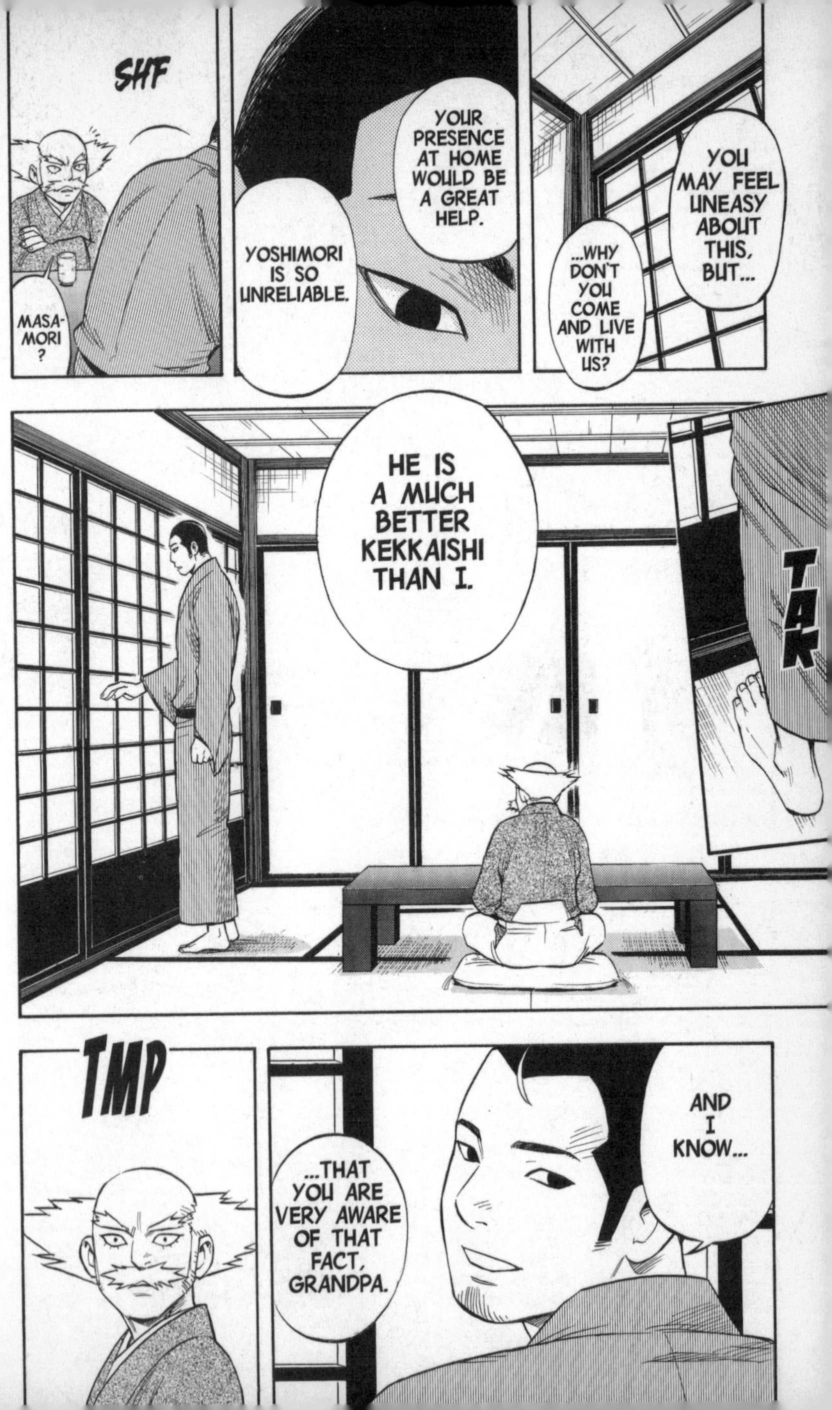
YOU MAY FEEL UNEASY ABOUT THIS, BUT...
...WHY DON'T YOU COME AND LIVE WITH US?
YOUR PRESENCE AT HOME WOULD BE A GREAT HELP.
YOSHIMORI IS SO UNRELIABLE.
SHF
MASA-MORI ?
TAK
HE IS A MUCH BETTER KEKKAISHI THAN I.
AND I KNOW...
...THAT YOU ARE VERY AWARE OF THAT FACT, GRANDPA.
TMP

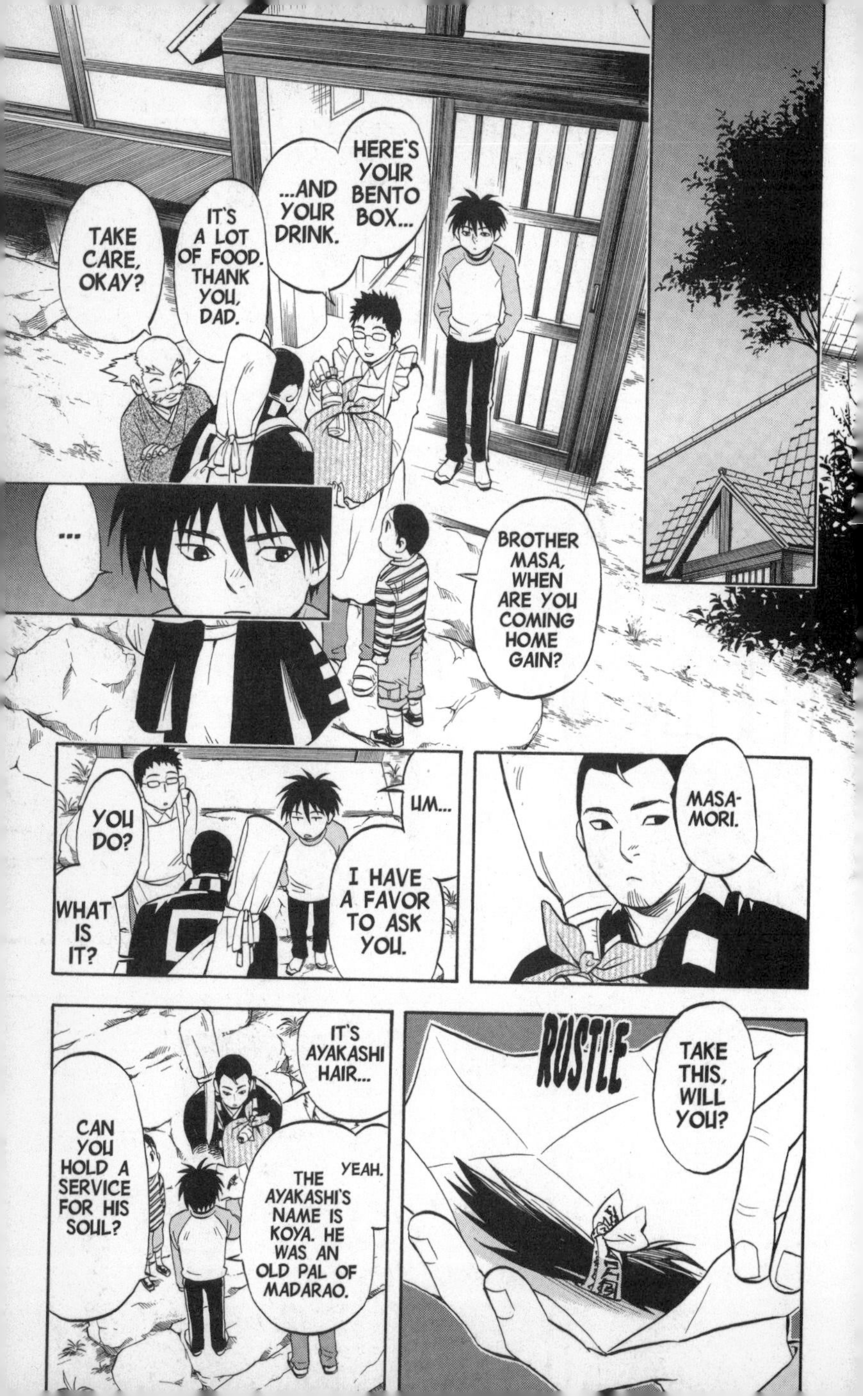
HERE'S YOUR BENTO BOX...
...AND YOUR DRINK.
IT'S A LOT OF FOOD. THANK YOU, DAD.
TAKE CARE, OKAY?
BROTHER MASA, WHEN ARE YOU COMING HOME GAIN?
...
MASA-MORI.
UM...
I HAVE A FAVOR TO ASK YOU.
YOU DO?
WHAT IS IT?
RUSTLE
TAKE THIS, WILL YOU?
IT'S AYAKASHI HAIR...
YEAH.
THE AYAKASHI'S NAME IS KOYA. HE WAS AN OLD PAL OF MADARAO.
CAN YOU HOLD A SERVICE FOR HIS SOUL?

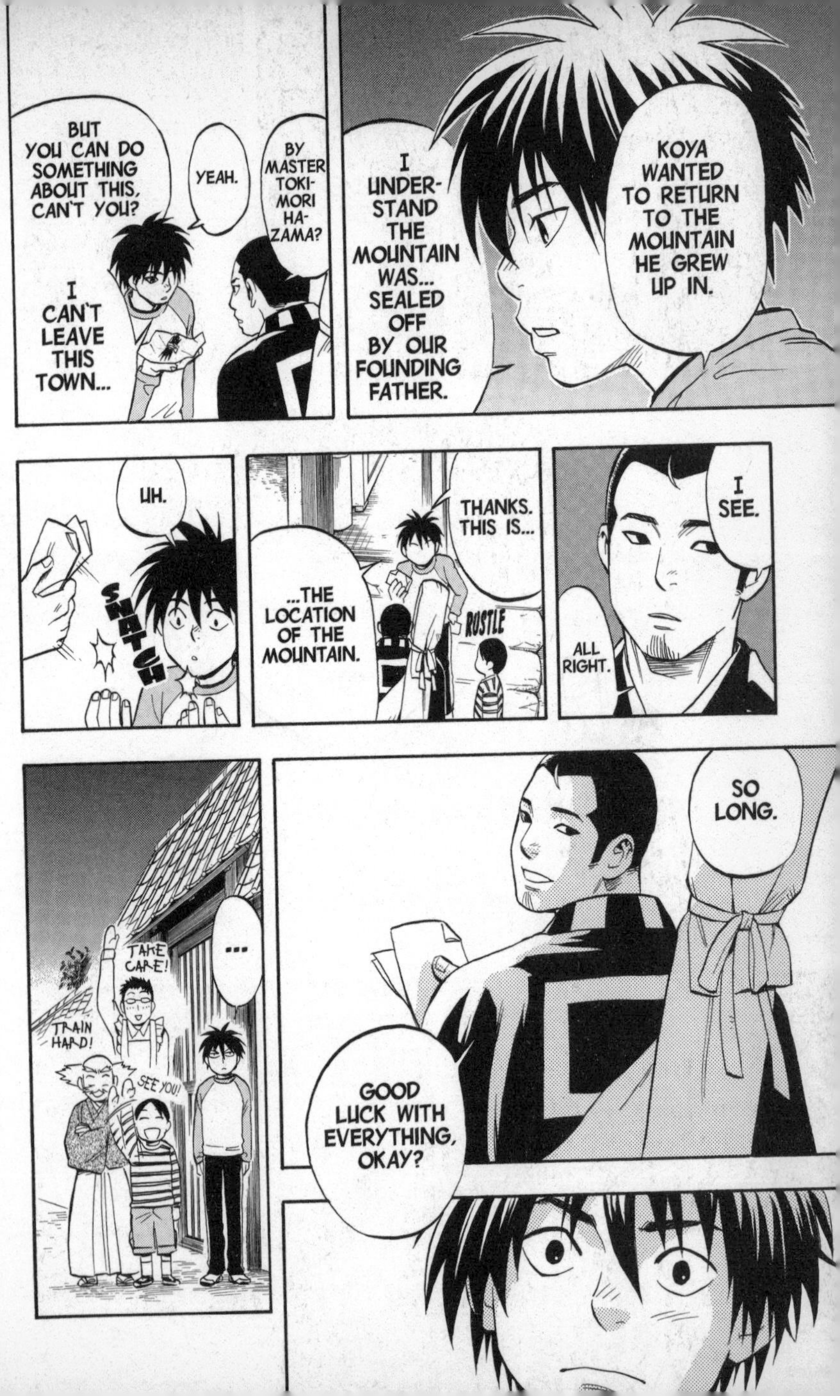
KOYA WANTED TO RETURN TO THE MOUNTAIN HE GREW UP IN.
I UNDERSTAND THE MOUNTAIN WAS... SEALED OFF BY OUR FOUNDING FATHER.
BY MASTER TOKIMORI HAZAMA?
YEAH.
BUT YOU CAN DO SOMETHING ABOUT THIS, CAN'T YOU?
I CAN'T LEAVE THIS TOWN...
I SEE.
ALL RIGHT.
THANKS. THIS IS...
...THE LOCATION OF THE MOUNTAIN.
RUSTLE
UH.
SNATCH
SO LONG.
GOOD LUCK WITH EVERYTHING, OKAY?
...
TAKE CARE!
TRAIN HARD!
SEE YOU!

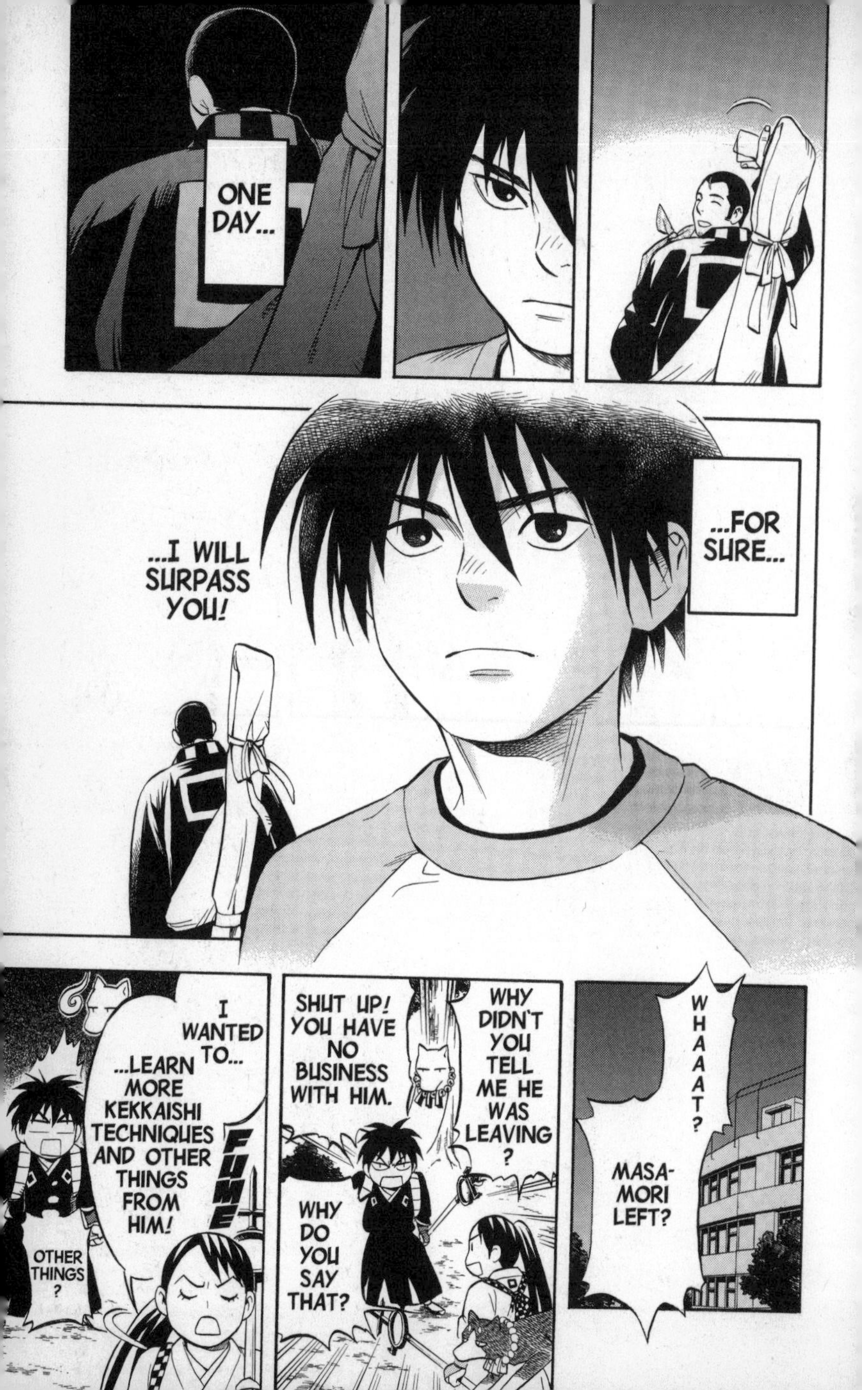
ONE DAY...
...FOR SURE...
...I WILL SURPASS YOU!
WHAAAAT?
MASA-MORI LEFT?
WHY DIDN'T YOU TELL ME HE WAS LEAVING?
SHUT UP! YOU HAVE NO BUSINESS WITH HIM.
WHY DO YOU SAY THAT?
I WANTED TO...
...LEARN MORE KEKKAISHI TECHNIQUES AND OTHER THINGS FROM HIM!
FUME
OTHER THINGS?

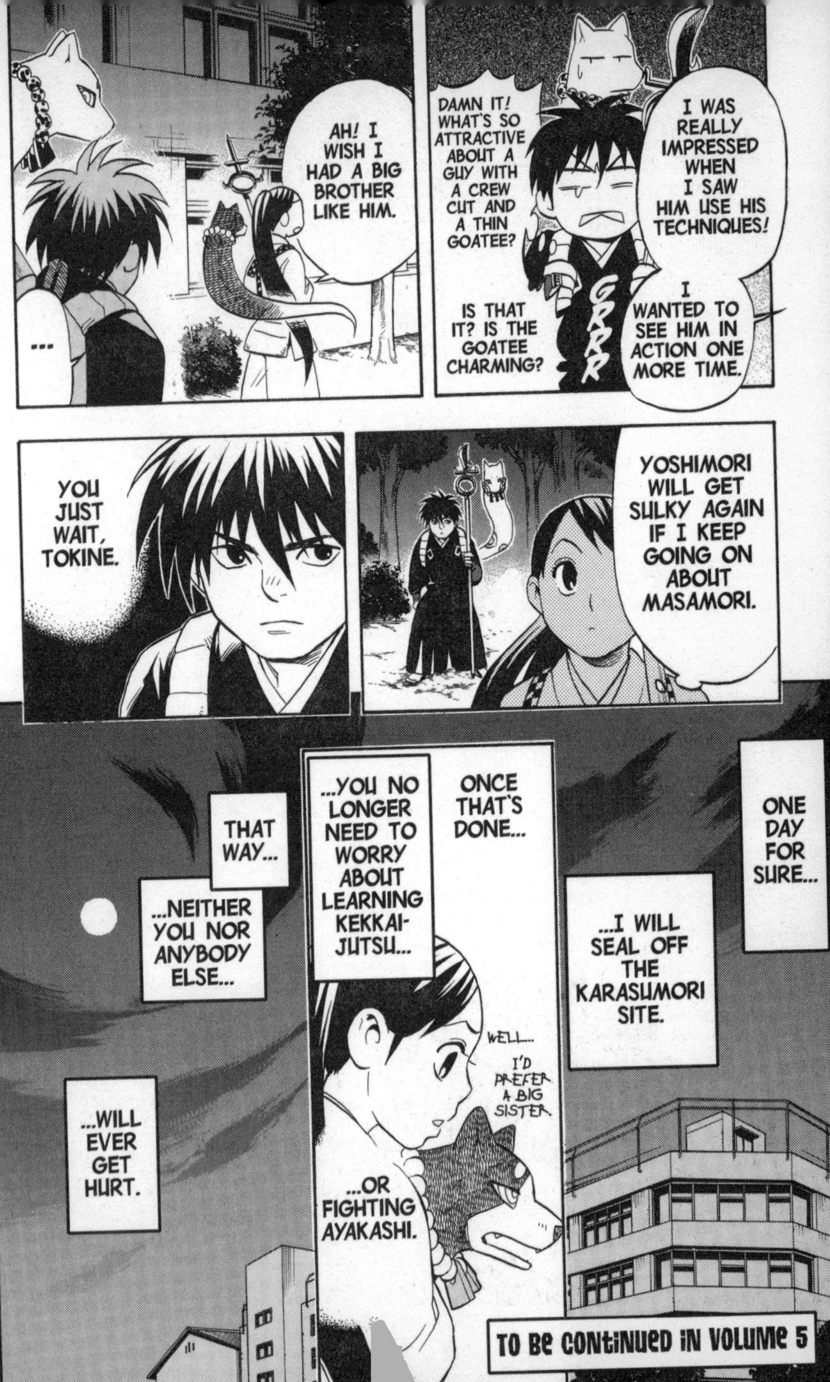
I WAS REALLY IMPRESSED WHEN I SAW HIM USE HIS TECHNIQUES!
DAMN IT! WHAT'S SO ATTRACTIVE ABOUT A GUY WITH A CREW CUT AND A THIN GOATEE?
I WANTED TO SEE HIM IN ACTION ONE MORE TIME.
GRRR
IS THAT IT? IS THE GOATEE CHARMING?
AH! I WISH I HAD A BIG BROTHER LIKE HIM.
...
YOSHIMORI WILL GET SULKY AGAIN IF I KEEP GOING ON ABOUT MASAMORI.
YOU JUST WAIT, TOKINE.
ONE DAY FOR SURE...
...I WILL SEAL OFF THE KARASUMORI SITE.
ONCE THAT'S DONE...
...YOU NO LONGER NEED TO WORRY ABOUT LEARNING KEKKAI-JUTSU...
...OR FIGHTING AYAKASHI.
WELL... I'D PREFER A BIG SISTER.
THAT WAY...
...NEITHER YOU NOR ANYBODY ELSE...
...WILL EVER GET HURT.
TO BE CONTINUED IN VOLUME 5

結界師

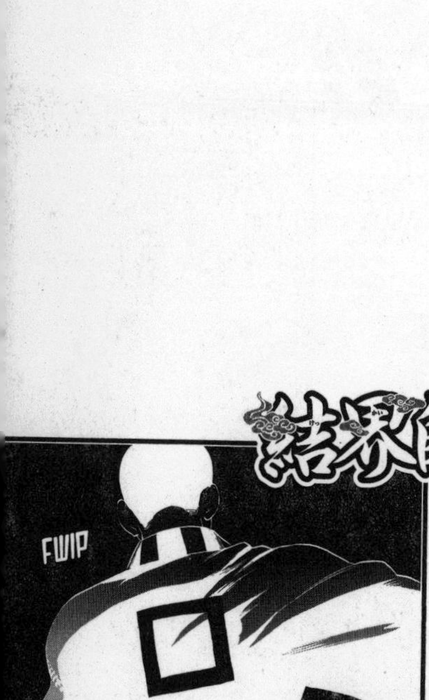
FWIP

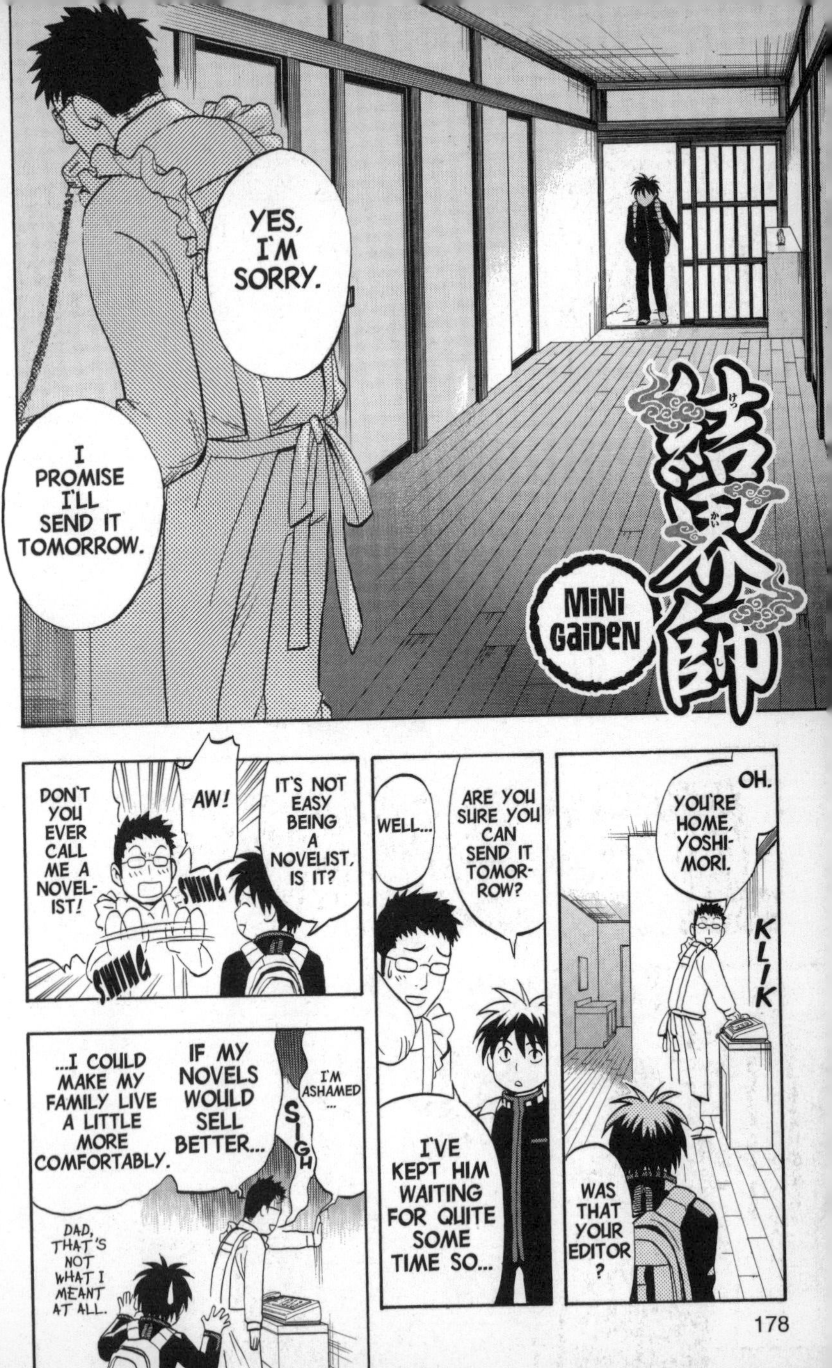
YES, I'M SORRY.
I PROMISE I'LL SEND IT TOMORROW.
結界師
けっ かい し
MiNi GaiDEN
OH. YOU'RE HOME, YOSHI-MORI.
KLIK
WAS THAT YOUR EDITOR?
ARE YOU SURE YOU CAN SEND IT TOMOR-ROW?
WELL...
I'VE KEPT HIM WAITING FOR QUITE SOME TIME SO...
IT'S NOT EASY BEING A NOVELIST, IS IT?
AW!
DON'T YOU EVER CALL ME A NOVEL-IST!
SHING
SHING
I'M ASHAMED...
SIGH
IF MY NOVELS WOULD SELL BETTER...
...I COULD MAKE MY FAMILY LIVE A LITTLE MORE COMFORTABLY.
DAD, THAT'S NOT WHAT I MEANT AT ALL.

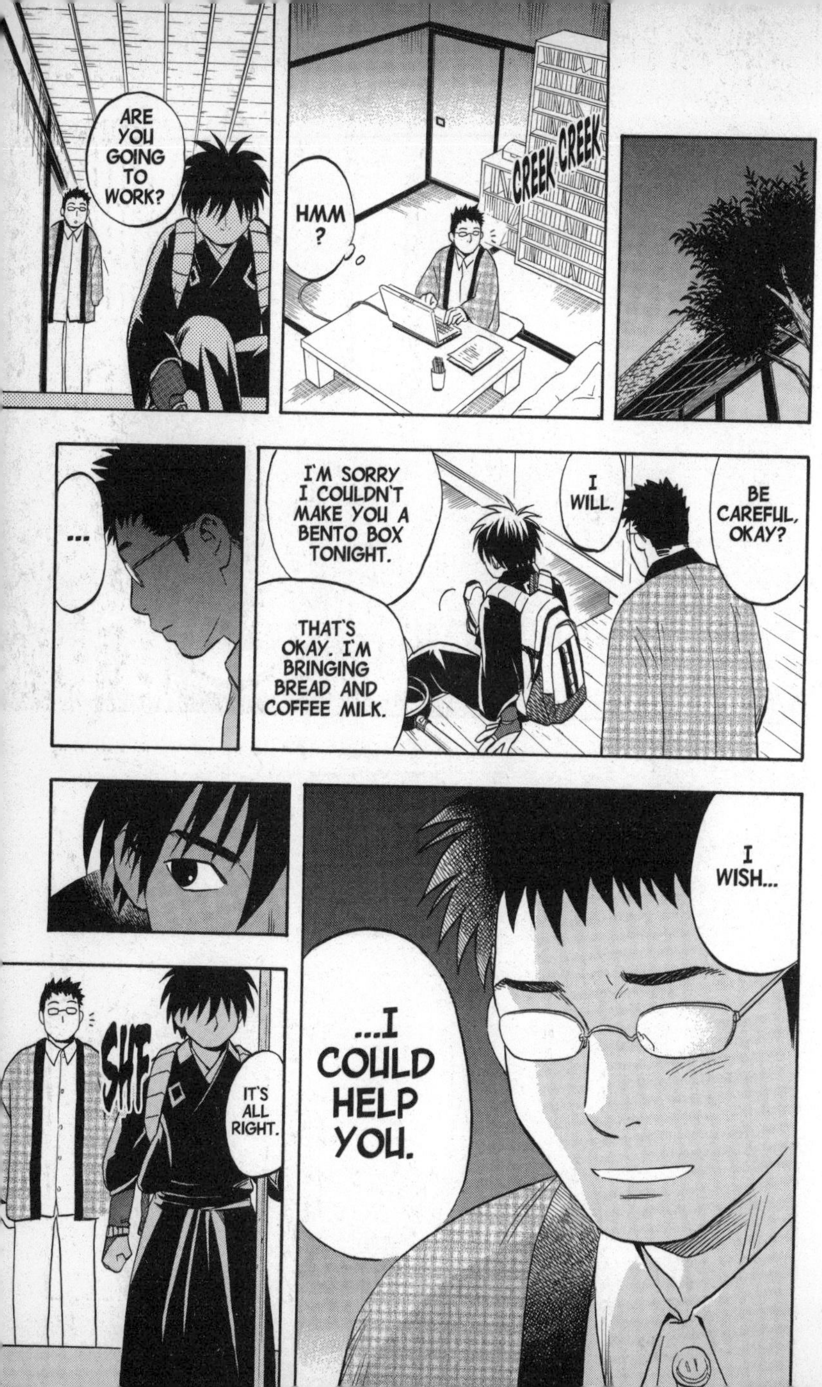
CREEK CREEK
HMM?
ARE YOU GOING TO WORK?
BE CAREFUL, OKAY?
I WILL.
I'M SORRY I COULDN'T MAKE YOU A BENTO BOX TONIGHT.
THAT'S OKAY. I'M BRINGING BREAD AND COFFEE MILK.
...
I WISH...
...I COULD HELP YOU.
SHF
IT'S ALL RIGHT.

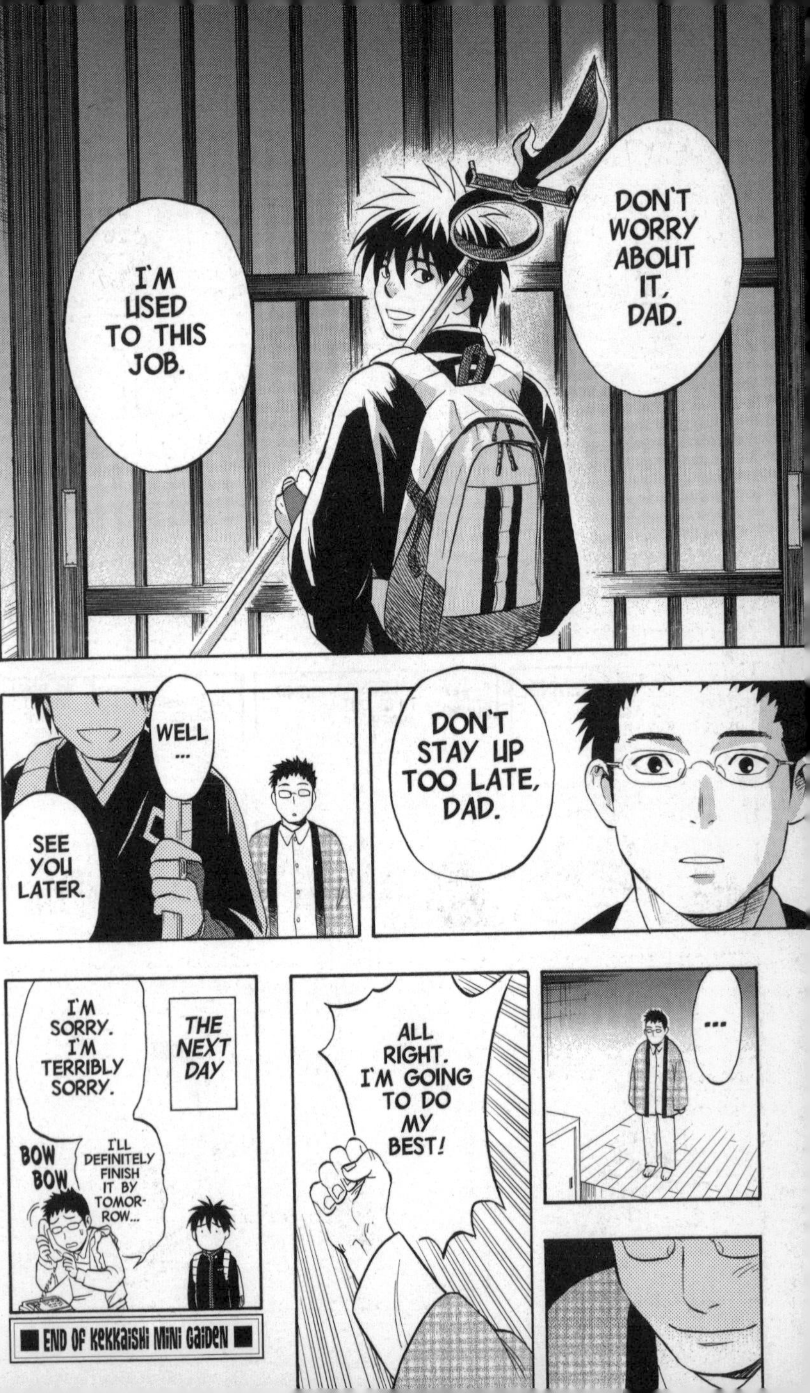

DON'T WORRY ABOUT IT, DAD.
I'M USED TO THIS JOB.
DON'T STAY UP TOO LATE, DAD.
WELL ...
SEE YOU LATER.
...
ALL RIGHT. I'M GOING TO DO MY BEST!
THE NEXT DAY
I'M SORRY. I'M TERRIBLY SORRY.
BOW BOW
I'LL DEFINITELY FINISH IT BY TOMORROW...
END OF KEKKAISHI MINI GAIDEN

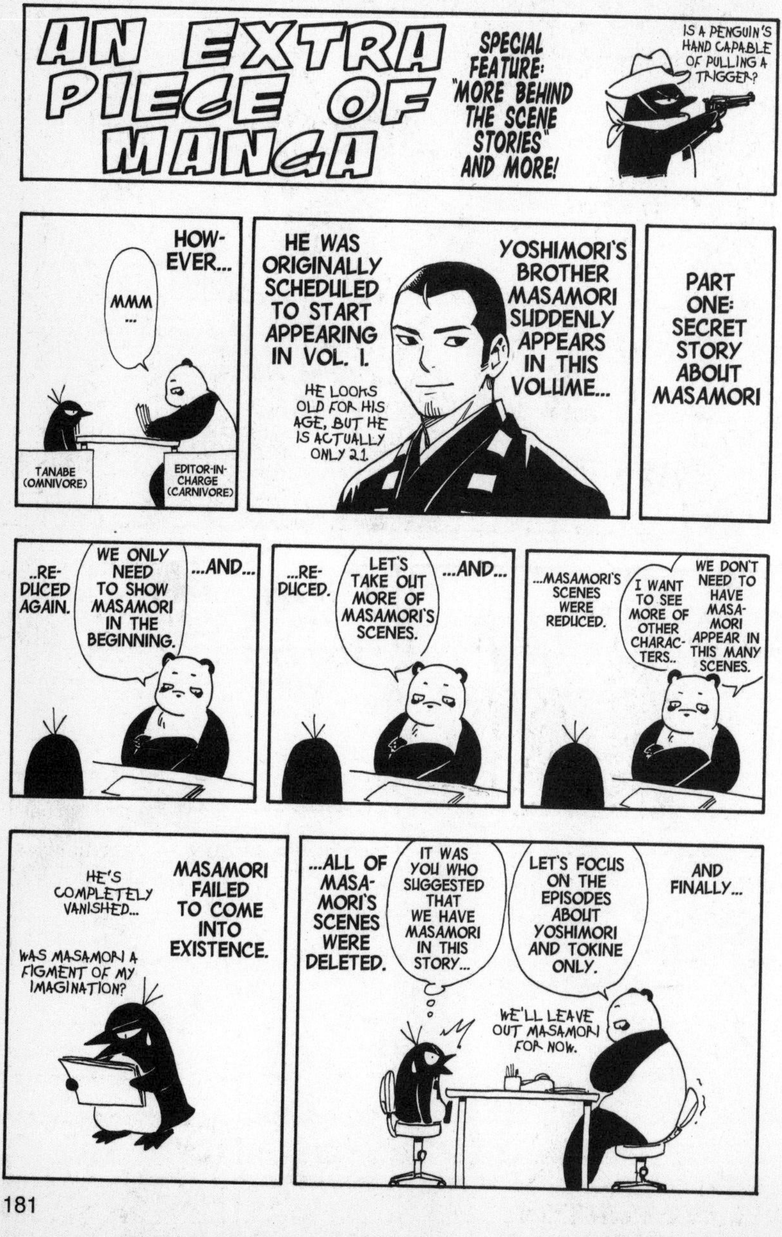
AN EXTRA PIECE OF MANGA
SPECIAL FEATURE: "MORE BEHIND THE SCENE STORIES" AND MORE!
IS A PENGUIN'S HAND CAPABLE OF PULLING A TRIGGER?
PART ONE: SECRET STORY ABOUT MASAMORI
YOSHIMORI'S BROTHER MASAMORI SUDDENLY APPEARS IN THIS VOLUME...
HE WAS ORIGINALLY SCHEDULED TO START APPEARING IN VOL. 1.
HE LOOKS OLD FOR HIS AGE, BUT HE IS ACTUALLY ONLY 21.
HOW-EVER...
MMM ...
EDITOR-IN-CHARGE (CARNIVORE)
TANABE (OMNIVORE)
WE DON'T NEED TO HAVE MASA-MORI APPEAR IN THIS MANY SCENES.
I WANT TO SEE MORE OF OTHER CHARAC-TERS..
...MASAMORI'S SCENES WERE REDUCED.
...AND...
LET'S TAKE OUT MORE OF MASAMORI'S SCENES.
...RE-DUCED.
...AND...
WE ONLY NEED TO SHOW MASAMORI IN THE BEGINNING.
..RE-DUCED AGAIN.
AND FINALLY...
LET'S FOCUS ON THE EPISODES ABOUT YOSHIMORI AND TOKINE ONLY.
IT WAS YOU WHO SUGGESTED THAT WE HAVE MASAMORI IN THIS STORY...
...ALL OF MASA-MORI'S SCENES WERE DELETED.
WE'LL LEAVE OUT MASAMORI FOR NOW.
MASAMORI FAILED TO COME INTO EXISTENCE.
HE'S COMPLETELY VANISHED...
WAS MASAMORI A FIGMENT OF MY IMAGINATION?

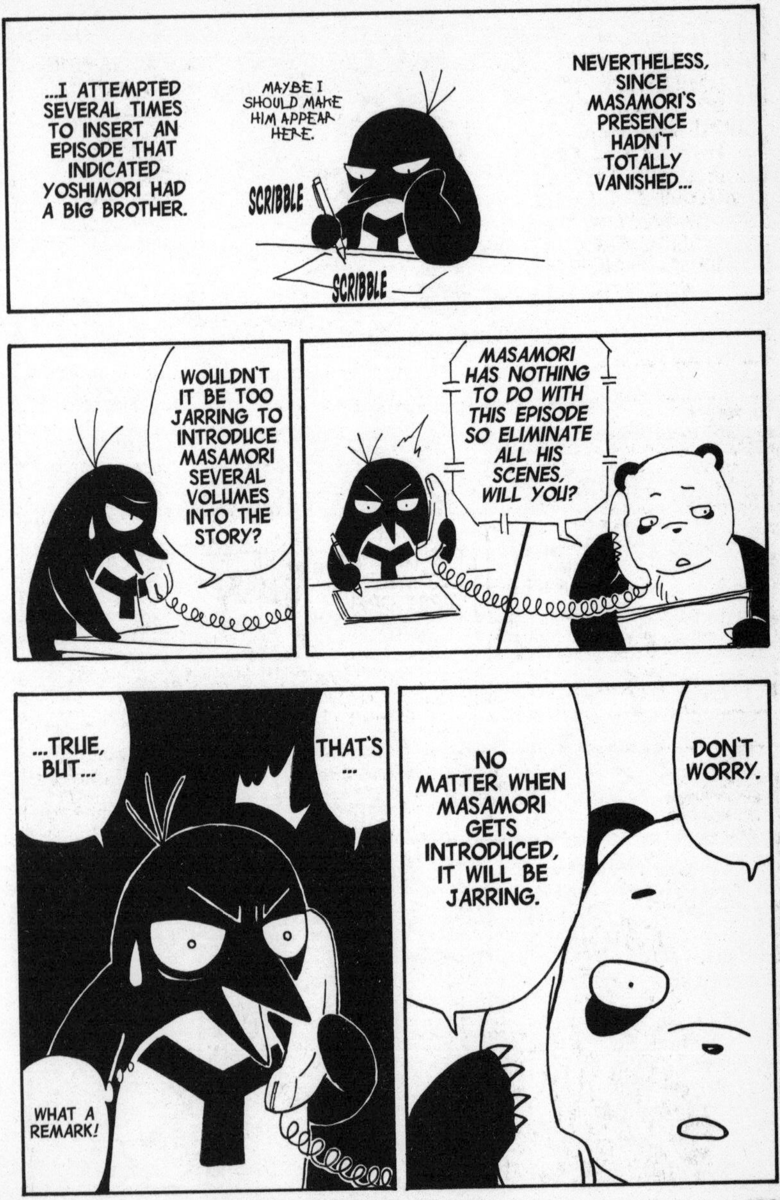
NEVERTHELESS, SINCE MASAMORI'S PRESENCE HADN'T TOTALLY VANISHED...
MAYBE I SHOULD MAKE HIM APPEAR HERE.
SCRIBBLE
...I ATTEMPTED SEVERAL TIMES TO INSERT AN EPISODE THAT INDICATED YOSHIMORI HAD A BIG BROTHER.
SCRIBBLE
MASAMORI HAS NOTHING TO DO WITH THIS EPISODE SO ELIMINATE ALL HIS SCENES, WILL YOU?
WOULDN'T IT BE TOO JARRING TO INTRODUCE MASAMORI SEVERAL VOLUMES INTO THE STORY?
DON'T WORRY.
NO MATTER WHEN MASAMORI GETS INTRODUCED, IT WILL BE JARRING.
THAT'S ...
...TRUE, BUT...
WHAT A REMARK!

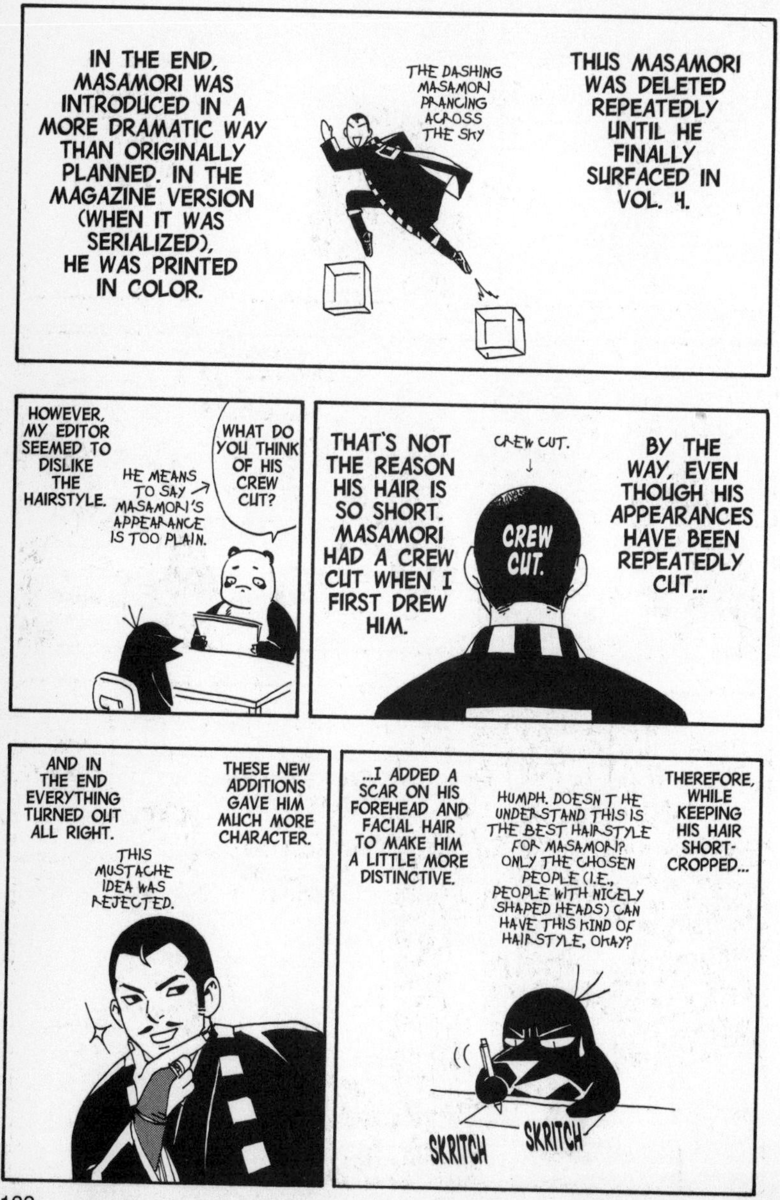
THUS MASAMORI WAS DELETED REPEATEDLY UNTIL HE FINALLY SURFACED IN VOL. 4.
THE DASHING MASAMORI PRANCING ACROSS THE SKY
IN THE END, MASAMORI WAS INTRODUCED IN A MORE DRAMATIC WAY THAN ORIGINALLY PLANNED. IN THE MAGAZINE VERSION (WHEN IT WAS SERIALIZED), HE WAS PRINTED IN COLOR.
BY THE WAY, EVEN THOUGH HIS APPEARANCES HAVE BEEN REPEATEDLY CUT...
CREW CUT.
CREW CUT.
THAT'S NOT THE REASON HIS HAIR IS SO SHORT. MASAMORI HAD A CREW CUT WHEN I FIRST DREW HIM.
WHAT DO YOU THINK OF HIS CREW CUT?
HE MEANS TO SAY MASAMORI'S APPEARANCE IS TOO PLAIN.
HOWEVER, MY EDITOR SEEMED TO DISLIKE THE HAIRSTYLE.
THEREFORE, WHILE KEEPING HIS HAIR SHORT-CROPPED...
HUMPH. DOESN'T HE UNDERSTAND THIS IS THE BEST HAIRSTYLE FOR MASAMORI? ONLY THE CHOSEN PEOPLE (I.E., PEOPLE WITH NICELY SHAPED HEADS) CAN HAVE THIS KIND OF HAIRSTYLE, OKAY?
...I ADDED A SCAR ON HIS FOREHEAD AND FACIAL HAIR TO MAKE HIM A LITTLE MORE DISTINCTIVE.
SKRITCH
SKRITCH
THESE NEW ADDITIONS GAVE HIM MUCH MORE CHARACTER.
AND IN THE END EVERYTHING TURNED OUT ALL RIGHT.
THIS MUSTACHE IDEA WAS REJECTED.

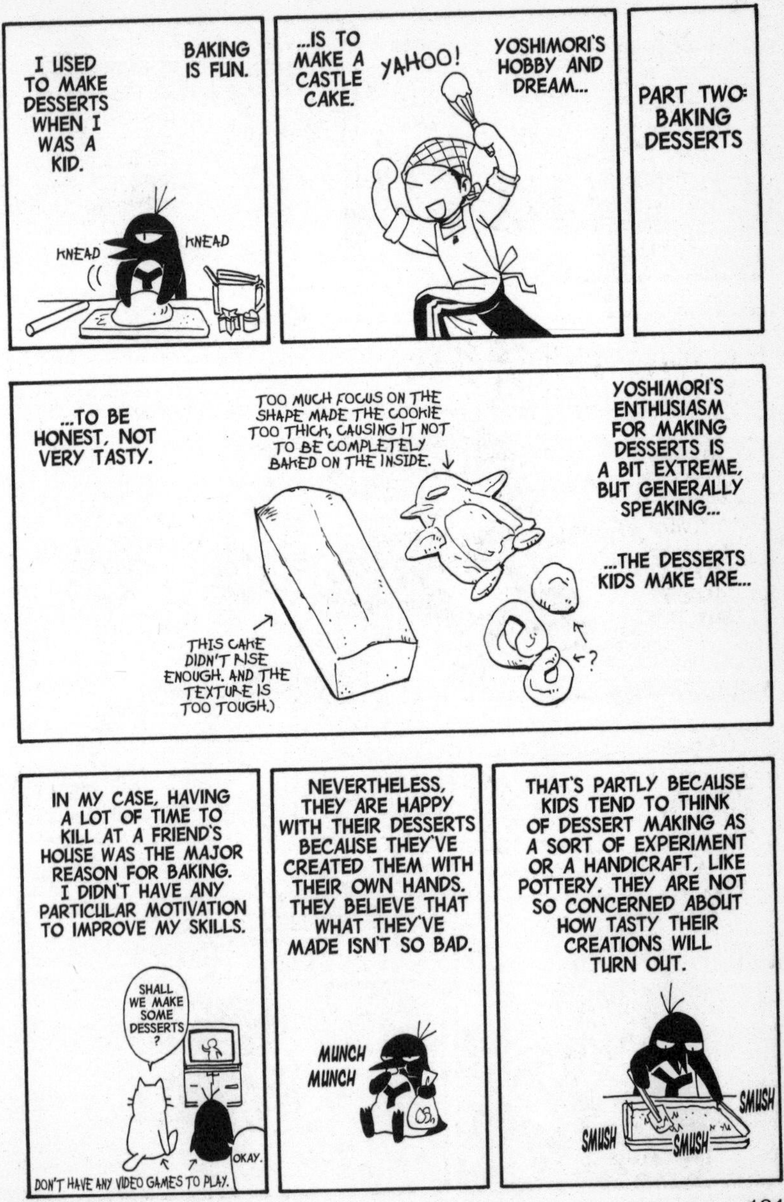
PART TWO: BAKING DESSERTS
YOSHIMORI'S HOBBY AND DREAM...
YAHOO!
...IS TO MAKE A CASTLE CAKE.
BAKING IS FUN.
I USED TO MAKE DESSERTS WHEN I WAS A KID.
KNEAD
KNEAD
YOSHIMORI'S ENTHUSIASM FOR MAKING DESSERTS IS A BIT EXTREME, BUT GENERALLY SPEAKING...
...THE DESSERTS KIDS MAKE ARE...
TOO MUCH FOCUS ON THE SHAPE MADE THE COOKIE TOO THICK, CAUSING IT NOT TO BE COMPLETELY BAKED ON THE INSIDE.
?
...TO BE HONEST, NOT VERY TASTY.
THIS CAKE DIDN'T RISE ENOUGH. AND THE TEXTURE IS TOO TOUGH.)
THAT'S PARTLY BECAUSE KIDS TEND TO THINK OF DESSERT MAKING AS A SORT OF EXPERIMENT OR A HANDICRAFT, LIKE POTTERY. THEY ARE NOT SO CONCERNED ABOUT HOW TASTY THEIR CREATIONS WILL TURN OUT.
SMUSH
SMUSH
SMUSH
NEVERTHELESS, THEY ARE HAPPY WITH THEIR DESSERTS BECAUSE THEY'VE CREATED THEM WITH THEIR OWN HANDS. THEY BELIEVE THAT WHAT THEY'VE MADE ISN'T SO BAD.
MUNCH
MUNCH
IN MY CASE, HAVING A LOT OF TIME TO KILL AT A FRIEND'S HOUSE WAS THE MAJOR REASON FOR BAKING. I DIDN'T HAVE ANY PARTICULAR MOTIVATION TO IMPROVE MY SKILLS.
SHALL WE MAKE SOME DESSERTS?
OKAY.
DON'T HAVE ANY VIDEO GAMES TO PLAY.

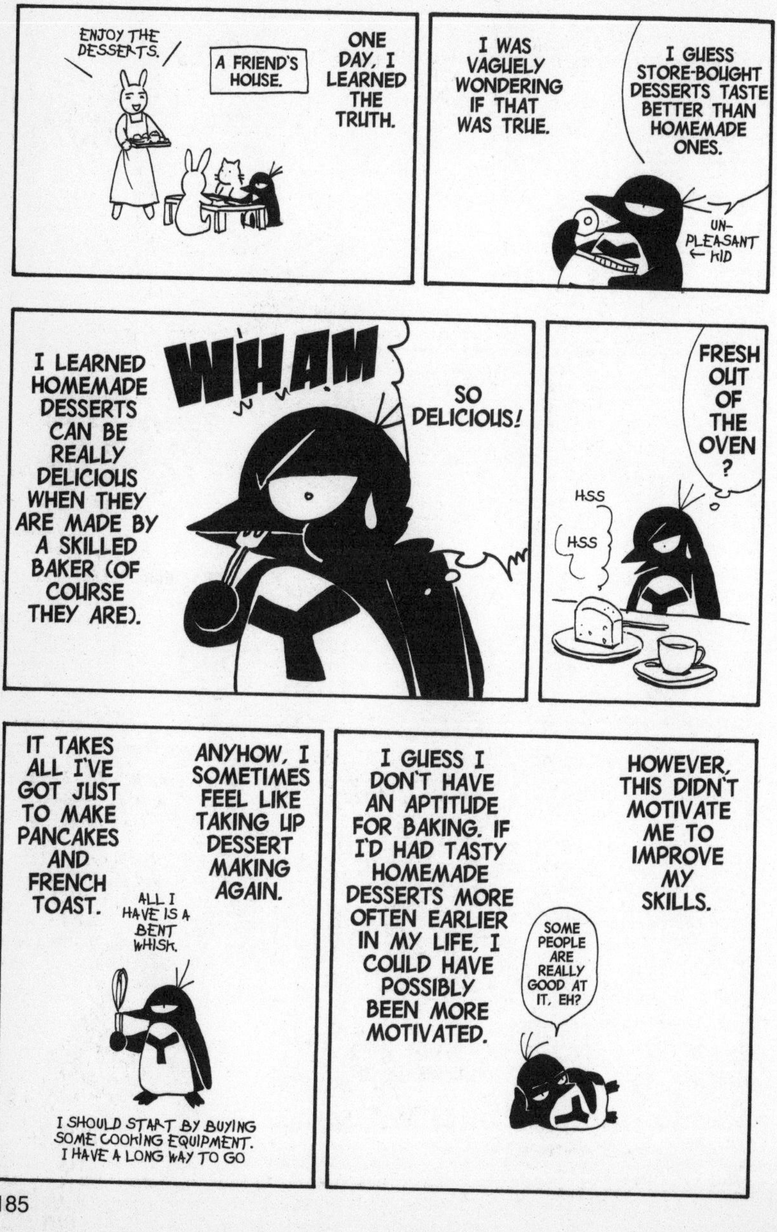
I GUESS STORE-BOUGHT DESSERTS TASTE BETTER THAN HOMEMADE ONES.
I WAS VAGUELY WONDERING IF THAT WAS TRUE.
UN-PLEASANT ← KID
ONE DAY, I LEARNED THE TRUTH.
A FRIEND'S HOUSE.
ENJOY THE DESSERTS.
FRESH OUT OF THE OVEN ?
HSS
HSS
SO DELICIOUS!
WHAM
I LEARNED HOMEMADE DESSERTS CAN BE REALLY DELICIOUS WHEN THEY ARE MADE BY A SKILLED BAKER (OF COURSE THEY ARE).
HOWEVER, THIS DIDN'T MOTIVATE ME TO IMPROVE MY SKILLS.
I GUESS I DON'T HAVE AN APTITUDE FOR BAKING. IF I'D HAD TASTY HOMEMADE DESSERTS MORE OFTEN EARLIER IN MY LIFE, I COULD HAVE POSSIBLY BEEN MORE MOTIVATED.
SOME PEOPLE ARE REALLY GOOD AT IT, EH?
ANYHOW, I SOMETIMES FEEL LIKE TAKING UP DESSERT MAKING AGAIN.
IT TAKES ALL I'VE GOT JUST TO MAKE PANCAKES AND FRENCH TOAST.
ALL I HAVE IS A BENT WHISK.
I SHOULD START BY BUYING SOME COOKING EQUIPMENT. I HAVE A LONG WAY TO GO

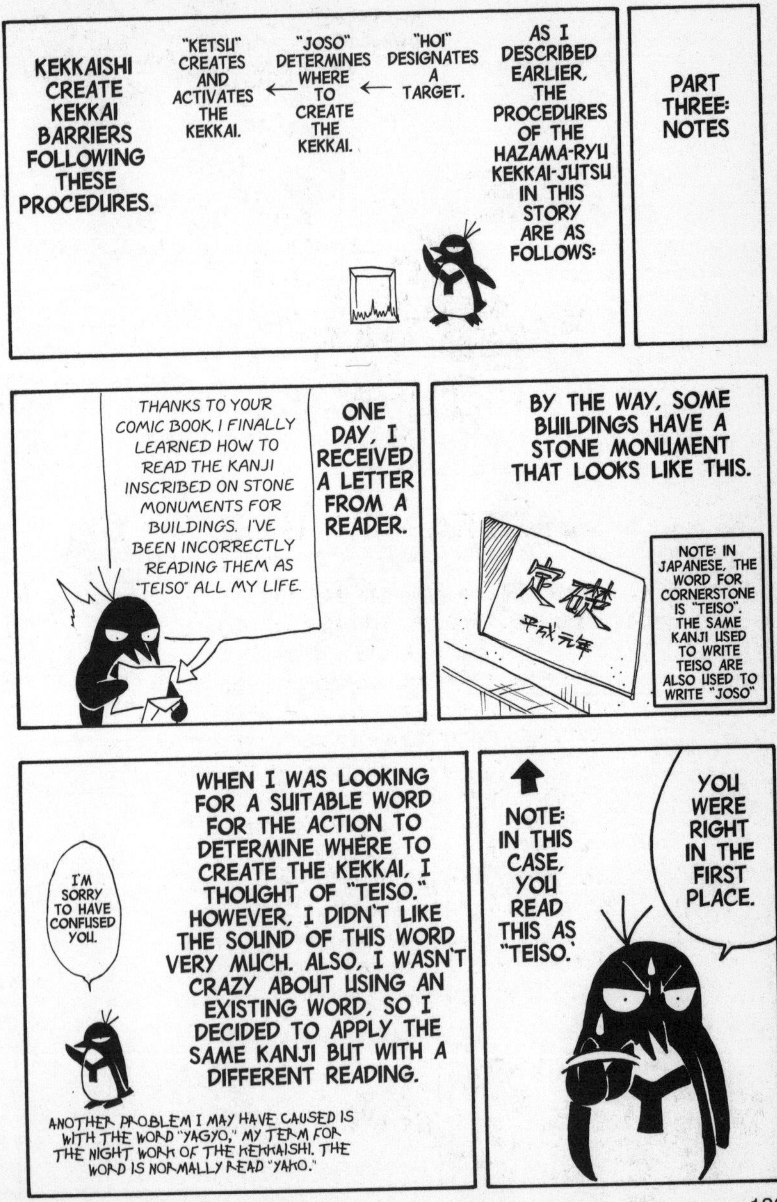
PART THREE: NOTES
AS I DESCRIBED EARLIER, THE PROCEDURES OF THE HAZAMA-RYU KEKKAI-JUTSU IN THIS STORY ARE AS FOLLOWS:
"HOI" DESIGNATES A TARGET.
"JOSO" DETERMINES WHERE TO CREATE THE KEKKAI.
"KETSU" CREATES AND ACTIVATES THE KEKKAI.
KEKKAISHI CREATE KEKKAI BARRIERS FOLLOWING THESE PROCEDURES.
BY THE WAY, SOME BUILDINGS HAVE A STONE MONUMENT THAT LOOKS LIKE THIS.
定礎
平成元年
NOTE: IN JAPANESE, THE WORD FOR CORNERSTONE IS "TEISO". THE SAME KANJI USED TO WRITE TEISO ARE ALSO USED TO WRITE "JOSO"
ONE DAY, I RECEIVED A LETTER FROM A READER.
THANKS TO YOUR COMIC BOOK, I FINALLY LEARNED HOW TO READ THE KANJI INSCRIBED ON STONE MONUMENTS FOR BUILDINGS. I'VE BEEN INCORRECTLY READING THEM AS "TEISO" ALL MY LIFE.
YOU WERE RIGHT IN THE FIRST PLACE.
NOTE: IN THIS CASE, YOU READ THIS AS "TEISO."
WHEN I WAS LOOKING FOR A SUITABLE WORD FOR THE ACTION TO DETERMINE WHERE TO CREATE THE KEKKAI, I THOUGHT OF "TEISO." HOWEVER, I DIDN'T LIKE THE SOUND OF THIS WORD VERY MUCH. ALSO, I WASN'T CRAZY ABOUT USING AN EXISTING WORD, SO I DECIDED TO APPLY THE SAME KANJI BUT WITH A DIFFERENT READING.
I'M SORRY TO HAVE CONFUSED YOU.
ANOTHER PROBLEM I MAY HAVE CAUSED IS WITH THE WORD "YAGYO," MY TERM FOR THE NIGHT WORK OF THE KEKKAISHI. THE WORD IS NORMALLY READ "YAKO."

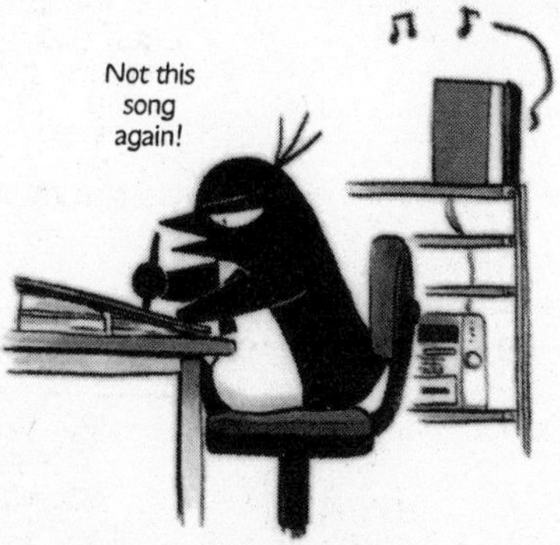
Not this song again!

MESSAGE FROM YELLOW TANABE

For a while now I've had the habit of listening to the radio while working on my manga. I grew up watching a lot of television, so I rarely listened to the radio in the past. Anyway, I find radio interesting because most of the shows are live and this creates a kind of intimacy between the program hosts and the listeners. Also, by listening to the radio, I get to hear many different types of music. When I hear something I like very much, I buy the CD. It amuses me when I find that the images on the covers of these CDs are very different from the pictures I had imagined while listening to the music on the radio.

KEKKAISHI

VOLUME 4

STORY AND ART BY YELLOW TANABE

Translation/Yuko Sawada
Touch-up Art & Lettering/Stephen Dutro
Cover Design & Graphic Layout/Amy Martin
Editor/Andy Nakatani

Editor in Chief, Books/Alvin Lu
Editor in Chief, Magazines/Marc Weidenbaum
VP of Publishing Licensing/Rika Inouye
VP of Sales/Gonzalo Ferreyra
Sr. VP of Marketing/Liza Coppola
Publisher/Hyoe Narita

Printed in Canada

Published by VIZ Media, LLC
P.O. Box 77010
San Francisco, CA 94107

VIZ Media Edition
10 9 8 7 6 5 4 3 2
First printing, January 2006
Second printing, November 2007

VIZ media
www.viz.com

RATED T FOR TEEN

PARENTAL ADVISORY
KEKKAISHI is rated T for Teen. Contains fantasy violence. Recommended for ages 13 and up.

ratings.viz.com

LOVE MANGA? LET US KNOW!

☐ Please do NOT send me information about VIZ Media products, news and events, special offers, or other information.

☐ Please do NOT send me information from VIZ Media's trusted business partners.

Name: _____

Address: _____

City: _____ **State:** _____ **Zip:** _____

E-mail: _____

☐ Male ☐ Female **Date of Birth** (mm/dd/yyyy): ___ / ___ / ___ (Under 13? Parental consent required)

What race/ethnicity do you consider yourself? (check all that apply)

☐ White/Caucasian ☐ Black/African American ☐ Hispanic/Latino

☐ Asian/Pacific Islander ☐ Native American/Alaskan Native ☐ Other: _____

What VIZ Media title(s) did you purchase? (indicate title(s) purchased) _____

_____

What other VIZ Media titles do you own? _____

_____

Reason for purchase: (check all that apply)

☐ Special offer ☐ Favorite title / author / artist / genre

☐ Gift ☐ Recommendation ☐ Collection

☐ Read excerpt in VIZ Media manga sampler ☐ Other _____

Where did you make your purchase? (please check one)

☐ Comic store ☐ Bookstore ☐ Grocery Store

☐ Convention ☐ Newsstand ☐ Video Game Store

☐ Online (site:_____) ☐ Other _____

How many manga titles have you purchased in the last year? How many were VIZ Media titles?
(please check one from each column)

MANGA
- ☐ None
- ☐ 1 – 4
- ☐ 5 – 10
- ☐ 11+

VIZ Media
- ☐ None
- ☐ 1 – 4
- ☐ 5 – 10
- ☐ 11+

How much influence do special promotions and gifts-with-purchase have on the titles you buy?
(please circle, with 5 being great influence and 1 being none)

1   2   3   4   5

Do you purchase every volume of your favorite series?
- ☐ Yes! Gotta have 'em as my own
- ☐ No. Please explain: _____

What kind of manga storylines do you most enjoy? (check all that apply)

- ☐ Action / Adventure
- ☐ Comedy
- ☐ Fighting
- ☐ Artistic / Alternative
- ☐ Science Fiction
- ☐ Romance (shojo)
- ☐ Sports
- ☐ Other _____
- ☐ Horror
- ☐ Fantasy (shojo)
- ☐ Historical

If you watch the anime or play a video or TCG game from a series, how likely are you to buy the manga? (please circle, with 5 being very likely and 1 being unlikely)

1   2   3   4   5

If unlikely, please explain: _____

Who are your favorite authors / artists? _____

_____

What titles would like you translated and sold in English? _____

_____

THANK YOU! Please send the completed form to:

NJW Research
42 Catharine Street
Poughkeepsie, NY 12601

Your privacy is very important to us. All information provided will be used for internal purposes only and will not be sold or otherwise divulged.